Fabricating
Transnational
Capitalism

THE

LEWIS HENRY MORGAN

LECTURES

Robert J. Foster & Daniel R. Reichman, Co-Directors

Fabricating Transnational Capitalism

A Collaborative Ethnography of

Italian-Chinese Global Fashion

LISA ROFEL | SYLVIA J. YANAGISAKO

with an essay by Simona Segre Reinach
and a foreword by Robert J. Foster

DUKE UNIVERSITY PRESS *Durham & London* 2019

Designed by Matthew Tauch
Typeset in Minion Pro by Westchester Publishing
Services

Library of Congress Cataloging-in-Publication Data
Names: Rofel, Lisa, [date] author. | Yanagisako, Sylvia Junko,
[date] author. | Segre, Simona, writer of supplementary
textual content.
Title: Fabricating transnational capitalism : a collaborative
ethnography of Italian-Chinese global fashion / Lisa Rofel,
Sylvia Yanagisako ; with an essay by Simona Segre Reinach ; and
a foreword by Robert J. Foster.
Description: Durham : Duke University Press, 2018. | Series:
The Lewis Henry Morgan lectures | Includes bibliographical
references and index.
Identifiers: LCCN 2018020449 (print)
LCCN 2018028965 (ebook)
ISBN 9781478002178 (ebook)
ISBN 9781478000297 (hardcover)
ISBN 9781478000457 (pbk.)
Subjects: LCSH: Clothing trade—Italy—History—20th century. |
Clothing trade—China—History—20th century. |
Fashion—Italy—History—20th century. |
Textile industry—Italy—Prato—History—20th century. |
Chinese—Italy—Prato. | Italy—Relations—China. |
China—Relations—Italy. | Entrepreneurship—China.
Classification: LCC HD9940.I82 (ebook) | LCC HD9940.I82 R64
2018 (print) | DDC 338.8/87174692—dc23
LC record available at https://lccn.loc.gov/2018020449

Cover art: Student-designed fashion show at Donghua
University, Shanghai, 2008. Photo by Sylvia J. Yanagisako.

Contents

Foreword

Lisa Rofel and Sylvia J. Yanagisako visited the University of Rochester as the Lewis Henry Morgan Lecturers for 2010, continuing an annual tradition that began in 1963 with Meyer Fortes's inaugural lectures on kinship and the social order. They delivered a public talk on the evening of October 20, taking turns reporting on eight years of joint research into how Italian textile and clothing firms since the 1980s have relocated manufacturing to China and, more recently, turned to China as a growing consumer market for Italian fashion brands. On the following day, Rofel and Yanagisako participated in a lively workshop devoted to consideration of an early draft of two chapters of their manuscript-in-progress. Robert Foster, Harry Groenevelt, Eleana Kim, and John Osburg from Rochester and David Horn (Ohio State), Rebecca Karl (New York University), and Andrea Muehlebach (Toronto) served as formal discussants.

Fabricating Transnational Capitalism is the culmination of Rofel and Yanagisako's project, a creative ethnography of Italian-Chinese collaborations in the global fashion industry. It is a much-anticipated and most welcome addition to the book series associated with the Lewis Henry Morgan Lectures. Morgan (1818–81) was an attorney, scholar, and founding figure in American anthropology who enjoyed a close relationship with the University of Rochester, to which he bequeathed a sizeable estate and impressive personal library. He might have appreciated this book as someone who believed that commerce promoted social progress and who himself had experienced both the failures and rewards of several business partnerships. Readers today will readily appreciate the book's innovative methodology and critical reframing of the study of capitalism.

The role of transnational commodity chains in the expansion of capitalism has long been recognized, and their proliferation also acknowledged as a defining feature of economic globalization. Until recently, however, anthropologists have not taken up the serious methodological challenge that such commodity chains present to the convention of a sole anthropologist doing fieldwork in a single place. *Fabricating Transnational Capitalism* advances the move toward collaborative, multisited ethnography by grounding itself in the long-term engagements of Rofel and Yanagisako with China and Italy, respectively. It is difficult to imagine a team of two anthropologists, assisted by a fashion studies scholar (Simona Segre Reinach), better equipped to meet the logistical and conceptual demands of a historically informed, thickly described account of capitalism in the making.

The historical depth of Rofel and Yanagisako's perspectives makes it difficult to see the manufacture of Italian luxury fashion in China as the sign of a new neoliberal economic order of outsourcing and privatization. There are no radical ruptures of world-historical significance here. Instead, Rofel and Yanagisako offer insight into how particular historical legacies of Chinese socialism and Italian state enterprise shape the ways in which an array of actors—managers, owners, and workers—do business with each other in the present. These actors bring different concerns and capacities to their uneasy encounters, a double-sided condition that Rofel and Yanagisako were well positioned to appreciate through on-site interactions in China and Italy, and extensive interviews conducted in Chinese and Italian as well as English. *Fabricating Transnational Capitalism* thus renders in unusual detail, as described in the introduction, "the actions and reactions, interpretations and misinterpretations, understandings and misunderstandings through which the Italians and Chinese in . . . transnational business collaborations reformulate their goals, strategies, values, and identities."

Doing business is often messy, and it is this messiness that a feminist substantivist approach to capitalism refuses to erase (see Bear et al. 2015). Put differently, Rofel and Yanagisako choose to treat capitalism as something other than a singular logic. They emphasize, rather, the contingent convergence of various life projects, pursued across domains not always recognized as "economic," out of which the accumulation and distribution of capital emerges. Take kinship, for example, a domain of obvious importance for understanding the operation of family firms. Think of how the transfer of inherited wealth underscores the significance of kinship in reproducing and nurturing twenty-first-century income inequality. Or, more pertinently, think of how an Italian manager of a joint-venture fashion firm prefers to raise his young daughter in Shanghai in order to endow her with the cultural capital and cosmopolitan sensibilities deemed necessary for future success. Actual situated practice—entangled with family and fortune as well as race, gender, and nation—eclipses the clean abstractions of both the economists ("the market") and their critics ("post-Fordism" or, for that matter, "the Law of the Tendency of the Profit Rate to Fall"). Separating the economic from the noneconomic makes no sense (other than ideological) in this analysis.

If capitalism is to be understood as made and remade in actual situated practice, then attending to the specificity of such practice is crucial. The same can be said for transnational collaborations. The collaborations at issue in *Fabricating Transnational Capitalism* are not only Italian-Chinese collaborations but also fashion industry collaborations that entail a specific asymmetry between China's reputation as a source of cheap labor and Italy's reputation as the home of tasteful design. This asymmetry defines a struggle that inhabits Italian-Chinese collaborations in the production, distribution, and marketing of clothing. Different commodity chains, different asymmetries. As the authors explain in the introduction: "Had we studied the production and distribution of computers, cell phones, steel, automobiles, or solar panels, these asymmetries would have been significantly different."

Rofel and Yanagisako's observation bears upon the enduring question of how value is created in capitalism. Their compelling discussion of the negotiation of the relative value of managerial labor, with which the book opens, illustrates what ethnography can contribute in this regard. Italian managers attempt to assert the primacy and superior value of their own embodied *Italianità*, which Rofel and Yanagisako describe as "an intuitive feeling for design, fashion, and, more broadly, aesthetics that they construe as having acquired by growing up in Italy." Chinese managers (and "entrepreneurs") in return assert their own cosmopolitanism, worldly knowledge that "encompasses their abilities to transcend culture to embrace the seemingly universal aspects of capitalist business practices" and thus to facilitate business with foreigners. Rofel and Yanagisako in effect reveal an ongoing competition played out under the guise of working together—a tension that surfaces, for instance, in Chinese owner Huang Huaming's angry response when Rofel inadvertently mentioned that his Italian partners were seeking other joint ventures. Both Italian and Chinese managers seek to qualify not only the products and brands associated with luxury fashion but also themselves as particular kinds of laboring subjects. These qualifications of themselves and each other, moreover, frequently obscure the labor of other subjects to whom the managers are connected in the same commodity chain.

For Karl Marx, the question of value in capitalism was one of extraction, that is, of how to extract ever-greater surplus value from the peculiar and generic commodity called labor power when that commodity is put to use, regardless of the particular use. It is a question of more or less. For Rofel and Yanagisako, the use value of labor power matters. This use value is not given but is actively negotiated, for example, through the invidious comparisons that Italian and Chinese managers make in their encounters with each other. It is a question of defining and ranking the qualitatively different resources— Italianità or cosmopolitanism—that are converted or translated into luxury fashion through transnational collaboration.

These two approaches are neither mutually exclusive nor contradictory, but Rofel and Yanagisako's approach considerably broadens the scope of what one must address in taking up the question of value. By insisting on looking beyond the so-called economic domain for what motivates the heterogeneity and mutability of use values, *Fabricating Transnational Capitalism* demonstrates the centrality of history and culture and therefore anthropology to the study of contemporary capitalism.

Robert J. Foster

Codirector, Lewis Henry Morgan Lecture Series

Acknowledgments

This book has benefited enormously from the support of numerous friends, colleagues, and institutions. We thank the Wenner-Gren Foundation and the National Science Foundation for the generous grants that made this research possible. We are also grateful to our respective institutions, the University of California, Santa Cruz, and Stanford University, for the faculty research funds that supported the preliminary research for this project. Fellowships from the Stanford Humanities Center and the Michelle R. Clayman Institute for Gender Research provided crucial support for Sylvia Yanagisako's writing. The Shanghai Social Sciences Institute was an ideal host for our research in Shanghai. We especially thank Li Li for help with introductions.

The invitation to present the Lewis Henry Morgan Distinguished Lecture of 2010 gave us the opportunity to present an early analysis and framing of our ethnographic material. We thank Robert Foster and Thomas Gibson and their colleagues in the Department of Anthropology at the University of Rochester for extending this invitation to us. The astute commentaries on our Morgan Lecture by Robert Foster, David Horn, Rebecca Karl, Eleana Kim, John Osburg, and Andrea Muehlebach were invaluable in the development and writing of this book.

Donald Donham, Leiba Faier, James Ferguson, Gillian Hart, Gail Hershatter, George Marcus, Megan Moodie, Donald Moore, Anna Tsing, and Mei Zhan read various chapters and gave the kind of honest feedback that makes all the difference. Conversations with Gopal Balakrishnan, Laura Bear, Christopher Connery, Karen Ho, Dai Jinhua, Keir Martin, and Massimilliano

Mollona invigorated our analyses of transnational capitalism. Our graduate students engaged in lively discussion with us and offered support in numerous ways: at the University of California, Santa Cruz: Patricia Alvarez, Gillian Bogart, Zachary Caple, Rebecca Feinberg, Alix Johnson, Caroline Kao, Sarah Kelman, Kali Rubaii, and Aaron Wistar; and at Stanford: Hannah Appel, Hilary Chart, Eda Pepi, Maron Greenleaf, and Vivian Lu. Elena Glasberg served as Lisa Rofel's writing angel. We especially thank Vivian Lu and Eda Pepi for their tireless work in getting this manuscript in order.

The audiences' lively engagement and questions in response to our talks at the following universities and institutes led to important revisions in our analysis and the writing of this book: Autonomous University of Barcelona, University of Bergen, Cornell University, University of California, Berkeley—variously at their Department of Anthropology, Center for Critical Theory, and Center for Chinese Studies—University of California, Davis, University of California, Irvine, University of California, Los Angeles, Centre National de la Recherche Scientifique in Paris, Centre Norbert Elias of the École des Haute Études en Sciences Sociales (Paris and Marseille), Chinese University of Hong Kong, University of Colorado at Boulder, Duke University, Fromm Institute at University of San Francisco, Harvard University, Johns Hopkins University, Leiden University, London School of Economics, Nanjing University, New York University, Norwegian Institute for Social Research, University of Oslo, Shanghai University, Southern Methodist University, University of Texas, Austin, and University of Virginia. Sylvia Yanagisako's participation in the following workshops and conferences provoked critical thinking of how this study fit into broad areas of scholarship on labor, kinship, capitalism, and transnationalism: the workshop on Kinship and Modernity at the School of Advanced Research organized by Fenella Cannell and Susan McKinnon, The Reconfiguring of Labor at the University of Oslo organized by Christian Krohn-Hansen and Penelope Harvey, Global Relations: Kinship and Transnationalism at Brown University organized by Jessaca Leinaweaver, Speculation: New Vistas on Capitalism at the London School of Economics organized by Laura Bear, and Risk and Uncertainty in the Economy organized by Jens Beckert and Hartmut Berghoff.

Our collaboration with Simona Segre Reinach has been crucial to the research we conducted in China and Italy and to the writing of this book. Her deep understanding of the history of fashion, Italian fashion, transnational and global fashion, and fashion studies scholarship contributed enormously to our understanding of the Chinese-Italian joint ventures we studied. We are grateful for her patience and generosity in tutoring us in the contemporary fashion industry.

Last but not least, we thank our partners and families for their love, support, and understanding of the amount of time it takes to conduct ethnographic research and write a book. Lisa thanks Graciela Trevisan, and Sylvia thanks John Sullivan, Emi Sullivan, and Nathan Sullivan.

Introduction

The women and men were tall, thin, and dressed in the latest Italian fashion. They paraded in a circle on the stage to the beat of blaring rock music with the identical expression of stern hautiness that was de riguer among professional models at the time. With the exception of two Italians, all were Chinese. The audience of about one hundred was itself almost entirely Chinese—women and men from the world of textile and garment production who had been invited to this event in the spring of 2007, held at the swankiest, new luxury hotel in Shanghai. By good fortune, this fashion show, titled Prato Excellence, coincided with the first week of our longest stint of fieldwork in Shanghai. Alessandro Panerati,[1] the director of international relations at the Confartigianato (the association of artisans and small businesses) of Prato, a textile-producing city in Tuscany, Italy, had invited us to the show. For several years, Panerati's job had been to develop Prato's business ties with China, and Prato Excellence was the culmination of a collaboration between the Confartigianato, Prato's Chamber of Commerce, and Polimoda, the premier fashion school in the nearby city of Florence.

Just before the fashion show, we chatted with Panerati and the president and vice president of the Prato Chamber of Commerce at a reception in which wine, risotto, and other artisanal products from the Prato area were displayed. The reception served double duty: first to set the stage for the Italianness of the fashion show, which featured clothing made from Prato's textiles; and second to introduce the Chinese in attendance to products from Prato and the region of Tuscany. Panerati and the officials from the Chamber of Commerce

Intro.1 Prato Excellence fashion show, Shanghai, 2007.

were eager to promote these products for the sake of the region, whose economy had recently been in decline. In case the Italian origins of the products had been lost on the guests, the dinner between the reception and the fashion show had begun dramatically with waiters sweeping in bearing steaming plates of pasta to the strains of "La donna e mobile," the lyric aria from Verdi's opera *Rigoletto*.

While the clothing modeled at the fashion show had been designed by students of Polimoda, Prato itself had never been known as a site of Italian fashion design. Instead, it had a long history of textile production.[2] Indeed, it was not until the arrival of Chinese immigrants in the 1990s that garment manufacturing flourished in Prato. Hired initially as workers in textile manufacturing, in most cases in small subcontracting firms, the Chinese moved quickly to producing ready-to-wear clothing for the lower-middle range of the European clothing market. By the time of the Prato Excellence fashion show, there were around 1,900 Chinese firms in this sector and approximately 20,000 Chinese people in the city and its environs. Despite being widely resented by many Pratesi (inhabitants of Prato) for having displaced the local labor force, the Chinese, Panerati explained, had initiated an entirely new sector of production, thus completing the fashion production chain in Prato.

Some of these Chinese firms had taken the spaces vacated by the textile firms, however, adding to the local perception of displacement. Given the resentment toward the Chinese in Prato, the irony of the leaders of Prato's business associations drumming up business in China was not lost on us or on Marco—a Chinese import-export entrepreneur we had met in Prato—who was attending the event in the interest of hiring students from Donghua University's fashion institute as designers.

We happened to sit at the table of Professor Hu Jihong, whom we later spoke with many times, who taught about regional factors in the textile industry at the business school at Donghua University. Donghua, which had been the textile engineering school in the socialist era, had become not a fashion design institute but a business school. Around Professor Hu were arrayed his former students, all of whom were working in one phase or another of textile and garment production for export. We later got to know them as well. Indeed, everyone at the table—ourselves included—was exchanging business cards to facilitate future connections or, as they say in Chinese, *guanxi*. After all, Chinese entrepreneurs need connections with one another to do any sort of business in China and classmates are the ideal sorts of guanxi.

Prato Excellence exemplified the not-always realized hopes, fantasies, and expectations motivating the Italian-Chinese collaborations we analyze in this book. Panerati and the other representatives from the Prato business associations hoped to entice Chinese companies to buy Prato's textiles to produce garments in China and in doing so to revitalize a manufacturing industry that had declined as a result of competition from China. The Chinese in the audience were hoping to find Italian partners with whom they could collaborate to manufacture clothing in China that could then be exported to Europe through these Italian firms, some of which had sent representatives to the fashion show. The latter were on the lookout to build the guanxi they needed with Chinese to conduct business in China. Over the years that we conducted research for this book, some of these hopes and fantasies were realized, sometimes in unexpected ways; others were not.

This book is a collaborative ethnography of Italian-Chinese ventures in the fashion industry that offers a new methodology for the study of transnational capitalism in a global era. It offers an innovative approach to analyzing the transnational capitalist processes that are shaping people's lives around the globe. We investigate how transnational relations of production and distribution are forged by people with different historical legacies of capital, labor, nation, state, and kinship. Rather than begin with a focus on presumed core structural features of capitalism, we ask what the Chinese and Italians who engage in these transnational ventures seek in them and how the constantly shifting asymmetrical field of power in which they interact leads them to reconfigure their goals, strategies, and practices.

Let us be very clear: this is not a comparative study of Italian and Chinese capitalisms but a study of the coproduction of Italian-Chinese transnational capitalism.[3] Indeed, what we offer here is an alternative to the conventional comparative method in anthropology—one that is better suited to the modes of cultural production and transformation prevalent in the world today. Instead of comparing different "cultures" or "cultures of capitalism"—a methodology that has proven as unfruitful as the static, bounded model of culture in which it is rooted—we offer a historically informed, ethnographic analysis of the formation of Chinese-Italian transnational capitalism. We do not envision these transnational ventures as the negotiated outcome between two distinct "dreams of capitalism." Rather than essentialize "Chinese capitalism" and "Italian capitalism" as distinctive cultural forms and thereby merely assert that the core features of capitalism are instantiated in culturally diverse ways, we argue that in these collaborations between Italian and Chinese entrepreneurs, new forms of value, accumulation, inequality, and identity are created, and eventually new projects are generated.

Our study demonstrates the ways in which specific national/transnational histories and legacies shape transnational capitalist engagements and collaborations, including their modes of engagement, conflicts, and shifts in relations of production over time. Both Italy and China developed their industrial production capacities through transnational engagements with markets and resources, as Immanuel Wallerstein's early insights (1974, 1980, 1989) about the modern world-system of capitalism predicted. Wallerstein's analysis, however, emphasized how the relations between core/semi-periphery/periphery reproduce the world system structure, with less concern for the historical contingencies that led particular places outside Europe to end up in any of those categories.[4] He argues (1989) that a previously "external" place becomes incorporated as the periphery when it becomes a source of raw materials. Although Wallerstein emphasizes that this process of incorporation is relational, he places the initiative with European countries without examining how the histories of specific places play a role in this process. In contrast, our study shows how the specific histories of capitalism, industry, state, and kinship in Italy and China have shaped their changing relations over time in ways that cannot be contained within a core/semi-periphery/periphery model of the modern world-system of capitalism.

This book advocates a new methodology for studying capitalism in a global era. We argue that collaborative research of the sort we have pursued generates analytical insights that lead to the reconceptualization of transnational capitalism in the current era. We offer and advocate here not merely a method but a methodology that is more than a strategy for data collection. It is an approach to the study of cultural production that entails both methods and concepts. Critical to this collaborative research is the ethnographic capacity to listen to and understand the multiple parties engaged in transnational capitalism. Until the present, almost all anthropological research on transnationalism, whether focused on capitalism, religion, or media, has been conducted by one ethnographer.[5] In these studies, the lone ethnographer focuses primarily on one of the parties in the encounter, thus overlooking (or even misconstruing) the goals, commitments, and historical legacies of the other parties. Few researchers, after all, have the linguistic skills to engage in dialogue and participant observation with more than one set of participants in transnational encounters who are not from their own background, let alone the area expertise to understand the historical legacies they bring to the encounter. Collaborative research by two or more anthropologists with complementary linguistic skills and area expertise provides a more robust way to investigate these transnational encounters. In the current case, Lisa Rofel's (1999, 2007) area expertise and past research in China and Sylvia Yanagisako's (2002, 2012) area expertise and past research in Italy provided us with knowledge of the legacies of capital, labor, kinship, gender, politics, and the state crucial to a comprehensive ethnographic analysis of Italian-Chinese ventures.

We have pursued this collaborative ethnographic research over more than a decade by following Italian firm owners, Chinese and Italian production and distribution managers, and Chinese entrepreneurs, officials, factory workers, retail clerks, and consumers engaged in these ventures. During this time, much has changed, including the transnational field of power in which these Chinese and Italians are situated. As a result, we have become especially interested in how relations between these Italians and Chinese have been shaped by the shifting asymmetries of power between them. Transnational capitalism, after all, is a historically situated form of unequal social interdependence in which people produce forms of labor, value, inequality, and identities, along with commodities. All of these are mediated by the form of their social interdependence. We ask rather than assume which processes of social mediation are being constituted in these transnational relations of production. Thus, rather than emphasize capitalism's unity or how it reproduces itself—an analytical approach that assumes capitalism has a stable core—we focus on the dynamics of capitalism that are key to transformations in a particular historical moment and how the people who participate in these transformations are also changed by them. Our approach addresses inequalities produced through capitalism in the same way: we do not assume a fixed basis to the forms of inequality that emerge in transnational capitalist relations but rather examine how they are constituted through diverse processes.

Our analysis highlights the ways in which capitalist practices emerge in relation to nationalism, gender, kinship, politics, the state, and social inequality. While this point has been made by others, these supposedly "noneconomic" relations and practices generally tend to be treated as either historical backdrop or as determined by "capitalism" reified as a social actor. Neither do we hew to a classic dialectical materialist approach (e.g., Harvey 2005) in which history plays an important role but then is overcome in a new era of capitalism. Rather, we argue that historical legacies play a key role as Chinese and Italians bring reinterpretations of their pasts—including past social inequalities and transnational histories—into their formulations of capitalist action. We do not, moreover, merely demonstrate how the distinctive histories of Italian and Chinese entrepreneurs form an assemblage or are articulated in these transnational collaborations. Our collaborative research enables us to show how their interactions also produce the significance and meaning of these histories.

Our approach both overlaps with and diverges from the recent emphasis on how economic knowledge practices produce economic reality, the ontologies of subjects who enact these realities, and value (Callon 1998; Stark 2009). We do not take for granted what counts as or should be included in "the economic." Nor do we assume there is a singular logic of value being enacted. Indeed, our collaborative research on the transnational negotiations over what gets to count as "value" emphasizes the ongoing processes that bring together different historically and culturally informed knowledges into these negotiations. We do not assume that one need only understand formal economic models and market devices to understand capitalism. Informed by feminist analyses, we bring together processes within and outside what conventionally gets bounded as an economic domain with a singular logic. Bear et al. (2015) call these "conversion processes between diverse life projects."[6] In what follows, we discuss the key processes on which this book focuses, the historical context of these Chinese-Italian collaborations, including our own research collaboration, and the major themes of the book's three sections.

Five Dynamic Processes in Italian-Chinese Transnational Capitalism

In contrast to economistic analyses of global and transnational capitalism, we approach capitalism as an assemblage of cultural practices in which culturally mediated human capacities—including beliefs, sentiments, values, and knowledge—operate as forces that incite, enable, constrain, and shape production. Rather than treat transnational capitalism as structured by a single logic or as the articulation of several distinct logics, we view it as an unstable, contingent assemblage of heterogeneous and sometimes conflicting visions of capital, labor, inequality, accumulation, property, kinship, and personhood that are continually being reformulated—in this case by both Italians and Chinese. The unfolding of capitalist dynamics between Italians and Chinese is contingent, as is all capitalism. Indeed, we posit that there is no universal capitalism or singular "modal" form stripped of multiple social, cultural, and political dynamics. Just as anthropologists have realized the analytic futility of identifying the universal or essential form of the family, marriage, and gender, so we contend that there is no pure form of capitalism or even neoliberal capitalism that can be usefully abstracted from historically specific relations. If there is no pure form of capitalism, it follows that there are no invariable elements that are always and everywhere key to it or its emergence and transformation.

Regnant theories of capitalism commonly identify four structural features that lie at the core of capitalist relations: the wage-labor relation, the pursuit of profit, private property, and inequality. Our study challenges the idea that these four features constitute a universal core or that they are instituted in a culturally homogeneous manner. Rather than begin with these structural features, we focus on five key dynamic processes that we discovered to have been central to the Italian-Chinese transnational collaborations we studied. In tracing these dynamic processes, we do not intend to merely replace core structural features with dynamic processes. Rather, our aim is to demonstrate how eschewing a structural model of capitalism opens up our analytic frame to render these key dynamic processes visible. These processes are so closely intertwined that by identifying them, we risk a misreading of them as distinct dynamics. Yet we think that the analytic benefits of our discussion below outweigh this risk.

The five key dynamic processes are privatization and the public/private division, the negotiation of labor value, the rearrangement of accumulation, the reconfiguration of kinship, and the outsourcing of inequality. Attending to these processes highlights the contingent nature of capitalist activity and the nondeterministic manner in which capitalist actions and relations are forged. At the same time, we show that none of these processes are independent of the state. On the contrary, the state is integral to all of them. While our research did not initially focus on the state, we found it to be critical to understanding the formation of Italian-Chinese capitalism, especially as both Italy and China have undergone marked transformations since the 1960s with regard to the role of the state in the pursuit of profit, capital accumulation, labor-capital relations, forms of inequality, and private property.

Privatization and the Public/Private Division

The concept of "privatization" has often been invoked to describe a new relationship between private economic interests, public resources, and the state since the beginning of what has become known as the neoliberal era (Heynen et al. 2007; Linder 1999; Mansfield 2009; McCarthy 2004). More recently, detailed studies have revealed rather complex private/public arrangements around the world, moving away from claims of wholesale "privatization" toward an emphasis on hybrid forms.[7] These studies demonstrate how the public sector has become financialized and thus profoundly oriented around profit-seeking. They also point toward a wide range of private/public relations, with different aims, meanings, and understandings of "partnership."[8]

Yet most of these more nuanced studies continue to assume that this hybridization indicates a novel trend toward a greater insertion of private interests into the goals and management of public resources and institutions. They tend to assume, moreover, that what counts as "private" and what counts as "public" are analytically distinguishable, if difficult to disentangle. They trace, for example, how a "private" company pairs with a "state," which is supposed to represent the public.

Our research challenges these assumptions. Our argument is not merely that there exist hybrid entities of public/private arrangements. We have two related arguments. We argue first that there is a history of state-private enterprises that long predates neoliberalism. We offer Italy's post–World War II industrial history as an example (see chapter 5). Second, we argue that in contemporary China, these are not simply "hybrids." More importantly, it is often impossible to assess or distinguish, much less disentangle, which aspect of a corporation is "public," or the state aspect, and which is "private." This blurring of the distinction is a deliberate strategy for multiple reasons (see chapter 2).[9]

Our analysis of "privatization" draws on the long-standing critique of the distinction between the private and the public developed by feminist anthropologists, other feminist theorists, and feminist activists. While some initial explorations of gender inequality were framed by a domestic/public distinction (Rosaldo 1974), there soon emerged a consensus among feminist anthropologists that this dichotomy was analytically unproductive and empirically unfounded (Rapp 1978, 1979; Rosaldo 1980; Yanagisako 1979).[10] Rayna Reiter (1975), for example, presented a compelling ethnographic analysis of how this ideological distinction legitimized both the authority of men in the "private" domain of the family and of the French state in the "public" domain. Studies of women's "domestic" activities disclosed them to have political as well as social reproductive consequence, leading to the conclusion that the dichotomy was "a cultural statement masking relations which are highly problematic" (Rapp 1979).[11] The assertion that it was invariably men who linked women to people outside their domestic group was refuted by studies of women's involvements in exchange transactions, informal women's communities, and kin networks (Guyer 1984; Stack 1974; Wolf 1972; Yanagisako 1977). Domestic relationships, moreover, were often so inextricably intermeshed with political alliances that to separate the domestic from the political was to misconstrue them (Strathern 1988). Feminist activists and theorists challenged the ideological constructions of private/public by drawing attention to the public import of actions ranging from domestic violence to sexuality in the seemingly private sphere of the home.[12] Black feminist scholars further highlighted how the "private" was never an attainable sphere for black women and families in the United States.[13] These findings led to the realization that the concepts of "domestic sphere" and "domestic relations" are part and parcel of the political ideology of a society. In addition, both John Comaroff (1987) and Yanagisako (1987) argued that the domestic/public distinction was rooted in a tautology that defined "domestic" as the activities of mothers and children, thereby constructing an inherently gendered dichotomy between domestic and public that made it analytically impossible for women to escape.

Feminist historians reached a similar conclusion, reevaluating histories of what were called "separate spheres" and showing that this metaphor always involved exclusions as it was based largely on white, middle-class women's experiences (Kerber 1988).[14] Antoinette Burton (1998) further challenged feminist historiography by emphasizing the centrality of colonialism to ideas about emancipation of women from the domestic/public division. Burton argued that racial anxieties in nineteenth-century Britain that centered on women's neglect of upholding the race if they entered the public sphere, and feminist responses to that anxiety, relied on a clear sense of distinction from and superiority to colonized female subjects. By the 1980s, scholars and activists engaged in the "Wages for Housework" movement had effectively challenged the ideological distinction between "reproductive" labor and "productive" labor, arguing that both produce value and, indeed, productive labor depends on reproductive labor.[15]

Curiously, however, when social analysts turn to the private/public division in capitalist socioeconomic relations, they assume they know precisely what this division means without further investigation. While there certainly are compelling historical studies of the privatization of public commons (Boyle 2003; Thompson 1974), and these processes continue today, we still tend to assume that once undertaken they are fully realized and that what counts as private is clearly delineated from what counts as public. This distinction, after all, is often inscribed in law.

Our ethnographic research, informed by these feminist analyses, led us to question the existence of a clear division between private and public in capitalism. Instead we realized that what counts as private and what counts as public are forged by historically specific processes, including the formation of differentiated transnational capitalist projects. This enables us to see that "privatization" is not as clearly delineated a project, nor as singular in its meaning, as is often assumed (even by those who disagree about the extent of privatization that has occurred in recent times). Rather, "privatization" has multiple meanings and can be instituted in various ways, which must be examined by historically and ethnographically informed studies.[16] In the current case, the transnational relations of production between Italian firm owners and managers and Chinese entrepreneurs and managers are central to how private and public relationships are evaluated, debated, and arranged.

In our ethnographic encounters with Chinese companies that do business with Italian textile firms, we found a range of situations along the spectrum from fully private to hybrid public/private to completely ambiguous and blurred statuses. In their interactions with Italian firm owners and managers, for example, Chinese managers in state-owned enterprises often portray their company as having "privatized." Yet, upon close examination, the situation is revealed to be more complex. For example, former state-run factories, the lowest strata of state bureaus under the socialist planned economy, have been sloughed off by the state, "sold" to former managers who became the owners and were made to be fully responsible for their own profits and losses. This process represents what we conventionally understand as "privatization." At the same time, however, state bureaus themselves have incorporated and become profit-seeking entities still situated within the state. Along with the import-export companies under their aegis, they have become blurred entities in which profit-seeking is central to each semiautonomous office within these corporations, yet the corporation is owned by the state.

The division between the private and the public, moreover, is often ambiguous. As much literature on China has pointed out (Ernst and Naughton 2008; Green and Liu 2005; Guthrie 1999; Hsing 2010; Huang 2008; Naughton 2007, 2008; Naughton and Tsai 2015; Nee and Opper 2012)—and sometimes decried—the state is very much involved in capitalist activity and the line between public and private, or state-owned and independently owned, is much less precise than one would assume from an analysis based on a supposed modal type of capitalism.[17] For that reason, there is a great deal of debate among scholars about the exact role of the Chinese state in the development of the Chinese economy. Some stress the ongoing dominance of the market economy by the state (Huang 2008). Others emphasize the increasing importance of private firms in stimulating economic growth (Lardy 2002).[18] Indeed, the reliance on an ideal type model of capitalism has hindered studies of capitalism in China, leading to the conclusion that China presents a special case of capitalism by virtue of the state's deep involvement in the market economy.

We found, moreover, that Chinese state officials have pursued projects of "privatization" to prove their worthiness to foreign investors by demonstrating they are not entangled in a state bureaucracy that is a holdover from the socialist past. This process has created entities that blur the line between the "private" and the "public." Blurring this distinction is the means by which government officials move beyond the socialist past while retaining some of its institutional legacies. The legal definitions of social relationships, however, do not wholly define the reality of those relationships. Indeed, legal definitions are often ideological statements of dominant beliefs that leave a great deal of room for interpretation. The motivation to ensure that China is not overtaken by the International Monetary Fund (IMF) or World Bank—or more broadly is not undone by the dictates of the world economy—leads many in China to hold onto certain legacies of the socialist past, particularly a strong state. Privatization is thus not as unambiguous or uniform a process as is often assumed in discussions of neoliberalism. Further, the search for "true" private capitalism in China or elsewhere can turn into a red herring in investigations of exactly how profit-seeking occurs. This deep blurring of the distinction means measuring China against such an ideological model might be a distraction from examining actual capitalist practices, which are always inventive.

China is hardly unique in this regard. While China's historical legacies have shaped the manner in which the state is involved in the market economy, this does not make for a special kind of "Chinese capitalism." The state, after all, is involved in structuring capitalist relations in myriad ways—whether through financial institutions and regulations, state-owned enterprises, or private-public collaborations (W. Brown 2001, 2015; Harvey 2005; Polanyi [1944] 2001). The widespread notion among both scholars and the popular media that the state ownership of enterprises (whether wholly state-owned or mixed state-private) in China represents a unique form of capitalism is not surprising, especially from the perspective of the U.S., where mixed private-public ownership of business has been rare, at least until the 2008 financial crisis. As Mariana Pargendler (2012, 2942) points out, however, while China is the site of the "most recent large-scale experiment" with state-operated enterprises, it is far from alone in this. State-owned enterprises have figured prominently in twentieth-century Europe, for example, where in 1997, 38 percent of the top fifty largest industrial companies in Europe were state owned (Pargendler 2012, 2948).

The Italian state, like many other European states, has been deeply involved in structuring capitalist enterprise. This has entailed not only regulating markets, banks, and labor-capital relations but also operating state enterprises. State enterprises and mixed state-private companies have played a major role in Italian capitalism, including the launching of the Italian "miracle" of economic development after World War II (Ginsborg 2003, 214). As early as 1907, in response to a liquidity crisis, the Italian state took over industries, including railroads, banks, and insurance, which had been previously run by private companies. In 1933 the state's share in private enterprise increased significantly when three of the most important banks in Italy were nationalized and their shares in private enterprise companies were transferred to the Istituto per la Ricostruzione Industriale (IRI) (K. Holland 2012, 1). IRI's main activities were steel, engineering, shipbuilding, electricity, and telephones. It was also a highly diversified, multisectoral holding company with a controlling interest in three of the largest national banks, Alitalia airline, Italy's main shipping companies, Italian radio and television (Radio Audizioni Italiane, RAI), a large part of the Italian telephone system, and the Alfa-Romeo automobile company. What was envisioned initially as a temporary response to economic crisis (Pargendler 2012, 2948) created enduring public-private enterprises in modern manufacturing and services (S. Holland 1972, 1). As Europe's "largest market-disciplined public enterprise" (Layton 1972, 47), IRI attracted considerable international attention after World War II as a model of state enterprise in a democratic, capitalist society. Indeed, in the 1950s and early 1960s it was touted as an example of state enterprise that was as efficient and dynamic as private enterprise, and its model of procuring the majority of its financing on the open market rather than from government grants was deemed a success (Ginsborg 2013, 283; S. Holland 1972, 1). During this period, public managers and entrepreneurs with close ties to the dominant political parties formed what Guido Carli, the governor of the Bank of Italy from 1960 to 1965, called "a state bourgeoisie" (Ginsborg 2003, 284).

State ownership declined significantly in the late 1960s (Ginsborg 2003, 283) when the major programs developing steel and the building of the national highways came to an end and IRI became mired in failure. Although scholars continue to debate the reasons for this decline, there is no doubt that between 1990 and 2005, the state's overall equity interest in publicly traded companies nearly halved. In spite of this, in 2001 the publicly listed firms controlled by the Italian government still accounted for 22.4 percent of total market capitalization (Pargendler 2012, 2951). While this is considerably less than the 80 percent of market capitalization held by government-controlled firms in China (Pargendler 2012, 2918), the difference is one of degree rather than of two entirely different types of relations between state, private enterprise, and market.

In the case of the Italian textile and clothing sector, however, state involvement has been limited to labor regulations, import-export controls, and taxation. The vast majority of financing for textile and clothing firms has come from family loans and firm profits, and there have been no state enterprises or mixed state-private firms. Indeed, Italian firm owners and managers in this sector are quick to contrast their independence from the Italian state with the involvement of the Chinese state in their partners' firms. Entrepreneurial autonomy is central to their claims about the value they bring to their joint ventures with Chinese. At the same time, as we shall see in chapter 3, the history of state enterprise in Italy is an integral part of the legacy that these firm owners and managers have brought with them to China.

In sum, together, feminist theory and our own ethnographic research lead us to emphasize that "public" and "private" are historically contingent ideological and political categories that obscure their deep entanglement, whether they refer to domestic and public life or capitalist processes. Our study includes a discussion of the blurring of this distinction as an important ethnographic aspect of the transnational encounters and negotiations among the Italians and Chinese involved in producing Italian fashion.

The Negotiation of Labor Value

Our conceptualization of the transnational production of "Italian" fashion in China as a particular form of social interdependence that shapes people's practices, dispositions, and identities led us to scrutinize the processes through which workers' labor power and value are constituted. We soon recognized that we could not understand these processes without bringing managers into the picture. Although Marx was not concerned with the labor power of managers, we discovered that an analysis of managerial labor power was indispensable to understanding the production of both value and subjectivities among managers and workers. In part I, we expand on Marx's argument that commodities are not the only things made in the production process. These include, as well, labor power and value, inequality, and identities. Critical to the transnational collaborations of the Chinese and Italians are the processes through which people actively assert, evaluate, contest, and renegotiate their respective contributions to the production and distribution of commodities. The continually changing field of power in which negotiations over the value of their labor take place, and which shape these negotiations, does not only include the asymmetrical power relations between the Chinese and Italians. It also includes those among the Italian managers and firm owners, among different types of Chinese managers and entrepreneurs, and between all of these different social actors and Chinese workers.

Although the story that Italian managers and Chinese entrepreneurs tell themselves is that they came to the work encounter with preexisting skills and knowledge, we contend that their labor power is constituted through the specific relations of their transnational collaboration. Our analysis reconfigures the conventional Marxian approach to the relation between labor power and value. Rather than begin with a conception of labor power as a transhistorical force of production through which value is produced, we trace the way in which labor power is produced through negotiations and contestations over labor value. We show that it is in the negotiation over the value of their respective contributions to the production and distribution of commodities that the knowledge and social powers of Italian managers and Chinese entrepreneurs congeal into their respective labor powers. Instead of being guided by Marx's idea that capital imposes and requires the abstraction of labor in order to make possible the generalized exchange of commodities, we focus on the processes through which people situated in asymmetric fields of power formulate and impose abstract categories of labor on both themselves and others as they negotiate and struggle over their comparative value. The heterogeneous skills and knowledge of Italian managers crystallize into a culturally specific labor power through negotiations over the value of their contribution to the Chinese production of commodities infused with Italianness. Chinese entrepreneurial labor, on the other hand, is made through a discourse of cosmopolitanism that they view as essential for transnational capitalism in China. Thus, Italian and Chinese managerial and entrepreneurial labor power and value are forged through transnational encounters rather than being brought to their collaboration already formed.

Our research demonstrates that the production of capitalist value is always a process of negotiation. This process is not simply a direct effect of capitalist investments or the result of a global stage of capitalism in which the presumed stable core of the production of value has become unhinged but rather an outcome of how people assert the value of their cultural capital, including their identities, knowledge, and habitus.[19] Our interest in the negotiation of value is thus focused not on the exchange value of the textile and clothing commodities they produce but on the relative value of the skills and knowledge, identities, classes, and cultures that are produced through their production relations.[20] We eschew a functionalist approach that characterizes differences as existing to serve capitalism, and argue instead that capitalism does not merely appropriate local difference, nor does it just link different cultural histories. Instead, we show that difference is both brought together in unequal transnational relations and hierarchies of value and generated in the process of creating and maintaining these production relations and hierarchies.

We see several advantages to the approach to labor power that we employ in this book. First, it avoids an objectivist perspective that treats labor as commensurable and measurable by a universal standard. We argue that labor power—whether managerial, entrepreneurial, or that of workers—exists neither independently of specific relations of production nor apart from culturally meaningful processes of formation. Second, the approach we have employed brings "power" into the concept of labor power, which is ironically absent in many Marxian uses. Labor power, we contend, is not a universal, transhistorical force of production but is itself culturally produced within a field of power. Third, our analysis of how inequalities of labor power and value are themselves shaped by the historically and culturally specific manner in which production relations are developed enables us to bring the state, which has not received sufficient attention, into the picture.

The Rearrangement of Accumulation

The accumulation of capital to invest in the pursuit of further wealth is generally considered to be the core of capitalism. A common approach in analyses of capitalism is to emphasize how the domination of this goal over others leads to the rearrangement of social life, which in turn creates specific relations of inequality. Virtually all aspects of social life in capitalist societies are viewed as being shaped by the pursuit of profit and the primary goal of capital accumulation. Certainly, much of social life has been rearranged in China to encourage the accumulation of wealth, including, most importantly, relations of inequality and class. Yet our approach and, in particular, our analyses in part II emphasize the multiple facets of this process, highlighting how the accumulation of wealth is itself rearranged in the pursuit of culturally meaningful goals.

The accumulation of wealth in China occurred under socialism as well, although it was directly organized by the central government and distributed in quite a different way. An overriding goal of the Chinese Communist Party (CCP) in the post-Mao era has been to keep itself in power, and one of its means for doing so after the 1989 Tiananmen demonstrations has been to encourage both nationalism and consumer culture. After those demonstrations, the Chinese state rearranged the means for the accumulation of wealth in order to avoid political upheaval. They thus further encouraged the devolution of some of the central government controls over wealth accumulation and distribution to local governments, the emergence of independent enterprises, and the production of consumer goods. With a novel emphasis on consumption, the government also promoted the rearrangement of social life, including the privatization of real estate and the development of consumer-rich middle-class aspirations. After China's 2001 entry into the World Trade Organization (WTO), even as local governments continued their control over local economies, central government bureaus reasserted their hegemony in key sectors over the accumulation of wealth, this time as corporate entities and without the accompanying commitment to wealth distribution prevalent under socialism.

While the political goals of the state mediate the way they encourage wealth accumulation, ordinary citizens still harbor a diffuse sense of the need to address inequality. This is reflected in the heated debates about corruption, especially corruption among party officials, which has led to constant rearrangements—on the part of citizens as well as the state—of licit and illicit means for accumulating wealth. "Corruption" is a key discourse that addresses new forms of inequality, the issue of guanxi, or social relationships of mutual advancement, and the role of family and kinship in wealth accumulation. Hence, the rearrangement of accumulation in China has been mediated by ongoing negotiations over proper and improper family and other relations of social interdependence. In response to numerous protests by rural and urban citizens, moreover, the state has brought back some of the welfare provisions it had discarded. The pursuit of transnational Italian-Chinese collaborations in the fashion industry is also motivated by Chinese entrepreneurs' and managers' nationalist desire for cosmopolitanism as signified by fashionable clothing as well as relations with a European nation. Thus in China, the rearrangement of social life and the pursuit of culturally meaningful social goals have overlapped as China has embraced a capitalist world economy.

The Reconfiguration of Kinship

As mentioned above, family and kinship have been pivotal in the negotiations over acceptable forms of the accumulation of profit and wealth in China. In light of the different historical legacies of the Chinese and Italians engaged in the transnational business ventures we studied, the ways in which kinship shapes the accumulation of profit among them varies. As will be seen in part III of this book, the Chinese and Italians hold different conceptions of the proper relation between family, business, and the state. These extend to their very definition of a "family firm" or "family business." Yet, in spite of these differences, kinship pervades their transnational business ventures and is an inextricable part of the processes through which financial, cultural, and social capital are converted into each other. Hence, it is crucial to the development of inequality and the reproduction of social class among both Italians and Chinese.

The pursuit of profit and accumulation of wealth by the Italian family firms engaged in collaborative ventures with Chinese partners is constituted by powerful kinship and gender sentiments and commitments. Kinship has been central to capitalist accumulation and a force of production in Italy for centuries and continues to be so today in a country where family firms constitute an overwhelming majority of all registered firms.[21] It is no less central in the transnational expansion of Italian family firms in the fashion industry that have outsourced manufacturing to Chinese factories, forged joint ventures with Chinese firms, and set up distribution chains in China. Indeed, Yanagisako argues that Italian family firms are as much "kinship" projects as "economic" ones. Thus, while transnational expansion has created more managerial positions for nonfamily members, it has not resulted in a shift toward control by professionally trained nonfamily members. Those firms that have been successful in transnational expansion have been able to incorporate more generations, thereby postponing division of the firm and its patrimony.

Kinship is likewise central to aspirations of accumulation among the Chinese engaged in these transnational enterprises. Given their recent socialist legacy, however, the link between family and business is fraught with ambivalence and the potential for accusations of corruption. This is especially true of firms that have developed out of formerly state-run enterprises, where the involvement of family members treads on connections between family and state that are seen as a major cause of corruption. A "family firm" in and of itself can thus be viewed as a sign of corruption. These accusations of corruption, in turn, are a central aspect of debates in China about novel relations of inequality that emerged with the introduction of the market economy. The Chinese firms that engaged in collaborative ventures with the Italians thus felt pressed to provide narratives addressing these potential accusations. Rofel found that these narratives were sometimes surprising and unexpected. They ranged from denials that they were family firms (despite having family members working in the firm), to denials that they had evolved from state-owned enterprises (despite clear evidence to the contrary), to claims of regional cultural essentialism. Only those firms that had been started by Chinese who had lived in Italy—what Rofel calls Chinese-Italian Chinese firms—felt relatively at ease about displaying the fact that they were indeed family firms.

The centrality of kinship to these profit-seeking transnational business ventures challenges models of capitalist modernity that posit the separation of kinship from the economy. Although kinship had been central to earlier anthropological models of social structure, when the discipline expanded its scope to include capitalist societies, kinship was relegated to the margins of social theory and located firmly outside the economy. In doing this, anthropology too readily accepted dominant theories of modern capitalism—whether Durkheimian, Weberian, or Marxist—that posited the decline in the significance of kinship in the face of the emergence of a rational market and modern institutions of governance despite the continuing prevalence of family businesses in many societies and the fact that many leading transnational corporations (e.g., Walmart, Murdoch News Corporation) are family firms. Our study demonstrates unequivocally that kinship continues to be a constitutive force in contemporary capitalism.

The Outsourcing of Inequality

The dynamic processes discussed above have also shaped the formation and interpretation of inequalities in both Italy and China since the 1980s. This highlights our point that we cannot begin with a foundational premise about capitalist inequalities, such as the capital/labor relationship, but must instead investigate how this relationship is shaped by other key political, social, and cultural dynamics. The ongoing negotiations over the value of the various contributions of Italians and Chinese to their relationship both indexes and constructs transnational inequalities. The ability to impose abstract categories of labor and hence shape inequalities takes place in a constantly shifting field of power. While the Italians (at least initially) brought the capital, Chinese managers and entrepreneurs insist on the fact that without their contribution, the production of "Italian" fashion in China could not proceed. The exploitation of Chinese workers' labor occurs in multiply mediated commodity chains, enabling a displacement of the source of their exploitation.

As we stated above, this includes the significant role of the state. The "privatization" process in China, which in fact blurs the boundary between private and public, is one means by which state corporations and government officials take advantage of their positions to garner a great deal of the new wealth. Paradoxically, the way in which a majority of citizens have been led to accept capitalist means of creating wealth and its attendant inequalities is to displace a critique of inequality onto the socialist past.[22] The widespread anger about corruption focuses on the wealth accumulation of officials' families and kinship networks, which is said to be a holdover from that past.

The state, moreover, has been central to the way in which foreign investment has evolved in China. The Chinese state first set the terms of that investment, delineated its parameters, and gradually changed the means and mode of that investment. The Chinese state evacuated its socialist protection of workers in the interest of increasing this investment. And it has been state policies, dating back to the 1950s, that have instituted inequality between rural and urban areas in China in the interest of rapid industrial development. The continuing division between rural and urban has made urban workers more highly valued than rural migrant workers. In the current era, it has created a pool of cheap labor as migrant workers from the countryside fill the multinational factories. Yet urban residents blame these migrant workers for being "backward" (*luohou*). With few exceptions, they do not identify with migrant workers' dilemmas. It is not uncommon for urbanites to treat them as if they literally come from another country (an impression fostered by the numerous dialects people from different regions speak). But again, it is the state that has protected China from becoming dominated by Western countries and the international organizations the latter have constructed in the name of free trade.

State policies that have favored foreign direct investment (FDI), including tax holidays and gifts of real estate, along with China's entry into the WTO, have meant that China's domestic economy has become inextricably intertwined with the global economy. The nationalism fostered by the state in the wake of Tiananmen along with histories of the colonial past have led Chinese entrepreneurs to blame current inequalities on their international partners, including the Italians, who often bring the capital, while Chinese workers, managers, and entrepreneurs supply the labor that has turned China into the workshop of the world.

The Italian firm owners and managers in these transnational ventures, conversely, attribute the inequality between themselves and their Chinese partners to the inexperience of the Chinese in capitalism and their lack of understanding of Western fashion. In conceding to the Chinese the technical skills of manufacturing, they simultaneously deny them the creativity needed to successfully compete in the global fashion industry. Hence, inequalities between Italians and Chinese in these collaborations are viewed as a logical outcome of their different histories and experiences and therefore their different roles in production and distribution. Whether they naturalize this difference as a consequence of Italian and Chinese proclivities or historicize it, they view it as a reasonable basis of inequality.

When it comes to the inequalities experienced in Italy, Italian firm owners and managers once again view this as a consequence of the globalization of the economy and China's role in it. They are fully aware that both workers and managers in Italy face greater job instability and financial vulnerability than they did in the boom years of the 1960s and 1970s. On the one hand, they resent the emergence of China as the preeminent site for the manufacture of commodities, including textiles and clothing, viewing it as a threat to the integrity of both Italian fashion and an Italian way of life that preceded the move toward outsourcing in the 1990s. On the other hand, they blame Italian workers, labor unions, and the regulations of the Italian state for raising the cost of production in Italy and, in their view, driving firms to manufacture in China in order to be competitive in the global market. For them, the divergent trajectories of success and wealth between those Italian family firms that have profited from the outsourcing of manufacturing to China and other countries and those that have not are a collateral effect of globalization. The same is true of their views of the decline in opportunities for creating new family firms.

We call this mutual displacement among Chinese and Italians the outsourcing of inequality. This outsourcing derives both from the way in which commodity chains in the transnational production of fashion have evolved and from the particular histories the Chinese and Italians bring to their encounters.

All five dynamic processes that we discuss here are mediated by powerful cultural sentiments and commitments that are usually excluded from analyses of capitalism. Whether these commitments pertain to kinship, gender, value, nationalism, or identity, the dynamic processes they generate are not embedded in either "economic" or "noneconomic" relations; they are constitutive of them.

Historical Context

Despite popular images of China as a "closed" society that has only recently opened to the West, both the historic silk road and contemporary transnational capitalist relations remind us that China and the West have long been active business partners. Among the many manufacturing sectors and markets connected today by the twenty-first-century silk road are the Chinese and Italian fashion industries, which stand in relation as both competitors and collaborators. In 2008 Italy was the leading European exporter of textiles and apparel and second only to China in terms of global market share. With 50,000 enterprises employing over 500,000 workers, this sector has been a major contributor to Italy's balance of trade, compensating for the negative balance in other sectors such as power and food (Greta and Lewandowski 2010, 20–21). When it comes to luxury fashion, moreover, Italian firms consisted of one-third of this sector (Riello 2012, 153). Ten Italian companies were estimated to control as much of 20 percent of the global luxury market, manufacturing goods valued at 40 billion euros (Greta and Lewandowski 2010, 20–21).

Beginning in the 1980s and increasingly in the 1990s, Italian textile and clothing firms outsourced manufacturing to lower-wage countries, including Romania, Bulgaria, Turkey, and China.[23] More recently, China has become both the major manufacturer of Italian textiles and apparel as well as the most promising market for Italian fashion brands. Yet long before the current era, links between Italy and China were integral to the production of Italian silk, which has been a staple in fashion clothing. Even after the Italians learned sericulture (the raising of silkworms) from the Chinese, the importation of Chinese silk to Italy, which began in the Roman period, continued along both the maritime route around Southeast Asia and the historic silk road through Inner Asia and the Middle East (J. Abu-Lughod 1989; Arrighi, Silver, and Brewer 2003; Rofel 2012). These trade ties continued to be important even after the industrial manufacturing of silk developed in Como in the northern Italian region of Lombardy in the late nineteenth century. European colonialism in the mid-nineteenth century intensified China's economic relations with European countries. Although sericulture was practiced in Como in both preindustrial and industrial periods, raw silk was also imported from Japan and China, and by the 1930s the decline in local sericulture led to the importation of most of the raw silk from these countries. After World War II, Italy relied almost entirely on China for raw silk and increasingly for already spun silk thread. All other phases in the production of silk fabric in Italy continued to be undertaken in Como—including the twisting of silk thread, its texturization and dyeing, and the weaving, dyeing, and printing of fabric.

After China's 1949 socialist revolution, the socialist world economy, especially aid from the Soviet Union, helped China recover from a century of instability and war and pursue industrialization-led development.[24] Owing to the U.S. embargo of China, a dominant assumption in the United States is that in the socialist period (1949–84), China had economic ties only with the socialist and nonaligned Third Worlds. In fact, China had well-developed trade ties with Italy and other European countries as well as Japan through the Ministry of Foreign Trade, exporting mainly textiles and other raw materials (Hsiao 1977; Mah 1971). Hong Kong served as a key conduit of indirect trade with Western and nonsocialist countries (Eckstein 1966). Italy became an even more important trading partner after the 1960 Sino-Soviet split (Eckstein 1977; Hsiao 1977; Mah 1971).

Silk had long been produced in China in household spinning and weaving businesses. Under European colonial organization, silk production, especially in the Lower Yangzi River region of Shanghai, Hangzhou, Jiaxing, and Suzhou, began to take place in large factories geared toward export. After the socialist revolution, all production was moved into large, vertically integrated state-run enterprises (Rofel 1999). In Italy, in contrast, the industrial manufacture of silk was spread over a loosely organized network of firms, the vast majority of which usually undertook only one phase of the production process (Yanagisako 2002). "Converter" firms initiated production by procuring orders from fabric wholesalers and garment manufacturers and then paying subcontracting firms to complete one of the phases in the production process. A move to centralize production in vertically integrated firms was initiated in the 1950s and 1960s, but this was soon abandoned in response to the labor conflicts of the late sixties and the rising labor costs and global recession of the early seventies, all of which underscored the advantages of decentralized but coordinated networks of small firms (Yanagisako 2002, 30). In the 1980s, some Como firms began importing unprinted silk fabric from China, and by the 1990s, they were importing printed fabric.

When Como's silk firms and other Italian textile and clothing firms began moving manufacturing to China in the 1990s, China was on its way to becoming known as the workshop of the world. Like capitalist firms in other countries, Como's silk firms as well as Italian firms producing wool, cotton, and linen fabric and apparel were initially lured to China by the low cost of labor and, subsequently, by its huge potential domestic market. The investment in production and sales in China was a significant shift in the strategy of Italian textile and clothing manufacturers. Even as they began outsourcing production to China, these firms complained about China as a source of inferior products and unfair competition. By the late 1990s, the increasingly favorable environment for foreign investment and trade created by various levels of the

Chinese government made China the most-favored nation for the outsourcing of some or all phases of the production of Italian textiles and clothing. The divergent interests of Italian brand owners and manufacturers became apparent as the number of textile and clothing manufacturing firms declined dramatically in the three decades between 1980 and 2010, while Italian fashion consumption expanded globally.

At the same time, a sea change swept through China since the beginning of the 1990s. This was an acceleration of what in China is known as "economic reform"—a broad set of policies begun in the early 1980s to rid China of Maoist socialism in all aspects of life through the decentralization of economic planning, the end of collective enterprise, the promotion of a market economy, and the steady move toward the domination of social life by profit-seeking, including some privatization (Naughton 1995, 2007; Oi and Walder 1999; Wang Hui 2003; Wank 1998). While the state gradually retreated from a centrally planned economy, it continued to participate strongly in the market economy. Indeed, one striking aspect of economic life in China today is the intimate involvement of all levels of the state in profit-producing enterprises (Naughton 2007).[25] As described above, a large number of profit-oriented businesses are mixtures of government and private ownership and management. These are joined by the vast number of state bureaucracies that own and operate for-profit businesses. Finally, the central government's decision to maintain a strong hold on key resources has led to state monopolies in critical sectors of the economy.[26] Thus the Adam Smithian opposition of the market versus the state does not help us understand the nature of capitalist activity in China today.[27] These changes in the role of the state in the market brought an increasingly visible amount of what gets labeled "corruption" among political officials, as they began to position themselves advantageously in relation to the market economy. The redistribution of some public resources under the rubric of privatization created new inequalities, as the urban/rural divide widened and the gap between the newly enriched classes and the poor grew exponentially.[28]

After the political crisis of June 4, 1989, known in the West as the Tiananmen demonstrations, then leader Deng Xiaoping and his supporters took advantage of the crisis to accelerate market-based profitization. Only during this post–June Fourth period did the state begin to encourage large-scale foreign investment in China.[29] This "opening" of China that Western commentators so frequently describe is more accurately understood as a turn away from post-Bandung commitments to the nonaligned and Third World and toward closer involvement with the United States, Europe, Japan, and the four East Asian newly industrialized countries (Taiwan, Hong Kong, Singapore, and South Korea).

During these early years, the foreign-invested enterprises were kept separate from the domestic economy. All foreign firms were required to invest in joint ventures with the Chinese government, initially with the central government but then increasingly with local state entities. In 1999 the prohibition on foreign economic cooperation with private enterprises in China was lifted (Rofel 2007). By 2000, in a significant reversal, the government stipulated quotas of foreign investment that *all* areas had to fill. With its eye toward joining the WTO, the central government allowed foreign companies to establish wholly foreign-owned enterprises without joint Chinese state ownership. Larger amounts of foreign investment translated into more local financial and political autonomy and greater prestige for local officials.

By 2002, after joining the WTO, China had surpassed the United States as the most favored destination for foreign direct investment (Gallagher 2005, 34).[30] Compared to other large developing countries, China is in a league of its own.[31] These shifts in Chinese policies, along with the 2008 lifting of the WTO import quotas imposed on China in the Multi-Fiber Agreement (MFA), led to a further increase in Italian textile and clothing firms engaged in manufacturing and distributing their products in China, through a variety of forms of collaboration with Chinese partners.[32]

When we began this project, we could not have predicted that China's economy and world economic presence would grow and transform as quickly as it did in the first decade of the twenty-first century. Since Italians began moving production to China, the relations of production, marketing, and distribution have changed faster than perhaps anyone could have imagined. The rapid growth of the Chinese market, the government's emphasis on consumer culture, the rise in the wages of workers as the government enforces a new labor law, the state's recent emphasis, following Europe and the U.S., on developing a "knowledge economy" and the "culture industries," and the increased presence of Chinese state-owned and private companies in all regions of the world have all contributed to the realization by the Chinese and Italians that their relationship, from the beginning of the 1980s, has always been in flux. Yet this much-discussed "rise" of China has not erased China's role in supplying workers in labor-intensive industries, including textiles and garment production.[33] Here we continue to find variegated forms of transnational capitalism emerging in relation to one another.

Collaborative Ethnographic Research

Since 2002, we have been investigating the formation and transformation of the transnational relations of production, distribution, and marketing of "Italian" fashion among Chinese and Italians in the unique historical context we outlined above. Our research has been conducted primarily in two sites: the eastern coast of China around Shanghai, which has served as one of the central locations for Western foreign involvement in China, particularly for labor-intensive industries such as textiles geared for export; and the Como-Milan area of the province of Lombardy in northern Italy, which is the center of the Italian and silk fashion industries. Italian and other foreign firms initially located themselves in Shanghai while establishing enterprises throughout the larger area, including the cities of Hangzhou and Jiaxing. The transnational collaborations we have studied thus link Shanghai and its environs to northern Italy and, through distribution networks, eventually to other areas of Europe and the United States.

Our collaborative project arose through the convergences of our respective previous research. Rofel began her research in Hangzhou's silk industry in 1984, just as economic reform was taking off in China's urban centers. She witnessed the devolution of central planning, the ability of state-run silk factories to pursue profits, the beginnings of hiring migrant labor, and the desires of some of the young urban factory workers to leave the factory and become entrepreneurs (Rofel 1999). These silk factories sold their silk garments and silk quilt covers to a domestic market that was just beginning to develop. They also surreptitiously sold goods through Hong Kong but otherwise had no direct contact with foreign businesses. The city of Shenzhen, on the border with Hong Kong, had just been invented to be the sole, cordoned-off location in China to experiment with foreign direct investment. In the same year, Yanagisako began her research in Como, Italy, on family firms in the silk industry. Like all textile industries in Italy, Como's silk industry had been composed almost entirely of family firms throughout both its preindustrial and industrial history.[34] Although the industry was thriving in this period, anxieties about competition from China were already pervasive—so much so that some firm owners initially harbored suspicions that Yanagisako was a spy for the Chinese silk industry.

By the late 1980s, Rofel began to find foreigners investing in the Lower Yangzi River region but always in joint ventures with some counterpart of the Chinese government, whether municipal, provincial, or central. Foreign trade was overwhelmingly controlled by state-owned import-export bureaus. The silk factories where Rofel had done research were finding themselves flourishing through foreign trade but also pinched by competition from rural-based silk factories, with their significantly lower wages, that had sprung up around the more loosely controlled rural industrialization efforts. Only in the 1990s were foreigners allowed to make direct arrangements with textile factories. By the late 1990s, Chinese factories were vigorously searching for foreign production and trade partners. At the same time, silk began a precipitous decline. Together with foreign companies, Chinese factories began to combine silk with other fabrics. By the turn of the century, most of the fifteen main silk factories Rofel had researched in the mid-1980s had closed, merged, privatized, become joint ventures with foreign firms, or begun to produce almost solely for export.

Meanwhile, the Italian silk industry suffered a significant decline in the 1990s, much of which the Como manufacturers blamed on "unfair" competition from China. They accused China of having intentionally flooded the global market with cheap silk garments, undercutting the prestige of silk. At the same time, they acknowledged that changes in lifestyle in Europe and the U.S. were also crucial in the decline of silk consumption. The increase in women's employment meant that women no longer had the time or the interest in caring for silk clothing, including silk lingerie, and the shift toward more casual fashion meant that fewer men were wearing silk ties on a regular basis. Throughout the 1990s and in the first years of the next decade, Como's leading firms experimented with a variety of strategies, including new fabric mixtures and outsourcing manufacturing to Romania, India, and China. None of these efforts were successful in turning around the decline of Como's silk industry, in which the number of firms was cut in half between 1981 and 2001.[35]

The collaborations between Italian and Chinese entrepreneurs in silk thus led to our own collaboration in research. In 2002 we began preliminary research in the Shanghai area, tracking those Como silk firms and other textile producers that were outsourcing manufacturing or forging joint ventures with Chinese firms. We were joined in this by Simona Segre Reinach, an anthropologist and fashion studies scholar, who had worked before with Yanagisako and who helped us understand how these transnational collaborations fit into the history of Italian fashion. As our research proceeded, so did the numbers of Italian textile and clothing firms outsourcing production in China, actively seeking joint ventures, and opening retail stores. Having discovered that Como's silk firms made up only a small part of the Italian-Chinese collaborations in fashion, we broadened our study to include the manufacture and distribution of Italian fashion brands.

As we mentioned at the beginning of this chapter, one of the benefits of our collaborative ethnographic research has been our ability to listen to both parties in these transnational encounters. Most research on transnationalism has had access to only one of the parties in these encounters, which too often results in analyses that overlook the intentions, meanings, and interpretations of other parties. Listening to both sides of the conversation has placed us in a better position to forge a more comprehensive, interactional analysis of the actions and reactions, interpretations and misinterpretations, understandings and misunderstandings through which the Italians and Chinese in these transnational business collaborations reformulate their goals, strategies, values, and identities. We pursued ethnographic research in China both together and separately among firms in the greater Shanghai area, including Hangzhou and Jiaxing, and in Wenzhou. Lisa Rofel also conducted interviews and participant-observation among workers in the factory she wrote about in her first book, in a silk yarn factory, and in a business that has textile, dyeing, and garment factories, and she followed the networks of entrepreneurs connected to one another in the export of fashion clothing. We did a small amount of research together in Italy—in particular, on the *pronta moda* (fast fashion) industry in women's clothing in Prato, which has been developed by the largest Chinese community in Italy. Finally, Sylvia Yanagisako and Simona Segre Reinach followed the Italian firms back to their headquarters and production sites in Como, Milan, and Rome and also interviewed industry representatives and government officials.

On a more humorous note, we should add that another benefit of our research collaboration was the amusement and bemusement we generated for our informants in both Italy and China. Most perceived Sylvia Yanagisako to be Chinese, even after discovering that she neither speaks Chinese nor has Chinese ancestors. (We often explained that she was born and raised in Hawai'i to underplay her Japanese ancestry.) Lisa Rofel, on the other hand, can easily be mistaken as Italian, even though she does not have Italian ancestors, nor does she speak Italian. On several occasions, Chinese entrepreneurs, managers, and workers continued to address their responses to Yanagisako, even after Rofel asked the questions in Mandarin and translated answers into English for Yanagisako. These confusions, along with the way in which translation impeded the flow and intimacy of conversations, eventually led us to cut down on conducting bilingual joint interviews and participant observation. Yanagisako and Segre Reinach, however, continued to interview some Italian speakers together in Italy and China.

China Rising, but in Fashion?

The ubiquity of clothing made in China and sold in markets throughout the world has become a constant reminder of China's rise as a powerful force in the global economy. Yet despite having become the primary site for the manufacture of textiles and clothing, along with a plethora of other commodities, China is far from being viewed as a primary mover in the global fashion industry. Indeed, its reputation as the "workshop of the world"—or, in less flattering terms, the "sweatshop of the world"—has undercut the prestige value of "Chinese fashion." Hence, the asymmetry between the Chinese and Italians in the collaborations we studied has been shaped by the specific history and structure of the fashion industry. Had we studied the production and distribution of computers, cell phones, steel, or solar panels, these asymmetries would have been significantly different.

Fashion, with its claim to aesthetic distinction, identifies design as the key component in the production of value. To put it more strongly, the value of fashion is said to reside in design. The fashion industry's celebration of the fashion designer as a creative artist who produces an innovative collection of clothing obscures the fact that design is a complex, interactive process involving many participants. In fashion industry representations, other indispensable links in the global supply chain of producing and distributing clothing fade into the background in comparison to the work of design. Having established Italy as a center of fashion design, especially after World War II, Italian brands and firms have been able to make strong claims for the value of their contribution to Italian-Chinese collaborations in clothing manufacture. Likewise, Italians claim greater knowledge and expertise in the distribution and marketing of fashion. As will be seen in the chapters to follow, including the chapter by Simona Segre Reinach on Chinese-Italian sensibilities in producing Italian fashion, this fashion history has restricted what Chinese entrepreneurs have been able to claim about the value they contribute to the global chain of production and distribution.[36]

The dynamic field of power in which the Italians and Chinese in our study collaborate is shaped by the particularities of the fashion industry in yet another significant way. The vast majority of Italian textile and clothing firms are family owned and managed, while the Chinese firms in this sector are characterized by a wider variety of arrangements, from state-owned to public-private to completely private. The latter include family firms but also many that are not family owned or managed. The Italian family firms that have been successful in the global fashion industry, especially those in the luxury sector, have emerged over the last three decades as the new bourgeois aristocracy of Italy. Whereas before the 1980s, families in other sectors, such as banking, energy, and automobiles, were the most prestigious in Italy, since the 1980s this older bourgeoisie has been eclipsed by families in the fashion industry, especially those whose surnames are identical to the brand. Not only are these Italian families much more wealthy than their Chinese partners, but they are recognized both in Italy and China, as well as globally, as fashion celebrities. In comparison, their Chinese partners have, at best, reputations as regionally successful entrepreneurs. Others are known only as the owners of subcontracting factories. As such, they can hardly claim the distinction that their Italian partners enjoy. This prestige hierarchy also shapes the claims Chinese entrepreneurs and managers make about their cosmopolitanism and the value they bring to the production and distribution process.

As we have noted, the asymmetries in the field of power in which these Italian-Chinese collaborations operate have been constantly changing. This is true of the fashion industry as well. Whereas the Chinese government's major strategy in the early 1990s was to encourage vast amounts of foreign investment geared mainly toward foreign export by providing low-cost labor, their most recent strategy has been to develop domestic consumption among a growing Chinese middle class, build the infrastructure of the inland areas away from the coast in order to raise the standard of living in inland provinces, and raise China from the level of low-cost labor provider to producer of knowledge that can claim a greater share of the profits from capitalist production. The rapid growth of the Chinese market, the rise in the wages of workers as the government enforces a new labor law, and the state's recent emphasis, following Europe and the U.S., on developing a "knowledge economy" and the "culture industries" all contribute to the understanding among Chinese and Italians that their asymmetrical relationship is neither fixed nor stable. For their part, Chinese entrepreneurs in the fashion industry are frustrated that their contribution to the production, marketing, and distribution of Italian fashion brands is not sufficiently recognized by their Italian partners. The unstable dynamic of their continually changing relations provides the context for ongoing Italian and Chinese negotiations over the value of their respective contributions to "Made in Italy" in China.

We are, of course, far from experts in the field of fashion studies. As the global fashion industry has developed, so has this interdisciplinary field of scholarship. From the outset of our research, we recognized that we needed the knowledge and expertise of a fashion studies scholar to situate the transnational collaborations between the Chinese and Italians in the history of fashion production. Our work with Segre Reinach has been integral in enabling us to understand how the moniker "Made in Italy" has, since the end of World War II, linked ready-to-wear design with industrial production and, moreover, has depended on transnational relations of production, consumption, cross-cultural borrowings, and valuation of aesthetics.

Collaborative Writing and Outline of the Book

In cowriting this monograph, we have not sought to present a single narrative voice. While we convey our shared theoretical framework and integrated analysis in the introduction to this book, in the introductions to its three parts, and in the chapter in part I, we have retained our different narrative styles in writing the separate chapters in parts II and III. While this may have resulted in an unevenness, for example, in our description of Italian and Chinese informants, we value this difference in representation and its reflection of both our different styles of ethnographic analysis and writing as well as those among the people we studied.

Three core themes that emerged through our collaborative research and analysis provide the framework for our analysis of transnational capitalist processes and the organizational structure of this book.

Part I, which is coauthored by us, addresses the negotiations over value between Italian firm owners and managers and Chinese entrepreneurs, the asymmetries in their relations that shape these negotiations, and how they justify or hope to transform them. We analyze the various emphases that Italian owners and managers and Chinese entrepreneurs and managers place on their respective national and cultural identities, historical legacies, relationship to fashion, and place both within China and beyond it. As stated above, in this first part we argue that the production of the value of labor and labor power is always a process of negotiation within historically specific fields of power. The interactive character of this process both enabled and called for an integrated analysis of the Chinese and Italians engaged in them, even as their perspectives, legacies, and identities differ.[37]

In part II, we trace the historical legacies and revisionist histories through which various Chinese and Italian social actors established their collaborations, as well as how they interpret their respective individual, family, class, and cultural-national histories to explain their current situation and their hopes and concerns for the future. We examine the importance of these legacies and revisionist histories for the way in which their transnational capitalist projects are forged. In contrast to part I, part II includes a coauthored introduction, a chapter by Yanagisako on the Italians, and a chapter by Rofel on the Chinese. This format allows us to trace the ways in which transnational collaborations are formed without fragmenting our analysis of how they are shaped by the respective historical legacies of the Italians and Chinese. A deep understanding of these respective historical legacies is crucial to understanding the different ideas about labor, inequality, commodities, nation, state, and family they bring to their collaborations.

Segre Reinach's chapter, which falls at the end of part II, interrogates "Italian fashion" as simultaneously a discourse, a product, and a national brand. As an anthropologist and fashion studies scholar, she examines the evolution of the relations between Italians and Chinese in fashion production through three forms of collaboration: sourcing, in which Italians procured both raw materials and labor in China; fashion production, in both its material (manufacturing) and immaterial aspects; and branding, the distribution of fashion products through the signifier of the brand. Her essay elaborates on the changing tensions in their relations as the Italians and Chinese negotiate the transformations in both China's economy and Italy's global fashion industry. The latter, Segre Reinach argues, has been undergoing an identity crisis as the globalization of "Made in Italy" has dismantled the original fashion-production model rooted in the alliance between *stilismo* and large-scale industrial manufacturing that created its success. As financial investment has become increasingly significant in the survival of fashion companies, China has become increasingly important to the future of Italian fashion.

Part III focuses on the kinship and gender relations that are critical to, but have different valences for, the Italians and Chinese and the manner in which they develop collaborative relationships. While the Italians tout the family-based nature of their firms, Chinese entrepreneurs often have a more ambivalent and ambiguous relationship to claiming they are a family firm, in large part due to the way public discourse about corruption pinpoints family favoritism. Given the different historical legacies that shape Chinese and Italian ideas about the nexus of family, business, and state, part III, like part II, includes a coauthored introduction, a chapter by Yanagisako on the Italians, and a chapter by Rofel on the Chinese. This enables our respective chapters to focus on key kinship and gender sentiments, concerns, and aspirations of the Italians and Chinese without being constrained by a conventional comparative analysis. For example, in her chapter, Rofel asserts that for the Chinese, "corruption" is a key frame through which family business is construed, and she shows how this shapes and constrains their approach to family business. "Corruption," however, is not a salient issue for Italian family firms because the link between family and business has been normalized and has become normative in Italian capitalism.[38] Consequently, any attempt to pursue a parallel analysis of corruption and Italian family firms would distort our understanding of the concerns and issues that Italians bring with them to their transnational collaborations and encounters. Instead, Yanagisako's chapter analyzes two distinct processes of generation that are critical to understanding Italian family firms, both their historical persistence and the generation of new ones. She shows how the transnational expansion of the Italian textile and clothing industry has had different consequences for these two integral processes of generation and, consequently, for Italian family firms in both Italy and China.

We offer a brief conclusion that reviews our main arguments about transnational capitalism and then discuss the transformations that have occurred since we completed our fieldwork. China's so-called rise, which signals its increased investments abroad and its growing domestic market catering to the expanding middle classes, and the economic, political, and social challenges that Italy, along with other countries in the European Union, has faced in the past five years indicate that Italian-Chinese collaborations will undoubtedly experience change. Most notable is the growing emphasis on Chinese consumers. Yet China has not ended its role as workshop of the world, a role that sits alongside its transnational investments, and the Italian fashion industry will continue to be produced through transnational collaborations.

1 The Negotiation of Value

Given the multiple chains and intervening links of production and supply entailed in transnational capitalism, the issue of value has risen to the fore. Our focus in this first part of the book is on the negotiations between Italian managers and Chinese entrepreneurs over the value of their contributions to the Chinese production of Italian fashion and the changing asymmetries in their relationships that shape these negotiations. Critical to the outcome of these dynamic entanglements of transnational capitalism are the cultural processes through which Italians and Chinese actively construct their actions, dispositions, identities, and labor power. Through these interactive cultural processes, they assert, evaluate, justify, contest, and renegotiate the relative value of their contributions to the production and distribution of textiles and clothing.

Our ethnographic analysis in this chapter shows how labor power and value are forged through the encounter between Italians and Chinese rather than brought to it already formed. We argue that the formation of labor power and value and the transformation of the cultural dispositions, identities, and practices of actors through transnational processes of production is part of the vast reorganization of global production that has challenged our understanding of the relationship between capital, labor, and the value of the (other) commodities it produces. Yet our analysis challenges the idea that the question of value has only become a problem with neoliberal capitalism. All value, whether quantified or not, depends on the cultural valuation of specific practices, as well as on institutionalized powers of law and formal practices such as accounting and the measurement of GDP. The asymmetries in access to capital, institutional power, cultural and political histories, and the flux of emergent relations shape the dynamics of these transnational processes of production but cannot fully determine them.

As we delineate in the introduction to this book, since the Italians began moving production to China in the 1980s, the rapid growth of the Chinese market, the rise in the wages of workers as the government enforces a recent labor law, and the state's recent emphasis, following Europe and the U.S., on developing a "knowledge economy" and the "culture industries" all promote an unstable field of power in which Italians and Chinese negotiate the value of their respective contributions. We argue that the explicit emphasis that Chinese and Italians place on the value of their contribution to the production, distribution, and marketing of fashion clothing labeled as Italian is shaped by these unstable asymmetries and the continually changing field of power.

Our interest in the negotiation of value focuses not on the exchange value of the textile and clothing commodities they produce but on the relative value of the skills and knowledge, identities, and cultures that are produced through their production relations.[1] As we argue in the introduction, transnational capitalism is a historically situated form of social interdependence in which culturally specific actors produce selves, forms of labor, and collectivities, along with commodities, all of which are mediated by the form of this social interdependence.

In part I, we are primarily concerned with two groups of social actors whose interactions and negotiations are central to the production and distribution of Italian fashion in China: Italian managers and Chinese managers and entrepreneurs. We trace key processes through which these Italian and Chinese managers and entrepreneurs negotiate the value of their respective contributions to the transnational production of commodities and profit in the fashion industry and, in doing so, constitute their respective labor powers. These managers and entrepreneurs work in a range of business collaborations in the textile and clothing industries.

It should be noted that when we use the terms "manager" and "entrepreneur," we do not approach these categories as either universal or static. To the contrary, their historically specific meanings for Italians and Chinese are part of what shapes people's subjectivities and the negotiations over the value of their respective contributions. As Yanagisako (2002) has argued in her previous work, distinctions among capitalists, managers, and workers are not always stable; one must take a diachronic approach to people's work and class trajectories over time.

Negotiating Value and Constituting Labor Power

Our discussion of what Italian managers and Chinese managers and entrepreneurs say about the value of their respective contributions to the production, distribution, and marketing of textiles and clothing leads to our analysis of managerial labor power. We are aware that Marx was not concerned with managers' labor power and that it will seem peculiar to some that we employ this concept in our discussions of managers and entrepreneurs. We find it useful, nonetheless, to pursue an analysis of labor power among managers and entrepreneurs because it shows how subject-making is part of the production process for managers as well as for workers. As Marx argued and we underline in the following chapter, multiple things are made in the production process—including fabric, garments, labor power, and identities.

In Marxist theory, labor power refers to human capacities. Marx distinguished between the capacities of human beings to engage in certain kinds of labor and the actual labor they perform. He made this distinction in order to demonstrate the amount of exploitation involved when capitalists extract the capacity to labor from workers. He also hoped to indicate the political struggles that could ensue as workers realize they can resist the efforts of capitalists to exploit their capacities. Since Marx treated capitalism as a social whole, the shaping of labor powers outside the workplace was, for him, directly linked to the labor that occurred inside the workplace.[2]

In his reinterpretation of Marx's theory of labor, Moishe Postone argues that "the meaning of the category of labor in [Marx's] mature work is different from what traditionally has been assumed: it is historically specific rather than transhistorical" (1993, 5). In other words, Marx did not construe labor as a universal, goal-directed social activity that creates specific products in order to satisfy universal human needs but rather as a "historically unique form of social mediation that, though socially constituted, has an abstract, impersonal, quasi-objective character" (5). Labor in capitalism is "a historically determinate form of social practice that structures . . . people's actions, worldviews, and dispositions" (5). As Postone writes, "The theory of alienation implied by Marx's mature critical theory does not refer to the estrangement of what had previously existed as a property of the workers . . . ; rather it refers to a process of the historical constitution of social powers and knowledge that cannot be understood with reference to the immediate powers and skills of the proletariat" (5).

Like Postone, we are interested in the processes through which the social powers and knowledge of workers are constituted. We extend the range of the people engaged in these relations of social interdependence, however, to include managers and entrepreneurs. Postone's concept of labor power offers a productive lens through which we might view the historic constitution of the social powers and knowledge of managers and entrepreneurs. Our concern here is with understanding how the transnational relations entailed in the production of "Italian" commodities in China are a historically specific form of social interdependence that produces social practices that, in turn, shape people's actions, worldviews, and dispositions. Unlike Postone, we do not approach this question inductively by theorizing it as a process of objectification through which social powers and skills become quasi-independent of workers, leading to their estrangement from these very social powers and knowledge. Instead, our approach is to ask how these social powers and knowledge are constituted, and how, in the process, people's actions, worldviews, and dispositions are transformed.

Our work examines how labor power develops not just outside the workplace but through the interactions, negotiations, and practices that occur within the relations of production proper. These cultural processes entail conceptualization and interpretation as well as instantiation. Thus, it would be a mistake to view managers and entrepreneurs' insistence on the value of their contributions as mere conceptualization that stands apart from the actual capacities they demonstrate. These are not just discourses about labor power but the materially instantiated labor power that, in the view of managers and entrepreneurs, produces the value of Italian-labeled fashion.

Asymmetry and the Unstable Field of Power

Like Chinese and Italian firm owners, managers, and entrepreneurs, we must grapple with the significant differences between the histories, structures, strategies, and dynamics of Italian capitalist firms and their Chinese partners. Perhaps the most significant difference is that while the vast majority of Italian textile and clothing firms are family-owned and managed, the entrepreneurial entities in China have a wider variety of arrangements, from state-owned to public-private to completely private. The latter include family firms but also many that are not family invested or family owned. Even those that are privately owned usually maintain close relationships with government entities in order to facilitate doing business in China. Put more strongly, it is virtually impossible to do business in China without close relationships with government officials at various levels. Italian firm owners too have an interest in cultivating close relations with government entities in Italy at several levels (commune, provincial, regional, and central state), but there are no state-owned companies or hybrid public-private firms in the fashion industry. Some government entities promote and support the transnational business activities of Italian firms, but firm owners and managers generally view this help as marginally effective at best. Many consider the efforts of Italian government entities a waste of time and money.

The Italians and Chinese engaged in these collaborations bring different historically informed concerns as well as differential access to forms of capital to their encounters. These include differential access to financial capital, cultural capital (e.g., brand reputation and knowledge of Western fashion), and social capital (in the case of Italians, access to distribution networks and the Western market; in the case of Chinese, knowledge of Chinese tastes, the Chinese market, state agencies, and party officials). In addition, Chinese and Italians bring to the encounter different understandings and histories of production relations; the role of the state; the relations between firm owners, managers, and workers; the power of capital investment; how particular markets operate; as well as different historical experiences of capitalism. The rules and regulations of the World Trade Organization, along with labor laws in both Italy and China, also shape their encounters. Finally, for the Italians working in China, obviously China looms large, while the Chinese working with Italians in China tend to place Italy and Italians into a broader category of "foreigners" or Westerners.

The systemic framing of the asymmetries between Chinese and Italians in our study is additionally conditioned by the specific industry in which they are involved—namely, the fashion industry. Relative to other industries, fashion places particular emphasis on design. The celebration of the fashion designer as an individual creator obscures the actual complex process of design that entails the interaction of a range of participants. The ownership of famous brands by Italians enables them to make a stronger claim to design and creativity than their Chinese partners and thus to the value of their contribution to the collaboration process. This, in turn, shapes how and what Chinese entrepreneurs can claim about the value of their contribution to the production, distribution, and marketing of fashionable clothing.

The Chinese who participate in this production process with the Italians, especially the entrepreneurs and managers, bring a strong sense of nationalism, fostered especially since the end of Maoist socialism in China, as well as knowledge, learned formally in school, about the colonial history of China in relation to the West. That this production process occurs in China also means that both the Italians and Chinese must contend with the Chinese state, which, even though it has had to accede to rather harsh WTO rules specified for China, is still stronger than most states in the Global South. Finally, both Chinese and Italians are immersed in larger public discourses—within Italy, about the presence of growing numbers of Chinese immigrants, many of whom work in the textile and garment industries; and in China, about the role of foreigners in relation to visible inequalities both within and beyond China.

The location of the production process in China also shapes the shifting and emergent character of the encounter between Chinese and Italians in the fashion industry. Whereas the Chinese government's major strategy in the early 1990s was to encourage vast amounts of foreign investment geared mainly toward foreign export by providing low-cost labor, their most recent strategy is to develop domestic consumption among a growing Chinese middle class, build the infrastructure of the inland areas away from the coast in order to raise the standard of living of inland provinces, and raise China from the level of low-cost labor provider to producer of knowledge that can claim a greater share of the profits from capitalist production. Both the Chinese and the Italians in our study work with the realization that their relationship is in rapid flux.

Italians in the fashion industry are both hopeful and anxious about these changes. On the one hand, they view the Chinese market as the salvation of "Made in Italy"—especially the luxury brands. On the other hand, they are anxious that as their Chinese partners learn more about Western tastes, design, branding, and marketing, they will take over more of the fashion market—both in China and the West. For their part, Chinese entrepreneurs in the fashion industry are frustrated that their contribution to the production, marketing, and distribution of Italian fashion brands is not sufficiently valued by their Italian partners. The unstable dynamic of their continually changing relations provides the context for Italian and Chinese negotiations over the value of their respective contributions to "Made in Italy" in China. Our analysis of this unstable dynamic also challenges the idea that a unified transnational managerial class has emerged. This unstable dynamic was manifest in the four main types of collaboration we found in our research (see the appendix for a description of the four types and the names of the firms in each type).

In the following chapter, we address the formation of the respective labor powers of Italian and Chinese managers and entrepreneurs by tracing their relations both with one another and with relevant others. In the case of Italian managers, this includes their relations with Italian firm owners. In the case of Chinese managers and entrepreneurs, this includes their relations with government officials and with people who are not from Shanghai. We analyze Italian managers' emphasis on *Italianità*, an intuitive feeling for design, fashion, and, more broadly, aesthetics that they construe as having acquired by growing up in Italy. This self-perception of embodying Italianità contrasts with their alternating praise and complaints about Chinese workers and managers, illustrating how the division of labor between the partners shapes their perceptions of each other. Not only do Italian partners have greater control over crucial phases of production, but they view themselves as evaluating the quality of Chinese work rather than the other way around. Finally, by affirming and elaborating the claims of Italianità touted by the widespread "Made in Italy" campaign, managers appropriate the fetishized powers of the commodity to constitute their own labor power. At the same time, however, in their relationship with Italian firm owners, these managers find themselves confronting changing class trajectories. They have possibilities for job promotion in China or other countries but little hope of advancement in Italy because of the decreased market for luxury fashion in Europe and the U.S., the "kinship class ceiling" (Yanagisako 2002) that makes it difficult for them to advance in their employers' family firms, and the decreased opportunities for starting their own firms in Italy.

In the case of Chinese managers and entrepreneurs, we discuss the assemblage of skills and knowledge that they emphasize in their work with Italians and other foreigners. These skills and knowledge can succinctly be labeled as "cosmopolitanism." This cosmopolitanism, or worldly knowledge, encompasses their abilities to transcend culture to embrace the seemingly universal aspects of capitalist business practices, to discern the cultural peculiarities of various foreigners' conduct of business, and to engage in the multitude of practices that facilitate the production of Italian fashion in China, including shepherding Italian managers through every step of the landscape of doing business in China. By contrast, they view the Italians as provincial. Their elaboration of their cosmopolitan abilities emphasizes the need for a broader view of the activities that constitute the production process, especially in transnational relations of production. They compare and contrast themselves not only to the Italians but also to other Chinese who are not from Shanghai, as a Shanghai identity is seen as de rigueur for conducting successful transnational business. Although they do not fetishize other aspects of their labor capacities of cosmopolitanism, having a Shanghai identity is one aspect they treat as an abstract, essentialized core of their abilities. While these Chinese entrepreneurs and managers view their relationship with Italians and other foreigners as ideally an equal division of labor, they often chafe at the inadequate recognition of the value of their labor by their foreign partners. Like Italian managers, the class mobility of Chinese entrepreneurs and managers is dependent on and realized through transnational production relations. Our approach to class is, therefore, both diachronic and interactional.

1 Negotiating Managerial Labor Power and Value

Lisa Rofel and Sylvia J. Yanagisako

As the CEO of a joint venture forged by a famous Italian menswear company and an up-and-coming Chinese manufacturer, Paolo Rinaldi embodied the urbane and elegant professionalism of the brand. From our first meeting with him at the sleek, ultramodern office in Shanghai, which served as both the headquarters of the joint venture Vinimoon and the Italian firm's regional office for China, Rinaldi was forthcoming about both the Italian firm's success in China and the challenges it faced in its joint venture. With over fifty stores in thirty Chinese cities, the Italian firm FGS was highly visible and often cited in the Italian press as evidence of the global success of Italian fashion. In the 1980s, it had been one of the first Italian firms to procure raw materials directly from sources in China rather than use Hong Kong intermediaries, and by the 1990s, it was opening retail stores in its major cities.

Rinaldi, who had a *laurea* (equivalent to a BA) in economy and business, had worked for the Italian firm for more than fifteen years before he had been assigned to Shanghai to lead the joint venture. In addition to working in the firm's headquarters in Italy, which was located in his home province, he had been head of operations in Turkey and director of finance and management in Mexico. Rinaldi's wife also worked for the firm in Italy and Mexico, taking time off for the birth of their two children, and in Shanghai she was put in charge of the operations department of another one of the firm's brands, where she managed logistics, import-export, and the distribution of the firm's products to retail shops.

When he arrived in Shanghai in 2005, Rinaldi's first task as CEO of the joint venture was to put in place an IT system for integrating sales and production and to merge the very different managerial structures of the Italian and Chinese firms. Vinimoon was divided equally between the Italian firm and the Chinese firm. Both firms were family owned and managed, although the Italian firm was in its fourth generation, while the Chinese firm, which was started by three brothers in the 1990s, was in its first.

Jiang Li, who chose the Italian first name Nico, was the cultural mediator for Vinimoon. The Chinese side of the joint venture had previously had a garment factory and also imported from Europe a variety of garments and accessories to sell in China. Jiang Li/Nico was in his early forties when we met him in 2008. He was slight, with thinning hair. Unlike some of the other Chinese entrepreneurs who work with the Italians, Jiang did not try to present himself as an exemplar of fashion. He dressed casually, in rumpled sweaters and loose-fitting pants. He was soft-spoken, with the air of a scholar. In fact, he used to be a high school teacher.

The first time we met Jiang was in the main offices of the joint venture in Wenzhou, a city famous for its family enterprises, located in coastal southern Zhejiang province. Jiang, who had lived in Italy for a decade and established a small business making silk ties for Italian firms, had his own office, adjacent to Paolo Rinaldi's office.

The eldest brother on the Chinese side of the joint venture, Cai Yiren, who had previously approached Jiang for help with his import business because they were from the same hometown, implored him to help establish this joint venture. While Jiang got involved initially only to help set up the business, the difficulties the Italian manager and the Chinese owners had in getting along led the Italian side, FGS, to ask him to work permanently for Vinimoon, at a salary comparable to his earnings in Italy. Interested in having his children educated in China, Jiang agreed to leave Italy and move back to China. Jiang credited himself with playing a central role in the success of this joint venture. He viewed himself as no mere language translator but as cultural cum business translator. This was reflected in his title, assistant to the general manager (*zong jingli zhuli*), which was a title distinct from other translators.

The management structure of this joint venture, which was the outcome of a year of negotiations between the Chinese and Italian partners, followed a clear transnational division of labor: the Italian firm was in charge of general direction, finance, operations, service, and export, while the Chinese firm managed the factory, production, personnel, and acquisitions. Although initially the Italian firm had sent Italian technicians to the joint venture's factory and had installed operations procedures used by their factory in Switzerland, by 2007 there was only one Italian production consultant at the joint venture's factory, leaving the Chinese partners in charge of the day-to-day management of production.

Our ethnographic analysis in this chapter shows how labor power and value are forged in capitalist enterprises through transnational relations of social interdependence rather than brought to them already formed. In doing so, it eschews the conventions of cross-cultural analysis that compares the cultural orientations of the Italians and Chinese engaged in them, whether to emphasize their similarities or their differences. Rather, our analysis of the negotiations between Chinese and Italians over the value of their respective labor powers demonstrates that the meanings of cultural dispositions and practices are constituted through the ongoing contingencies and instabilities of transnational supply chain capitalism. Our analysis of value, labor, production, commodification, appropriation, and abstraction is thus ethnographically attentive to these contingencies and instabilities. We trace the respective career trajectories of Italian managers and Chinese managers and entrepreneurs, their class mobility, their relations to their respective locations of origin and presumed national cultures, their critiques of one another and indirect responses to those critiques, and their comparisons of themselves to others in addition to one another, all of which figure into their assessments of the value of their respective labor powers. We conclude with a reprise of how they instantiate and enact those labor powers through the encounter rather than bringing them to the encounter already formed. This chapter illustrates how our method of collaborative ethnography facilitates our understanding of the negotiations, tensions, and differential claims over contributions to value in the production of Italian fashion in China.

Transnational Career Trajectories

This first section highlights the diverse backgrounds of the Italian and Chinese managers and entrepreneurs in order to illuminate the discussion that follows of how they forge, through their encounter, the value of their contributions to the production of Italian fashion in China. As this section demonstrates, some of the managers and entrepreneurs came with experience in transnational business or in the production of fashion textiles and garments, but just as many of them came with no experience in either of these fields.

Italian Transnational Managers

Paolo Rinaldi's colleague Gianfranco Naldi had arrived at his position as general manager of the joint venture through a very different career trajectory than Rinaldi. A strikingly handsome and impeccably dressed man in his early forties, Naldi appeared even more an embodiment of the brand. Yet given his training and degree in chemical engineering, his managerial position in a clothing firm had hardly been predictable. His first job had been in a petroleum company that operated in the U.S. and the UK and in which he became a supply coordinator for the U.S. and Asia-Pacific sector. He was then recruited by a large, global professional services firm to work on reengineering industrial and high-tech supply chains. After five years, Naldi made a radical shift and took a job with an Italian textile firm, where he became the purchasing officer, traveling to China to find sources of raw silk, yarn, and other fabrics. As a manager whose expertise lay in logistics and supply chains, he supplemented his résumé by directly managing raw material suppliers in China and supervising fabric quality control. In spite of his earlier work in engineering, when he was hired by the Vinimoon joint venture, he was put in charge of sales and customer service. Although he was initially assigned to manage international sales, the company soon discovered that having an Italian "face" boosted domestic sales among Chinese, who responded favorably to a joint venture that was perceived to be more of an "Italian company, with an Italian style" than a Chinese one. Naldi's movement from engineering to sales was topped off in our final year of research, when he was lured by an Italian luxury jewelry brand to be director of distribution and sales in China. Whereas our first meeting with him was at the joint venture's factory in Wenzhou, our last meeting with him was in the lobby of a luxury hotel in Shanghai where he had taken up residence.

Leonardo Benini, by comparison, had found his job in another Italian-Chinese firm by chance while he was searching for work in Shanghai. Benini, who is of Italian descent but a French citizen, had come to China to fulfill his civil service and had then remained to teach French at a university in Beijing. He and his wife had decided they wanted to stay in China for several more years. With his graduate degree from a French business school and his fluency in Mandarin, French, Italian, and English, Benini was an attractive hire for the Ferrari firm, which manufactured lingerie in its own garment factories outside Shanghai and also subcontracted manufacturing to Chinese firms. Although the Ferrari firm was a joint venture, its capital was originally entirely Italian. Its status as a joint venture was based on the marriage of the firm's founder, Luciano Ferrari, to a Chinese woman. The firm did not have its own label but produced lingerie for a number of well-known, high-end Italian and U.S. brands, as well as for lower-cost ones. Since the firm's design office was in Milan and the prototypes were made there by a staff that had been working with the owner for over twenty-five years, Benini, as well as Ferrari, Ferrari's son, and his wife, traveled constantly between Milan and Shanghai, as well as to the firm's customers in Europe and the United States.

After working for Ferrari for four years, Benini left to take a position as business development manager for another Italian clothing firm—this one specializing in denim. A little more than a year later, a managerial head-hunting firm recruited him to be a brand manager for yet another Italian family firm that was marketing three different labels in China. Although the firm had contracted with a Hong Kong company to give it the exclusive right to distribute the three labels in China, they hired Benini to ensure that the brands were presented as the Italian owners desired. Because he was constantly moving among the retail sites in Shanghai where the brand was sold, we usually met at the Starbucks coffee shop in one of the city's central shopping malls. As we shall see later, Benini's career trajectory and his move from arranging for the manufacture of Italian brands to protecting the brand image of an Italian brand reflects the directional shift of the Italian firms in the first decade of the twenty-first century from "Made in China" to "Made for China."

Silvana Salvianti, an attractive single woman in her early thirties who had been trained as an English-language interpreter in Florence, interrupted her workday to meet with our Italian colleague, Simona Segre Reinach, and Sylvia Yanagisako at their serviced apartment in Florence.[1] We were initially surprised at how quickly she had responded to our request for an interview, until we realized that she thought we were management headhunters for an Italian firm. In her twenties, Salvianti had worked at a number of short-term jobs in Italy before she was offered a stable position in a clothing firm that was based in the provincial capital near her hometown. The firm owned a number of brands, and in 2006 Salvianti was sent to direct the trading company that manages the sale of one of the firm's brands in China. She had already visited Shanghai in 2002, and she had liked the city so was happy to accept the job. As general manager, she was in charge of developing retail, training personnel, and dealing with department stores that were retailing the brand, which had a medium-high position in the market. In 2009, however, she left Shanghai to return to Italy to marry and have her first child.

As reflected in the preceding examples, three-fourths (fifteen of twenty) of the Italian managers we encountered were men.[2] Two-thirds were married or living with a steady partner, and all were between the ages of twenty-six and forty-five. The majority had earned the Italian equivalent of a bachelor's (laurea) or master's degree in business (economy and business, business management, or fashion business administration), although a few held degrees ranging from chemical engineering to Chinese language and literature.[3] Half of the managers had worked for their employer in Italy before being transferred to China, either to initiate operations or to join an already established office. The other half, like Gianfranco Naldi and Leonardo Benini, arrived at their jobs through more circuitous routes, for example by working for other firms in the same sector or as global supply chain managers in other sectors.

Managers view living in Shanghai with its European restaurants, large European expat community, sizeable Italian community (estimated at around one thousand), vibrant nightlife, deluxe shopping malls, and good international schools as a rich experience. Both single and married managers enjoy the lively social life offered by Shanghai, and they value their friendships with people from a range of countries. These include primarily Italians, other Europeans, Australians, and North Americans. Given the relatively low cost of living in comparison to Italy, managers who are single go out to dinner frequently with friends, and many live in serviced apartments in which daily maid service is included. After a couple of years of intense nightlife, single men tend to settle into a pattern of spending their weekends playing golf, visiting friends, or traveling to nearby Asian cities. Single women managers mentioned the advantage of Shanghai being a safe city, which makes going out at night easy for a single woman, in contrast to large Italian and European cities. Silvana Salvianti, who had been working in Shanghai for four years, said: "The social life is sparkling, international, I have a lot of foreign friends. Friendship is made everywhere. . . . There are lots of events, work dinners, and engagement. In the beginning, yes, you are hesitant, unsure, if you are a single woman. I was terrorized in the beginning. I came from a terrible experience in London where I was assaulted. Here instead it is very safe."[4] On the other hand, women managers claim that it is easier for single men to pursue their careers in Shanghai because they do not feel pressured to get married, even if they are in their midthirties. Women, in addition, are put off by the availability of Chinese women to European men, although they did not express an equivalent interest in Chinese men. One complained, "There is a lot of prostitution—very young, attractive women at bars who go out with horribly old European men just for a dinner at a beautiful restaurant or a small gift. It's not any different from Thailand." Most married managers with children live in expat compounds, which one manager self-consciously described as "our own international ghetto—a kind of Club Med for families." Given their relatively high salaries and the low cost of living, managers can easily afford to employ at least one domestic servant and some employ two: one to cook and clean and the other to help with childcare. Once their children were in school, their social life centered on the expat families whose children attended the same international school. Although the turnover in their children's classes is high—with as many as 50 percent of their classmates leaving each year—parents appreciate the benefits to both their children and themselves of having classmates whose parents are "at a high level in very important companies." They view attendance at a school where the students come from "all over the world"—including Chinese children from Hong Kong and Singapore—as providing their children with a head start in an increasingly global world. Massimo Soci, an Italian manager whose six-year-old daughter speaks Chinese, English, Italian, and Portuguese, felt that living in Shanghai and attending a school that had its origins in Hong Kong had given his daughter a mental agility superior to that of children of her age in Italy, even though she made small errors in speaking Italian.

In spite of their interest in providing their children with an "international experience," however, outside of their business dealings, few managers socialize with Chinese people. When they do, it is with the Chinese from Taiwan, Hong Kong, Singapore, or the United States—in other words, expats themselves. One exception was Leonardo Benini. He spoke Mandarin, lived in an apartment building near the city center with many Chinese neighbors, and expressed disdain for the narrow expatriate life of his Italian colleagues and friends. He was hopeful that his children's experiences growing up in Shanghai would prevent them from adopting the racist, anti-Chinese attitudes he had observed in Italy. The other two exceptions were men who had married or were engaged to Chinese women. One of them, Riccardo Ferrero, who worked and lived in an industrial city about sixty miles from Shanghai, had learned the local dialect by hanging out for four years with the technicians he managed before marrying a local woman.

All Italian managers consider the challenges of residing and working in China to be formidable. As one put it, "It is more interesting than beautiful." The air pollution, the language and communication difficulties, and the distance from family and friends in Italy are felt to be daunting. Many managers come from towns and small cities in Italy, and they sorely miss the beauty of the Italian countryside and the recreational activities (cycling, skiing, sailing) it offers them. In comparison to "second-level" (e.g., Hangzhou) or "third-level" (e.g., Wenzhou or Jiaxing) cities, however, Shanghai is viewed as a paradise. One manager described being assigned to a "third-level" city as equivalent to being condemned to "twenty years to life imprisonment." The absence of a European community and social life, the "ugliness" of the urban landscape, the "not-yet-modern mentality" of the Chinese residing outside major cities, and the lack of Italian food is experienced as a great hardship. "The body needs pasta and pizza!" one manager declared, although he also conceded, "You get used to it; humans can get used to anything."

Despite these hardships, managers have no doubt that the career opportunities offered them in China are better than what is available to them in Italy. Almost all of them acknowledge that had they remained in Italy, they would never have obtained a position or salary as good as the one they have in China. They have only to mention the slow rate of economic growth in Europe and the U.S. in contrast to the nearly 10 percent growth rate in China's GDP (at the time we did our research) and the comparative rate of growth in their firm's business in Europe as opposed to China to underscore their point. A distribution manager said, "There's no way I would have the opportunity to open thirty stores a year in Italy," adding, "here if you make a mistake you can recover." Gianfranco Naldi compared the pleasure of participating in the 20 percent annual growth in his firm's production in China to his previous job in a textile firm in Italy, which had consisted primarily of downsizing and working with the labor council to fire people. The greater freedom he had to make decisions in China, he said, also made him feel more like a firm owner than an employee.

Chinese Transnational Managers

Lou Jingxiao is a self-confident young woman who was in her midthirties at the time we met her in 2007. She had built her own successful small business, Xiaoyu Ltd., in Shanghai as a "mediator" shepherding the production process in China for well-known fashion firms. Lou is of medium height, with long, slightly wavy hair she wears partially pulled back. She was always stylishly dressed, in fashion clothing that made her stand out from others. She was a walking statement of her involvement in the Western fashion industry. In our first meeting, she was wearing a tightly fitting short black dress with yellow-striped high-heeled shoes she later said were from Italy. Though we rarely met in her firm's office suite, the few times we did allowed us to see that Lou's design for her office reflected her taste in high Western fashion, with muted but playful colors, though she also dotted the office with classical pieces of Chinese art objects. Lou studied at the business school of Shanghai's textile and fashion university, Donghua University, where she learned international trade and finance. She then went to work first for a Chinese state-owned textile import-export company and later for a Korean company making textiles in China. With the Korean company, she specialized in working with Italian customers. After ten years of work experience, Lou decided to open her own business, specializing in arranging in China the production of fashion clothing mainly for Italian firms but also for French and Dutch companies. She brought 10,000 RMB (US$1,666) of her own capital into the business, half of which was her own savings and half of which was from her parents, who are living on small retirement pensions. She also managed to bring with her many of her Italian customers who had been working with the Korean company. For the first five years, her company was actually legally registered under the aegis of a state-owned municipal import-export company. However, her capital was at direct risk, because she bought the goods from the Chinese factories and sold them to the Italian firms. She also received a commission from the Italian firms. After the end of WTO quotas on textile imports from China, Lou separated her company from the state-owned company.

General Manager Li Linfeng was in charge of the Hangzhou-based joint venture Hui Hua Yi/Silk Nouvelle with Roberto Canclini, the owner of a well-known Italian fashion firm. When we met him in 2008, Manager Li (as his colleagues referred to him) had worked for the Zhejiang provincial silk bureau—now called corporation—for forty years. At fifty-eight, Manager Li looked quite fit. He also looked like someone who was a party cadre. His manner of dress (somber, nondescript clothing), his mode of interaction (no nonsense), and his air of authority all bespoke that background. He did not try to display himself as a consumer. To the contrary, his whole demeanor spoke of a no-corruption attitude. Rofel met with him numerous times over the following five years, as he became increasingly intrigued with her knowledge of Hangzhou's silk industry and her fluency in Chinese.

As he tells it, Manager Li worked his way up the hierarchy in the Zhejiang silk industry. He began in 1964 as an ordinary worker learning how to sew embroidered clothing in one of Hangzhou's silk factories. He had entered the factory because his parents worked there. Such a factory job was much coveted at that time by urban youth. Belonging to a state-run work unit represented what the socialist state prided itself on as distinguishing it from capitalist exploitation. Manager Li's climb continued as he became a shift leader, then a workshop head, and eventually he moved out of the factory to do sales for the provincial silk bureau. At the time we met him, Manager Li had been doing import-export work for twenty-two years.

Manager Li's narrative implicitly emphasizes that he is no party hack but someone with deep knowledge and experience in the silk industry. Also striking in Manager Li's narrative are the key pieces he left out: his family background as working class, which potentially gave him a distinctive affective relationship to the socialist past and the state; and the factors that led to his steady rise, which surely included party membership and struggles during the Cultural Revolution and its aftermath. Manager Li's narrative as well as the parts he chose not to emphasize signal the fact that he is someone the Zhejiang silk corporation trusts to work with foreigners and still keep the state's interests as his primary goal.

These examples represent the range of Chinese entrepreneurs engaged in transnational supply chains of Italian and other European fashion. In contrast to the Italian managers, their Chinese counterparts owned their own firms, were managers or employees in state-owned corporations, or served as mediators in joint ventures in which they took advantage of their position to nestle their own private firm within the joint venture. Also in striking contrast to the Italians, those who owned their own business were in their midthirties or younger. They—and their parents—agreed that the older generation, who had lived all their lives under socialism, did not have the knowledge, experience, and, most importantly in their view, the willingness to take the risks involved in engaging with this kind of entrepreneurship. These young entrepreneurs were the first generation of private, transnational entrepreneurs since the turn to a market economy in China. As we will see, they offer a marked contrast with the officials/managers who run the state-owned enterprises. Given the burgeoning economic growth in China (China's rate of GDP growth in 2008 was 9.6 percent; today it is 6.5 percent; World Bank n.d.b) and the end of state involvement in job assignments, this younger generation had become used to "jumping into the sea," as the common phrase had it. If they failed, they felt they could always find other work. And indeed, Lou Jingxiao, in contrast to Li Linfeng, had continuously changed workplaces—though not sectors—until she opened her own business.

All of the younger generation of entrepreneurs involved in transnational supply chain work in the textile industry, with the exception of one who had family involvement in one of the state-owned import-export corporations, had degrees from Donghua University's business school. As Donghua University specializes in the textile and garment industries, and now has a fashion institute, their training in business school focused on these sectors. Thus, they felt they were knowledgeable about both business and textiles and garments. But many of them additionally gained knowledge and experience from working for state-owned import-export corporations as their first job. They invariably felt this experience was more valuable to them than their classes in business school.

These young entrepreneurs comprised the burgeoning middle class in China. They were the ones who accumulated enough wealth to eat out regularly at fancy restaurants, vacation as a group both abroad and within China, join health clubs, and send their children to private schools or at least pay for a myriad of private tutoring in English, piano, and other talents. Unlike their parents, displays of consumption were an important aspect of their social status.[5]

By contrast, those in the highest positions in the state-owned import-export corporations, at least at the time we did our research, were all of an older generation who had risen through the ranks of the party-managerial ladder common under socialism. They learned through experience how to engage in sales. Given that the state held control of all the major import-export corporations in this sector, these managers did not worry about finding Italian or other joint venture partners, about putting their own capital at risk, or about losing their jobs if the state-owned company did not turn a sufficient profit. Yet they also had below them in the corporation many younger managers who had received the same kind of training as Lou Jingxiao and on whom they depended to carry out the bulk of the import-export labor.

In contrast to the middle-class lifestyle of the private entrepreneurs, top-level managers in state-owned corporations did not flaunt their levels of consumption or taste, owing to the ongoing public criticism of the corruption of public officials (see Rofel's chapter in part III). They considered themselves, however, to be entrepreneurs rather than merely officials, though the blurring of the status of the companies they represented made their own status unclear (this will be discussed more in Rofel's chapter in part II).

At the beginning of our research, both private and state-run Chinese companies eagerly sought out foreign investment. But by the end of our research, these entrepreneurs and officials, like their Italian counterparts, increasingly turned to the Chinese domestic market. This was in part due to rising middle-class consumption in China but also due to the 2008 financial crisis that had a direct impact on exports from China. Hui Hua Yi/Silk Nouvelle, for example, while it did not abandon its joint venture or export business, began to create brand clothing for the Chinese domestic market.

Given that this period of our research reflects a major transformation in China, a word is in order about the term "entrepreneur" within China. As with most categories of personhood related to capitalism, the term "entrepreneur" is historically multivalent.[6] Joseph Alois Schumpeter, one of the most well-known theorists of entrepreneurialism, argued that entrepreneurialism was the key to the creative destruction that propels capitalism forward (Medearis 2013).[7] Certainly, these beliefs—or ideologies—about entrepreneurial innovation were fostered in China beginning in the early 1980s, when post-Mao economic reforms began. There was much ambivalence at that time about the existence and role of the entrepreneur. They were viewed in official and popular discourse simultaneously as innovators but also as unsavory characters using immoral means to take advantage of people (see Hsu 2006; Tsang 1996). With the expansion of the regime of private property, the meanings and practices of "entrepreneur" have also expanded (see Huang 2008). If it can be said to have a core meaning, it would be "to make a living."[8] "Entrepreneur" can thus mean owning one's own company to make a living and be one's own boss; it can also mean to engage in trade and exchange, or buying and selling. Some entrepreneurs own the means of production, but others have a company that operates as a node in a chain of subcontracting arrangements and own no means of production.[9] It is not an exaggeration to say that nearly everyone in China today dreams of becoming an entrepreneur, from migrant workers on the shop floor, to farmers, to managers and white-collar professionals of all sorts, even, dare we say it, intellectuals.[10] The post-Mao state encourages this dream, through various institutionalized forms of support for creating wealth.[11]

The category of entrepreneur also includes state cadres who combine governance with doing business. The officials representing state-owned import-export companies, however, had an ambivalent approach to their work. They viewed themselves as still representing the state, as under socialism, but now a state that itself was seeking profit. Nonetheless, to present themselves as entrepreneurs would have fed into the loud public discourse about the corruption of government officials.[12] Emphasizing the semiotically rich meanings and practices of "entrepreneur" as they have historically emerged in China in this most recent period is critical to understanding that the dynamic and unstable nature of the negotiations between the Chinese and Italians is in part due to the expansive nature of this category.

Thus, those we include in the category of Chinese entrepreneur in the transnational fashion textile and garment industry are situated in a wide array of business arrangements, much broader than one might initially assume from the term "entrepreneur." Those who own private firms tend to have small companies that specialize in connecting foreign companies with sources of raw materials and with factories that produce high-quality yarn, fabric, and garments appropriate for fashion clothing. Also included in this category, however, are managers/officials as well as office employees in state-run import-export trading companies who manage their offices in a semiautonomous manner; managers of factories owned by the state; managers of factories that were state-owned but have recently privatized; translators working in the offices of Italian firms located in China as well as translators in joint ventures between Chinese and Italians, who take advantage of their position to set up their own small firms; managers in Italian firms with offices located in China; and those who work directly for Italian firms as managers of Italian-owned factories or as overseers of quality control for the whole production process.

The Spatial and Social Mobility of Managers

The spatial and social mobility of Italian and Chinese managers is a key aspect of the formation of their respective labor powers through their relations of social interdependence. For Italian managers, their relationships with firm owners are a critical aspect of this social mobility. For Chinese managers and entrepreneurs, their relationships to state-owned corporations is analogous to, though quite distinct from, Italian managers' relations to firm owners in shaping their social mobility. Finally, the social mobility of both Italian and Chinese managers is formed in relation to one another and the transnational nature of the production and distribution of made-in-China Italian fashion. The complex interaction of these various relations shape but also are reconfigured by their mutual relations of social interdependence.

Italian Managers

As family firms began outsourcing production to China in the 1980s and forming transnational joint ventures in the 1990s, the shortage of Italian managers in China strengthened managers' ability to negotiate with firm owners for salaries and benefits. The small- and medium-sized firms that made up the majority of manufacturing firms in Italy initially found it difficult to hire Italian managers willing to staff their offices and production units in China. Until 2004, industry and commercial consultants in Shanghai agreed that the greatest obstacle facing Italian firms in China was the shortage of "human resources." What they meant by this was the shortage of managers in whom firm owners could place their trust, with whom they could communicate, and who shared their cultural sensibilities. Not only did these firms lack the recruitment capabilities of large companies, but they were less attractive because they offered more limited opportunities for job advancement.

In the first few years of the millennium, the shortage of managers was so acute that some companies resorted to hiring academics who originally came to China to study Chinese language and literature. As we saw earlier, Leonardo Benini, who had come to China to teach French and had no previous experience in the clothing sector, was able to easily land a managerial position in the Ferrari firm. Rosanna Potenza, who had studied sinology in Italy and theater in Beijing, was hired in 2002 by the owner of a clothing firm who met her while she was working as the manager of an Italian restaurant. She soon found herself in charge of supervising five Chinese quality control technicians. After 2004 the shortage decreased as a growing number of university graduates sought work in China rather than face unemployment in Italy. Managers who had been in China for several years commented on the noticeable increase in the arrival of Italians, especially in Shanghai. While earlier arrivals had been recent college graduates seeking jobs, managers reported lately encountering ones who were even willing to take an unpaid internship in hopes of building their resumes.

Despite this increase in Italians willing to work in China, the pool of Italian managers with experience and knowledge of China remained small. By early 2010, in the midst of the economic downturn in the U.S. and Europe, moreover, Italian and other European luxury brands were expanding their distribution in China. The combination of the downturn of sales in Europe and the U.S. and the stimulus incentives offered by the Chinese government had further increased the importance of the growing Chinese market in these firms' global business plans. For example, before the economic downturn, the joint venture Vinimoon had been exporting 70 percent of its luxury menswear and selling only 30 percent in China. After the downturn, exports had decreased dramatically while the Chinese domestic market had grown, so the ratio of foreign to domestic sales had become 50:50. Italian firms, especially luxury brands, accordingly began shifting more resources and energy to the Chinese domestic market. They began actively wooing experienced managers from other companies in the same and related sectors. In the spring of 2010, several of the managers who worked for FGS had been lured away by very attractive offers from other companies, including an Italian luxury jewelry brand, a luxury Swiss watch company, and other Italian luxury clothing brands. The Italian luxury jewelry company had offered one of the FGS managers twice the salary he had been getting, because his experience and contacts, especially in second-level cities in China, made him an ideal candidate to lead their expansion. Thus, even with the decline in the shortage of "human resources," Italian managers with experience in China have gained bargaining power in relation to firm owners.

Managers are not optimistic, on the other hand, about their prospects of returning to Italy or Europe to move up the managerial hierarchy in the firm. To the contrary, they express little hope of returning in the near future. There are several reasons for this. First, as has been mentioned, in the first decade of the twenty-first century, the European and U.S. markets for luxury goods declined. Even before the global recession of 2009, jobs in this sector were shrinking throughout Europe and the United States. Second, a horizontal move to a comparable position in Italy would mean a significant drop in purchasing power, lifestyle, and social status. No dining out at fancy restaurants; no chauffeurs, maids, nannies, or social life in a vibrant international community; no international schools where one's children rub shoulders with those of diplomats and international entrepreneurs and gain the trilingual language skills and cosmopolitan sensibility that one hopes will give them a head start in the global economy. Third, the cultural and local knowledge gained by living in China, while viewed as invaluable for producing and marketing the brand in the country, is not seen as useful for producing and marketing the brand in the U.S. and Europe. Finally, the chances of a manager advancing to a better position in the firm's home office are slim and, in some cases, nonexistent. Managers are well aware that their advancement to the highest levels of management in a family firm is limited by "the kinship glass ceiling" (Yanagisako 2002, 138). Consequently, the most promising opportunities for career advancement lie in being assigned to lead the firm's expansion whether in manufacturing or sales in another country (e.g., Turkey, Vietnam, India) or in being recruited by a firm in a related sector in China.

The limited opportunity for promotion in Italy whether by their current employer or another firm is compounded by the fact that these transnational managers are blocked from another path of career advancement that has been an avenue of class mobility in Italian industrial districts. This is the option of opening a firm of their own. Yanagisako's research on family firms in the silk industry of Como, Italy, showed that in the period from the end of World War II until the 1980s, the continual creation of new firms by managers and technical directors in the same sector in which they had been employed was responsible for a good deal of the dynamic character of the industrial district (Yanagisako 2002). The existence of small, specialized firms alongside larger, more vertically integrated firms enabled ambitious employees who found themselves being blocked from promotion by the kinship glass ceiling to start up their own firms, sometimes by taking some of their former employers' clients with them. Ten of the fifteen founders of subcontracting firms in that study had worked for a firm in the same sector before opening their own firms, and three more had been employees of firms in another sector of the industry (Yanagisako 2002, 123). Other studies likewise discovered a high degree of upward mobility in localized industrial districts, particularly in central and southern Italy, but also in the north (Martinelli and Chiesi 1989, 121).

The capital required to open a small, subcontracting firm was limited and came mostly from the firm founder's own savings and small loans from relatives and business associates. What was indispensable was the labor of family and relatives, as well as business and support from other firms in the district that needed their services. Family and relatives made up a significant part of the firm's workforce in its early years (Yanagisako 2002, 129). It was common for a wide range of relatives to work in the firm. The employment of relatives increased the labor flexibility of the firm because they could be asked to work extra hours when needed. Relatives could also be trusted with managerial and administrative tasks, and so were a more flexible workforce that could move between shop floor and office depending on the need.

As Yanagisako argues in chapter 5, the outsourcing of manufacturing to China has largely closed off this avenue of career advancement and class mobility to managers. As large, vertically integrated firms have sent subcontracting work overseas, the opportunities for opening small, subcontracting firms in industrial districts like Como have shrunk. Transnational managers are in an especially weak position to embark on this path of occupational and class mobility as they lack the social networks on which to draw in their home communities in Italy and in China. They have neither family labor nor industrial networks that would afford them the labor and capital resources to open a firm. Initiating a business in China without these resources requires a large amount of capital, much more than they have access to. Their expat social network, while useful for finding other managerial jobs, does not provide resources for opening a new firm. With one exception, the Italian managers we spoke with in China did not consider a start-up a viable option. The exception is telling. Riccardo Ferrero—who had learned the local dialect, married a local woman, and developed a local network of male friends in the industrial district where his employer's factory is located—was the only one who said that he was considering opening his own firm if his employer sold his or shut it down.

The boundary between Italian firm owners and managers, which was unstable and permeable in Como and other Italian industrial districts characterized by decentralized production, has become more stable and impermeable as a result of the outsourcing of manufacturing. Thus, in contrast to the blurring of these boundaries among Chinese entrepreneurs, the distinction between capitalists and managers among Italians has hardened. This hardened boundary in turn shapes how Italian managers in the transnational production of Italian fashion in China configure the value of their labor power.

Chinese Entrepreneurs and Managers

The young entrepreneurs in China who dominated the transnational business in the textile and garment industries were the first generation of transnational entrepreneurs owning their own businesses since the initiation of post-Mao economic reforms beginning in the 1980s. Thus, unlike many of the Italian owners who formed their own firms after having gained experience working for another firm owner, these entrepreneurs either gained experience working in state-owned import-export companies or went to business school and then worked in a state-owned import-export company. Like Italian firm owners, all of them also had to rely on their own savings and funds from their families to start their own businesses. But in the Chinese case, it was because the state banks generally offer loans only to state-owned companies (Tsai 2004).[13] And unlike Italian family firms in the textile sector, most of these small firms initially had to have a close relationship with the state, as they had to nestle their firms within a state-owned import-export company to be allotted a portion of the textile import quota imposed on China by the WTO until 2008. Some of these business school graduates continued to work in these state-owned companies, because they received job security, a steady and reliable income, and guaranteed benefits.

Their social mobility is part of a radical transformation in class and social inequality in China since the end of socialism. As many scholars have described (Anagnost 1997; Kelliher 1992; Lin 2006, 2013; Rofel 2007; Walder 1986), inequality under socialism was based not on the accumulation of wealth but on the accumulation of power. Those like Li Linfeng rose up by moving through the party-state ranks. Their status was based in part on the class labeling system under socialism that was periodically reinvoked. Their access to power led to privileged access to resources but not to dramatically differentiated divisions based on wealth. With the end of socialism, the state redistributed some means of production and treated social resources, such as housing—now called real estate—as new sources of wealth accumulation. There emerged the marketization of power, inequalities in distribution and rent-seeking behavior, increasingly polarized incomes, the abolition of security in employment, and a decrease in state-provided social benefits (Rofel 2007, 9; Wang Hui 2003). Labor also became commodified. Rural residents who migrate to urban areas for work comprise the new underclass. Some have argued that China has transformed from one of the most economically egalitarian societies to one of the most unequal (Sun and Guo 2013, 1). This inequality is manifested in employment, housing, healthcare, education, and social welfare. It is spatially and regionally differentiated, particularly between rural-urban and inland-coastal. We did our research on the eastern coast, where a greater proportion of the wealth is concentrated.

According to the website created by Thomas Piketty and his colleagues, in 2015 the top 1 percent of the population in China owned 12.7 percent of the wealth, while the bottom 50 percent owned 15.1 percent of the wealth (World Wealth and Income Database n.d.).[14] This top 1 percent are overwhelmingly composed of officials/entrepreneurs, including the sons and daughters of those who founded the socialist state, who are party members and CEOs of state-owned corporations. The bottom half is composed mainly of migrant workers from the countryside, who are denied legal status in the cities and thus work mainly in the construction and service sectors. (For more on migrant workers, see Rofel's chapter in part II.)

Inequality in China is thus shaped by the state. That is, even as increasing numbers of what we would conventionally consider private firms have appeared, state-owned corporations have a strong presence in profit-seeking activities. As some have pointed out, an individual's relationship to state-owned corporations still plays a defining role in inequality. Beibei Tang and Luigi Tomba have argued that the distinction between those who work within state enterprises and those who do not continues to determine privileged access to resources, "amplifying the effect of market transition" (2013, 91), and also is still decisive in an individual's ability to move up the social ladder. This inequality refers not only to the older generation of officials, like Li Linfeng, but to the many younger generation employees who do not want to take the risk of turning their labor power into marketized labor and who embrace the security of employment and benefits of a job within the state.

The Chinese managers and entrepreneurs we interviewed and came to know were not part of the top 1 percent of wealthy elites. Yet they could all aspire to middle-class status. They experienced social mobility and yet—at least those with their own firms—resented the uneven opportunities in relation to officials/entrepreneurs in state-owned corporations. They were at the forefront of the broad public discourse on official corruption. Even those who worked in state-owned companies could be quite vocal about the corruption in their own offices. As explained more in Rofel's chapter in part II, "corruption" is a semiotic site through which licit and illicit forms of profit-seeking are debated. In self-conscious contradistinction to state officials, then, who are regularly accused of corruption,[15] these young, private entrepreneurs viewed themselves as the vanguard of building a new, morally appropriate China. Those engaged in transnational business viewed themselves even more so as the vanguard of a new China, as they uniformly agreed that China's future lay in intimate entanglements with a capitalist West. Their career trajectories as well-to-do middle-class professionals also depended on these transnational relations, as they would not have been able to create as much wealth for themselves in the domestic market at that time, with the state dominating many of the paths to that wealth creation.[16]

Guardians of *Italianità* versus Chinese Cosmopolitanism

Italian owners and managers and Chinese entrepreneurs and managers continually engage in processes of negotiation in their transnational relations. In part, these negotiations entail drawing up contracts and making commitments about production and distribution goals. At the same time, they equally entail configuring the importance and value of their mutual contributions to the process of producing Italian fashion in China. These negotiations continue even after contracts have been signed, with the various interlocutors keeping an eye to the future. These social relations of interdependence can be simultaneously smooth and tense, certain and uncertain, clear and ambiguous. As we shall see, Italian managers emphasize their "Italianness" and embodiment of Italianità as central to Italian fashion and as something Chinese managers cannot attain, while Chinese managers and entrepreneurs emphasize their cosmopolitanism, without which they believe Italians would not be able to function in China. Their elaboration of this cosmopolitanism highlights the multiple steps in the commodity chain of producing and distributing Italian fashion made in China. Both sides insist their contributions are essential to the value of Chinese-made Italian fashion.

The oppositions in which Italian managers characterize the differences between Chinese managers and themselves are hardly unfamiliar to us. Although Italy did not have colonial projects in China or any other areas of Asia, Italians are well steeped in nineteenth- and twentieth-century Orientalist discourse on the Far East. Thus, it is not surprising that oppositions between tradition and modernity, despotism and democracy, collectivity and individualism, authority and creativity underlie a good deal of what they have to say about their experience of working with the Chinese. Other complaints, however, are more specific to the sector of production in question.

Lack of fashion sense is perhaps foremost among these. Italian managers are quite capable of viewing some areas of difference between themselves and the Chinese in cultural relativist terms casting neither as objectively better than the other. This is true even when it comes to fashion. At the same time, however, they have a decidedly unilineal view of the evolution of fashion and its global diffusion. According to Italian managers and firm owners, it will be many years before the Chinese will be up to understanding the semiotics and sensibilities of Western fashion. The Chinese, they say, are still in the phase of copying, much like the Japanese were in the 1980s, and it will take another generation before they get beyond this. They are resolute in their prediction that the Chinese will inevitably adopt "modern" (i.e., European) fashion; the only question is how long it will take them. If Chinese consumers are not enthusiastic about the newest colors and styles in Italian fashion trends, it is because they have to be taught a more modern fashion sensibility. If they do not like bold plaids, checks, and stripes, it is because they have yet to evolve out of their preference for black suits, which Italians moved away from years ago. If they are too focused on comfort, they have to realize, as one

Italian distribution manager put it, that to be fashionable you cannot "dress like you are going to the gym."

Given the underdeveloped state of Chinese fashion sensibilities, Italian managers view themselves as crucial to guaranteeing quality control, brand management, and effective marketing. Whether they are overseeing a factory in a joint venture, arranging for subcontracting by Chinese factories, or setting up franchise retail outlets, Italian managers feel they must be constantly vigilant in order to maintain the quality and prestige of the brand. The greatest fear of Italian firms—and one that kept some firms from engaging in production and distribution in China for years—is that their brand image will be damaged, whether by shoddy presentation or by having their designs stolen and made into cheap copies. Leonardo Benini pointed out that since the "Chinese only started to have their brands in 1993/1994, that's too short a time to become good at retail." Hong Kong distributors, in contrast, are considered knowledgeable about fashion and skilled at retail. Many Italian firms rely on Hong Kong distributors whose services include brand management and procuring the best locations in shopping malls, shopping streets, and department stores, as the risks of going it alone in an unfamiliar social landscape are daunting. Having a good location in a shopping mall or in a department store is key to success and having a distributor who is working with several brands puts you in a better spot. A few Italian firms, however, are still reluctant to work with Hong Kong distributors, because they want to retain strict control of the brand themselves.

The need for brand management by Italians is all the more critical because, according to Italian managers, the Chinese (as opposed to "Hong Kongesi"[17]) not only do not know which colors and fabrics go together but also do not know how to combine items of clothing into an outfit and present them attractively in retail stores (called visual merchandising). Chinese store managers have to be taught the concept of a "collection" with its style coherence and color theme. In the eyes of Italian distribution managers, the Chinese make the mistake of cramming their stores full of racks with thousands of unnecessary options. For example, they will present the same design with pockets or without pockets. The ill-conceived assemblage of a hodge-podge of styles results in, as one distribution manager put it, "a horrifying kitsch." Chinese distributors and retailers need to be trained to understand "mood directions," seasonal trends, and how to attract customers' interest by taking risks in their window displays.

Unlike Italians, who managers say are used to wearing fashionable clothing and who, consequently, have an intuitive taste for fashion, the Chinese have yet to acquire this. As evidence that the Chinese themselves recognize their undeveloped fashion sense, Marzia Bordogna, an FGS merchandiser who did market research and created retail collections, pointed out that Chinese customers are more willing to follow suggestions from sales clerks as to which items to buy together. In Italy, she noted, customers go into the store to purchase just one item, which they put together creatively with other pieces of clothing because they have confidence in their fashion taste. Interestingly, there was no significant gender difference on this topic. Both male and female Italian managers agreed with Gianfranco Naldi (trained in chemical engineering), who asserted, "Since I'm Italian, I have always known about fashion."

Above all, the Chinese cannot be trusted to preserve the brand's Italianità. This includes not only the quality of the manufactured product but the design features that convey the Italianità of the brand. In the view of Italian production managers, Chinese production supervisors and workers simply do not have the ability to recognize the small but crucial details of Italianità—such as the positioning of a pocket or the alignment of a zipper. Likewise, even while they concede that Chinese managers have a better understanding of the Chinese market, Italian distribution managers see them as falling far short of knowing how to effectively market Italianità in China.

This is not to say that Italian managers biologize Italianità. While a couple of managers mentioned that Italianità is "in our DNA," they appeared to mean this metaphorically. Monica Campani, who had studied Chinese language and literature and worked as an intermediary between an Italian design studio and Chinese clients, stated, "we Italians have a culture of fashion that I would say is almost genetic." Although Italianità is cultural rather than genetic, it is not something that can be taught in ten easy lessons. Just as creativity cannot be learned in school, neither can Italianità. None of the managers spoke of acquiring Italianità through schooling or job training. Instead, like Gianfranco Naldi, they recounted how they had acquired an intuitive feeling for design, fashion, and, more broadly, aesthetics by growing up in Italy.

In contrast to their Italian counterparts, Chinese entrepreneurs did not emphasize their "Chineseness" as that which marked the value of their contribution to transnational relations of production and distribution. At the time we did our research, Chineseness represented cheap labor and a "backwardness" in relation to the West—a revival of colonial evolutionary notions of culture. Certain people in China also embraced this discourse.

That image is one that Chinese entrepreneurs especially in the fashion industry had to work against in order to convince their Italian counterparts they were worthy partners as well as to create a higher valuation of their own labor power.[18] Chinese entrepreneurs and managers thus tended to emphasize the extent to which they had transcended their national-cultural identities. The kinds of skills and knowledge Chinese entrepreneurs claimed they had that were essential to these transnational relationships can succinctly be put as "cosmopolitanism."

Despite the disparate locations in which they labored, these Chinese entrepreneurs sensed that the Italians tried to portray themselves as creating the value of their labor power from within a world of their own, not in relation to their Chinese counterparts. As explained above, Italian managers actually do both: They describe their Italianità as intuitive, a result of growing up in Italy. But they also implicitly create the value of that Italianità in relation to their evaluation that their Chinese counterparts have very little fashion sense.

Chinese entrepreneurs, by contrast, necessarily viewed themselves as forming nearly all aspects of their cosmopolitan identity in relation to the Italians and other foreigners. This relationality in their self-definition resulted from both the structural nature of transnational commodity chains, in which China was seen as the workshop of the world, and from China's long colonial history, which is still at the forefront of many Chinese people's evaluations of China's place in the world—at least in a postsocialist, U.S.-dominated capitalist world.

They sensed, moreover, that most foreigners viewed them as "merely" Chinese. Sometimes they complained to Rofel that their Italian partners did not sufficiently acknowledge their cosmopolitanism, that there appeared to exist an impermeable barrier to this recognition. This barrier, they implied, also created constraints on how they could translate their labor power into greater value.

Cosmopolitanism is necessarily formed through relationality. It is a claim about an ability to interact with a wide range of foreigners and therefore be a "worldly" citizen. Thus, Chinese entrepreneurs were self-consciously aware of how their skills and knowledge were in fact formed within a specific social and historical context. Yet there was one key aspect of their labor power that they, like the Italians, congealed into their personhood. As explained below, that aspect was their Shanghai identity, which they felt enabled them, in contrast to other Chinese, to succeed at embodying cosmopolitanism. Their elaboration of a Shanghai identity is analogous to Italianità.

In stressing cosmopolitanism as the most vital aspect of the value of their contribution, Chinese entrepreneurs both implicitly and explicitly pointed out that the production and distribution of Italian fashion in China required many steps in the process that went well beyond a narrow focus on design and brand. These steps, as elaborated later in this chapter, included translation, both linguistic and cultural; the sourcing of raw materials and fabric; the choice of trustworthy and capable factories; the shepherding of Italians and other foreigners through the landscape of China, both physically and metaphorically; the constant, weekly need to oversee quality control in the factories; and navigation of the Chinese state. These skills did not reside in the mere fact that they had grown up in China but rather, in their view, in their cosmopolitan approach to acquiring a wide range of abilities necessary for shepherding foreigners and fashion garments through the commodity chain process.

All of the Chinese entrepreneurs readily admitted there are skills and knowledge they learn from the Italians, such as certain notions about fashion. But they viewed their cosmopolitanism as giving them the ability to learn and apply this knowledge of fashion. Some entrepreneurs also claimed a knowledge of fashion and credited themselves with helping designers create a fashion garment that would succeed in terms of the kinds of fabrics that could go together or the layout of zippers or collars. Thus, the Chinese entrepreneurs were convinced that they brought skills and knowledge without which the Italians would simply be unable to proceed at all in the production and distribution processes—at least distribution in China, which was becoming an increasingly important market for the Italians. In their view, a fundamental feature of their cosmopolitanism was their ability to grasp the seemingly universal aspects of conducting transnational business. That is, they embraced a predominant capitalist belief that creating value and profit transcends culture. This cosmopolitanism, they said, enabled them to engage with a wide range of foreigners. Yet, despite this belief, they also interpreted culture as playing a key role in transnational business, as they could readily discern that the broad range of foreigners who conduct business in China have some distinctive ways of going about it. Thus, an important corollary is that their cosmopolitanism further enabled them to handle the particularities and peculiarities of how foreigners interacted with them. That is, they believed there are nonculturally marked ways of doing business that they assume everyone must understand but then they also realized that there are distinctions among foreigners in how they go about actually conducting their businesses. Although they tended to fold Italians into the broader category of "foreigner" or "Westerner"[19]—in part because there were relatively few Italians working in China—they also thought the cultural particularities of Italians' business practices lay in their relationship to time. The Italians, they felt, were constantly changing designs and plans up to the last moment—and still expecting an on-time delivery of the garments.

Chinese entrepreneurs' close involvement in the production process begins with their ability to choose the appropriate factories for producing fashion clothing. These factories are judged to have this ability if they have the proper kind of weaving or knitting looms for fashion clothing, if the factory owner or manager understands and appreciates the demand for a certain level of quality control, if the factory does not subcontract out to other factories of lesser ability, and, ideally, if the factory manager or owner is part of the entrepreneur's network of guanxi, or connections, so that they can be prevailed upon to make these entrepreneurs' orders a priority.

Chinese entrepreneurs also did a great deal of work overseeing quality control in addition to the general oversight of the Italian managers. Quality is the crux of whether Chinese entrepreneurs will have a successful business.[20] Italians first want to see a sample of the proposed product. Chinese entrepreneurs must therefore contract with a factory to make a sample, though the factory might not end up producing the product if the sample is not accepted. This is all the more reason why the connections, or guanxi, between these entrepreneurs and the factory owners are important, for the factory is basically doing free labor in the hope of a future (sub)contract. One Saturday night, Rofel stayed up until midnight with Wang Shiyao, who works for a Shanghai state-owned import-export company, because he had to wait for a prototype to be delivered from the factory so that he could check the quality before the factory produced any garments. The mediator entrepreneur spends a great deal of time on the prototype, negotiating between the subcontracted factory and the Italian firm to ensure quality control.

The sample itself might have problems. Entrepreneurs with a background from Donghua are attentive to new fabrics being developed as well as the quality of well-known fabrics and which kinds of fabrics might actually work well together as opposed to what the designer imagines might work. In working with Italian and other foreign fashion firms, these entrepreneurs often take it upon themselves to suggest new fabrics to try out. In the case of the Molteni firm, for example, the entire work of the Chinese textile engineer they hired is to go around to different factories to sample the fabrics they are making.

Moreover, the Chinese entrepreneurs and managers travel to the factories at least once a week to ensure proper production. If the production lags behind, then the Chinese entrepreneur must pay extra costs for special shipping or, as written into their contracts with the Italian firms, they lose some of their payment if they are late. They must ensure that the production of the fabric or garments will meet the deadline. Time is treated as of the essence. The latter is especially significant because the tempo of transnational fashion production demands an uneven time schedule. Italian and other foreign textile and garment firms often demand a quick turnaround in production. Moreover, they often keep making last-minute changes to a design that then require changes in the production timetable. Finally, the production of fashion clothing must meet an established deadline each season when the new fashions are introduced into the European and U.S. markets. The Chinese entrepreneur who has strong guanxi with factory owners can convince a factory owner or manager to make her production order a priority.

Li Yue, for example, and his wife (he never mentioned her name) are owners of a small factory (two hundred workers) in Hangzhou, Molto Bene Ltd., that produces fashion clothing solely for Italian companies. Li was in his midforties when we first met. A tall, well-built man who looked younger than his age, Li dressed in the most fashionable of Western-style menswear. Li and his wife got into the business of fashion garment production circuitously. Li had studied tourism and hotel management in college. His wife, originally from Wenzhou, had been living in Italy running a restaurant since 1983. She speaks fluent Italian. They met in China and after they married, Li went with her to Italy, in part so they could give birth to their two children there. Li sees Italy as a country with an old civilization, while he sees China as undergoing a vast transformation to become a new country. He and his wife want their children to have connections to both types of culture.

Li and his wife first started out helping Italian companies in various industrial sectors transport goods to and from China. Then they set up a consulting company (zixun gongsi) to help Italian companies find the right counterparts for production as well as marketing in China. In 1994 he became the consultant for top fashion companies in Italy, in charge of quality control. He got these customers through the Italian embassy. As he put it, "I was like their eyes. Because they couldn't be here all the time and they couldn't communicate very well." In 1999 Li and his wife decided to open their own factory, mainly to be able to control the quality. They have a direct link with the Italian companies, bypassing the government trading companies. They also refuse to have domestic customers, in order to protect the intellectual property of the designs of their Italian customers.

Other Chinese entrepreneurs work with the Italians to market their fashion clothing in China. They assert that when the Italians want to distribute and market in China, they need them not only to shepherd them around China but also to work with them in designing clothing appropriate for the Chinese market. One day, Jiang Li/Nico, for example, laid out ties produced for Chinese consumers versus those exported to Europe. He pointed out the differences in color, pattern, and style between the two markets. Lou Jingxiao saw herself as essential to the design process as well as the production process. She repeatedly stressed that Italian designers were often not sufficiently familiar with the different qualities of fabrics. She stressed her knowledge of new fabrics being experimented with in China and whether they would work in combination with older ones. Chen Rongfen (who goes by the first name Nicole) works for a Chinese import-export company, FuHua Co. Ltd. (Grand China), that specializes in helping foreigners market their goods in China. When we met her, Chen Rongfen/Nicole had been working with Italians for a number of years. Chen emphasized that without someone like her, the Italians would have no way of understanding how to produce for Chinese taste. She saw herself as absolutely essential to the process of designing and producing fashion garments—for a Chinese market.

Finally, in addition to the question of quality, Chinese entrepreneurs help factory managers solve a range of other problems. One is the sourcing of fabric. Recently, one Chinese entrepreneur complained that the timetable was going to be a headache on one particular order because the Italian firm had insisted on buying part of the fabric from a firm in Hong Kong. The Italian firm thought the Hong Kong firm had access to better quality fabric. But the Hong Kong firm lagged behind in the order and indeed had forgotten about it entirely. This resulted in a late shipment. Consequently, this entrepreneur had to insist the Hong Kong firm share the penalty of a lowered payment with her. These issues are pressing for mediator firms because they operate by buying the garments from the factory and selling them to the Italians. Thus, their capital is directly at risk.

The structure of their transnational relations, including the various links in the commodity chain, lead Italian managers and Chinese entrepreneurs to highlight their differences, even as they claim overlapping terrain. In the fashion industry, emphasis on Italianità is closely tied to the importance of branding and therefore quality control. By contrast, Chinese entrepreneurs must demonstrate how they transcend "Chineseness," given its associations with low-cost production. While this section has presented a contrast in the various emphases Italian and Chinese managers and entrepreneurs placed on the value of their contributions to the Chinese production of Italian fashion, the next section reveals their common emphasis on the importance of cultural interpretation and translation.

Cultural Translation

Italian managers working in joint ventures frequently characterized their job as being a cultural interpreter between the Italians and Chinese. They identified culture as "a fundamental element" in these relations, with much more being involved than language translation. Along with cultural interpretation comes their responsibility for facilitating negotiations between the Chinese and Italian collaborators. Andrea Politi, who represents a large, multibrand Italian firm in its joint venture with a Chinese manufacturer, explained: "My work as deputy general manager is one of consultant, support, advice, communication, and ambassador of Italianità. . . . You have to propose, suggest, advise; there are always compromises. The Chinese listen until a certain point. . . . They think that Italians are stupid and that Italians think the same of them! I am between the two sides, regardless of coming from the [Italian] side; but I act as a buffer between the sections." Several managers emphasized the need for compromise between Italian and Chinese ways of doing business. Paolo Rinaldi declared that he had to constantly use his "emotional intelligence" to maintain the balance between the two partners.

> It is easier to move the firm ahead, but much more difficult to mediate the cultural aspects between [the partners]. One has to come to compromises, and often you have to have long, exhausting meetings about things that seem minor, for example how much an employee can speak on the telephone or how much can be spent at a restaurant or what the benefits are for the director. These are things that are of great importance to the Chinese partner that are very minor to us.

Leonardo Benini explained that he had to help Chinese understand the needs of Europeans and Americans and help Europeans and Americans understand the character of production in China. This, he said, might entail something as seemingly minor as convincing the Italian firm that they must use mannequins in China despite their aesthetic judgment not to use them in their European stores. He explained to the Italian firm that the Chinese want both the top and bottom displayed on the mannequin so they can see how the outfit goes together. After working in China for more than ten years, Benini felt that companies had come to understand that knowing China was much more important than having a master of business administration (MBA). As a result, companies were doing more recruiting locally rather than in Europe, and he was constantly receiving calls from companies who knew about his work. Although he had studied economics, he reported that if he could do it all over, he would have studied language and literature.

Being a cultural interpreter and facilitator of communications also entailed participating in Chinese social activities, which managers admitted could become tiresome after a while. Gianfranco Naldi described how he had to participate in KTV (karaoke parties) with their Chinese partners several times a week. "I have to do this. For them, having dinner and then after-dinner social activities are important. Otherwise, they will always view you as an outsider. We drink wine, beer, maotai [sic]. Sometimes the families do business this way. If you don't do this, they might trust you but they don't appreciate you."

The work of cultural interpretation also has its frustrations. Paolo Rinaldi offered,

Of course, working with the Chinese is more complicated. First, there is the language. Then there is the mentality. It is about their approach to everything, not just business. . . . Usually, I would break down problems into smaller problems and then solve one at a time. But with Asians, they like to solve everything together, not piece by piece. For example, when you are choosing the buttons and the fabric, they want to do it all at the same time. You can go crazy. Too often they [Chinese] think, "They are not right, we are better." To tell you the truth, we have the same feeling. But for Italians it is a conflict of mentality. I try to approach it by saying that it's not "We're right, they are wrong," but it's difference. It's a more flexible way of dealing with difference.

Translation, like all work processes, must be managed. At times this requires leaving things out. A couple of managers reported that they did not always tell their Italian employer or the Chinese partner everything that had been said by the other party. Massimo Soci went so far as to admit that he sometimes lied to facilitate negotiations. During the two months that he sat with the Chinese firm owner and the interpreter to work out the terms of the joint venture, he occasionally lied to keep the process going rather than get hung up on some minor issue.

A cultural mediator in a joint venture may also be perceived as a spy for one of the partners. Relations between partners can be fraught with suspicion when they are collaborators and competitors at the same time. For example, six years after its creation, the joint venture Pure Elegance began promoting a youth-oriented brand that was becoming a likely competitor of a brand owned by its Italian partner. While the two firms had initially cooperated in arranging their locations in department stores, over time the threat of competition had raised questions as to whether it was in the interest of both firms to continue this practice. This put Andrea Politi, who was the Italian firm's representative in the joint venture, in a difficult position. If his colleagues in the Italian firm asked him where the joint venture was going to open a shop, he could not tell them. He claimed: "I maximize the role of [the Italian partner] in the joint venture, but I'm not a spy." Antonio Peroni, who had the double role of being the CFO of the Italian firm FGS in China and the CFO and deputy general manager of the firm's joint venture with its Chinese partners, appeared to be joking when he said that when he visited the Shanghai offices of the joint venture, it was to spy on its operations. There was considerable ambiguity as to how much truth there was in the joke.

The Chinese entrepreneurs and managers equally viewed themselves as cultural translators and cultural mediators. One quotidian way in which they acted as cultural mediators was through code-switching. They do so through their own names as well as the landscape of Shanghai. Lou Jingxiao, for example, goes by the name of Maggi Lou with her Italian and other foreign business customers. She is not alone or unusual in this practice. These days, it seems everyone—of a certain generation—dealing with foreigners has taken a Western name and reversed the order of their surname and given name (surnames come first in Chinese). Lou Jingxiao chose the name Maggi because she admires Margaret Thatcher—a strong, female model, as she viewed her. Rofel met several other Maggis, as well as George, Nicole, Alex, Henry, Ross, JoJo (actually a clever riff on her Chinese name), and so on. These young Chinese entrepreneurs (older entrepreneurs did not tend to take English names) had no difficulty moving back and forth between their Chinese and English names—using their English names for business and among most foreigners and their Chinese names among family and friends. No Chinese worker, by contrast, ever introduced themselves to us with an English name. (Nor do intellectuals in China tend to take on English names.) Perhaps it goes without saying that most foreign entrepreneurs working in China do not take a Chinese name.

Over dinner with Rofel one night, Lou Jingxiao/Maggi and Wang Shiyao/George, a classmate of Lou's from Donghua University's business school who now works in one of Shanghai's major municipal import-export companies, Three Swords, explained that foreigners have a hard time pronouncing their Chinese names. But they also felt it gave them an identity that signified the ability to do business internationally and thus made Italians and other foreigners feel more comfortable doing business in China.[21] The joint venture companies Chinese and Italians have established also have two different names, one in English (but not in Italian) and one in Chinese. And again, the Chinese entrepreneurs fluidly move between the names, depending on their interlocutors.

The whole architecture and landscape of Shanghai also engages in code-switching. We realized this aspect of life in Shanghai one day when we tried to figure out the location of an office building in which an Italian firm was located. The English name for the building that Yanagisako had been given bore no relationship to the building's Chinese name. We had to find a Chinese person who knew both names. In China, people tend to move around cities through landmarks rather than through street names. Thus, the names of buildings are critical to finding one's way. This name-switching of landmark buildings functioned to create parallel worlds in which expatriates living in Shanghai move around comfortably in English while the majority of the Chinese population blithely ignore the English. Chinese entrepreneurs move around between these worlds. In fact, they need to be able to move across the various geographical and cultural borders in Shanghai to manage the full range of the supply chain in Italian fashion.

As with the Italian managers, Chinese entrepreneurs also viewed themselves as cultural translators in the broadest sense. They viewed their work as "translating" both the physical and cultural landscape of China for the Italians and other foreigners. Of course, while the Chinese entrepreneurs did not view themselves as mere "translators" for foreigners, all the Italian firms and joint ventures have translators, who work by the side of the Italian managers and go with them everywhere. They believed the Italians need them to "translate" China, because the Italians and other foreigners view China as a mostly impenetrable country.

Jiang Li/Nico, introduced at the beginning of the chapter, is one such translator. He emphasized that he was the only person in the Vinimoon joint venture capable of taking on the role of cultural mediator because he was the only one fluent in both Italian and Chinese and the only one, with perhaps the exception of one of the Italian technicians who had married a Chinese woman, who was familiar with living among both Italians and Chinese. Recall that Jiang had lived in Italy for ten years; yet he did not describe his cosmopolitanism as having grown out of merely being in Italy. Rather, in his interpretation, it was the other way around. He brought a certain open-mindedness to his journey to Italy: "I wanted to learn about everything in Italy. I did not bring Chinese things with me but learned how they do things in Italy. Of course, I brought some things from China, like *renqing*, *limao* [the proper way to conduct human relations, to be polite]. But there were things worth studying from Europeans."

Joint ventures can give rise to the most fraught relationships between Chinese and Italians. This joint venture was no exception. Not a few joint ventures have dissolved in the face of ongoing disputes, and few foreign firms choose to engage in joint ventures in China now that they are no longer required to do so. The different emphases that each side in Vinimoon placed on what was good for the business did not always coincide and indeed sometimes caused dissension. (See Rofel's chapter 6 for further discussion of Vinimoon in relation to kinship.) One example Jiang gave was the question of buying a company car. The Chinese owners wanted to buy a car for the company. But they wanted to buy a Mercedes. Jiang explained the problem this way:

> The foreigners don't usually buy a car for their companies. When they need to pick up a guest at the airport or take them around, they go to a rental car company. But they realized that China doesn't have rental car companies and that the company needed to buy a car. But then when you buy a car, of course, you have to hire a driver and also buy gas. The driver doesn't cost that much. But the foreigners thought that the company needed to buy new equipment and not spend all the money on the top-brand car. The company should buy new equipment and concentrate on making the best product possible. The high-quality product will attract customers. They thought buying the top-brand car was a waste of money. The Chinese believe that the image [*xingxiang*] is important. They think the company will attract customers if they have the right image. I think the foreigners were right. So I convinced the Chinese they shouldn't emphasize the empty surface [*xu*] but reality [*shi*]. So the company bought a Buick, which is half the price.

In this way, Jiang saw himself as a cultural broker. He continued: "All the way up to today, there are still difficulties. The Chinese side thinks foreigners waste a lot of money. For example, the foreigners want to get the best talent and hire the best managers. But the Chinese think it is not necessary to spend so much money because they can hire a Chinese person much more cheaply." Jiang thus viewed himself as absolutely central to the ability of this joint venture to proceed and prosper. As he explained his abilities: "I try not to have either side make a sharp, definitive decision [*panjue*]. I slowly try to bring them to see each other's point of view. I use time and also persuasion."

Another, more explosive reaction of a translator occurred in Rofel's conversation with Shu Hailun, the translator for the joint venture Pure Elegance. Rofel and Shu had several prior conversations and had become comfortable acquaintances over the course of several years. One evening over dinner with Rofel, Shu announced that he had just resigned from his job that day. Rofel was quite surprised, so she asked if this was a good thing or not. "A very good thing," he replied. "I have 'liberated' [*jiefang*] myself. I am now free [*duli*]." The term he used for "to liberate," *jiefang*, was first popularized by the Communist Party to mean liberation from class exploitation. Shu's use of it had the connotation of liberating himself from some kind of oppression. He said Mr. Politi, the new Italian manager he had been working with, accepted his resignation. But then he launched into a long complaint about this manager and spent most of dinner complaining about him: "He is too arrogant. He thinks he is better than everyone else. He thinks he is always right and that what he says should go." "He's not like Soci," he added. (Soci was the previous Italian manager). "Soci is an ordinary employee [*zhiyuan*]. This guy thinks of himself as at the top [*gaodeng*]." Then for a few moments we chatted about what he would do in the future. But then he went back to his complaints:

He likes to take care of too many things. He wants to be the one to decide everything. And he wants to know what you are doing every minute. He called once to say he wasn't coming into the office. So then he shouldn't care what I am doing if he's not coming into the office. But he called me later that day and said, Where are you? I said I went to the bank. He said I have to tell him where I am going every time I step out of the office. Should I tell him when I have to go to the bathroom, too? Soci wasn't like that.

Thus, both Italian managers and Chinese entrepreneurs and translators mediated, experienced, and embodied the ongoing negotiations over the value of their respective contributions to the production and distribution of

Italian fashion through assertions about cultural translation. The Italian managers viewed their cultural mediation as essential to the labor process. Chinese entrepreneurs and translators also viewed their capacity to be cultural translators as contributing to the value of Italian fashion. These capacities of their labor power were formed through the negotiated encounters rather than already congealed in their persons.

Mutual Criticisms: Chinese Lack of Managerial Creativity versus Italian Provincialism

In negotiating the value of their respective labor powers, Italian managers and owners and Chinese entrepreneurs, translators, and officials not only overlap in their claims to certain skills necessary to a transnational commodity chain, such as cultural mediation. They also point out the shortcomings of their partners in contrast to themselves. These contrasts serve to highlight the centrality of their own skills and knowledges. Yet these skills and knowledges are constituted through this very relation of mutual interdependence.

Italian Evaluations of the Chinese

Praise for Chinese Workers

Italian managers as well as firm owners generally have strong praise for the technical skills and abilities of Chinese workers, whom they describe as very good at adapting Italian machinery to meet local production needs and quick to learn computing tasks. This is a dramatic shift from the attitudes toward Chinese workers expressed by Italian managers and firm owners in the 1980s and 1990s when Yanagisako conducted her research on family firms in the silk industry of Como in northern Italy. At that time, Como's silk manufacturers derided the technical capabilities of the Chinese, characterizing them as far inferior to Italian ones. By the fall of 2004, however, both managers and firm owners reported that as a result of acquiring state-of-the-art machinery and technical know-how, Chinese productive capacity had improved so rapidly that they could now produce textiles and clothing equal in quality to Italian ones. According to Danilo Marsili, distribution manager for an Italian brand in Shanghai, "Chinese are very quick; they are faster than Italians when it comes to computer work, IT work, and doing analyses. We Italians are still faxing things!" While in the 1990s and first years of the new millennium, his textile firm had sent technicians to train their Chinese counterparts to operate, adapt, and repair the latest equipment, in 2007 Nicolò Marazzi stated, "Now it's not worth it to send technicians. There are great technicians in China. Our partners are at a very high level technically. And in China the phrase 'I can't' doesn't exist."

Although these claims about the increased proficiency of Chinese workers must be assessed in the context of the shift to overseas production that occurred between the 1980s and 2004, they are not merely a justification for the high price of clothing designed in Milan but sewn in Hangzhou. The change in Italians' assessment of Chinese textiles and clothing is also a consequence of the investments in both equipment and technical expertise that Italian firms have made in China. In addition to sending technicians to their Chinese partners, Italian firms have also sent better equipment. Whereas in the 1980s, Italian textile manufacturers sold to Chinese manufacturers only looms they were replacing with newer equipment, by 2006 those who had started joint ventures or their own wholly owned factories were sending state-of-the-art, high-speed looms.

Praise for the technical skills and work ethic of Chinese workers by Italian managers, as well as by firm owners (from whom we shall hear in part II), was often paired with criticisms of Italian workers, who were characterized as less industrious and unwilling to engage in hard work. These complaints about the degradation of the Italian workforce are hardly novel. In the 1980s and 1990s, Yanagisako had heard similar lamentations by firm owners in the silk industry of Como, many of whom blamed the labor unions and the legislation that had gotten passed in the 1970s for causing the decline of the quality of labor in Italy. These complaints must be situated in the post–World War II history of Italian capital and labor, which we mentioned in the introduction to part I and which will be discussed in greater detail in part II. For now, suffice it to say that for Italian firm owners and managers, the industriousness of Chinese workers represents precisely what they view as the deficiencies of Italian labor—which is what they say drove them to relocate production to China in the first place.

The Shortcomings of Chinese Managers and Entrepreneurs

In comparison to their praise of Chinese workers, Italian managers are much less complimentary in what they say about Chinese managers and entrepreneurs. On the one hand, they construe their relation with the latter in terms of a functional division of labor, with each party having managerial knowledge and skill that complements that of the other. Paolo Rinaldi, the CEO of the joint venture Vinimoon, summed up this division of managerial labor in the following terms:

> Our managerial know-how is important, but theirs is even more so—their relations with the workers, their social connections, the dinners with customs officials and tax officials. They know the market well and they manage relations well. There are two different managerial capacities: ours and theirs and both are necessary because it's difficult to work in China. They pay very close attention to cost more than we do. And they know how to read the Chinese market much better than me. We put into the product a certain Italianità and sophistication. They harmonize it with the Chinese market. They are an important asset in the joint venture; and in this way we succeed in managing the company day by day.

At the same time, Rinaldi and other Italian managers had a bevy of complaints about the shortcomings of Chinese entrepreneurs and managers. Among these were their poor planning skills, lack of initiative in problem-solving, inflexibility, lack of creativity, and lack of familiarity with management systems.

> The Chinese are not able to plan. They do not have that planning capacity. They can work when they have orders. The Chinese in the production unit often don't understand how what they are doing fits into the larger picture: they just focus on their small part of the process and don't think about how it fits into the rest. They don't really understand what they are making or how it should look as a finished product. (Gianfranco Naldi, general manager of Vinimoon)

> Once, I discounted the price from 1,000 to 500. We printed everything and sent it to the store, but first I reviewed it. I noticed an error. I asked why it was still written 1,000. The Chinese workers told me that they realized it was an error but since I did it they didn't correct it. To me this was absurd; if you see a mistake, you have to correct it; even I can make a mistake. (Silvana Salvianti, general manager of Felsari)

Paolo Rinaldi expressed a common complaint about the inflexibility of the Chinese and their unwillingness to make any exceptions: "The Chinese want precise procedures and rules and don't want any exceptions. If someone asks me to substitute a Monday for Saturday—this is a real example that actually occurred and I gave him permission—this causes great unhappiness." Rinaldi went on to suggest that one of the reasons Americans do not work well with the Chinese is "because they lack the necessary flexibility to understand the inflexibility of the Chinese." Hence, despite his efforts to be open to cultural difference, Rinaldi admitted:

> From a cultural point of view, it's been a shocking experience. Things that are natural to me upset them. You think you understand them [the Chinese], but it's not true. After three years, I have to say that I am back at point zero. . . . Think about how there was the Cultural Revolution and the type of school they went to didn't teach them how to manage choices. If you give them more choices, they are unprepared. They don't have mental elasticity. For me to feel good, I have to invent something every day; but [here] I also have to invent things for them.

Rosanna Potenza, who had majored in Chinese studies and who had gone to Beijing to study Chinese theater before she was hired to manage quality control for an Italian company, reported that although she had been enthusiastic about the Chinese when she was a student, she had grown somewhat disappointed. She described her relationship with China as a love-hate one. She concluded that the Chinese "remain Chinese as far as mode of thinking. They need to be guided; they don't take the initiative and they have to be given instructions for everything." Even though she knew the language, she felt that the major problem she faced was communicating with the Chinese. She explained that she is Pugliese (i.e., from Apulia, a province in southern Italy) by birth, adding, "It is said that people from southern Italy are slow and show little initiative, but the Chinese are even worse."

Lack of analysis is another frequent theme in Italian managers' complaints about the Chinese. According to an Italian distribution manager, for example, her Chinese assistant had trouble deciding on her own whether to ship an order by plane or truck, although a simple cost analysis would have made it clear what should be done. "You have to give them very specific instructions," she said. She was quick to add that she did not view this as a fixed trait of the Chinese, stating, "I am sure there will be Chinese managers in the future who can plan—those who travel abroad."

Italian managers commonly attribute the lack of "mental elasticity" and "creativity" of the Chinese to Communist education and policies. Chinese people over the age of forty are considered incapable of being adept entrepreneurs or managers. Commenting on the lack of capable managers in their fifties, one manager noted, "Mao prohibited them from reading and writing, so they don't have the head for running a firm." Another said, "The fact is that the clothing industry is in the hands of ex-peasants who are forty-five years old and have a mentality that was formed in the past. As long as you tell them precisely what to do, it's fine."

Although they attributed Chinese lack of creativity to the Communist state and school system, it was unclear from managers' comments whether creativity could be taught. One manager said in the same breath, "[The lack of creativity] is a problem of the school system; the Chinese schools don't encourage creativity. And creativity is something you are born with; you can't be taught it. The Chinese don't have this capacity."

Italian managers also lament the poor communication skills of Chinese managers and employees. Since few Italian managers (four of twenty in our sample) speak Mandarin or any other Chinese language or dialect, they either rely on Chinese translators or, more commonly, communicate with Chinese staff in English. Italian managers frequently complain about the poor English-speaking ability of their Chinese staff. The English-language abilities of both Italians and Chinese vary widely, so it is not surprising that misunderstanding between them was common. Many of the Chinese staff speak what is best described as "business English," which they learned in business school, while most Italian managers had acquired English through a combination of language study throughout their education and on-the-job training.

Another common complaint of Italian managers involves the Chinese reliance on email rather than direct verbal communication. Several Italian managers expressed exasperation that Chinese employees would send them emails rather than speak to them, even if they were sitting in the next room. Marzia Bordogna explained that she tried to communicate verbally with the rest of the staff in her office because email could result in delays in the work process. When you have to wait for others to read your emails and reply, it takes too long, she reported. In addition, people get so many emails that they do not pay attention to them right away, so, she argued, it is more efficient to walk a few steps and talk to people.

Bordogna was not entirely oblivious to the relation between language and power and the likelihood that Chinese employees preferred to rely on written communication to minimize the risk of misunderstanding or being accused of misunderstanding. She added that even when she gave verbal directions, she followed up with emails and documents as attachments. At the same time, she interpreted the lower rate of direct verbal communication by Chinese staff as a sign of their lack of trust.

Finally, several managers commented on the short-term perspective of Chinese managers and entrepreneurs. They were particularly critical of their Chinese partners' unwillingness to make long-term investments, especially when it came to investing in the design and image of a brand. Gianfranco Naldi explained that when it comes to retail strategies, Italians place more importance on managing the brand image even if this means opening fewer retail stores. In comparison, the Chinese are unwilling to spend money on advertising and instead want to maximize their profits in every store. Monica Campani, who was working with her boss in Milan to promote a new line of retail stores in China, lamented:

> They are good with hardware, but not with software. . . . If they have to buy equipment, they will spend millions of euro. But when it comes to hiring a designer who will teach them about international tastes that they don't understand, they have a difficult time understanding the value of this. . . . They always search for quick results, things they can touch with their hands, when instead learning how to put together a collection takes time season after season.

Antonio Peroni also complained about the short-term perspective of the Chinese in comparison to the Italians. In contrast to others, however, he attributed these differences not to culture but to the respective activities and experiences of the parties in the joint venture: "We [Italians] go far but we go slowly. The joint venture is just at the beginning of this process. It takes time and it's difficult especially for people like them [the Chinese partners] who were successful by having a factory. It's not because they are Chinese but because they are manufacturers, and so they want to see something tangible. Whereas a brand is intangible and you can't see the result of the investment right away."

Peroni's remarks highlight the way in which the division of labor between the partners shapes their perceptions of each other. Both joint ventures and outsourcing relations connect Chinese manufacturing firms to an Italian firm that owns and promotes one or more clothing brands or textile lines. In the case of clothing brands, the Italian firm's design office in Italy comes up with the styles and produces prototypes for each garment, including specifying the types of stitching to be used in various parts of the garment. The prototypes and directions for cutting the fabric and sewing are sent to the Chinese manufacturer—either directly from the design office in Italy or via the joint venture or the Italian firm's office in Shanghai. In some cases, an Italian designer or production manager travels to China to instruct the manufacturer as to how to put together the garment. Whether manufacturing is done by a partner in a joint venture or a subcontractor, the Italian firm monitors the manufacturing process and oversees the quality control of the product.[22] Likewise, in the manufacture of textiles, the Italian firm's home office designs the fabric—including the weave and color—and the prototype is usually woven first in Italy. It is only after the prototype has been checked and refined that the design is sent to the Chinese manufacturer via computer-aided design (CAD). Here again, quality control is managed by Italians.

The division of labor between Italian and Chinese partners and collaborators in the management of the various phases of production of textiles and clothing sets up an asymmetry in their relative power to control design, quality, brand image, distribution, and profits. Not only do Italian partners have greater control over these phases of production, but it is they who evaluate the quality of Chinese work rather than the other way around.

It is worth noting that Italian firm owners' evaluation of Chinese entrepreneurs and managers is more mixed than that of Italian managers. Firm owners who had joint ventures with Chinese firms praised not only the technical skill and industriousness of Chinese workers but also the qualities of Chinese managers, entrepreneurs, and even the Chinese state. In addition to lauding the discriminating taste of Chinese customers and their appreciation of quality, Alessandro Bossi, one of the owners of FGS, declared, "The Chinese are extraordinarily entrepreneurial and organized." In direct contradiction to the complaints of managers working for his company in Shanghai, he added, "Planning is the great power of China." Indeed, he suggested that the Italians should learn from the Chinese. At the same time, however, he asserted that the Chinese have no respect for rules, and for this reason their work has to be controlled and supervised. Renato Costa, who has a joint venture with a formerly state-owned and state-managed factory, offered a similarly complex and inconsistent assessment. Chinese schools, he argued, are producing not only very well-prepared technicians but "extraordinary" university graduates. He not only defended the Chinese copying of designs, pointing out that the Japanese had also copied things at the beginning of their industrial success, but also stated that when the Chinese copy fashion designs, they make them better. "Before long," he said, "a Chinese Armani will appear." In spite of this prediction, however, he concluded that at present Chinese designers are merely technicians who can execute a design rather than create it and that "design is still something they have to develop."

The ambivalence captured in these firm owners' comments about their Chinese partners and clients reflects both their hopes and anxieties about the future, in which China looms large as a key market but also as a competitor. Their positive comments about the sophistication of Chinese taste clearly speak to their exuberance for the expanding Chinese market in luxury goods. Like other Italian luxury brands, their hopes for survival and expansion hinge on the market in China and the sixty million Chinese tourists that Alessandro Bossi estimated would shortly be traveling the globe and shopping in his firm's stores. Tourists, especially Asian tourists, visiting Europe have been a mainstay of Italian luxury brands, and with the saturation of the Japanese market, China has become the industry's salvation.[23]

Chinese Critiques of Italians

Chinese entrepreneurs who work together with the Italians to produce fashion textiles and garments know they do not enter into contractual relations with the Italians on the basis of equality. They have learned, in their business school training or through experience, that in a capitalist world of private property, the fact that the Italians bring the capital and usually the brand name (though sometimes the brand name is a joint venture between them for the Chinese market) shapes the claims Chinese entrepreneurs can make about the value of their labor power and thus their contribution to the production and distribution of fashion clothing. Not only with the Italians but with most other foreign partners, Chinese managers and entrepreneurs feel they bump up against the "Chinese glass ceiling" and that they will not be able to advance very far in a foreign-owned firm. Yet they also are cognizant that their own career and class trajectories are necessarily bound up with transnational business relations in that China's ability to maintain its high growth rate is dependent on deep immersion in a global economy. At the time of our research, the growing elite class in China was predominantly composed of those involved in global business rather than those who focused solely on the domestic market.

Not all Chinese entrepreneurs, however, have the same reaction to the asymmetry in their relationships with Italians. While they all recognize the existence of that asymmetry, there are a range of responses that have changed over time. Factory owners and managers who subcontract for the Italians have the most distant relationship to the Italians in this commodity chain. When they have complaints, they will more often be directed against the Chinese state import-export company that has given them the production contract. Those who act as mediators between Italian companies and Chinese producers have a different relationship to the Italians than those who establish joint ventures with the Italians. Among the latter, there exists a further differentiation between those who are private entrepreneurs and those who represent the government. Those who seem to have the most strongly felt frustration and sometimes even explosive reactions to their asymmetrical relationship with the Italians are the private entrepreneurs in joint ventures with the Italians. This is especially true when the fashion clothing is directed toward the Chinese market. Yet others, including factory owners and mediators as well as translators, also voiced frustration from time to time about the difficulties in asserting the appropriate value of their contribution to the production of Italian-labeled fashion or changing the asymmetry in the relationship. Government officials, by contrast, were keenly intent on convincing the Italians they were worthy partners and not mere representatives of the corruption that seems so pervasive throughout state corporations. Thus, both the structural and emergent aspects of the encounters through the fashion industry highlight the repeated emphasis and attention that Chinese and Italians both place on the value of their respective labor powers.

When they talk about themselves specifically in relationship to the Italians, Chinese managers and entrepreneurs tend to emphasize that the Italians are not as cosmopolitan as they are. They see the Italians' relative lack of cosmopolitanism in various ways detailed below, but one prominent way is how the Italians naturalize their manner of doing business, which Chinese by contrast see as particular and specific. Most of the entrepreneurs described the peculiarities in the way the Italians conduct transnational business as having to do with their style of last-minute planning or last-minute changes that make it difficult to organize factory production. A variety of Chinese people who work with the Italians, including those Chinese who work at the Italian embassy but also those working in the textile and garment industries, complained that the Italians often change their plans at the last moment and yet still expect Chinese factories to produce according to the original time schedule. They also complained that the Italians, since they are focused on production, are always looking for the lowest price and do not always invest in thinking about the long-term benefit of their partnership with the Chinese. Again, particularly private Chinese entrepreneurs emphasized that it is their own cosmopolitanism that enables them to handle these peculiarities of the Italians and allows Italians to function in China.

Other entrepreneurs, including government officials, also saw that the Italians have difficulty distinguishing among Chinese—which ones are good at business and which ones are not, which ones are trustworthy and which ones are not—whereas they, Chinese entrepreneurs, see themselves as able to distinguish among various foreigners. They often pointed out, in contrast, how foreigners, including but not only Italians, were unable or unwilling to make themselves more cosmopolitan by learning Chinese. Indeed, one entrepreneur commented at one point that some of the Italians, especially the Italian designers, do not speak very much English, so she had started learning Italian. (The Italian designers usually travel once or twice a year to China along with firm owners.)

Chinese entrepreneurs also viewed a majority of the Italians as provincial, in that they hailed from small towns and had quaint ideas about the Chinese that harked back to nineteenth-century colonial histories.[24] The tone Chinese entrepreneurs used in mentioning these aspects of working with the Italians was not one of belittlement but rather either amusement or historically inflected resentment at the sense they are being taken advantage of and have to put up with it because of the asymmetrical relationship they perceive they have with the Italians.

One of the most iconic stories in this regard was told by Chen Rongfen, who goes by the name Nicole when dealing with foreigners. Chen told a humorous story of her first encounters with Italians. She said that when she first went to Italy, the Italians were very naïve and ignorant about Chinese people. They asked her why she was not wearing her Chinese "costume." They thought, she said, that she would come wearing the clothing of the Chinese imperial household, costumes that they must have seen in martial arts or other films portraying an ancient Chinese past. They knew nothing about us, she concluded. In telling this story, Chen laughed appreciatively.

Some entrepreneurs commented on the condescension of the Italians in less humorous terms. Jiang Li/Nico, the cultural mediator/translator of Vinimoon, once offered Rofel the following unsolicited comment at the end of a discussion that had stretched over a whole morning. In their conversation, he had painted a picture of himself as an urbane gentleman who knows how to adjudicate between the Italians and Chinese and can see the positive and negative of both sides. Rofel was therefore a bit taken aback when they were saying good-bye and she was already walking away from his office in Shanghai.

Suddenly he launched into a different tone and stated forcefully: "Foreigners need to learn how to treat Chinese people with respect. Otherwise, they will never succeed in doing business in China." Only much later did Rofel finally learn the personal reason for Jiang's outburst. (See Rofel's chapter in part III.)

Some of these Chinese entrepreneurs further contrasted their worldliness with that of the Italians they have worked with in China by uniformly portraying the Italians as not understanding how to work with foreigners, such as Chinese people, and as relatively unfamiliar with, uncomfortable with, unable, and in some cases unwilling to learn how to move around in a foreign country or foreign culture such as China. Those who have their own private firms in particular viewed the Italians in this way because the latter are generally unwilling to leave their narrow, expatriate worlds. In the view of these Chinese entrepreneurs, the attitude, or assumption, on the part of Italians that being Italian or European is sufficient in itself is precisely what makes them parochial. The Italians tended to keep themselves sequestered in expatriate communities without reaching out to make contacts with Chinese people outside of business dealings, or they were reluctant to live in China full-time and thus only come to visit periodically. Thus, some of these entrepreneurs viewed the Italians as more limited, and less cosmopolitan, in this respect than themselves. Again, this was especially true of Chinese private entrepreneurs who, in searching for business clients, had to reach out and work with a wide range of foreigners.

The recently gentrified landscape of Shanghai reinforced these segregations. In the past twenty-five years, Shanghai, a port city on the eastern coast and home to some twenty-seven million people, has regained its presocialist reputation as the commercial and financial center of China. Shanghai has fashioned itself as the exemplar of a twenty-first-century city. The downtown area that had once been carved into colonial extraterritorial concessions has been preserved. This area is where the foreign expat communities live, including those from Taiwan and Hong Kong. Starting in the 1990s, all other buildings, including all homes, were systematically razed to the ground as Shanghai experienced a radical cosmopolitan makeover, centered in the downtown areas and partially but unevenly spreading to other areas of the city. Longtime downtown residents were pushed out by municipal officials who took advantage of the emergent real estate market. Shanghai is now a study in contrasts. Its downtown center is virtually a showcase of the latest in architectural design. Even middle-class Chinese people cannot afford to live in this rebuilt downtown. The Chinese entrepreneurs and managers we interacted with lived in the west and north of the city, as well as the newly developed Pudong area to the south (which had recently displaced farmland). Conversely, very few Westerners live in these other areas, although there are communities of ex-pat Taiwanese and Japanese in the west and north, respectively. The gentrification of Shanghai was simultaneously its postsocialist reworlding of China.[25]

Chinese entrepreneurs move around and between these worlds. In fact, they need to be able to move across the various geographical and cultural borders in Shanghai. Italians and other foreign entrepreneurs living in downtown Shanghai learned how to move around a limited pathway among those buildings and landmarks incorporated into the code-switching, as described above. But the Italian and other foreigner entrepreneurs often have to step outside this narrow pathway in order to carry out their business. Thus, even with this parallel world constructed for them, most foreign entrepreneurs, including the Italians, need their Chinese counterparts to act as their cultural and physical guides in China. This was especially true of the many Italians and other foreign entrepreneurs who come to China periodically but do not live there. Chinese people who work with foreigners, including the Italians, thus feel that they are essential every step of the way.

"Step" is the key term here. Some of the Chinese entrepreneurs' commentary on their Italian counterparts consists of matter-of-fact, casual descriptions of their responsibilities in the context of transnational commodity-chain labor. One time-consuming responsibility is to shepherd Italians and other foreigners around the physical landscape of Shanghai and its environs. JoJo, for example, would plan our meetings around her need to shepherd foreign entrepreneurs for merchandising. She complained not about the foreigners per se, since she took for granted this aspect of her job, but about the unrewarding aspect of this task. Lou Jingxiao similarly frequently commented on her need to take foreigners around for the entirety of their visits. The latter is especially true of those Italian and other owners who do not live in Shanghai but come for infrequent visits. The daughter of a very close friend of Rofel's in Hangzhou eventually gave up her independent business because she never had time to see friends or family, instead describing her life as a whirlwind of shepherding foreign businessmen (and they are mostly men). They shepherd them to visit factories for production and shopping malls to establish retail outlets. They take them on excursions and organize their meals.

But even if the Italian managers lived in Shanghai, the Chinese entrepreneurs and managers felt the need to shepherd them around the city. Though this practice might seem simple at first glance, it lies at the heart of conducting business. All aspects of the Italians' and other foreigners' ability to conduct business in China depends, of course, on their ability to physically maneuver around China. This includes finding raw materials, finding appropriate factories to subcontract with, and setting up stores to market Italian fashion in China. This seemingly simple yet essential part of their labor reinforces Chinese entrepreneurs' views of themselves as having essential cosmopolitan skills without which the Italians could simply not function in China. Indeed, they feel that the Italians would be literally lost in China without them. This view was reinforced for us by the perhaps apocryphal story told to us by an Italian in Shanghai's Italian consulate who helps Italians establish businesses in China. He mentioned a businessman who came from Italy to set up a business. He set up a factory outside Shanghai and then went home. The next year, when he returned to China, he had no idea how to find his own factory.

Chinese entrepreneurs and managers must also navigate the Chinese state for their Italian partners.[26] Opening stores in China, for one, is not purely a commercial or business matter. It always involves local government officials as well. After the central government decentralized a large portion of government functions to local officials, they began a process of privatizing urban land and buildings, which became "real estate."[27] Local officials who oversee the use of most urban real estate expect to profit from the development of shopping malls, among other real estate projects. The matter of placing one's retail outlet thus involves multiple layers of bureaucracy as well as the company that owns or leases the shopping mall (which is often, though not always, a state-owned company). The multitude of social skills involved in this process necessarily calls for someone who is sufficiently cosmopolitan to navigate multiple and quite distinct social relationships. These entrepreneurs tend to have the view that it is not merely their "Chineseness" that enables them to navigate this terrain but their cosmopolitan abilities to mediate between foreigners and the Chinese state. This is true even of state officials involved in the import and export of Italian fashion clothing. In their case, they wish to avoid overemphasizing that they represent the state. Hence, they, too, emphasize their cosmopolitanism, which, they imply, makes them less corrupt than other Chinese officials.

A final commentary on the Italians was about their perfidy. One particularly explosive reaction of a Chinese entrepreneur about his mediating role occurred in an interview with Huang Huaming, the Chinese owner in the joint venture Yufei/Pure Elegance. Rofel had gone through his Italian partner, Rinaudo, to get an interview with him. She found him strangely tense throughout the interview, and when she asked why he decided to set up a joint venture with Rinaudo, the whole tone of the interview changed. At first, he remained calm and polite. He explained that the benefit for him was that it is difficult to become a big business in China.[28] Huang added that Rinaudo could train his company in fashion and management. He explained that the advantage for Rinaudo is that it wanted to bring its labels to the Chinese market and it could do so through Yufei.

Huang then launched into a paean to the joint venture, pointing out its success for both his firm and the Rinaudo firm, with over three hundred stores all over the country. At this point he felt it necessary to comment on a subject that Rofel had not yet asked about: "In terms of the management, it is we Chinese who are the main managers. I make all the decisions." Rofel asked, "And then what is the Italian [manager] doing here?" Huang replied, "He helps. He makes communication easier." Huang must have realized the last comment might sound too dismissive of his Italian partners, so he added: "In the contract, it says that the board of directors will meet several times a year to make the major decisions, like starting a new label or investing in something new. We discuss the overall budget. We meet four times a year. But the other decisions, I make them. Like where to open a store."

He then once again went back to amplifying his decision-making powers: "Also, I might decide to make new investments. With the funds that are in our own company, which is called Hua Ziyi. Our portion of the ownership of Yufei is under this company. I might take those funds and invest in something else, like tourism or a chain store. I haven't decided yet, but it is always better than just leaving the funds sitting in the bank." But then he went back again to emphasizing the solidity of the joint venture: "Our relations are not bad with them. You can see that because the business is expanding. In the last year, our profit was 7 yi [Y 700,000,000, US$101,449,275]." When Rofel asked him about challenges the company faces, he answered indirectly by emphasizing that "the key thing is in one's thinking: to share one goal together. Each side has its strengths [youdian]."

Rofel did not know there were any problems between the Rinaudo managers and Huang until she very matter-of-factly mentioned that she understood the Italians were looking for other joint ventures. This statement produced a dramatic change in him. He was already tense but up to this moment had been trying to present a smooth picture of their working relations. Once Rofel made this statement, it was as if she had put her finger on a sore tooth. He let loose with a torrent of angry commentary.

> I told them this was the wrong thing to do. This will not help our business. In our contract, we negotiated this point and I had to give up on insisting that they not do this, because I wanted their help. But they should not be doing this. This is not good. Last year, they started looking in Hangzhou. I complained, so they stopped. But this year they are starting again. They have not told me directly but of course I know. People come and tell me. Do they really think I won't know who they are talking to? This is not good for Pure Elegance. First, others will start to wonder: Why is Rinaudo looking for other partners? Are they having a problem with us? They will wonder. It will make people think our business is not doing well or we are having difficulties with each other. It is going to influence the reputation of our business. Second, they will most likely not succeed. You see many foreigners open businesses here and they fail. It is very hard for foreigners to be successful in China. They don't know how to do business here. You know, many Chinese don't like to work for foreigners. They don't want to have a foreign boss. These foreigners give orders but they don't know how to get things done here. Third, this is going to influence my own thinking [*wode xinli*—literally, what is in my heart, and here he even pointed to his heart].

> Without me, they would be nothing. They have only been successful because of me. Why do they want to go around finding other partners? No matter how it ends, this is not good for us. You see all these foreigners. You see all these Koreans who open businesses here. They fail. Why? They do not know how to do business here without us. This will not be good for us. If they succeed with the others, then people will think we are not as good anymore. But if they fail, then it will reflect badly on us also. Either way, it is not good for us. Do they think I don't know about this? Of course, I know. I know who they are talking to. They cannot succeed with those people.

The Italians working in the production of Italian fashion in China and their Chinese partners are aware of the criticisms that each has of the other. As evident from what has already been described, they sometimes indirectly respond to those critiques: Italian managers emphasize their worldliness by virtue of living in China even if they usually live alongside other non-Chinese residents; Chinese entrepreneurs emphasize their ability to engage with fashion and design and the regular and intensive work they do with quality control. In their enactments of the respective value of their labor powers, Italians and Chinese further compare themselves not just with one another but with other others.

Comparisons with Other Others

Even as Italian managers and Chinese managers and entrepreneurs compare themselves to one another and develop critiques of one another to make claims about the respective value of their labor powers, they also compare and contrast themselves to relevant others who populate their worlds. The social world of producing made-in-China Italian fashion in which they situate themselves encompasses a range of others who, indirectly, also enhance the value of their own labor powers. For the Italian managers, this includes Italian firm owners, whom they consider to be provincial. For the Chinese managers and entrepreneurs, this includes non-Shanghai Chinese, whom they also consider to be insufficiently cosmopolitan.

The Provincialism of Italian Firm Owners

Although China has become both a favored site of production and the promised land for sales, it is still viewed by most Italians as something of a hinterland. The fact that firm owners do not live in China attests to this. Only one owner of the ten Italian firms in our study regularly resides in China—in this case, at his factory for two months each year. The others limit their visits to their firms' offices, production sites, and shops in China to a week or two at a time. Neither do any children or other members of proprietary families have any plans to move to China to develop the firm there. Consequently, the managers who oversee these firms' activities in China have developed a critique of the "provincialism" of firm owners and their children. As one Italian manager of a firm on the outskirts of Shanghai put it, the children of the Italian bourgeoisie are hardly willing to give up pasta and parmigiano to live in China. An official in Italy's foreign commerce institute expressed a similar sentiment when he said, "The children of the entrepreneurs either have to stay in Italy because there are not enough people to run the company at home, or they are too spoiled to come to China and prefer to spend their time in Monte Carlo or Portofino. They miss prosciutto and mozzarella and don't want to struggle with chopsticks."

Although they are understandably cautious about openly discussing the provincialism of their employers, managers squire around members of the proprietary family during their visits and serve as intermediaries between firm owners and their Chinese partners to enhance their sense of themselves as more worldly actors who are capable of transcending the limitations of Italian family capitalism, much as the new generation of Chinese entrepreneurs view themselves as transcending the limitations of China's socialist past. While their characterization of proprietary families as "provincial" is clearly self-serving, it is not cut entirely out of whole cloth. As shall be seen in chapter 5, all the Italian textile firms and a majority of the clothing firms doing business in China originated in small towns and semirural provinces rather than in major urban areas of northern or central Italy. These sites were, after all, close to the raw materials (silk, wool, linen), water, and labor power they needed to initiate the industrial manufacture of textiles.[29] After World War II, some of the most successful textile firms expanded into clothing manufacturing, thus moving up the commodity value chain. The most successful of these, in turn, transformed themselves into luxury designer brands or national (and now international) retail chains (see Yanagisako's chapters in parts II and III for a history of the emergence of these family firms in the context of Italian industrialization and transnational expansion).

The ascendance of these family firms was achieved over the course of three to four generations, and their provincial roots are still apparent in many of them. In fact, their provincial origins are celebrated alongside claims of their success in globalizing Italian fashion. Even those proprietary families that have offices and homes in major cities such as Milan and Rome maintain homes and reside for at least part of the year in the small cities and towns where the family's business originated and where their place at the top of the social hierarchy is unchallenged. The family's enduring connection to its provincial origins is, moreover, often publicized as a testament to the authenticity of the artisanal origins of the firm and its enduring commitment to high quality. The marketing of these luxury brands, in particular, frequently employs images of rural aristocracy and gentry, including photos of the extended family, their friends and dogs in their elegant homes and gardens (Segre Reinach 2010).

The display of the familial and provincial origins of these firms has become all the more important given the resentment and anger that has emerged in

Italy over the outsourcing of manufacturing to China and other countries. This anger over outsourcing is exacerbated by, and often confounded with, the circulation of "fake" or "counterfeit" products, some of which have fake brand labels and others that falsely claim to be "Made in Italy." Since the 1990s, campaigns against the "unlawful exploitation" of the "Made in Italy" label have been launched by a number of regional governments, labor unions, and business associations in Italy. Drawing on this outrage, in the spring of 2010, Italy passed the Reguzzoni-Versace Law, which limits the "Made in Italy" label to shoes, leather, textiles, and clothing in which two of the four phases of production have taken place in Italy. The firm owners' continuing residence in their provincial homes symbolically grounds their claim to the deep historical roots and, consequently, the authenticity of the brand even while it is being manufactured in China. The employment of nonfamily managers, who lack the symbolic capital to anchor the authenticity of the brand, protects the proprietary family's provincial identity and the potential taint on the national purity of the brand. The occasional visit of firm owners to China, on the other hand, serves to publicize the brand.

Although half the Italian managers in our study come from the same or nearby communities as their employers, they consider themselves professional managers who are better able to confront the challenges of living and working in China. Many of them obtained their jobs through local social networks, but the longer they live abroad the less they feel they have in common with family and friends back home. The work and social life to which they grow accustomed in China is a far cry from their experiences growing up in their small towns of origin. Not only do they become accustomed to the class privileges of the services of drivers, maids, and nannies, but their social life in Shanghai is centered on the European expat community. When they return to Italy on vacation, many discover their old friends to be rather close-minded: in a word, provincial. Marzia Bordogna, for example, reported that her friends had told her she was crazy to go to China. She described them as being so attached to their hometown that they would not even take a job in Milan, where they would have higher pay, more interesting work, and better career prospects. In comparison to her friends, she felt herself to have become more flexible and open-minded as a result of living and working in China. Like many managers, she found herself increasingly impatient with the challenges of daily life in Italy. Her colleague Antonio Peroni exclaimed, "When I go to Italy it suddenly occurs to me that 'THIS is the Third World!' My thoughts are always in Italy because my parents are there. But when I go to

Milan, there isn't any service any more, they lose your luggage at the airport, and they burn your pizza at the autogrill. Italy scares me; it makes me more anxious than China does."

Managers are, in addition, painfully aware of the family sentiments and commitments that shape the strategies and decisions of firm owners, including decisions about promotion and succession. These they view as unfortunate impediments to the transformation of the firm into an efficient business that could compete successfully globally. In less guarded moments, they speak of their desire to restructure the firm along the lines of management models they had learned in business school, in which there was a CEO, a CFO, division heads, and so forth, each with clear job descriptions, domains of responsibility, and relations of reporting and accountability. They complain about the impediments to their attempts to "managerializzare" the firm (to institute a professional managerial structure) and rid it of the "extraneous" family emotions and dramas that they feel get in the way of efficiency and profits.

The argument about the need to further "managerializzare" family firms is not limited to managers but has been in wide circulation in Italy for at least the past thirty years. One can hardly open a business journal or newspaper in Italy without encountering discussions about the merits of reorganizing family firms into more "modern" business organizations. The owners of family firms themselves participate in these discussions. Rather than challenge this vision of entrepreneurial modernity, they speak of the ways in which they have incorporated modern management techniques and structures into their firms to forge a "modern family capitalism." After all, they and their children also have degrees in business and finance, information technology, marketing, and economics.

Shanghai Identification

While Italian managers contrast themselves with the provincialism of Italian firm owners as well as their own family and friends located in Italy, their Chinese counterparts contrast themselves not with state-owned firms—whom they view as hopelessly corrupt—but with others located in regions of China outside Shanghai. In this sense, both the Italians and the Chinese use regional or place identifications to assess their own transcendence of others. For Italians, however, this transcendence of their own backgrounds is achieved by moving outside the nation (in this case, to China), while for their Chinese counterparts, this entails a historical reinvigoration—by way of transnational relations—of what they often treat as an ontological, or essential, identity: that of being a Shanghai person. One could view this ironically as a counter-provincial exceptionalism that connotes its own kind of narrowness (see J. N. Brown 2017).

Being a Shanghai resident or, more accurately, a "Shanghai person" (*Shanghai ren*) is another key marker of the cosmopolitanism that the Chinese entrepreneurs view as part of the essential skills and knowledge they bring to their business ventures with foreigners, including the Italians. Indeed, it is perhaps the central aspect of these entrepreneurs' cosmopolitanism, for Shanghai signifies worldliness. This is true not only today but historically as well. Shanghai, one of the world's largest cities, constitutes a "global city" that scholars have remarked upon as a key node of transnational capitalism. It acts as a central location through which transnational corporations conduct business in Asia. The vast majority of Western foreigners who do business in China today situate themselves in Shanghai.[30]

Among a wide range of those living in Shanghai, both those who identify as "Shanghai people" and those who have become residents of Shanghai in order to work in international business, there appear to be two basic interpretations of Shanghai's history, held simultaneously: they are proud of its cosmopolitan roots, enmeshed as it was with the West from the very beginning, and also critical of certain colonial aspects of that history. Everyone knows the story of the famous signs along the Shanghai riverfront, known as the Bund, that used to say "No Chinese Allowed." But they also know that Shanghai embodied—and has recaptured—a dynamic world of cosmopolitan knowledge and identity. (For more on nostalgia for Shanghai's past, see Rofel's chapter in part II.)

In the view of these Chinese entrepreneurs, a Shanghai identity means the difference between being a savvy partner for foreigners, someone who can help foreigners maneuver among the potential shoals of doing business in China, or being someone who might get taken advantage of by both other Chinese people and foreigners. Embodying a Shanghai identity means a worldliness that enables these Chinese entrepreneurs to maneuver not only within the complexities of doing business in China but also among the numerous foreigners who congregate in the "Pearl of the East."

Shanghainese are famous in China for their entrepreneurial skills. To be a "Shanghai person" is thus automatically to be seen as someone who is astute in international commerce. Shanghai dialect is still de rigueur among Chinese living in Shanghai, for using it marks one as an insider and not an outsider. The distinction can often mean a difference in the price one pays for goods as well as a more favorable contract. Those who move to Shanghai to engage in business are often judged on how well they have learned to speak Shanghai dialect.[31] For those who were not born in Shanghai, their ability to attend school in Shanghai and subsequently find work in Shanghai is, for them, a sign of their cosmopolitan success. Wang Shiyao/George, for example, grew up in a rural area near Ningbo (in southern Zhejiang province). But he went to Shanghai's business school, Donghua University, and then landed a job in a state-run Shanghai import-export company. He considers himself to have become nearly a Shanghai person over the years—though not quite—garnering praise for his ability to speak some Shanghai dialect.

In addition to comparing themselves to others who move to Shanghai but who cannot quite seem to fully embody a Shanghai identity, Shanghai-based entrepreneurs and managers contrast themselves with other regions of China.[32] Those from Shanghai are proud to characterize themselves as astute entrepreneurs. They view those from other places, such as Beijing, or other regions, such as inland provinces, as by turns simple, slow, or too honest. The entrepreneurialism of Shanghai people is seen as distinctive by other Chinese people as well, who emphasize the negative side of the characterization, that is, that Shanghai people are opportunistic, manipulative, and devious.

This is not merely a contrast with small towns and rural areas. Rofel often heard these stereotypes voiced by friends and strangers, in everyday conversation in places like Beijing. For example, Rofel once had a conversation with a friend who teaches at the premier Beijing University, about a Chinese scholar teaching in the United States. They were discussing the varied and controversial assessments of his character. This friend concluded the discussion as follows: "Well, you know he is from Shanghai. That explains everything about his character." Tang Shan, who works at the Zhenfu silk factory in Hangzhou that Rofel wrote about previously (1999), once remarked quite casually that "we" people from the south (*nanfang ren*) are much sharper than people from the north (*beifang ren*). And of course, all the urban residents along the eastern coast distinguished themselves from rural residents and migrants living inland. These two groups similarly viewed one another as virtually coming from another country.

Yet Shanghai-based entrepreneurs nonetheless singled out Shanghai as an exceptional place-based identity differing even from their close neighbors in Hangzhou. While they viewed the other aspects of their cosmopolitanism as necessarily relationally produced and verifiable only through those relationships, a Shanghai identity was treated as something inherent. One either has it or one does not. Just learning Shanghai dialect is insufficient, for one embodies a Shanghai identity in all aspects of daily life. So strong is this identity that one entrepreneur insisted that when she went to Japan, she did not identify with other Chinese people there. She stated unequivocally that she only feels an identity with Shanghai, not with all of China.

A Shanghai identity is both embodied and abstracted. That is, a Shanghai identity is not fully naturalized, as most Shanghai residents recognize that their parents and grandparents migrated to Shanghai from other regions of China. A Shanghai identity needs to be imprinted through regional dialect and intimate experiences of living in Shanghai through one's lifetime. Yet, analogous to national identities and to the Italians' approach to Italianità, Shanghai-based entrepreneurs tend to treat their Shanghai identity as an abstract form of their labor power that other Chinese have difficulty embodying.

The Enactment of Respective Labor Powers

The Value of *Italianità*

Italian managers' evaluation of the technical competence of workers, the shortcomings of Chinese managers and entrepreneurs, the provincialism of Italian firm owners, and their own role in the production of Italianità must be situated in the history of the "Made in Italy" marketing campaign that has been key to the success of Italian fashion since the 1980s (see Segre Reinach's chapter in this volume for further discussion of the history of Italian fashion). Since its inception in the 1980s, the "Made in Italy" campaign of the Italian Trade Commission has achieved great success in the marketing of a national brand. The Italian fashion industry, which was the major beneficiary of this campaign, saw its textile and garment exports triple in that decade. This was not, of course, the first time that the Italian national brand in fashion had been promoted. During the fascist era, Mussolini had issued dressmaker quotas through his National Fashion Authority and its trademark, Ideazione e Produzione Nazionale (Conceived and Made in Italy). His attempt to create *la linea Italiana* from homegrown styles, materials, and methods of manufacture conformed to his policy of autarky, which aimed at national self-sufficiency (Ross 2004; White 2000).

The "Made in Italy" promotional campaign launched in the 1980s has continued through the first two decades of the twenty-first century. In 2008, for example, the Italian Trade Commission announced that it had recruited the iconic "Italian-born actress, model and business entrepreneur Isabella Rossellini as a spokesperson for the new 'Made in Italy' advertising campaign to be presented in the U.S." In their press announcement, the trade commission stated: "In this new campaign, Isabella Rossellini challenges Americans to 'Let yourself be charmed by an Italian,' highlighting the perfect style and passion for hand-crafted detail that makes Italian products so special and unmistakable" (Italian Trade Commission 2008). Rossellini went on to say: "Italian style signifies quality. Quality gained from centuries of work by artists and artisans and combined with Italian charm, humor and warmth. It is an irresistible combination."

The press release describes "Italian-made products" as having been "coveted by discerning American consumers for their fine tradition of hand craftsmanship, attention to detail, pioneering design and use of the highest-quality materials." Along these lines, when Salvatore Ferragamo celebrated its eightieth anniversary by inaugurating an exhibition in Shanghai in April 2008, prominently displayed along with the vintage shoes manufactured by the company was the tableau of a workshop in which two Italian artisans dressed in white lab coats were crafting shoes by hand. In September 2009, the luxury menswear brand Ermenegildo Zegna conveyed a similar message by constructing a tailor's workshop in their flagship store for Milan's Fashion Night Out (Segre Reinach 2010).

The evocation of Italian artisanal and craft traditions that can be traced back to the Renaissance endows "Made in Italy" commodities with a rich cultural heritage, which in turn legitimates their high price. As Segre Reinach (see her chapter in this book) has noted, however, the artisanal labor celebrated by the "Made in Italy" campaign is a historical fiction.[33]

The '80s model, in fact, on which "Made in Italy" made its name, was the first model of creative industrial fashion. After Florentine luxury prêt-à-porter, with aristocratic couturiers with names such as Marchese Emilio Pucci, Donna Simonetta Colonna di Cesarò [made] the first attack on French hegemony, Italian fashion left the aristocratic Florence, city of art, and moved the fashion shows to Milan, the city of commerce. The result was the ready-to-wear hallmarked by the so-called "industrial aesthetics," with its Fab Four: Armani, Ferré, Missoni and Krizia . . . the creators of "Made in Italy." (Segre Reinach 2010, 210)

The industrial aesthetic that became a model for modern fashion combined clothing designed for mass production with a system of sizes that could be accurately reproduced.

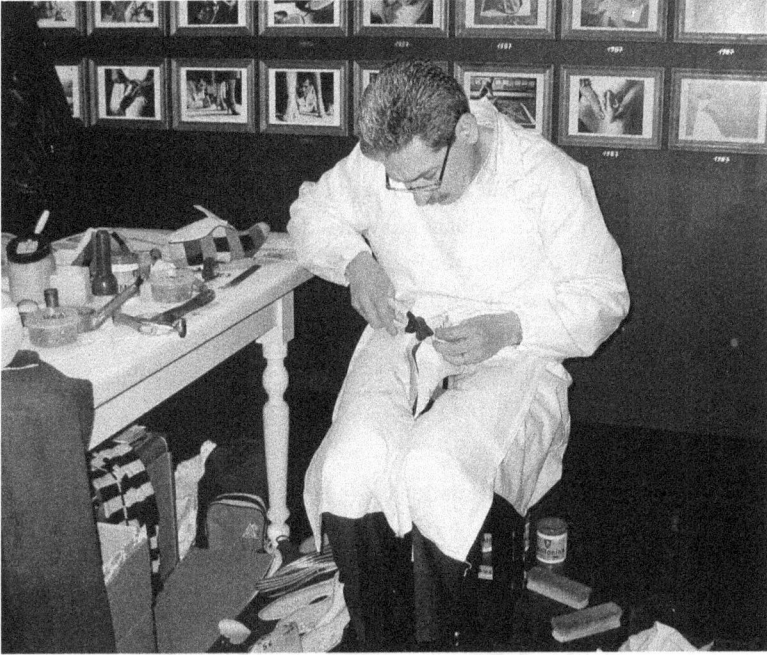

1.1 Italian artisan demonstrating shoemaking at the Salvatore Ferragamo eightieth anniversary exhibit, Shanghai, 2008.

"Made in Italy" also trumpets the "Italianness" captured in commodities that have been produced within an imagined culturally saturated "Italian" space. In a charming illustration of commodity fetishism, the cultural characteristics of the producers and their location are embedded in the commodity itself. In claiming to have captured the labor of Italian workers in the commodity, "Made in Italy" appears to epitomize the fetishism of commodities. At the same time, however, the culturally specific character of Italian workers purportedly captured in the commodity would seem to impede the kind of abstraction of labor that Marx identified as central to capitalist relations of production. In Marx's formulation, the "socially necessary labor" transformed into abstract labor by industrial capitalism is construed as universal, not culturally specific. In this case, the abstraction of labor takes a particular nationalist form and what is constituted is an abstract Italian labor.[34]

Before Italian textile and garment manufacturers began outsourcing production overseas, "Made in Italy" fabric and clothing relied largely on the labor of women—some of whom worked in factories and others who worked at home in a cottage, putting-out system. In this earlier phase of domestic outsourcing, the abstraction of labor entailed a disguising of the gender of workers, for behind every imagined Italian craftsman stood a female factory worker. Once production was outsourced to China, the abstraction of labor added a transracial twist. The labor of Chinese men and women became disguised as the labor of Italian men through a process that we might call "industrial drag."[35] This transnational industrial drag echoes Chinese managers' critique that their Italian counterparts create the value of their labor within a world of their own—that is, Italianità—even as we can see the abstraction process entailed. However, Chinese managers also occlude Chinese workers in this critique: it is their own labor as managers and entrepreneurs that they refer to, thus also disguising the labor of Chinese workers.

The Appropriation and Instantiation of *Italianità*

Given that the exchange values of the commodities produced through Italian-Chinese collaborations in China are inextricably linked to their Italianità, it is hardly surprising that Italians claim that their labor—whether in design, manufacturing, branding, or retailing—is more valuable than the labor of the Chinese. Less expected is the discovery that in the overseas manufacture of "Made in Italy," Italian managers have become the surrogates of Italian workers. Although the "Made in Italy" marketing campaign highlights the artisanal craft and skill of Italian workers, in the transnational production and distribution process, Italian managers have become indispensable to infusing commodities with Italian charm.

By affirming and elaborating the claims of Italianità touted by "Made in Italy," moreover, managers appropriate the fetishized powers of the commodity to constitute their own labor power. In appropriating the value of Italianità, managers produce an interesting twist on Marx's model of commodity fetishism. Whereas in Marx's model of commodity fetishism the social powers of workers are captured in the commodity, in this case the social powers attributed to commodities are recaptured in the labor power of Italian managers. In constituting themselves as the guardians of a legacy of artisanal production and claiming its productive powers for themselves, Italian managers obscure the industrial labor of Chinese workers.

Italian managers' emphasis on the cultural knowledge, information, communication skills, and creativity they bring to the production process, interestingly, parallels Michael Hardt and Antonio Negri's (2004) argument that information and communication have become key to the global economy in the "postindustrial age." Like the discourse of Italian managers, these claims of an epochal shift to a "knowledge economy" in which "immaterial labor" is hegemonic conceal the industrial labor of workers in countries to which manufacturing has been outsourced. While the "Made in Italy" campaign locates the production process in a preindustrial epoch of craft production, Hardt and Negri's and other scholars' claims about the rise of "immaterial labor" locate it in a postindustrial age, thus skipping over the current industrial age in which it is, in fact, located. Yanagisako (2012) has argued elsewhere that Hardt and Negri mistakenly treat the distinction between material and immaterial labor as an objective one, rather than as we have shown here, an ideological distinction that is actively made in encounters along with hierarchies of value and forms of inequality. Missing in their discussion of "affective labor," which they highlight as a form of "immaterial labor," is a critical recognition that the distinction between the "instrumental action of economic production" and the "communicative action of human relation" is itself an ideological construct that obscures the communicative dimension of all human activity, whether it is labeled "economic activity" or otherwise.[36]

The appropriation of Italianità by managers is, in part, an intended consequence of the collaborative project of firm owners and managers to imbue commodities manufactured in China with Italian character. Although the goals of firm owners and managers differ, they are complementary. By claiming that these commodities meet Italian standards of quality and design, firm owners cast managers as guardians of Italianità. Managers, for their part, find the value of their labor enhanced by claims that their managerial skills guarantee "Italian quality" even when commodities are produced in China.

Managers' discourse of Italianità draws on both the long history of Italian achievements in art, craftsmanship, and design and the more recent promotional campaign of "Made in Italy," as well as on their own experiences in China. They arrive in China well steeped in this broader history as well as with specific knowledge and skills they acquired through their upbringing, education, and work in Italy. As we have seen, however, these vary widely given their diverse educational backgrounds and job experiences. Some clearly knew a great deal more than others about textiles, fashion, clothing, distribution, and marketing when they began their jobs in China. Through their managerial practices and experiences—situated in the asymmetrical field of power of their relations of production with the Chinese—Italian managers acquire the cultural powers of Italianità.[37] Put another way, Italianità is not what managers bring to their work in China but what they constitute through their work in China. Rather than a "skill set" that managers arrive with or that they acquire on the job, Italianità is instantiated through the managerial work process and experienced by managers as an integral part of their cultural being and cultural life.

Given the ways in which the Italian managers speak of their key role in planning, information, fashion knowledge, creativity, and communication, one might be tempted to view this as a claim to managerial skills that can be utilized across a range of corporate settings in the global economy. These are, we suggest, not usefully viewed as either a "skill set" or a Foucauldian technology of the self but rather as the reification of hierarchical work relations, which transforms relationality into cultural subjectivity. As a cultural-nationalist discourse of the "managerial self," moreover, Italianità does not fit easily into models that predict the formation of a global, transnational managerial class (Sklair 2001).

Italian managers, not surprisingly, are hardly interested in reducing their labor to a skill set that can be taught to others, such as Chinese managers. Yet it is not mere self-interest that keeps them from construing their labor in these terms. Rather, they are keenly aware that it is through their situated work relations with Chinese managers and workers that their knowledge, creativity, and organizational skills are constituted. In other words, they come to know themselves and the character and value of their labor through their hierarchically structured relations of production. At the same time, the notion that they embody Italianità does not preclude managers' recognition of its effectiveness as a marketing strategy. As one manager, whose assignment was to raise the market position of a brand in China, candidly put it, "Italianità is the card to play." It is what enables both Italians and Italian commodities to "charm" us.

Chinese Cosmopolitanism and the Commodity Chain

The Chinese entrepreneurs and managers' emphasis on cosmopolitanism must be placed in a wider context of China's reworlding of itself (Zhan 2009) in the post-Mao era. One way to reject the socialist past is to paint China as a closed nation that only recently "opened up" to the world. This portrait erases a rather large socialist international world of which China was once a part. It creates an affective reorientation of China toward the West. It portends an overcoming of the antagonisms of the Cold War. Perhaps not surprisingly, then, this language was shared by both Western commentators and public discourse in China (though the former sometimes add some Orientalist twists). It was especially prevalent at the time we did our research. Now it seems to have been overtaken by a worldwide commentary on China's increasing presence in other countries around the world.

Those entrepreneurs and managers who work with Italians and other foreigners emphasize their cosmopolitanism because they believe these qualities define them as savvy, capable entrepreneurs who are not "merely" Chinese. These cosmopolitan qualities of entrepreneurship are developed, reworked, and reformulated in their interactions with Italians and other foreigners. That is, working with the Italians and other foreigners seems merely to confirm a prior cosmopolitanism that they bring into the relationship. In fact, while they bring some of this into the relationship, their ability to work with the Italians actually confirms—that is, produces—them as the cosmopolitan people they thought they already were when they entered the relationship. The qualities of cosmopolitanism that Chinese entrepreneurs emphasize—their ability to code-switch and to shepherd foreigner entrepreneurs through the process of setting up business in China, including everything from eating, to finding appropriate factories, to quality control, to offering knowledge on Chinese taste for the Chinese market, to translation in the broadest sense—all of these cosmopolitan abilities, in the view of these Chinese entrepreneurs, define the value of their labor power.

Labor power, we should recall, is not the actual labor performed. As we argue in the introduction to part I, in Marxist theory, labor power refers to capacities. Marx construed these capacities as preexisting the social relations of labor, whereas we assert the opposite: that these capacities develop through the production relationship. This development entails an interpretation that is instantiated through practice. Thus, it would be a mistake to view Chinese entrepreneurs' insistence on the value of their labor power as mere conceptualization that stands apart from the actual capacities they demonstrate. These are not just abstract conceptions of labor power but the actual labor power that, in their view, creates essential value in the production of Italian-labeled fashion. In other words, their descriptions of their cosmopolitan abilities are at the same time descriptions of the labor power they contribute in the transnational production processes with foreigners.

To go a step further, these are descriptions of the production process as well. In other words, Chinese entrepreneurs describe simultaneously their capacities for creating successful transnational businesses and the actual practices they are engaged in. Maneuvering through Chinese bureaucracies, for example, is not just a capacity but an essential component of the production of, in this case, Italian-labeled fashion. Shepherding foreigners around Shanghai and its environs is an instantiation of their labor power. Translation is the sine qua non of production processes not only in China but in global supply chains more generally. Indeed, given their embrace of capitalist ideologies, these Chinese entrepreneurs believe that these activities lie at the heart of the production process. Hence, while they acknowledge the labor that factory workers perform, these Chinese entrepreneurs view themselves as the central node in the production of Italian-labeled fashion, thus partially effacing factory workers. Yet their insistence on the key value of these steps in the production and distribution of made-in-China Italian fashion reveals the hierarchies of value that emphasize only a few steps of the transnational commodity chain: design and branding. These are, as earlier noted, those aspects closest to "immaterial labor."

At the same time, these Chinese entrepreneurs' close involvement in the production process leads them to view their relationship with the Italians as ideally not one of hierarchy but of an equivalent division of labor. Each side, they say, has its responsibilities in order to make the transnational encounter work properly. Problems occur when the divisions of these responsibilities are not clear or when one side feels it has been taken advantage of by the other. Their sense of their own cosmopolitanism thus involves understanding how to properly carry out their side of this division of labor and avoid reifying the hierarchy of labor value entrenched in commodity chains. The frustration they feel about the lack of sufficient recognition from their foreign partners about the value of their labor power is fueled by the recognition that their class mobility within China is dependent on the success of these transnational business ventures. This entangled hierarchical relationship brings some entrepreneurs to comment periodically on the condescension Italians and others feel toward Chinese people, which reminds them of China's colonial history.

As these Chinese entrepreneurs negotiate their periodic frustrations with the asymmetry in their relationships with the Italians and other foreigners, as they struggle with being seen as "merely Chinese" rather than cosmopolitan, as they press the fact, in their view, that the value of their labor power is insufficiently recognized, they simultaneously use their experiences in the fashion industry to position themselves as entrepreneurs of their own, apart from the business they do with Italians. Virtually all of those who own factories that produce fashion clothing for Italian firms, for example, have also begun to develop their own clothing brand for the domestic Chinese market, even as they continue to produce for Italian firms. They are moving themselves up the ladder of profitable activity, as they see that subcontracting for foreign firms is becoming more expensive in China and more competitive globally. The Chinese side of the joint venture firms have always had their own lines of clothing and have continued to develop those lines. Lou Jingxiao/Maggi has begun a unique web company targeting professional Chinese women to help them buy fashion clothing. She operates both this company and her mediator firm simultaneously. She is trying to convince Wang Shiyao/George to leave the municipal import-export business and take over her mediator company. Li Yue has developed his own brand, which he is marketing domestically. Even the cultural mediators and translators engage in entrepreneurial activities on their own: Jiang Li/Nico has a tie business, subcontracting for the joint venture he works for as a cultural mediator. Another translator for another joint venture has opened small shops selling fashion clothing in the outlying towns outside of Shanghai.

These multiple entrepreneurial activities contribute to the sense of ongoing flux in the encounters between the Chinese and Italians. They thus intersect with the structural constraints delineated at the beginning of this chapter, feeding the ambivalence Chinese entrepreneurs tend to feel when working with Italians and other foreigners and the anxiety Italians feel that the Chinese will eventually pass them by. The attempts by their Chinese collaborators to move themselves up the supply chain are hardly foreign to the Italian partners. As Yanagisako shows in her chapters in parts II and III, those Italian family firms in textiles and clothing that have been successful enough to expand beyond their regional and national origins to produce in China are themselves the product of such strategies.

Conclusion: Constituting Managerial Labor Power

In the introduction to part I, we suggested that Moishe Postone's approach to Marx's concept of labor power offers a productive lens through which we might view the historic constitution of the social powers and knowledge of managers and entrepreneurs. In construing labor in capitalism as a "historically unique form of social mediation," Postone emphasizes the meaningful, social process through which labor is constituted rather than as something that existed previously as the property of workers (1993, 5). Asking how the specific forms of social interdependence entailed in the transnational production of "Italian" commodities in China shape Italian managers' and Chinese entrepreneurs' practices, worldviews, subjectivities, and dispositions has led to our analysis of Italian managers' appropriation and instantiation of Italianità, on the one hand, and Chinese entrepreneurs' emphasis on and instantiation of cosmopolitanism, on the other. As we suggest in the introduction, the cultural processes through which labor power develops both outside the workplace and within the relations of production proper entail instantiation as well as conceptualization and interpretation. Italian managers' and Chinese entrepreneurs' labor power is instantiated through their daily work practices of overseeing production and distribution of Italian brands in China.

This approach to labor power might lead one to expect that the abstraction of sentiments, sensibilities, and aesthetics entailed in the Italian managers' appropriation of Italianità and Chinese entrepreneurs' emphasis on cosmopolitanism would result in their estrangement from their authentic cultural being. As we noted in the introduction to part I, however, here our analysis diverges from Postone's conceptual framework. In contrast to Postone, we do not approach this question inductively by theorizing it as a process of objectification through which social powers and skills become quasi-independent of workers, leading to their estrangement from these very social powers and knowledge. Instead, we ask how these social powers and knowledge are constituted, and how, in the process, people's actions, worldviews, and dispositions are transformed. In this chapter, we have seen how the instantiation of Italianità through managers' labor in the production process impedes a process of estrangement of the sort that turns the labor power of workers into something alien to them. In other words, the dual processes of abstraction and instantiation of Italianità among managers constitutes it as an inextricable and inalienable quality of their labor, rendering it impervious to estrangement.[38] The instantiation in the production process of the culturally specific powers and knowledge they construe as embodied by a self that was forged through their intimate and public life in an Italian cultural habitus enables managers to both objectify these social powers and knowledge and naturalize them in ways that resist estrangement.

Chinese entrepreneurs have not abstracted their cosmopolitanism as directly from the product of their labors. They viewed their cosmopolitanism as necessarily constituted through the transnational work relation rather than brought to it already fully formed. Thus, they tried to challenge the hierarchical work relation, not by transforming relationality into cultural subjectivity but by emphasizing the two as co-constituted. Their claim that cosmopolitanism lies at the heart of their labors also leads it to be an inextricable part of their labor, thus also resisting estrangement. In this sense, the way they constitute their labor power shares both the historical specificity as well as the abstraction that Postone (1993) emphasized, although the abstraction is not estranged from them but rather part of their self-constitution.

Through these cultural processes of production, a diverse array of sentiments, sensibilities, orientations, and knowledge congeal into a managerial labor power that is indistinguishable from their cultural being. For Chinese entrepreneurs, the intertwined processes of social constitution through relationality and instantiation have produced a congealed Chinese entrepreneurial labor. For Italian managers, the intertwined processes of abstraction and instantiation, objectification and naturalization have produced an abstract Italian managerial labor that Italian managers experience as an inherent aspect of their cultural lives, which were, after all, made in Italy.

II Historical Legacies and Revisionist Histories

The outburst of Huang Huaming of Pure Elegance about the perfidy of his Italian partner Rinaudo, which was described in chapter 1, elicited a surprisingly sympathetic response from the Italian manager, Andrea Politi, who had been assigned to replace the earlier Italian manager in the joint venture. Politi conceded that Huang's anger was understandable. Drawing on the marriage metaphor that Italian managers frequently used when speaking of these joint ventures, Politi opined that Huang must feel like a newlywed who has discovered that his spouse is already searching for a lover. He felt that Rinaudo could have moved forward to search for other joint ventures in a manner that did not infuriate Huang. Although he hoped Huang would "get used to it," Politi acknowledged that Huang's resentment was exacerbated by the inequity spelled out in the fifty-year contract of the joint venture, which prohibited Huang from forming any other joint ventures for five years while placing no such constraint on Rinaudo. At the same time, Politi agreed with Rinaudo's top management that they could hardly be satisfied with just one joint venture in China. Rinaudo, after all, was one of the largest Italian fashion firms—with $1.3 billion in annual sales worldwide. As phenomenal as the growth in Pure Elegance had been, its annual sales were less than 4 percent of Rinaudo's.

The feelings of betrayal that Huang vented about Rinaudo's search for another joint venture were part of a pervasive lack of trust between the partners in this joint venture. While the complex relations of collaboration and competition between the Italian and Chinese partners in Pure Elegance might appear to be an anomalous recipe for distrust and conflict peculiar to transnational joint ventures, knowledge of both Rinaudo's and Pure Elegance's histories reveals quite the contrary. In this part of the book, we argue that historical legacies of capital, labor, property, kinship, and the state are ongoing forces in transnational capitalism. We trace the ways in which historically sedimented practices combined with interpretive narratives about the past have generated and continue to shape the capitalist interdependencies of Chinese-Italian collaborations.

Conventional social science analyses tend to emphasize a "rupture" between the current era of transnational capitalism, variously called global capitalism or neoliberalism, and the preceding period of capitalism, granting the latter status as a precipitating force, but one that is resolved with the emergence of novel capitalist arrangements. These analyses herald proclamations of the new. While we acknowledge the importance of identifying what is distinctive about any historical moment—and the Italian-Chinese collaborations we have studied are novel for all involved—the tendency to emphasize rupture underestimates the ways in which historical legacies continue to shape practices, memories, and narratives. Our argument here is that, contrary to much that is now being taken for granted in our understandings of neoliberal capitalism, history matters not just to the present but in the present. Thus, one cannot understand the actions of the parties to these transnational—and translational—relations without knowing the respective histories of labor, capital, state, and kinship that led to and continue to inform these collaborations. To reduce these actions to utilitarian strategies or to the clash of different "cultures of capitalism" is misleading. These historical legacies and revisionist histories are both structural and contingent, both sedimented in institutions and laws and constantly in flux in relation to other cultural practices that together produce transnational capitalism.

Our approach to neoliberal capitalism is shaped by the historical legacies and revisionist histories of the Chinese and Italians in these transnational business collaborations. "Globalization" and transnational capitalist collaborations clearly arose in response to the economic crises of the 1960s through the 1980s, including in the West the collapse of the Bretton Woods[1] international monetary system, financial deregulation, and subsequent international currency turbulence; labor conflicts; neoliberal state policies; and in China the Cultural Revolution, the subsequent transition to a market economy, and an engagement with the Western-dominated global economy. Yet neoliberal capitalism did not wholly overcome the past.[2] In the chapters to follow in part II, we show how these Chinese and Italian legacies are not simply resolved in the collaborations between Chinese and Italians but continue to motivate them. Given their significance in shaping how Chinese and Italians comprehend and frame their understandings of production relations, the role of the state, the family, the relations between firm owners, managers, and workers, and the power of capital investment and how particular markets operate, it would be a distortion to incorporate them into a shared transnational capitalist or managerial perspective. This section of our book argues that, contrary to the idea that capitalism operates in cleanly divided eras and overcomes past conflicts, histories continue to play a vital role in shaping the kinds of capitalist practices that are encouraged, endorsed, sought out, legalized, or even accepted in a "gray" zone of illicit activity. These histories shape how people come to embrace certain forms of capitalist practices rather than others, what they view as "corrupt" versus "ethical" entrepreneurial activity, and how they evaluate inequality.

Italian owners, managers, converters, and technicians bring a number of legacies of capitalism, state, and kinship to their collaborations with their Chinese counterparts. First and foremost among these are the structure and dynamics of Italian industrial districts in which specialized, small- to medium-sized family firms were embedded in production networks rooted in kinship, friendship, and local community relations that engendered both cooperation and competition, trust and betrayal (Yanagisako 2002). Each industrial district specialized in a particular cluster of commodities with the firms in them linked in decentralized production chains that were sometimes orchestrated by a converter firm. As such, they constituted a localized supply chain. These networks existed alongside larger, vertically integrated firms; indeed, the two were dependent on one another. Some of these districts had existed since the beginning of industrialization in Italy in the late nineteenth century. Their decentralized structure had been reinvigorated in the 1970s in response to the struggles between labor and capital and the rising cost of oil. Other districts emerged in the 1970s as part of the industrialization in what is called the "Third Italy" (i.e., neither the large-scale mass production in the industrial north nor the agricultural production of the agrarian south). In all industrial districts, the decentralized structure of production shaped strategies of firm survival and expansion. Key among these strategies was the expansion of small firms into adjacent sectors of production.

This meant that subcontracting firms that provided manufacturing services for other firms commonly became the competitors of their former clients.

Thus, key to capital-labor relations in Italian industrial districts was a process of class mobility by which labor could be converted into capital. The labor of family members and relatives enabled the accumulation of profits that could be used as capital and reinvested in productive resources (land, buildings, manufacturing equipment, hiring wage labor) in order to expand the firm. Those firms that were more successful in this expansion process could, in turn, buy the manufacturing services of smaller, less-capitalized family firms that aspired to follow the same path to upward mobility. The conversion of family labor into capital was central to the dynamic structure of Italian industrial manufacturing districts. Together with the first chapter of this book and chapter 5, chapter 3 by Yanagisako demonstrates that the boundary between labor and capital cannot be assumed as fixed and stable but rather is continually remade through particular, situated historical processes.

Yanagisako's chapter shows that when Italian firms like Rinaudo arrived in China, they engaged not only in the manufacture of garments but also in various allied sectors and phases of the clothing production and distribution chain, including the sourcing of fabric, the production of multiple brands, licensing of their original brands, buying local brands, and acting as a trading company for other Italian firms. In other words, they continued to pursue the strategies that had been integral to their success in Italy—operating in, and attempting to gain control of, multiple phases of the manufacturing and distribution process without developing a vertically integrated firm. Italians' avoidance of vertically integrated firms derived not only from their lack of large amounts of capital but from an aversion to them stemming from experiences during the labor conflicts in Italy in the 1970s, when such firms were especially vulnerable to strikes and work stoppages. Instead of developing vertically integrated firms, Italian family firms forged multiple partnerships, some of which we will see were in competition with each other. Consequently, they brought to their transnational partnerships the complex relations of collaboration and competition that pervaded their home industrial districts. In China, however, these tense relations were not with family members or with neighbors and community members but with Chinese partners. In other words, the distrust and feelings of betrayal between Huang and Rinaudo were hardly novel to their transnational partnership or the result of intercultural misunderstandings and misperceptions but rather the continuation of a historical legacy of tension and conflict that had pervaded Italian industrial districts.

The historical legacy of capital-labor conflicts in Italy from the 1970s onward not only set the stage for the outsourcing of manufacturing to China by Italian textile and clothing firms and influenced their mode of investment in China; it also shaped their attitude toward Chinese workers. Whether they had experienced the labor-capital conflict in Italy first-hand—as had the entrepreneur Luciano Ferrari, whose career history is recounted in Yanagisako's chapter— or learned about it second-hand, Italian firm owners and managers expressed strong resentment of the power that Italian labor unions had wielded from the late 1960s forward. They attributed what they perceived as the declining work ethic in Italy first and foremost to the Italian labor movement and contrasted it to the willingness of the Chinese to work diligently.

China, for its part, is haunted by the socialist past. This past manifests itself in widespread public debate about the transition from a socialist command economy to a capitalist market economy. One of the most debated aspects of this transition is its attendant social inequality. There exists a range of interpretations of the socialist past among Chinese citizens today. Private entrepreneurs tend to thoroughly reject the socialist past. Analogous to the rise of the bourgeoisie in Europe, who exaggerated the aristocracy's failings in order to displace their political and ideological power, entrepreneurs in China portray the socialist period in exaggerated terms as having nothing of value worth maintaining or revitalizing. They blame the problems of inequality on the government as signifier of that past, thus displacing the question of capitalism's production of inequalities and enabling people to fantasize an ideal market economy that would be fair and equal. Government officials who engage in profit-seeking activities, on the other hand, while they portray themselves as having moved beyond the socialist past, do not condemn that past, for they hold onto its anticolonial nationalist aspirations as well as its institutional legacies. Yet official histories also offer revisionist interpretations of the past, evacuating it of class antagonisms. Migrant workers from the countryside in the textile and garment factories, in contrast to both of these other groups, do not draw a clear boundary between the socialist past and the present, making connections instead with different kinds of suffering their families have endured up through and including the present. Their dreams for the future, however, are constrained by the only thing available on the horizon: becoming an entrepreneur. These various revisionist histories together provide a means by which Chinese citizens are led to embrace capitalism.

Grappling with the socialist past looms over the interactions with the Italians. A thorough rejection of the socialist past is a force that motivates entrepreneurs to engage with the Italians and other foreigners, especially in Shanghai, a cosmopolitan city redolent of nostalgia for the presocialist era. Government officials also embrace collaboration with Italians as a means to demonstrate their ability to seek profit. For workers, however, whose labor in factories is variously situated within the commodity chain of Italian fashion production, entanglement with that production provides new means to evaluate how inequality is differentially formed within capitalism.

While engagement with Italians is one means to try to move beyond the socialist past, widespread corruption in China means that people have continuous conversations about the past, thus giving it an ongoing, palpable presence. Corruption is laid at the door of government officials who have used their political power to accumulate wealth for themselves and their families. Entrepreneurs attempt to draw a clear distinction between officials' pursuit of wealth and the profit-seeking activities of everyone else. Yet government officials, of course, have also tried to distance themselves from China's socialist past. Thus, the definition of "corruption" in relation to profit-seeking activities can be ambiguous, resulting in ambivalent evaluations of capitalist economic action. Moreover, these revisionist histories intermingle with historical legacies as well as novel practices. The former includes the role of the state at all levels, and the social and familial networks necessary to conduct business. The latter includes the institution of a property regime and the enormous rise of migrant labor from the countryside to the urban-based factories. Most striking is the emergence of profit-seeking entities that blur the division between "public" and "private."

Our knowledge of the historical legacies that the Italians and Chinese bring with them to their collaborations leads us to challenge other conceptualizations of transnational capitalism. Implicit in contemporary discourse about globalization is the notion that national economies predominated until the last decades of the twentieth century and have only recently evolved into a "globalized" economy. Both chapters in part II concur with Wallerstein's (1974) theory of a world-system of capitalism by demonstrating that Italians and Chinese developed their industrial production capacities through their transnational engagements with markets and resources long before forging Italian-Chinese business collaborations in the 1980s. Wallerstein paid close attention to the ways in which the interactions between European polities shaped the emergence of the Western core and how the hubs of European capital shifted over time, demonstrating the fluidity and interdependency of European capital (1974, 50–51, 197; 1980, 291). When he moved outward from Europe to recount how other regions become subsumed into the core/semi-periphery/periphery structures, however, the historical contingencies of the interactions between places were less specified. Our chapters place greater emphasis on the specificity of these national/transnational histories and the ways in which they shape these collaborations, including the problems they entail.

Our chapters also challenge the widespread notion that the cross-cultural character of transnational collaborations is in itself the source of the conflict they frequently entail. The historical legacies that impel these transnational relations produce both trust and mistrust, mutually beneficial dependencies and equally strong efforts to disentangle these dependencies. Yet, as our chapters show, the competition and distrust that sometimes emerge in Italian-Chinese collaborations are, on the one hand, a variation of the complex relations of collaboration and competition that were already present in Italian industrial districts and, on the other, a continuation of the ever-present Chinese memories of colonial encounters with Westerners and the Japanese. We conclude that it is not the cross-cultural character per se of the Italian-Chinese relations that produce conflict and distrust but the specific historical legacies they bring to them. In short, what are too readily interpreted by both scholars and subjects as Chineseness and Italianness are not enduring ahistorical, cultural characters but historical and institutional legacies.

Finally, as discussed in the introduction to the book, our essays challenge the idea that "privatization" or hybrid private/public entities mark a new era of neoliberal capitalism. We depart from this view in two respects. First, there is a history of state-private enterprises that long predates neoliberalism. As a corollary, we disagree that a critical difference between capitalism in China and Italy is that the state plays a central role in "Chinese capitalism." While the role of state bureaucracies in profit-seeking activities is at the core of debates about the nature of the market economy in China, historically, the Italian state has also been heavily invested in capitalist enterprises. The extent and mode of involvement of the Italian state differs from that of the Chinese state, but the distinction lies there and not in the presence or absence of active state involvement in profit-seeking activities. As we note in the introduction to the book, state enterprises and mixed state-private companies have played a major role in Italian capitalism, including the launching of the Italian "miracle" of industrial development after World War II (Ginsborg 2003, 214). Indeed, after World War II, the Istituto per la Ricostruzione Industriale (IRI) of Italy, whose enterprises ranged from steel to electricity and television, was widely touted as a model of state enterprise in a democratic, capitalist society (Layton 1972, 47). Italian state ownership of enterprises is now a little under one-fourth of total market capitalization compared to the 80 percent held by government-controlled firms in China (Pargendler 2012, 2918). But the difference is one of degree rather than of two entirely different types of relations between state, private enterprise, and market.

An awareness of this history of Italian state involvement in capitalist enterprises is also indispensable to understanding the Italians' desire to collaborate with nonstate entities, particularly "family firms," because of their own history of relations with the Italian state. As mentioned previously, Italian owners and managers characterize their move to China as freeing them from a period in which labor in Italy became too powerful and brought about increased state intervention and regulation. This unfavorable view of the Italian state has been pivotal in shaping their negative view of Chinese state agencies and state enterprises, which they interpreted as similarly dysfunctional. On the Chinese side, in order to attract foreign investors who do not want to work with the state, state-owned enterprises have begun to "privatize."

Our argument is not that things are just as they were before the Italians and Chinese began these transnational collaborations in the last decades of the twentieth century. These collaborations enable transformations that both Chinese and Italians seek and desire, as well as unexpected transformations. For Italians, these collaborations enable firms to outsource and decrease the cost of manufacturing and expand distribution to the global fashion market. This has strengthened the reproduction of those family firms that have been successful in globalizing the production and distribution of "Made in Italy." For Chinese, the ability to move beyond the socialist past depends, in part, on the success of their interactions with foreign investors from capitalist economies. So-called independent entrepreneurs and brokers attempt to fashion themselves in a revisionist image of the presocialist past, in which Shanghai was a cosmopolitan city filled with foreign colonial capital. Interactions with the Italians enable these entrepreneurs to imagine themselves as having no relationship at all with either the socialist past or with the current communist party state. Yet interactions with foreigners, particularly Westerners or the Japanese, ineluctably call forth the history of colonialism whenever the collaborations result in mistrust and interactions perceived as unfair based in unequal access to capital, skills, and knowledge. Thus, these entrepreneurs sometimes find themselves in a paradoxical situation of both desiring and rejecting these transnational collaborations.

Our second disagreement with arguments about privatization and neoliberalism, as inspired by feminist critiques, is with the underlying assumption that the categories "private" and "public," at least in relation to capitalism, are transparent and clearly delineated from one another. Even the category "hybrid" tends to imply the ability to distinguish them. To prove their worthiness to foreign investors, Chinese state officials working in export-oriented businesses have undertaken a process of "privatization" that has created entities that often blur the line between the "private" and the "public." Blurring this distinction is the way government officials get beyond the socialist past while holding onto some of their institutional and historical legacies. They hold onto the institutional legacies so that China will not be overtaken by the IMF or the World Bank. Rofel's chapter in part II demonstrates that "privatization" is not as transparent a process as often assumed in discussions of neoliberalism and, further, that the search for "true" private capitalism in China or elsewhere can distract from an investigation into exactly how profit-seeking occurs.

The types of collaborations we discuss in part II are inclusive of the four main types of collaborations we found in our research (see the appendix for a description of the four types and the firms in each). The joint venture between Rinaudo and Pure Elegance is an example of a joint venture with active management collaboration, in which both Italian and Chinese investors together make major decisions about production, management, and marketing. Another type of collaboration, a joint venture with a division of management labor, can be seen with Hui Hua Yi/Silk Nouvelle, which is more fully involved with the Chinese state. Indeed, it began under the aegis of the Zhejiang provincial silk corporation, as a collaboration with the Italian firm Float in the 1980s. As our research proceeded, the Chinese side of this collaboration "privatized," and the collaboration became a joint venture between the seemingly private company, Splendid China, and Float. Rofel describes the ambiguities in Splendid China's privatization process, as it tries to woo more foreign investors. The partnership of FGS with a private Chinese family firm, resulting in the joint venture Vinimoon, is a variation on the previous example. As in the former case, this venture is jointly owned by the Italian and Chinese partners but they leave each other to take full responsibility for their respective domains. The Italian capitalists and their managers are generally in charge of design and marketing while the Chinese entrepreneurs and managers are in charge of the production process. Finally, the chapters in part II describe yet another kind of transnational collaboration we found in our research: wholly Chinese-owned enterprises that provide subcontracting for Italians. Through the life history of one individual, Wang Shiyao, Rofel describes a Shanghai municipal-owned import-export corporation. As with Hui Hua Yi, this company retained certain aspects of its past as a socialist bureaucratic entity, with a vertical organization that included the ownership of factories for production and retail stores to sell its own line of clothing. Yet it combined these features with transnational subcontracting relationships with a wide variety of foreigners, including Italians.

This type of subcontracting had a private variation in China: "mediator" firms and Italian "converter" firms located in China that do not own any factories but organize production networks (although the import-export companies might both own factories and subcontract to other factories). The Italian converter firms usually work through the Chinese mediator firms. These firms take orders from European and U.S. designers and apparel makers and send detailed prototypes to the Chinese factories. They are also proactive about visiting the factories at least weekly to ensure that proper production is taking place. In the case of the Chinese companies, they buy from the factories and sell to the European and U.S. firms, thus putting their own capital at risk. They also collect a commission from the foreign firms. Yanagisako describes the entrepreneurial activities of Vittorio Segalini, who worked for a consultant for Chinese brands while also establishing his own menswear brand. Rofel further discusses the Jingyu broker firm run by Lou Jingxiao/Maggi, described in chapter 1. Lou is an example of someone who both despised the Communist Party and also was cognizant of the colonial history of commercial relationships in China. Again, as our research proceeded, these relations shifted subtly: the Italian converter firms seemed to become less important as the Chinese mediator firms gained in experience and began to work more directly with Italian and other foreign clients.

Finally, Yanagisako's chapter describes a private converter firm that had extended its operation to include the production of silk and polyester lingerie (plus a small amount of cashmere) for several well-known brands, Italian department stores, and retailers. Luciano Ferrari had developed this firm along with his Chinese partner, who became his spouse. Their subsequent disagreements about the firm—which also led to their divorce—offer a more literal example of the marriage metaphor used to describe the conflicts and betrayals that sometimes exist in these transnational collaborations.

In sum, our ethnographic analysis in this section of our book demonstrates that histories continue to play a vital role in shaping the kinds of capitalist practices that are encouraged, endorsed, sought out, legalized, or even accepted in a "gray" zone of illicit activity in Italian-Chinese collaborations. These historical legacies shape how Italians and Chinese involved in these collaborations come to embrace certain forms of transnational capitalist practices rather than others, what they view as "corrupt" versus "ethical" entrepreneurial activity, and how they evaluate inequality.

2   The (Re-)Emergence of Entrepreneurialism in Postsocialist China

Lisa Rofel

In some places and times, transformation is so imperceptible it barely feels noticeable. But in other historical moments, like the current one in China, the population as a whole has lived through life-altering transformations in everything from their experiences of their own bodies to their dreams of what a future might look like. One of the most debated aspects of this transition is its attendant social inequality. In public discourse and private conversation alike, people assess, defend, and denounce the inequalities that exist in China. To what extent are they part of the ongoing presence of the socialist past? Or to what extent are they novel emergences of the present? To what extent are they tied to China's decision to immerse itself in a global economy based in capitalism? The answers to these questions shape how those engaged in or aspiring to an entrepreneurial life evaluate their own economic actions and those of the people they interact with. Moreover, they shape how people embrace, contest, and produce these transformations.[1]

For Chinese entrepreneurs, participation in the transnational commodity chain of Italian fashion is intimately tied to ongoing evaluations of China's recent socialist past. Although China's socialist past might appear as if it has definitively ended, in fact its legacies continue to reverberate in the present. One of the primary goals of these entrepreneurs in China is to move away from the socialist past. Yet they bring socialist historical legacies with them, even as they do not wish to do so. Where does the socialist past lie? This question (and its intended pun) preoccupies many in the world of entrepreneurship, because of their desire to demonstrate how far China, one's company, and oneself have moved beyond that past.

Memories and legacies of the socialist past—and their rejection—are unequally distributed across the social landscape. Workers in China do not unequivocally reject the socialist past. As discussed below, they have a more ambiguous sense of continuity as well as change between the past and the present in their experiences and those of their families. Their relationship to future visions—the horizons of expectation that organize the lifeworlds of these different actors—is a mirror image of those of entrepreneurs. Throughout China, future visions have radically contracted because there is nothing but the fantasy of "entrepreneurship" that anchors them. The disposable labor force that sits at the bottom of the regimes of value and labor documented in this book, Chinese workers, are here revealed to be actors in their own right in that they consistently seek to escape factory work and imagine their freedom (in the limited terms provided). Even though this horizon is narrow, it nevertheless also makes for a highly mobile precariat that slips away from factory work. They are constantly in exodus from it.

Local government officials/managers also have a distinct relationship to the socialist past. Their desires to continue to build and support a strong state, coupled with their nationalist commitments and, for some, lingering ideals of resolving social inequalities, have led them to insist that it is possible to combine some aspects of the socialist past—such as structural and institutional legacies—with entrepreneurial, market economy activity in the present. The paradoxes they face in making this effort are, however, not easy to resolve.

Thus, there exists an ongoing tension between historical legacies and what I call revisionist histories. One of the main arguments of this chapter is that the encouragement to accept a thorough rejection of the socialist past—that it offers nothing of value worth maintaining or revitalizing—is a revisionist historical means by which Chinese citizens are led to embrace capitalism.[2] The rejection of the socialist past also encourages a fantasy that a capitalist market economy can promote fairness and equality. Conversely, these entrepreneurial engagements shape the way in which the socialist past is viewed. One could compare these transformations in China to the bourgeois revolution in Europe, in which the emergent capitalist class portrayed the aristocracy in exaggerated terms. To invoke the immanent logics of capitalism or the overwhelming power of the state to explain the transition from socialism to capitalism is insufficient. One needs to attend to this ideological and affective work involved in fostering the transition among a wide populace.

The analysis offered here raises the question of comparison with countries of the former Soviet Union. There seems to be a greater diversity of postsocialist evaluations of the socialist past in these countries than in China. They range from nostalgia for that past in light of widespread disillusionment in its aftermath (Alexievich 2016; Berdahl 1999; Kalb 2009; Pozniak 2013; Stenning 2000; Todorova and Gille 2010); to the opposite argument that the ghost of socialism—what Liviu Chelcea and Oana Druta (2016) call "zombie socialism"—is regularly kept alive as a disciplinary device to buttress neoliberal politics and inequalities; to the understanding that particular socialist institutionalized practices and imaginaries have in fact survived the demise of the socialist system (Atanasoski and Vora 2017; Caldwell 2011; Horvat and Štiks 2015). This latter argument echoes my argument in this chapter that revisionist histories appear in China alongside the continuation of various socialist practices. Alexei Yurchak (2006) presents the counterintuitive argument that socialism prepared people for their postsocialist lives in unexpected ways, in that the fundamental values of socialist life (such as equality, community altruism, and ethical relations) were of great importance, even as their everyday lives transgressed the norms of official state ideology.[3]

This latter argument leads to several caveats. First, the nostalgia that many experience is not for the socialist system tout court but for particular components of it. Although there does not exist widespread nostalgia for socialism in China, New Left intellectuals in China have also tried to resurrect a sense of that which is worth holding onto from the socialist past. Second, unlike in much of the former Soviet Union, the Communist Party is still very much in power in China. They have a strong hold on interpretations of the socialist past. Moreover, the Chinese state's power enables state officials to resist the kinds of World Bank and IMF-endorsed programs of wholesale privatization that have devastated Eastern European countries (Horvat and Štiks 2015). As a result, state-led capitalism in China has led to economic growth that has both improved overall livelihoods and created the greatest level of inequality in the world. This fact affects how the socialist past is evaluated. Finally, as Neda Atanasoski and Kalindi Vora (2017) have argued, "postsocialism" is not a unified phenomenon or experience. They emphasize, moreover, that, like the related term "postcolonialism," it is better to view postsocialism as an analytic rather than a fixed time period. As implied in this chapter, postsocialism as a category does not unite different experiences around the globe. Rather, the different kinds of transnational capitalist encounters in Eastern Europe and in China, and the differences, for example, in the state's role in capitalist development, will shape what the past means.

The collaborations between Chinese and Italians are the means and mode of making this transition. The collaborations with Italians in the fashion industry are vital to reimagining potential futures in light of the past. Moreover, Shanghai, as the major historical site of the colonial presence and the current center of both fashion and finance, figures centrally as an imagined cosmopolitan site par excellence.[4] Through transnational encounters, those engaged in or aspiring to entrepreneurial action revise their pasts and imagine their potential futures.[5]

These transnational encounters are intertwined with two other social forces that shape this transition from socialism to capitalism. One, as I have mentioned, is the intertwined relationship of historical legacies and revisionist histories. On the one hand, blurred public/private means of profit-seeking in China provide a structural combination of both past practices and novel ones.[6] This combination has led to what I consider to be red herring debates about whether China is following a "proper" capitalist path (for example, see Huang 2008). On the other hand, a revisionist interpretation of the past in only negative terms leaves people facing an ongoing paradox about inherited infrastructural means that enable profit as well as about how to discuss new forms of inequality. This revisionism further encompasses a reimagination by elites of the prerevolutionary past, especially of 1930s Shanghai. Indeed, the history of Shanghai figures centrally in how elites imagine the meaning and import of their eliteness. Workers, on the other hand, do not engage in this kind of nostalgic revisionism of a prerevolutionary moment. Instead, they blur the past and the present, thus implicitly echoing the critiques of the socialist past by elites but turning the force of those critiques onto the contemporary situation.

The second interlocking force is affective engagement. By affective engagement, I mean not with the product of one's labor nor with one's job but rather attachments to imagined temporalities.[7] One sees these affective engagements most notably—and differentially—in the nostalgia for the prerevolutionary past among private entrepreneurs, nationalist commitments by government officials, and aspirations to become future entrepreneurs on the part of workers. This heterogeneity in relation to temporality highlights the specificities of these transformations. The engagements of private entrepreneurs, government officials, and workers with the commodity chain for Italian fashion; historical legacies; and revisionist interpretations of the socialist past are distinct from one another, even as we find overlaps.

Rejection of the Socialist Past, Which Is Not Past Enough for Some

It might not seem surprising that entrepreneurs in China would want to distance themselves from the socialist past. What is perhaps unexpected is that in doing so, they contrast themselves not with the old socialist state-run enterprises, most of which do not exist any longer, but with contemporary capitalist practices carried out by government officials. Entrepreneurs who have "private" firms go to great lengths to distinguish themselves from state-owned corporations, even as they need to work with and through those corporations.

The contrast Chinese private entrepreneurs make between themselves and those whom they view as still representing the socialist past comes out most clearly in comments about business ethics. To appreciate these comments, it is important to realize there exists a widespread discourse about government corruption. This corruption is said to be the result of the degradation of political power during the Cultural Revolution (1966–76), when government officials were said to have used their power to gain privileged access to positions and resources. A common critique among private entrepreneurs is that state agencies such as import-export trading corporations continue to harbor this kind of corrupt behavior. Private entrepreneurs accuse state officials of focusing not on making a profit, which would be an appropriate goal in today's China, but on their own and their families' benefit, to the detriment of the company as a whole.[8]

As anthropologists have pointed out (Gupta 1995, 2005, 2012; Haller and Shore 2005), discourses of corruption signal contested and multiple visions of proper/improper and moral/immoral relations of citizens to their political leaders and their states.[9] Anthropologists have thus turned to analyzing what discourses of corruption produce (e.g., policies supporting neoliberal free trade, constructions of the state as an imagined entity).[10] This anthropological approach informs the way I interpreted the numerous conversations

I had with entrepreneurs about corruption in China. To anticipate, my analysis argues that what gets produced by discourses of corruption in China is the encouragement to embrace a thorough rejection of socialism and, concomitantly, an affective attachment to the capitalist pursuit of profit.

One such conversation—or series of conversations—about corruption occurred with two young entrepreneurs who had been classmates at the business school of Donghua University, Shanghai's textile university. Both of them were in their early thirties when I first got to know them in 2007. I introduced Lou Jingxiao/Maggi in the previous chapter. To recall, Lou ran her own small business, Xiaoyu Ltd. (named by combining her name with her daughter's), as a mediator firm helping Italian fashion firms find the right factories and ensure proper production quality. The other young entrepreneur is Wang Shiyao, who goes by the name George with his foreign clients. To recall from chapter 1, Wang works in one of Shanghai's large municipality-owned import-export companies, Three Swords, that specializes in textiles. This company has a long history in the socialist period and before; indeed, they kept the name of the company they nationalized, whose owner had fled to Taiwan. It still owns thirty factories. In contrast to Lou, Wang dressed in a casual, almost sloppy manner. Tall and wiry with glasses, Wang obviously did not think his dress reflected on his business acumen or his ability to attract clients. This has to do with the fact that he works for a state-owned company that quintessentially represents how capitalism within the state is developing in China today. One could view Wang as someone representing the state. However, Wang did not see himself this way. Nor did Lou view him in this way. He was not a party member. Nor did he get his job through connections, because he is not from Shanghai but from a village outside Ningbo, a medium-sized port city not far to the south of Shanghai. He viewed himself as having a secure job that shielded him from the vagaries of the job market and that would help him get permanent residency in Shanghai so that he could support his parents.

Three Swords is also public, which means it is listed on the Shanghai Stock Exchange. The company is required to be profitable in order to pay employees' salaries, including their year-end bonus. (They cannot rely on the central government to underwrite their debts.) Under socialism, the central government—and down through the hierarchy of bureaus (central, provincial, municipal)—used to organize production, distribute the product, and pay all the necessary expenses without regard to profit. This system has been somewhat, though not wholly, disbanded. The central government no longer covers many of the expenses of provincial and municipal government corporations, though it collects taxes. Under this rearrangement, the corporation that Wang works for has closed some of the factories under its aegis that were not creating enough profit to offset wages and benefits to long-term and retired workers. They merged the remaining ones and began to hire rural migrant workers.

As with many state-owned companies today, this corporation devolves the responsibility to earn a profit onto each office. Wang Shiyao is in charge of Office Number 5, which attracts a wide variety of foreign clients from Japan, Korea, Hong Kong, New Zealand, the United States, and Europe—including Italy. The factories still under its aegis produce textiles and garments that range from high-end fashion to sports clothing. This import-export corporation makes about 50 percent of its profit from production for the domestic market and 50 percent from production for the foreign market. For the domestic market, it produces its own brand of clothing. For the foreign market, it links the foreign client with its own factories or subcontracts out to other factories, depending on need and quality demand.

This import-export corporation also makes money by having companies like Lou Jingxiao's under its aegis. Such an arrangement means the state corporation deals with all the bureaucratic hassles on behalf of these smaller companies.[11] This work most especially includes cultivating guanxi, or connections, with individuals within various government corporations and bureaus who can help smooth over—or slow down—the process.[12] Indeed, three-fourths of this corporation's export business comes through companies like Lou Jingxiao's. At the time, this was due to the World Trade Organization (WTO) import restrictions on textiles from China. The central government textile ministry then dispersed export quota licenses. The quota allotment was based on the actual export business each state-owned company had conducted in the preceding year. It was difficult, though not impossible, for private Chinese firms to be awarded a quota amount. Thus, they had to operate through the government's quota system. Conversely, no government import-export corporation could possibly use up the quota it was given on its own, and actively courted private entrepreneurs to work through them. Wang Shiyao's company was therefore competing for as large a volume of export as possible, and companies like Lou Jingxiao's helped them out.[13]

Finally, like many other state-owned corporations in China, this import-export company also realized they can make a profit from the transformation of previously state-owned urban space into private real estate. Therefore, they have moved their offices and factories three times to make the most out of the downtown piece of real estate that they "own." I put "own" in quotation marks because in this new world of capitalism in China, the state still owns all the land and leases it to individual residents and companies for seventy years.[14]

The first time we all got together was a rainy Sunday evening in spring of 2007. After I asked a series of formal questions about the structure of his company, Wang as well as Lou jumped into a more general lament, one that I later realized was a familiar complaint: people in China, they said, think about material things and nothing else. They just want to make money. They do not have any principles.

Strikingly, Lou and Wang did not place this problem at the doorstep of capitalism but blamed it on what they viewed as the strong, ongoing, and seemingly invincible presence of the socialist past. I asked indirectly how this problem connected to Wang's company by asking about his company's future direction. Wang replied: "That is hard to say, because it depends on what the leaders are thinking. Maybe we should lower our voices here. Because the leaders actually don't always think about making profit when they decide things. Private companies are very clear—they need to make a profit and they need to be efficient about it. But with government companies, there is a lot of waste and other reasons why they do things. Leaders make decisions and we ordinary employees don't understand why." Then Lou chimed in: *pigu zai nar jiu juedingle* (whoever's ass is in the right place decides).

These two commentaries might seem opposed: that people only think about making money, and that Wang's company does not think about making a profit. But on closer examination, it becomes clear how Lou and Wang were relating these two comments: the individuals within the company definitely thought about nothing but their own interest at the expense of actually creating a profitable company.

A week later, Wang and I spent the day together. We talked about why he works so hard. Wang often stays in his office until well past midnight. I wondered aloud who would come to work in such a place. Are there people willing to work for your company, because it is a government-owned company? I asked. Yes, Wang replied, "they have connections, to the boss or someone else so they get a job there. Then they don't have to worry, or work very hard. I can't criticize them too much because of these connections" (see Tang and Tomba 2013).

Wang Shiyao feels the frustration of having to make up for the lack of diligence he sees in his bosses (the officials representing the municipal government) as well as in the children of officials who work there. He and Lou Jingxiao repeatedly complained about the fact that these officials do not know how to do the work; they have a sinecure; they get their sons and daughters into these jobs, who also do not want to or know how to do this work.

These complaints might sound familiar to those in the United States, who have long witnessed the career paths of children of the economic and political elite and have critiqued corruption based on the intimate connections of wealth and power. Yet, unlike in the United States, Lou Jingxiao and Wang Shiyao did not explain these problems as due to the inheritance of wealth nor even the inheritance of power but more specifically in the way they interpret Maoist socialism as having evacuated social life in China of any moral principles, leaving an ethical vacuum of mere selfishness. They have thus given a new ontology to the socialist past.

True entrepreneurialism, for them, signaled the opposite: the ability to express one's talents regardless of background, and the ability to gain elite status through one's own merits rather than through political connections. Yet in their dreamworld of capitalism, the goal is not personal freedom so much as a set of ethics not just in business but in social life more broadly. The set of ethics these entrepreneurs wished to reinvigorate was Confucianism.[15]

My conversations with these two entrepreneurs, echoed by many others, reflect an important piece of today's revisionist histories: "true" capitalism can only thrive in opposition to the socialist past. The lingering presence of the socialist past, they believe, not only contributes to but is the major cause of social inequality today. For these entrepreneurs, the vast inequalities in income, the corruption through money, and, paradoxically, the singular focus on material things and consumption are all blamed on the continuing presence of government officials in profit-seeking realms. Analogous to the history of the bourgeois revolution in Europe, in which bourgeois merchants contrasted their fight for freedom against a feudal system of inherited positions, here we see that this decided rejection of the socialist past that is still not past enough creates an affective attachment to the possibilities that capitalism seemingly provides, including the possibility of overcoming inequalities. In revisionist histories among entrepreneurs, the socialist past does not merely haunt the present; it invades the present.

Yet one can nonetheless discern historical legacies in the practices of these private entrepreneurs. One, discussed above, is working through government-owned import-export corporations. Another involves guanxi, or building networks. While entrepreneurs complain that government officials work through guanxi, these entrepreneurs do exactly the same—just with different kinds of networks. Their networks involve their business school classmates, some of whom, like Wang, have jobs within state-owned corporations. Yet, in their view, this networking is of a different quality, since it does not directly involve currying political favors. From another vantage point, however, the distinction between ethical and unethical networking is not always clear. While historical legacies are thus discernible in these private entrepreneurs' economic actions, it is also true that they do not have models of entrepreneurial activity per se from the socialist past. For that, they often turn to the presocialist era.

Neofeudal Nostalgia

What has replaced socialist ideals is of course the pursuit of wealth. But a bald pursuit of wealth, paradoxically, is the accusation many hurl against government officials. What do these young entrepreneurs in Shanghai admire? Among elites in Shanghai, there is a great deal of nostalgia for the presocialist elite life.[16] This celebratory nostalgia enables entrepreneurs to interpret their eliteness as distinct in kind from that of government officials. It also offers them a model of entrepreneurial economic action rooted in Chinese history. Finally, this nostalgia enables them to address social inequality in China without implicating themselves. I call this nostalgia neofeudal, or more precisely, neosemifeudal, given how socialist historians labeled the early twentieth century as the semifeudal era. One central aspect of this nostalgia is a desire to enact the kind of cosmopolitanism that prewar colonial Shanghai is reminiscent of, with its numerous international colonial communities. Engagement in the Italian fashion industry allows these entrepreneurs to make more claims on that history than if they were wholly involved in the domestic market or in another sector.[17]

I got a sense of this admiration in a conversation with Lou about her background. Her parents were labeled "intellectuals" during the Cultural Revolution and were sent down from Shanghai to the countryside of Jiangxi, a poor southern province to the west of Shanghai. After the age of three, she grew up with her mother's parents in Shanghai. Her maternal grandfather, an entrepreneur, was an important influence on her. Prior to the socialist revolution, he had a department store. After the revolution, he was labeled a capitalist and the new government took away his store. He became a manager of a state-run store. With the end of the Cultural Revolution, he opened his own store again, first a corner food and drink store and then again a department store. Her grandfather was very strict with her. He felt that his family had to be models for the other workers in the store. One day one of the workers offered her something to take out of the store. Her grandfather found out and made her kneel on a laundry board for several hours. With such a description of strict physical discipline, one might assume that Lou harbors resentment toward her grandfather. To the contrary, she places that kind of discipline in the realm of moral ethics: "My grandfather . . . taught me about proper conduct and about treating people equitably [heqi]. He used to say, Yishen wei ze, yihe wei gui [use yourself as an example, use harmony as the guiding principle]."

Lou Jingxiao reaches back to presocialist history to find a model of proper entrepreneurial behavior. These models did not exist under socialism, as entrepreneurial activity was often banned outright or usually under a cloud of deep suspicion and distrust.[18] The model of entrepreneurship that Lou learned from her grandfather includes hierarchical ethics, unswerving dedication to the business, and hard work. It is also a model of building from small to large and of changing types of business depending on opportunity and need. Finally, it appears as if her grandfather did not have any other family members involved in his business. Nor does Lou.

While Lou's narrative might not sound particularly nostalgic, what is striking is how she reaches back before the socialist era to a moment that represents for her the proper ethics, embodied by an entrepreneur targeted by the socialist government as an improper citizen who needed reeducation. Ethical entrepreneurs such as her grandfather appear to address and therefore resolve social inequality through their morally upright behavior. We could also view these ethics as more broadly a type of self-fashioning (reminiscent of Foucault's [1986] historical study of Greco-Roman self-fashioning), an ethos supposed to underlie all of one's behavior. But this ethos can only be embodied by a few; it is not for normalizing the population, nor for addressing structural problems such as inequality.

What drew my attention more explicitly to the neofeudal nostalgia pervasive in Shanghai was an exhibition I was invited to in the reconstructed art district north of the Suzhou River. Artists have taken over abandoned factory buildings in this area and installed art galleries and small boutiques. This art district in itself embodies the revisionist layerings of history. It constitutes a Benjaminian palimpsest of ruins. I was completely unprepared mentally and emotionally for this exhibit. Prior to this exhibit, Shanghai's early twentieth-century history still represented for me the life of what the Chinese Communist Party (CCP) called semicolonialism, with colonial industrialization, workers' unrest, and endless strikes as well as the location of the initial formation of the CCP.

Nothing of this history appeared in the exhibit. Instead, I found a space made over into a model of an elite entrepreneurial home circa 1930. The various open rooms were filled with furniture and items from what presumably were of 1920s and 1930s Shanghai vintage. There were the sofas, art deco style, the lamps designed to look like svelte women, the vintage phonograph player. There were reproductions of the kind of art an elite entrepreneurial family in the prewar era might have hung on their walls. Among the dense crowd, visual artists were showing off their latest nostalgia artwork. The whole scene exuded colonial cosmopolitanism. This is the world that contemporary elites try to fashion for themselves.[19]

The elite entrepreneurs this nostalgia celebrates arose out of the colonial treaty port system established in China after the Opium Wars in the mid-nineteenth century. Known as compradors in English and *maiban* (literally arranging trade) in Chinese, these entrepreneurs emerged as intermediaries for foreign firms.[20] Compradors assisted foreign firms to access marketing systems beyond the treaty ports for commodities such as tea and silk. Compradors also acted as financial guarantors when Chinese firms purchased imported goods, and their financial links allowed Western banks to provide loans to Chinese banks (*qianzhuang*) (Hao 1970).[21] Former compradors went on to become some of China's most successful industrialists in the early twentieth century.[22] Given their role in aiding foreign trade corporations, these entrepreneurs were labeled as traitors by the CCP. They were distinguished from the category of "nationalist capitalists" who were portrayed as aiding the country instead of supporting colonialism.[23] This socialist evaluation of pre-socialist entrepreneurs is being turned upside down by neofeudal nostalgia.

This nostalgia operates effectively, in fact, because Shanghai has actually rebuilt itself into a twenty-first-century urban commercial and finance center. It has also refashioned itself with a radical architectural makeover, at least in the downtown center.[24] Shanghai's downtown center is virtually a showcase of the latest in architectural design. In the evening, downtown Shanghai looks like a computer-generated world of light shows and videos playing off the outside of buildings. This current downtown center's striking high-rise buildings, designed by some of the world's most famous architects, are interspersed with gated high-rise apartment complexes and multiplex shopping malls selling designer brands. Elites in China nostalgically imagine that Shanghai might have continued this status without the hiatus of the socialist era.

2.1 The state and market economy come together visually on a famous Shanghai commercial street.

This nostalgia thus serves as an affective cultural and ideological resource for the contemporary celebration of entrepreneurial activity. It encourages people to dream of becoming entrepreneurs. It also seems to resolve the dilemma of examining the relationship between social inequalities that have emerged in China under economic reform and the entrepreneurial activities these elites engage in that might contribute to those inequalities. For the emphasis in this neofeudal nostalgia is on the glory of these prewar elites, which they embody not just for themselves but also for China. The nationalist sentiment in this prewar glory displaces the history of prewar inequality and exploitation that used to hold pride of place in official narratives. Indeed, that is the point.[25]

In this nostalgia for a revisionist history of prerevolutionary Shanghai, one finds the other piece of the origin story for contemporary China. These images exude affective loss, recovery, pleasure, and desire. They are embodied memories of a never experienced past. The affective attachment to this past is the means by which to leap over the socialist era, to trace an imagined linear path from then to now. Transnational engagements with the West are central here, even as nationalist sentiment both confronts and evades the colonialism that made Shanghai into an international city. Those who work in the transnational production and distribution of Italian fashion are in a particularly good position to embody this cosmopolitanism, given the high visibility of Italian fashion as signifier of elite cultural taste.

For elites in Shanghai, the intersection of origin stories in the presocialist past, affective attachments to memories of that past as currently reenacted, and transnational encounters with the West that lend themselves to a revised version of that past together create the conditions of possibility for moving from one world to another, from the world of socialism to that of capitalism. They seem to resolve, at least for elite entrepreneurs, the sticky question of China's evident and severe social inequalities. Those inequalities are laid at the door of the socialist past still invading the present, obviated in a decided rejection of previous official histories of Shanghai, and displaced in a Shanghai pride in being at the historical forefront of Chinese cosmopolitan, transnational life. Elite entrepreneurs have addressed China's inequalities with me directly in one way only: to the extent that these elite entrepreneurs feel that China is the sweatshop of the world on behalf of transnational entrepreneurs, they place themselves in a position analogous to China's workers, as those from whom transnational entrepreneurs extract surplus value. To this extent, they also tend to sympathize with the dilemmas workers face.

Blurring the Public/Private: Making State Corporations Profitable

It may appear to be commonsensical that those who cast themselves as "independent" entrepreneurs try to distinguish themselves as much as possible from government entities whom they accuse of dragging past degradations into the present. But government officials also try to distance themselves from the socialist past. As with these entrepreneurs, distancing oneself from the socialist past enables those working within state entities to craft a revisionist history of their position while also continuing with the legacies of certain historical and institutional practices. Government officials' efforts to move away from the socialist past is their way of dealing with the swirl of accusations against them—that they take advantage of their monopoly on power to create a monopoly on the creation of wealth: in a word, that which people in China consider to be corruption. Government officials thus distance themselves from the socialist past in order to shed that which the socialist past has come to represent—inequalities based in political networks.

One of their main means for doing so is to "privatize." As we argued in the introduction, feminist theorists and activists have long deconstructed the division between the private and the public. They have challenged the ideological constructions of the domestic/public or private/public by drawing attention to the wide variability across cultures and through history in what these categories encompass and represent. They have thus emphasized that the seemingly private sphere of the home is always part of the political structure of society.

In turning this insight onto capitalist practices, it becomes clear that the practice of "privatization" is not straightforward or singular in meaning. It entails a wide range of private/public relations, with different aims and import. It is thus important to examine how what counts as private and what counts as public are forged by historically specific processes, including the formation of differentiated transnational capitalist projects.

In contemporary China, the line between public and private, or state-owned and independently owned, is much less precise than one would assume from an analysis based on a supposed modal type of capitalism. There exists a range of situations along the spectrum from fully private to hybrid public/private to completely ambiguous and blurred statuses.[26] In terms of the latter, it is often impossible to assess or distinguish, much less disentangle, which aspect of a corporation is "public" or the state aspect, and which is "private." This blurring of the distinction is a deliberate strategy. The argument offered here is distinct from those who would accuse the Chinese state of obfuscation. Rather, this chapter argues that "privatization" has multiple meanings and can be instituted in various ways that make the distinction between public and private impossible to delineate and that consequently highlight their contingent meaning.

Government officials want to be seen as at the forefront of the current practices to create wealth for China, although they have a different view of their own practices than do independent entrepreneurs. Government officials working in state corporations also give a different valence to the question of— and concern for—inequality than do independent entrepreneurs. The pursuit of wealth on behalf of the state is the manner through which state officials cast their actions as demonstrating the continuing concern of the Chinese state for

its people. Indeed, appearing to move away from the socialist past is an important means of recasting the inequalities emerging in the present, inequalities
for which the state still feels obligated to respond and take some responsibility,
given its commitment to "market socialism" (Perry 2008). These officials' diffuse sense of seeking the welfare of—and wealth for—the nation, while it can
be interpreted as a continuation of the socialist past, is in fact their version of
a revisionist history that criticizes the socialist era through a developmentalist
logic: that the socialist era held China back from proper development.[27]

I present an extended ethnographic case of a provincial state bureau whose
"true" nature—that is, whether it had fully privatized or was still part of the
state—was difficult to discern even as it was clearly seeking to create profit. I
slowly came to realize that this state bureau is an entity that is profit-seeking,
partially privatized, and still part of the state. Rather than accuse the Chinese
state of not enacting "real" capitalism, an argument I find to be a red herring,
or try to parse whether such blurred boundaries are an evolutionary stage, or
even whether they prevent solid economic growth that might otherwise take
place, I argue that this ambiguous division between private and public constitutes "profitizing practices" through which the state moves beyond the socialist past while continuing to build on previous institutional practices viewed as
advantageous for pursuing wealth.

Li Linfeng, whom we introduced in part I, is in charge of the joint venture called Hui Hua Yi/Silk Nouvelle with Renato Costa, the owner of a well-
known Italian fashion firm. We always met with Li in the headquarters of Hui
Hua Yi/Silk Nouvelle, located on the outskirts of Hangzhou, in what used to
be the countryside. Hangzhou has incorporated this county, Xiaoshan, into its
city limits and turned it into a special development zone.

Profitizing the Zhejiang silk bureau has been firmly intertwined with the
export of silk. Mary Elizabeth Gallagher (2005) has insightfully argued that
with economic reform the Chinese government in fact initially encouraged
foreign investment in China in order to push poorly operating factories into
bankruptcy and close them. With Hui Hua Yi/Silk Nouvelle, we see another
side to this story: Li's tale of transformation emphasizes the moment of foreign trade with the West as key to the flourishing of the Zhejiang silk industry.

In our first interview with him, Li began the history of the joint venture
with Costa by detailing the export situation in China at that time. As he explained, in the early 1980s, the only way to export silk was through the central
government's All-China textiles import-export bureau. One point Li left un-
stated was that there was only one way to export silk in the 1980s *according*

to state regulations. As a result, numerous silk factories, including the factory I wrote about (1999), had established hidden connections to export silk to Hong Kong, making direct profits they did not share with the central government.[28] Silk factories that initially exported in this way did so under the guise of the state's efforts to decentralize management of factories, allowing them to make their own profit if they produced above and beyond their quota.

There is a common misperception both in China and elsewhere that prior to the 1980s, China had no trading relations at all with Western countries (as distinct from its trade with socialist and Third World countries). This is due to the fact that the United States placed a trade embargo on China until 1971. This misperception is evident in Li's statement that foreign trade with the West began in the 1980s. In fact, China continuously exported goods, especially foodstuffs and textiles, outside the Communist bloc. They did so mainly through Hong Kong. By the early 1960s, textiles constituted two-thirds of all exports. After the Sino-Soviet split in 1960, China's major trading partners became Japan, Hong Kong, and Malaysia-Singapore as well as Western countries such as Canada, France, West Germany, Italy, and the United Kingdom. After the United States lifted its trade embargo with China in 1971, the U.S. gradually became a major trading partner (Eckstein 1966, 1977; Riskin 1987).

Prior to economic reform, the silk industry was folded into state-run enterprises (see Rofel 1999). Since silk is such an important part of textile production in Zhejiang province, the province had its own silk bureau and, underneath that, each city in the province had a municipal silk bureau. With economic reform, these practices changed dramatically although slowly over the course of thirty years. The goals changed from need and international status to profit. Gradually state-owned trade corporations expanded dramatically as the central government allowed provincial bureaus to control their own import and export. Thereafter, factories could export silk directly or through the provincial bureau's trading company. In the mid-1980s, silk was one of the few exportable commodities in China. Conversely, the importance of foreign trade to this industrial sector has to do with the fact that silk was then an expensive commodity on the domestic market, rarely purchased by ordinary citizens in China, who considered it an unnecessary luxury. (Silk woven marriage quilts were the only exception.)

Li was in charge of this profitizing process for the Zhejiang provincial silk bureau. The silk bureau began this process by changing its name to the Zhejiang FuHua Silk Corporation. This was not mere nominalism: it was the first step toward changing the silk industry from a fully government-run planned economy to one in which profit-seeking activity would take a more prominent role in motivating economic production and exchange.

Renato Costa was one of the first foreign investment partners with the Zhejiang FuHua Silk Corporation; he has the longest history with them. They began working directly together in 1985, when Costa first came to China in order to import silk thread. Li waxed eloquent in our numerous conversations about his Italian partner "Renato," as he called him, because this relationship instantiates the kind of transformations toward profit-seeking that state officials see themselves as enacting, as mirrored in the trust that Costa evidently displays toward them. Since they were both doing well with trade, they decided to combine trade with production, setting up their own joint venture in 1993, Hui Hua Yi/Silk Nouvelle. Until China's 2001 entry into the WTO, all foreign investments in China (except in Shenzhen) had to be in the form of joint ventures with a state entity. Hui Hua Yi/Silk Nouvelle makes silk clothing not only for Costa's firm, Float, but also for customers in France, the United States, and Germany. They do not have any other customers in Italy. Li averred that it was not a good idea to have other customers in the same place as their partner.

> The first ten years of making silk clothing with Renato [i.e., 1993–2003] were great profits. At that time, we were still a planned economy, but even still because the quantity of silk was not great but the quality was high and he entered the market early on, so he could make a lot. In Rome, they used to line up to buy his clothing. We have real feelings with Renato, like family. It is real sentiment. Our relationship is based on trust. He lets go of looking over the management. I don't collect any wages from Hui Hua Yi. My wages do not come from Hui Hua Yi at all, so then Renato knows I am not trying to take anything from Hui Hua Yi and so he trusts me.

Li has always received his wages from the Zhejiang FuHua Silk Corporation. This issue, he states, is at the crux of why the joint venture of Hui Hua Yi has continued: trust. Implicit in his statement about the source of his wages and the issue of trust is the well-known accusation of corruption against government officials. Li emphasized this point by explaining that his relationship with Costa came about because Costa had actually been taken advantage of by others in Shanghai when he had invested in their factories that later went bankrupt. Then Costa found the Zhejiang FuHua Silk Corporation and Li. Although the joint venture had begun as a venture between the provincial government and Costa's Italian firm, Li obviously needed not only to continue bolstering Costa's confidence in their corporation but also to attract other foreign investors: hence, the move to "privatize."

Over subsequent interviews, Li began to explain how the Zhejiang FuHua Silk Corporation had "privatized." That is, he explained that the silk corporation was extricating itself from this joint venture, even though the joint venture was to continue. This story, as it unfolded, surprised me, as until that moment I had held onto my understanding that Hui Hua Yi was a joint venture under the Zhejiang FuHua Silk Corporation and was thus a partnership with a fully state-owned entity. But then Li explained what had happened with China's imminent entry into the WTO, which appeared to be a story of privatization: "Originally, the Zhejiang FuHua Silk Corporation was the partner in the joint venture with Renato Costa. But starting in 2000, they formed Splendid China because the government was trying to privatize the company and promote 'people's management.'" Splendid China is actually more akin to a general holding company. It has twenty to thirty ventures like Hui Hua Yi under its aegis. One of the reasons the silk corporation seeks to at least appear as if they have privatized is that Italian fashion firms and other foreign firms generally prefer to work with private companies in China over government ones.

The term Li actually used to discuss this process was not "privatize" but *minying*, which translates literally as "run by the people" or more colloquially as "people managed." Its colloquial translation can also be "privately run" but there is a different Chinese term that directly means privately owned by individuals: *siren* or *sirenban*. The Chinese term for "privatization" is *sirenhua*. "Minying" is meant to signal that the firm is not run directly by the state but by people who do not represent the state. There is a fine but distinguishable line between "managing" or running versus "owning" a firm. That Li did not use the term "sirenban" could signal the reluctance of state officials to speak of privatization directly, since the Chinese government's official discourse always speaks of the "socialist market economy" or "socialism with Chinese characteristics." But Li's reluctance to use the term "sirenban" could also have been due to the fact that this entity, Splendid China, was still part of the silk corporation but in a different relationship to it, that is, in a different relationship to the state. Li implied that the Zhejiang FuHua Silk Corporation is no longer the major partner in this joint venture, having been replaced by Splendid China. But the status of Splendid China gradually called forth more questions.

Thus, the meaning of "privatization" in Li's story is ambiguous. At the time that we spoke, I had assumed a clean, neat, and transparent definition of privatization. Either the Zhejiang FuHua Silk Corporation—or this entity

Splendid China—had fully privatized, or it was fully state owned. Li led me to abandon my initial assumption that the Chinese side of this joint venture was still state owned. However, through reviewing exactly what he said as well as eventually speaking with others related to Splendid China and the Zhejiang FuHua Silk Corporation, a more ambiguous state of affairs emerged.

As we argue in the introduction, while feminist scholars and feminist activists have long deconstructed the division between the private and the public, curiously, when we turn to the private/public division in relation to capitalism, we tend to assume we know exactly what this division means without further investigation. Numerous scholars have raised an important ethnographic question with regard to China: it is often difficult to discern whether a corporate entity is privately or state owned. Yasheng Huang (2008), for example, argues that one of China's largest corporations is actually a private corporation but must pretend to be state owned because, since its founding in the late 1980s, it has flouted many state regulations. This argument fails to answer the question of the relationship between public and private.[29]

In my research, I found the opposite tendency: that many state-owned entities try to dress themselves up as private. My question, then, is the opposite of Huang's: why would a state-owned corporation bother to dress itself up as a private one? In the course of my conversations with Li, the "true" nature of Hui Hua Yi, Splendid China, and the Zhejiang FuHua Silk Corporation were difficult to discern even as all three entities were clearly seeking to create profit. I slowly came to believe that this corporation, and many others in China, represents the kind of blurred entity that is profit-seeking, partially privatized, and still part of the state. I distinguish my argument from the idea that the Chinese state is disingenuous, that it "pretends" to privatize but does not really do so. More to the point, I distinguish my argument from those who argue that because the Chinese state has not followed a particular capitalist path toward privatization, it therefore has not truly instituted capitalism. Such a view universalizes the ideology of Adam Smith ([1776] 1998) about the particular path one must follow in order to foster profit-seeking activity. Analytically, this ambiguity in some state-owned corporations reveals the historically contingent and continuously changing nature of the private/public distinction within capitalism not only in China but elsewhere.

In China, many, though not all, enterprises that were formerly part of various state bureaucracies have been "privatized." Everything subsumed under a particular bureau, excluding labor, that once was considered "state owned" has been turned into "assets." These assets include not only the buildings, machinery, production networks that include smaller enterprises tied to state bureaus hierarchically positioned above them, reputation, and knowledge but also the land—now called real estate—on which these enterprises are located. These "assets" in turn have become "equity" that investors can buy and through which investors can seek profit, which can equally mean shutting down the enterprise and declaring it bankrupt or cutting costs (i.e., wages and benefits for workers, not to mention the workers themselves) along with finding myriad novel ways to create wealth. Often the latter means speculating in the real estate that these enterprises now own.[30] Equity, then, has turned into "securities." Thus, enterprises have been securitized so that the equity in what is now called a company or a corporation is distinctly held by various profit-seeking entities.[31] Instead of turning over all their proceeds to the state bureau above them and then having the state redistribute the necessary funds to them as under the planned economy, the owners and managers of the reconceptualized companies create "profits" and pay "taxes" to the state.[32]

Over the course of numerous conversations, Li spoke about various practices that would conventionally indicate privatization. One was a process in which employees were "encouraged" to buy stock in Splendid China. This stock-buying campaign did not make the employees into the owners of the company, or even into its managers. Like U.S. corporations, the fact that stockholders buy securities in a corporation does not mean that the corporation itself—or one of its holding companies—is no longer the major owner.[33] Needless to say, migrant workers in Splendid China's factories were not given the option to buy stock. Only office employees—the technicians, designers, marketing personnel, and managers—were part of this arrangement. This enforced share buying was supposed to encourage a shift in perception and affect on the part of employees about their relationship to the state—or more precisely, to the state's previous responsibility for their work and welfare. It was also supposed to create a sense that the responsibility for the survival of the corporation rests on employees' own shoulders.

At the time of our first interview with Li, the Zhejiang FuHua Silk Corporation still owned 51 percent of the stock in Splendid China. In later interviews, Li explained that Splendid China employees had bought about 44 percent of the Zhejiang FuHua Silk Corporation's stock. Splendid China was also required by government regulation to find a few other companies to buy their stock so that this process—whether privatization or profitization—did not look like stark originary accumulation. That is, it should not look as if the government handed over public resources to the top managers to make a profit for themselves. According to Li, three other companies bought a total of 5 percent stock in Splendid China. It is more than likely that these companies represent the Zhejiang FuHua Silk Corporation, as many state-owned corporations have pursued this strategy of creating multiple holding companies. As we know from cases in the United States and elsewhere, "holding companies" have become a favored practice of corporations to hide their monopoly—and otherwise sometimes illegal—holdings. In fact, in another interview, Li offered me not just one but several of his business cards, demonstrating the several hats he wore within the silk corporation. These cards revealed that Splendid China is a trading company under the aegis of yet another group—Southern Silk Ltd., which is undoubtedly a subsidiary of Zhejiang FuHua Silk Corporation and structured to stimulate profit. Thus, the Zhejiang FuHua Silk Corporation is most likely still the majority shareholder of Splendid China. Selling stock, then, can have multiple implications: it can indicate a "privatization" process, it can make the company "public" in the sense of appearing on the stock market, and it can mean "public" in the sense of still remaining under the aegis of a state-owned corporation. In Splendid China's case, it was not listed on the stock market; shares in the company were internally distributed.

Another telling ambiguity about the status of Hui Hua Yi and Splendid China surfaced in our discussion of branch trading companies. One was the joint venture with Silk Nouvelle. In response to my query to clarify "branch trading company," Li replied that Splendid China is a stock company (*gufen gongsi*). Under Splendid China, he clarified, there are eight branch companies, "or you could call them *bumen*." The word "bumen" is a key term that links Splendid China with the government. "Bumen" means department, or section, of a larger entity. It is a term that has been in use since the 1950s. Wang Shiyao, who appeared in this chapter's first section and who clearly recognizes his company as state owned, described his office within a Shanghai state-owned import-export company as a bumen. Branch companies, or bumen, under the aegis of Splendid China can engage in a wide variety of profit-seeking activities, including joint ventures, domestic production, and buying and selling of raw materials and fabric for the domestic market and also for export. None of the independent companies I encountered in China have anything they would call "branch companies." The larger nonstate private companies have established "franchises."

I had the opportunity to speak with one of the employees of one of Splendid China's branch companies, Lou Huayan. Lou Jingxiao/Maggi introduced me to her. They both worked with the same Italian procurer, but were not in competition because Lou Jingxiao handled knit clothing while Lou

Huayan dealt with woven garments. I met with Lou Huayan in Hangzhou, in a Singapore-run café where we had lunch and talked. Lou Huayan was a very young-looking woman, thirty-three years old when I met her in 2008, dressed casually, in jeans and sneakers. She had an easygoing manner. She peppered our discussion with business terms in English. Through the length of our long conversation, Lou Huayan clarified the relationship of these branch companies to Splendid China. Exactly as in Wang Shiyao's case in Shanghai, Splendid China had decentralized the finances of the corporation, so that each "branch company" was responsible for its own profits. While the base salary of each employee was guaranteed, the bonuses—the most important part of their income—were dependent on the profits they brought in (as in the manner of Wall Street firms). Thus, the bumen have definitely been "profitized." However, they were intimately tied together in one state corporation. "Branch company" is thus the term that indicates profitizing but not absolute privatization.[34]

Finally, Splendid China has eight "children companies" (*zi gongsi*), as Li Linfeng called them. As he explained to me, "These are not independent agents. We, Splendid China, own 70 percent of these companies, and the employee who runs one of these children companies owns 30 percent. In the future, we would like to change that to 50/50. This is a way to encourage our employees." He continued, "We help organize the customers for them, by sending them to exhibitions, fairs, and so on. The financial arrangements are all with us and the management structure is unified with us." If Splendid China were a fully "independent" or "private" company, it is unlikely they would encourage their employees to take potential profit away from them. However, given the greater likelihood that Splendid China is still under the aegis of the Zhejiang FuHua Silk Corporation, the fact that employees generate more profit on their own initiative can only be seen as a benefit for Splendid China/Zhejiang FuHua Silk Corporation.

In addition to the ambiguities I have pointed out, another telling characteristic is the power of appointments. In Splendid China's case, the power of appointment did not change. Li was clearly appointed as manager of both Hui Hua Yi and Splendid China by the Zhejiang FuHua Silk Corporation. Li stayed in those positions for eleven years. He emphasized his longevity to demonstrate the lack of corruption—both his own personal lack of corruption as well as that of presumably a state-infused profitized company. Li was required by the state to step down with retirement. His successor, then the vice manager, was similarly appointed by Zhejiang FuHua Silk Corporation.

"Privatization," I concluded, could have a wide variety of meanings. Splendid China is undoubtedly a "privatized" trading company within Zhejiang

FuHua Silk Corporation. It is "private" to the extent that it creates its own profit-seeking activities. It is also responsible for its losses, such that Zhejiang FuHua Silk Corporation will not lend a hand should Hui Hua Yi or the other joint ventures fail to generate profits. On the other hand, Splendid China generates profits that are partially used by Zhejiang FuHua Silk Corporation, especially to pay the salaries of those officials or managers working in Hui Hua Yi and Splendid China but also in other areas of the silk corporation.[35]

While the division between private and state owned is blurred in the case of Splendid China, I do not mean to suggest there is no capitalist "privatization" of the kind we more conventionally think of under that category. When I asked Li to review the history of what had happened to the silk factories I had known in the 1980s, thirty-seven of which were then under the Zhejiang FuHua Silk Corporation, he stated right away that none of them existed any longer: "All of these factories have been privatized [*minying qiye*]. They have to pay their own taxes and make their own arrangements."[36]

I asked him to explain the example of the factory I know best, Zhenfu. The Zhejiang FuHua Silk Corporation sold it to a group of Zhenfu's managers, who now wholly owned it. Moreover, the silk corporation had given Zhenfu the land it used to be located on, in the center of town, which they had transformed into a popular tourist silk market.[37] In return for getting all the profit from this real estate, Zhenfu's owners had to agree to keep paying the workers their salaries and take care of the pensions of retired workers. "But," he continued, "they have to take care of themselves. It used to be that everyone ate out of one big pot [*chi daguo fan*], but now the government [*guojia*] doesn't have that much money to give out to support everyone." He then added: "Now, the relationship with Splendid China has changed. Splendid China buys from these different factories; we are all on an equal footing. It is no longer like before, when it was a hierarchy of above and below [i.e., the Zhejiang FuHua Silk Corporation was above the factories and told them what to do]."

Thus, some parts of the Zhejiang FuHua Silk Corporation have fully privatized, if by "fully privatized" we mean that the state no longer is involved in any way in the generation of profits or the mitigation of losses, and no longer takes any responsibility whatsoever for workers' wages and benefits, including pensions. Most of this type of privatization has occurred at the bottom of the hierarchy of production, that is, the factories themselves.

I learned more details of this type of privatization from my old friends at Zhenfu. The most knowledgeable about this process was Tang Shan, the former Communist Party youth league secretary for the factory who later worked in Zhenfu's accounting office for many years. Improbably (because she was such an upright party member), we had become close friends. Zhenfu's managers—now the owners—always needed to consult with the accountants before taking any action. As Tang explained, she and other accountants tell their bosses what they should do with the money and when. Each time I go to Hangzhou, I visit with Tang. In one conversation where we went over the details of Zhenfu's privatization, she confirmed that everyone had been ordered to buy shares, including workers. Tang also confirmed that the provincial silk corporation decided that the then head manager would become the owner. He became the head of the Board of Directors (*dongshizhang*) and also general manager (*zong jingli*). This manager's ownership of this previously state-owned factory was facilitated by a loan from a state-owned bank. These banks facilitated the privatization process, basically handing over state-owned resources to individuals.

In asking Tang about the overall situation at Zhenfu, I tried not to sound critical, as workers and managers alike had long taken pride in its famous silk products. But my visit to the factory and my interviews with workers there, arranged by Tang, had given me the distinct sense that all was not well there and that Zhenfu was on the decline. One indication for me was that the majority of workers seemed to be older; there were very few younger workers who had come to work there. Tang explained that Zhenfu was shrinking: "Many do not want to come and work in the factory; the wages are not that high. And the three-shift system is very bitter [*xinku*]. They can now do other work for the same wages and they don't have to work the three-shift system." Zhenfu maintains the socialist three-shift system prevalent in the garment and textile industries: two days of day shift, two days of evening shift, and two days of overnight shift. Then two days of rest.[38]

The situation of Zhenfu complicates the story of postsocialist originary accumulation, or to use David Harvey's (2005) term, "accumulation by dispossession." We often hear stories of incredible wealth accumulated in former socialist countries by a few well-placed individuals who managed to acquire and turn into private property that which had formerly belonged to the state. Clearly, in China one finds individuals who have amassed wealth. But this story is complicated by the fact that often these individuals are still working within state-run corporations. By contrast, those who are given the "advantage" of turning former state-owned resources, especially factories, into their individual private property are in vulnerable industries with heavy welfare burdens. This is the case of the managers of the silk factories originally under the Zhejiang FuHua Silk Corporation. They were offered special conditions for becoming the owners of the factories. But this was still to the advantage of the state, which wanted to slough off the welfare obligations and difficulties of making a profit in a labor-intensive industry like the textile industry. Moving into export, especially export of fashion clothing, might save a few of these factories. But even this situation is precarious, as Li Linfeng admits.

Thus, the privatization of these textile factories has quite different implications from the ambiguous private/public status of Splendid China. The factories under the Zhejiang FuHua Silk Corporation have been "privatized" in the sense that they are fully responsible for their profits as well as losses—in addition to workers' welfare—without any support from the state corporation they used to rely on. They are then allowed—or forced—to find their own way toward profitizing, which is often difficult unless they are favored by the state corporation they used to be subsumed under with contracts in the commodity chain of production for foreign companies. Here, therefore, we see a revised relationship to the state, at the level of the factories. Most importantly, these privatized factories survive only by inserting themselves into the commodity chain of textile production largely controlled by the state corporation.[39]

This extended ethnographic view highlights how one corporate entity can be multiple things. I am not interested in discerning whether China has "true" capitalism because the latter comes in many forms, all of which involve the state in some manner (cf. Polanyi [1944] 2001). Moreover, these corporations, even if they are state owned, or partially state owned, are dedicated to seeking profit. Given the protean nature of privatization, it alone cannot be used as a proxy for the emergence and development of capitalism in China.

This gets us to the question of state officials' views on social inequality in China. If, as I have been arguing in this chapter, independent entrepreneurs create revisionist histories that displace their own role in the creation of social inequalities, then what of state cadres who participate in profitizing, like Li Linfeng? My conversations with Li were periodically interspersed with references to inequality. He repeatedly emphasized the need to raise the wealth of China overall and that raising China's wealth would improve everyone's lives—the official government position. This position cannot be dismissed out of hand, for it reflects a diffuse sense that the state will ensure a fairer distribution of the wealth. Li also spoke about workers' wages and the need to raise them to keep skilled workers, indirectly indicating that wages are low. On the other hand, the sloughing off of factories is the way the government can end their commitments to workers' welfare, which in the past was a means of mitigating social inequality. The third way he talked about inequality was to say that the textile industry overall was not making good profits in recent years, so they wanted to move their factories to the poor regions of China in the west. Here was an acknowledgment of poverty by region.

It is harder these days for anyone to stand up in support of the state. Li never made the kind of confident pronouncements about the government I used to hear in the 1980s. Yet Li clearly believes the state needs to be there to create wealth and that the state will make sure the underprivileged are also taken care of. Li thus retains the traces of the socialist past in the idea that the government should try to take care of its citizens. State cadres like Li have a diffuse sense of duty to the country and diffuse sense of nationalism that make them argue that profitizing is beneficial for the country and therefore, they imply, the inequalities that result are necessary, if only perhaps for a time.

Li is similar to independent entrepreneurs in another respect: both lay the principal responsibility for inequality in China at the door of global capitalism. They see China as being treated as the workshop of the world and, in that sense, like private entrepreneurs, they identify indirectly with workers. They feel China has to go through a "stage," as Li put it, of being on the bottom rungs of the ladder, and then move up and beyond this stage. Yet unlike independent entrepreneurs, Li never expressed nostalgia for the presocialist past. His comments that China still needs to raise itself up is also a continuation of what was always a nationalistic directive during the socialist era. Ideally, for government officials like Li, the state is still important for preventing the worst effects of the global economy for Chinese citizens. Moreover, Li knows full well through personal experience that inequality existed in the socialist period—even as socialist policies addressed presocialist precarities of life for a majority of Chinese citizens. The inequalities that existed under socialism were not primarily due to corruption—at least not at first—but due to the difficulties of changing historically sedimented social and economic relationships coupled with development policies pursued under socialism that favored rapid industrialization and therefore urban residents over rural citizens.[40] These policies created the rural/urban division, with its unequal distribution of resources and opportunities, that persists to this day; they fostered the emphasis on industrialization that established the horrendous working conditions for factory workers, even as the state gave workers a stable livelihood. Thus, Li compares today's social inequalities not to a period of no inequality but to one that had a different form even as its developmentalist ethos persists. His history of Hui Hua Yi/Splendid China is far from a neofeudal paean to a period in which entrepreneurs were valorized.

Where the socialist past lies for Li is obviously not exactly the same as where it lies for the independent entrepreneurs. For the latter, as I have argued, the socialist past lies in the continuity of the state officials, such as Li, the way they help their family members advance, and, most importantly, their ability to take advantage of their access to political power to become a profitable enterprise. For someone like Li, however, the socialist past lies in the nationalist pursuit of turning China into a powerful country, and the dedication of officials like him to place the good of the country as a whole before his own personal gain. The need to demonstrate that they have moved beyond the troubling aspects of the socialist past, the affective attachment to the nationalist goals of creating a China able to stand up for itself in the world of nations, and the desire to retain those infrastructural means toward profit that Li and others are convinced are essential to creating a strong economy not overrun by foreign investors (or the IMF or World Bank) have led to this blurring of private/public that is characteristic not only of the Zhejiang FuHua Silk Corporation but also of many similar entities throughout the various levels of government in China. Thus, even as they wish to signal they are leaving the socialist past behind, one can see that the historical legacies of socialist government organization have in fact led to a mixture of socialist legacies and capitalist practices.

For the perspective of those who struggle with the production of wealth and the ruins it leaves in its wake, I turn in the next section to workers in the Shanghai and Hangzhou textile factories that produce for export.

Blurring the Past, Present, and Future: Workers in the Italian Fashion Supply Chain

This last section addresses workers in factories geared toward export of Italian fashion clothing, the overwhelming majority of whom are migrants from the countryside. Multinational corporations, along with the involvement of various Chinese government agencies and independent entrepreneurs, have together produced the horrendous working conditions of today's migrant workers in China. Indeed, these transnational relations in what is conventionally called the global commodity chain are a key part of how workers experience China's current transformations.[41] The involvement of these corporations, however, is both revealed and obscured by the nature of the commodity chain, with its multiple intermediaries.

Italian fashion companies certainly participate in transnational supply chains that foster workers' difficult conditions of labor. However, it is also important to be specific about which industrial production sectors one is describing. The textile industry, in contrast to the electronics industry, for example, has a long history in China. It formed some of the initial basis of the socialist economy, providing export income, jobs, and social stability for the new socialist government, especially in urban areas. It is a labor-intensive industry that also has a well-developed domestic market. Thus, migrant workers in the textile industry can move about among different kinds of textile factories, some with working conditions that are better than others. The dyeing factories certainly deal with unhealthy chemicals; the spinning and garment factories less so. But all have both back-breaking work schedules as well as insecure working conditions. In textile factories for export, at least export of fashion clothing (in contrast to mass-produced garments), the problem is less constant overwork or even horrible factory conditions than the risk and insecurity workers face in relation to the uncertain and ever-changing schedules associated with fashion garment supply chains.

Throughout this chapter I have been arguing that those engaged in the export of Italian fashion, like many others in China, grapple with the relationship between the socialist past and the present. How they do so shapes the specificity of their encounters with Italian fashion firms. This is no less true of workers. Yet, in contrast to either independent entrepreneurs or government officials, workers blur the past with the present in their experiences of inequality, even as they do not wholly reject the socialist past. Moreover, in contrast to entrepreneurs, workers' affective engagements with temporality are not with the past but with struggling to imagine themselves as part of China's future.[42] Workers' ability to maneuver in the interstices between development and displacement is thus shaped not only by their encounters with the transnational supply chain for the Italian fashion industry and by their spatial migration but by a temporal movement as well. In the case of these migrant workers, their yearnings are for what is most hegemonic on the uncertain horizon of the future: that of becoming an entrepreneur. This dream of entrepreneurship is not just at the level of the social imaginary; it is also structured into the way in which labor in factories geared toward fashion clothing export is organized. Workers in this sector are essentially being taught to be entrepreneurial about their factory labor—to accept the risk and uncertainty as part of the very conditions of their labor. Thus, workers are treated as if they are already entrepreneurs of their own labor within the factories.[43]

The workers I discuss here worked in three different factories, each with a distinctive positioning in the transnational supply chain for Italian fashion. The first, Zhejiang New Dawn Group Ltd., has several holdings in the textile industry, including a large garment production factory in Tongxiang, an old canal town on the famous Grand Canal, located halfway between Shanghai and Hangzhou, that has been turned into an industrial zone. New Dawn Group was introduced to the Italian companies for which they produced garments through one of the Zhejiang provincial import-export corporations. The factory owner had met directly with the Italian customer, who wanted to see the conditions in the factories. The second, Style Company, a yarn spinning factory in Jiaxing, a city to the northeast of Hangzhou in Zhejiang province, was originally a joint venture between an Italian company owned by Mr. Luciano Marini and both the central Chinese and municipal Jiaxing governments. In the course of our research, Luciano Marini bought out the Chinese government partner and the factory became a wholly foreign-owned enterprise. The third is Hangzhou's Zhenfu factory, whose privatization I describe earlier in this chapter. The factory receives its production orders from the Zhejiang FuHua Silk Corporation. They do not know who their foreign customers are.

The Temporal-Spatial Past among Workers

Xiao Lan is a thin, lively worker who was thirty-seven years old when I met her in 2007. She was working in the Tongxiang garment factory for export.[44] Xiao Lan and I sat inside the Tongxiang factory offices and chatted about her life. She had grown up in Jinhua, another small town in Zhejiang province about five hours from Tongxiang. Her parents had been farmers. Her mother died when she was young and her father when she was eighteen years old. Her parents had lived in poverty, sometimes to the point of hunger. Xiao Lan came of age at the beginning of economic reform, when rural collectives were broken up, economic production devolved to the household, and rural residents could go into commerce. Xiao Lan's father opened a small store in Jinhua.

Xiao Lan has lived a life of constant movement, a narrative I heard from many workers. She, like these others, is considered a migrant worker. Xiao Lan had first worked in her hometown of Jinhua, in a factory that made clothing for export. She worked there for six years. But she worked there on and off because, as she described herself, she is someone who likes to "play" (wan).

She did not work there continuously but kept taking time off. She then moved from her hometown to the slightly larger town of Huzhou, also in Zhejiang, where she worked for one year in a factory that made high fashion women's clothing for export to Italy, Africa, and the central Asian countries surrounding China. Finally, the same year I met her, she moved to Tongxiang. In each of these towns, Xiao Lan has worked in garment factories for export. I asked how she had learned to make clothing. She said she had studied with a *shifu* (master craftsperson) for two years. That shifu had her own store. The shifu did not pay her but she helped the shifu with her business. By the time she moved to Tongxiang, Xiao Lan had been promoted to quality inspector. She walks around and checks on people's mistakes.

Xiao Lan describes herself as someone who, in addition to playing around, is also brave. By bravery, she meant she never worried about moving around from place to place and job to job. What struck me about Xiao Lan's movements, however, was not their spatial dimension but their ontological instability. Only when I asked about her plans for the future did Xiao Lan explain that in between working in the Jinhua factory, she had opened a restaurant and then a dance hall. She had the restaurant for three years. She really likes to cook. But then the owner of that building tore it down and sold the land to someone else to build a high-rise. Xiao Lan then opened a dance hall with her boyfriend, but they fought so she left. She decided to *dagong* (engage in manual labor) because it is less hassle (*mei fannao*). She would like to think about opening a restaurant again, this time in Tongxiang. Thus, she has moved back and forth between working in factories and being a small, independent entrepreneur.

Xiao Lan and other migrant workers I met do not engage in a fierce condemnation of the socialist past, as do elite entrepreneurs, but neither do they embrace it. They do not castigate the supposed lingering effects of socialism in the present nor do they imagine they are continuing a nationalist agenda. Xiao Lan's and other migrants' stories reflect a much more fluid and ambiguous sense of both continuity with and change from the socialist past.[45] Their stories are about moving away from their parents' and grandparents' memories of poverty under Maoist socialism, a poverty they experienced well into the post-Mao era. Moreover, they are moving away from the ontology of being a peasant, which has long signified backwardness and immobility (Anagnost 1997; Yan 2008).

One of the main reasons for the ambiguous sense of continuity with as well as change from the socialist past is the *hukou* system, a system of residency instituted by the socialist state in the mid-1950s that created a two-tier citizenship. Every person has a residency permit, and until recently they could only live in the area specified on their permit. This division had enormous consequences under socialism, as only urban residents got access to full social benefits and, importantly, food. The socialist state used this hukou system to pursue its developmentalist policies of urban industrialization, taking resources from the countryside to support the cities. This division still exists, in that rural migrant workers can get temporary permits to work in cities, but they do not receive any social welfare. Moreover, urban residents disdain rural migrants, accusing them of being responsible for the crime, dirt, and other social ills that plague the cities (L. Zhang 2001).

While the rural/urban division is prominent for migrant workers, as an overarching sense of division among citizens in China, these particular migrant workers have actually moved around in a circuit that, for the most part, did not include the major eastern coastal cities of Beijing, Shanghai, Guangzhou, or Shenzhen. Instead, they moved among small towns in the single province of Zhejiang—Jinhua, Huzhou, Jiaxing, Tongxiang, Wenzhou. Their discomfort in some of these towns had more to do with what they described as native-place prejudice. Xiao Lan, for example, said she was not comfortable in Huzhou, because when you did well, Huzhou people would be full of jealousy (*duji*), and if you made a mistake they would laugh at you. It is because they are *bendi* (local), she averred.

This division of rural and urban citizens is one of the key reasons that the socialist past and the postsocialist present have a more fluid and ambiguous temporal relationship for these migrant workers. If they are leaving the past behind, it is a past that spans the division. Unlike elite entrepreneurs, who insist the past should stay past though it frequently refuses to do so, for these migrant workers, it is a past whose elements, including most importantly social relations of inequality between urban and rural citizens, seamlessly blend pieces of socialism with the aftermath of socialism proper. These socialist and postsocialist elements coalesce for these migrant workers in a manner that puts off center the grand narratives of transition. They displace, as well, elites' stories about the origins of social inequality, implicating urbanites more directly in the experiences of migrant workers.

Affective Engagements with the Future

Xiao He was a young man around thirty years old when I met him in Tongxiang. He learned how to sew clothing when he was a little boy in Wenzhou, a city in southern Zhejiang province. I pressed him on this question of how he had learned to sew, since one aspect of the factories that struck me was the reentry of men into textile production.[46] In 2007 when I went into the textile factories for international export, I found that approximately 50 percent of the weavers and sewers were men. Xiao He responded to my question about learning to sew by expanding his narrative about his boyhood: when he was a little boy, he had an interest in sewing and occasionally, when he had nothing to do, he would sew a little. I asked when he started to work. His family was poor and he had a lot of brothers and sisters, so he was apprenticed out to a shifu at a young age to learn how to make clothing. This shifu had a small store. Xiao He spent one year there and together they made ordinary clothing. Then he spent another year in Shanghai with another shifu. With this second shifu he learned how to make Western clothing (*xizhuang*). I asked if there was any difference in learning how to make Western clothing. He said yes, it was hard to learn because you have to sew by hand. After that, he worked in Wenzhou for ten years in a factory that made Western men's suits for an Italian label as well as two other labels, one of which was for the domestic market.

Xiao He rose to become head of one of the factory workshops in Wenzhou. It was challenging, he said, because you have to figure out what workers are thinking, and they are not always happy. One issue workers were unhappy about was the lack of freedom (*ziyou*). I believe that by lack of freedom he meant workers were not able to move around in the factory or to come and go as they pleased. In other words, they could not be the master of their own time or movements, their quotidian temporalities. Of course, there are factory rules (*changgui*), he said, so there was nothing he could do to resolve that problem. The other issue was they want to make more money. He could do something about this. He told them if they raised the amount they were able to produce, then he could give them more money, and they were satisfied with that. He left that job and moved to Tongxiang to be with his wife, who had moved there to work in a garment factory.

Later in the afternoon, when I walked around the factory shop floor with Xiao He, I asked him why he thought men are willing to do this work. He replied, "We used to *zhongnan qingnü* [look up to men and look down on women]. That was in traditional society. But now people are freer, and they can make a choice." One might also infer that textile production is less onerous and less dangerous than construction work or other types of factory work, and therefore has attracted men.

I asked Xiao He if he had plans for the future. He said that he would like to stay in Tongxiang. He said some workers like to move around a lot, looking for better wages. But they are always unhappy. Really, he said, the wages are all about the same. This is a problem in their hearts (*xinli wenti*). I asked if he had any other plans for the future. In response, he began by saying he did not have any big ideals. He just wanted to lead a decent life (*shenghuo gaohao*). But then he added that he used to have his own shop. It was a small workshop; he worked for himself and had hired a few others. When factories had an order they needed to fill and were under pressure, they turned to these small workshops to complete the work. But it did not pan out. He would like to think about doing it again, but it is hard to save the money for that. Of course, he added, if you are someone with a lot of money, then it does not matter.

These workers' affective engagements are not with the past but with a fantasy of a future, one in which their ontology will not be that of a peasant, nor that of a migrant worker, but that of someone making a successful business on his or her own. I have often been asked why these workers put up with such horrendous working conditions. Of course, one could go a long way by answering that they have no choice. While that answer is important, it is incomplete. Workers are quite articulate about their horrible working conditions.[47] At the Tongxiang factory, workers described their working conditions to me very clearly: they get paid by piecework, and when there is work they have to work continuously, with no days off. Sometimes they even sleep by their machines, as they work overtime in twenty-four-hour cycles to finish the order for export. When there is no work, they get sent home, with no pay. They get about two days off from work each month, and often work from eight in the morning until nine at night. They work as many hours as needed to finish an order and then they get some rest time. They do not have a regular work week and they do not have regular days off. There is no guaranteed wage in factories for export that are privately owned. These working conditions in a garment factory geared toward Italian fashion export are somewhat distinct from the Jiaxing spinning factory or Hangzhou's Zhenfu fabric-weaving factory, though both also produce for export. As explained earlier in this chapter, these factories maintain the three-shift system. In the current transnational capitalist moment of commodity chain production, this shift system appears to workers to be relatively benign compared to the situation at garment production factories for export. Yet in all the factories, the inequalities of their daily work experiences are structurally visible to them, as many migrant workers have worked in three, four, or five factories. Thus, they do not blame individual factory owners but the whole factory regime.

In contrast to recent descriptions of labor protests, especially in southern China, in the lower Yangzi River delta area where we conducted our research, migrant workers mainly protested by leaving one factory for another.[48] Indeed, factory owners and managers' major complaints to me about production for export concerned the instability of their workforce. When migrant workers return to their hometowns and villages for the lunar New Year holiday, factories would typically lose about 20 percent of their workforce because workers would fail to return. Numerous factory owners have turned away from production for export and focused solely on the domestic market so that they can offer regularized working conditions and thus have less turnover.

While workers are quite clear about the depredations of their working lives, they move through this world in the hope of moving beyond it. While they have a clear critique of their labor conditions, and they often vote with their feet by leaving one factory after another, they refuse to embrace the ontology of being a worker. Under socialism, workers were touted as heroes and indeed at least for urban workers this official display of adulation did change the meaning of their demeaning factory work. But migrant workers from the countryside have never been celebrated in this way. In the post-Mao era, there is no glory in being a worker. On the contrary, workers are placed on the lowest rung of society, sometimes to be pitied, sometimes to receive some protection from the state, but mostly as those from whom others distance themselves and with whom they no longer see themselves as having any relationship. Thus, many workers included in their narratives a story about how they planned to move beyond working in a factory. Each and every worker told me how they used to have, currently have, or will have their own shop. Some had had small garment workshops like Xiao He, supplementing factory needs. But others, like Xiao Lan, opened or dreamt of opening restaurants or flower shops.

Tang Qing, from Sichuan province in the west of China, was twenty-three years old when I met her in 2008. She worked in the Jiaxing spinning factory. By that point, she had been working in several different kinds of factories for seven years. Her parents, she said, were peasants (*nongmin*) whose life was very bitter. They had only three mu of land (0.5 acres), on which they planted rice, wheat, and occasionally corn. These are staple crops that do not bring in a lot of income. Tang helps them out with the farmwork when she is home, and she also sends them as much money as she can from her wages.

She would have liked to continue in school but her parents were too poor to pay the school fees. So she began factory work. Initially, she worked in a factory near her home, but the deposit they required from workers (to try to keep them from leaving) was too expensive for her, so she left for Jiaxing. She started out in a shoe factory there, but there was too much overtime. She returned to Sichuan province but could not find work so came back to Jiaxing, where she ended up in the spinning factory.[49] Tang explained, "The work is not as tiring and we don't have to work as long. We don't have to work overtime. The wages are not so bad, but the prices of everything have gone up a lot." At the time we spoke, Tang was not yet married. She and her boyfriend planned to open a flower shop in his hometown in Jiangsu province, once they saved up enough money.

This affective engagement with a possible future in which one could have another mode of being is what pulls migrant workers through the present.[50] This dream of becoming an entrepreneur has been fostered for over a decade in both official and popular narratives. Soap operas, journalistic stories lauding successful wealthy businessmen (and they usually are men), autobiographical success stories by some of China's Fortune 500, and the CCP's decision to put its official imprimatur on entrepreneurs, admitting them to membership in the party as representatives of "the people," have conjoined to make the dream of becoming an entrepreneur the main road to self-development and seemingly the only possibility of having any future at all.[51] Indeed, there seems to be no other dream on the horizon at the moment.[52]

This alternative mode of being, however, is not just the *homo economicus* of classical economics, nor the one being lauded by the Chinese state. It is a mode of being in which migrant workers' lives and their very subjectivities are meaningful and socially validated. Thus, the quality of their desire to be moving into another way of life exceeds their existing mode of being. I have argued elsewhere that the socialist narrative of speaking bitterness engendered a desire among subalterns for a "historical imagination of overcoming" (Rofel 1999, 141)—in that case, overcoming the preliberation past by embracing the socialist present (see also Anagnost 1997). Migrant workers have developed another historical imagination of overcoming—in this case, the (harsh) present by embracing a possible future. Yan Hairong calls this an "ephemeral transcendence" (2008, 8), as most migrant workers will never be able to become entrepreneurs.[53]

There was an important exception among workers to this future-oriented affect centered on entrepreneurship: older workers who were married and had a child. Luo Ming was a thirty-five-year-old spinner at the Italian-owned Jiaxing yarn spinning factory when I met her in 2008. She was from a nearby township called Wanjiajing. Her father farmed, and her mother was a sent-down youth from Shanghai, who had stayed and was still working in a factory in Wanjiajing. Luo had been working in this spinning factory for eleven years. She was not good in school and did not like just sitting at home, so she entered the factory. Some of her friends had opened their own businesses but they had not done that well and also entered the factory. Luo had just signed a contract to become a permanent worker in the factory. When you get to be forty years old, she said, it is difficult to find work. She understood that she could retire at the age of fifty. Her husband also worked in a factory, one that made car parts. Luo pinned all her future hopes on her daughter, for whom she spent quite a bit of her wages to send her to the Youth Palace to learn how to study harder and to play the piano. She looked forward to her retirement.

Transnational Encounters

Xiao Zhan worked four years in a leather clothing factory in the town of Chongfu near Tongxiang, his hometown, before coming to the Tongxiang factory. His family had lost their land to the local government's real estate development plans. His father had subsequently opened a small shop to sell dry goods. Before working in the leather factory, Xiao Zhan had opened his own small workshop making clothing. He did not need any capital to open it; he had learned how to make clothing from his older sister and his older aunt's daughter. His workshop did well and he hired others to work for him. He ran the workshop for three years before going to work in a factory. Indeed, he still has the workshop, and his father helps look after it. He plans to expand it in the future. He only went out to do factory work, he said, because his mother wanted him to get some experience out in the world. He was twenty-eight years old when I met him.

Xiao Zhan, as with all the workers with whom I spoke, made a clear distinction between working on fashion clothing for export versus clothing for the domestic market. The former is more difficult, has a more onerous temporality, and the pay is less certain. Xiao said that with the latter, the quantity is large but the skill is not very high, while with high fashion clothing the quality is high and consequently you have to really make an effort. Making fashion clothing for export is more difficult because of the close attention to detail workers must give—how the garment is sewn, how the seam around the shoulder is put together, whether the seams are straight. Xiao He also echoed this point, noting that you cannot tear out the seam once the whole garment has been sewn; hence the importance of the job of constant inspection. Both Xiao Zhan and Xiao He emphasized that women's clothing for export was more difficult to work on than men's. The frequent changes in the styles of women's clothing require workers to continually learn how to sew new garments. Xiao He's view was that there should be a difference in pay between working on fashion clothing for export versus on what he and others called "ordinary clothing."

With fashion clothing for export, time schedules must accommodate the foreign customers' last-minute demands. Xiao Zhan stated unequivocally that the main problem he faces with this work is overtime, which is usually obligatory. Often, foreign customers only request a comparatively conservative order, and once it sells out they need a supplementary order on short notice. Alternatively, they may make last-minute changes to the design of the clothing. On those days, workers work twenty-four hours, sleeping intermittently near their machines. As Xiao Zhan averred, the foreign customer is the one who has the sole power to decide (*kehu shuole suan*). Thus, the boundary between work and nonwork time has become increasingly blurred. Indeed, to reiterate, the structure of labor in factories for export has required that workers treat their labor in an entrepreneurial manner. That is, they must take upon themselves the risks entailed with the factory's ability to make a profit. This means not only the sheer fact of employment and possible layoffs but also the way in which workers must be willing to do whatever it takes to create a commodity for export. Thus, workers go through "booms and busts" in these factories, in which they either work intensively throughout a specific time period or they have no work. In the latter periods, they also have no pay. They are "on call" to the factory owners at a moment's notice and must both find other means of survival in the interim and be ready to drop other arrangements when they are called in to work.

I asked workers which they would prefer to work on, fashion clothing for export or ordinary clothing. Most workers responded that they would prefer to work on ordinary clothing, because then they do not have to think so much about what they are doing. Xiao Zhan, in contrast, said he will work on whatever gives him food to eat, and concluded that if you cannot "eat bitterness" (*chiku*), then you cannot do this work. Xiao Zhan ironically used the primary phrase that the Communist Party had employed not only in its early organizing but also after it established the People's Republic of China (PRC), to describe the condition from which they had liberated China's masses.

Workers' transnational encounters are vivid but obviously of a different mode than those of elite entrepreneurs. Their encounters are with the materiality that links China with the Italian fashion industry, that is, the making of transnational garments. This constitutes a distinct means of encountering the foreign (cf. Rutherford 2003). The fact that Xiao Zhan's mother wanted him to "see the world" by going out to work in a garment factory for export alerts us to the importance of these encounters for migrant workers.

Since these migrant workers are also treated by urban citizens as though they are virtual foreigners, it is not entirely unreasonable to state that their transnational encounters also include their process of coming to live in China's cities. In the cities, these rural migrants learn a range of different forms of cosmopolitan knowledge they hope will help them become entrepreneurs: various forms of consumption and leisure activities (Pun 2003; Yan 2008), clothing styles, housing arrangements, as well as the temporality of labor, and various ways of making a living. Even in the more regional circuits that these particular migrant workers follow, they nonetheless learn these cosmopolitan knowledges. Often, they are moving to larger towns or cities than the ones they came from. Yan Hairong (2008) has shown how urban consumption, which signifies a modern subjectivity, is an important source of attraction for young rural women drawn to Beijing. She calls this a "mirage of modernity" (2008, 145). Pun Ngai has described how consumption is a new "technology of the self" for migrant women who desire to become modern urban subjects (2005, 157–63). While Yan insists that consumption does not resolve the contradictions these women face as marginalized workers from the countryside, Pun argues that consumption leads women away from a critique of the conditions of their exploitation.

Migrant workers also experience new modalities of inequality. Whereas in their home villages inequalities are centered on local officials, in Tongxiang, Jiaxing, Hangzhou, and other eastern coastal cities, these workers find themselves subsumed into the overarching category of the migrant. It is partially the experience of being "other" to urban and local citizens that blurs for these workers what urban elites take to be clear historical divides and thus shapes their interpretations of current social relations of inequality. Some workers attributed the disdain they experienced away from home as much to the small-town native place thinking of the citizens of Jiaxing or Hangzhou as to an "urban" experience.

Whereas elite entrepreneurs cast foreign transnational entrepreneurs in the lead role of exploiter, migrant workers link the conditions of working in an export-oriented factory to the domestic factory regime. The grueling conditions of factory work, urban and local citizens' disdain, and working for export within a local factory together shape the conditions of hardship that workers dream of leaving behind. Their stories regarding the rural life they are trying to move beyond, coupled with their imagined relationship to a possible future of becoming something beyond being a worker, provide an unstable but potent means of leading them to endure their current exploitative working conditions.[54]

Thus, to understand workers' experiences of social inequality in China today, it is important to pay attention to the specificity of their transnational engagements. While migrant workers across different kinds of industries certainly share overarching problems of exploitative and degrading working conditions, it also makes a difference exactly which kinds of working conditions they face, including the specificity of the sector in which migrant workers labor, the specific conditions of labor in the factories of that sector, as well as the materiality of the commodities they produce.

Migrant workers' interpretations of social inequalities in China thus meld together precisely what elite urban entrepreneurs keep apart—that is, the production of social inequalities through capitalism. It is precisely the commodity chain nature of their labor that makes these encounters formative in shaping how migrant workers dream about their futures. Their awareness of the various "elsewheres" that have changed life in China, their material involvement in garment production, their understandings of the challenges in this labor that gives them a modicum of pride in their ability to do it, their work rhythms, and their encounters with others within the factories shape the meaning of their own lives. Most importantly, for this generation of migrant workers, the distinctiveness of their lives when compared to those of their parents is thoroughly intertwined with that of transnational capitalism.

Conclusion

I began this chapter with the interlocking questions about where the socialist past lies, the role of transnational production in the Italian fashion industry in differentially framing how people try to leave that past behind, and the interpretations of social inequality in China today. My answer to these questions was to demonstrate the intertwined relationship of revisionist histories; affective engagements with temporality by way of history and memory; and transnational encounters, or "worlding projects," by which people construct and get pulled into a certain vision of what constitutes a meaningful world.

Elite entrepreneurs in the transnational commodity chain for the Italian fashion industry vehemently reject the socialist past even as they feel that past continues to live on in the present. They believe there should be a sharp division between then and now even as they are affectively engaged in a nostalgia for the presocialist past. Government officials engaged in import-export work do not renounce the socialist past, even as they, too, hope to leave it behind. Both of these groups utilize the infrastructure of the socialist past as well as certain practices essential for doing business in China. Migrant workers also do not renounce the socialist past, for the simple reason that the boundary between that past and the present is not a sharp one for them.[55] These three groups' engagement with history and memory moves them affectively toward either a reimagined past or a fantasy of a possible future. The one thing that seems visible on the horizon is that of becoming an entrepreneur. In contrast to elite entrepreneurs, who ironically resemble Hegelian Marxists in their belief that temporality and history should be properly linear and progressive and have a telos, these migrant workers could be seen as combining a certain Maoist approach to temporality—skipping among historical periods—with a Benjaminian view of the ruins of the past piling up at their feet. They do not embrace a telos as they face the precariousness of their futures, even as they hold out a measure of hope.

The three forces—the transnational supply chain for Italian fashion, historical legacies/revisionist histories, and affective temporal engagements—explain how each of these different groups with heterogeneous life experiences embrace and produce new modes of being in historically contingent, sometimes surprising ways. The dynamic engagement of these three forces points to the ways in which transnational encounters in the export of Italian fashion clothing structurally shape interpretations of the socialist past, even as affective engagements with the temporality of both past and future in turn shape interpretations of their current experiences.

Affective engagements with temporalities, with the past, present, and future, and with memories and revisionist histories are what compel elites and subalterns alike to reenvision the worlds they are both pulled into and create. They include embodied sensibilities that are not merely located within the individual body but also are produced in relation to others. Transnational encounters entail material encounters with the products of one's labor as well as the temporalities of foreign companies. Attention to these transnational encounters bridges the division between structural histories of socialism and capitalism, on the one hand, and the meanings people give to their labor and to the people, resources, and objects they encounter and produce, on the other. Such an approach helps us see unexpected outcomes, and articulations of multiple practices that make capitalism an ongoing process of creation and destruction rather than a singular, deterministic structure. The role that these transnational commodity chains play in the lives of migrant workers encourages us to reverse the way we approach transnational capitalism and neoliberalism, treating them not as external *context* for local enactments nor as sui generis phenomena but rather as the effects of social engagements that produce their nondeterministic systematicity.

3 Italian Legacies of Capital and Labor

Sylvia J. Yanagisako

The opening vignette in chapter 1, in which Huang Huaming vented his feelings of betrayal toward his Italian partner Rinaudo's search for another joint venture, was far from peculiar to their partnership. It merely dramatically conveyed the distrust that pervaded many of the Italian-Chinese collaborations we studied. While this distrust might appear to be the consequence of the transnational and transcultural character of these joint ventures, knowledge of the history of the Rinaudo family firm reveals quite the contrary. Like many other Italian firms that have been successful in the global fashion industry, Rinaudo's expansion into China was modeled on a system of production and distribution that it had relied on as it evolved from a provincial textile manufacturer to a global retail chain. As it moved beyond the borders of Italy, Rinaudo extended the spatial range of its supply and distribution chain and, along with it, the tensions and conflicts inherent in the complex and conflicted relations of cooperation and competition that pervaded it. It also generated new ones.

Just as Huang was wary of the potential betrayal by Rinaudo, so Rinaudo had been concerned from the start about Huang's integrity. Andrea Politi, the manager representing Rinaudo in the joint venture, explained that despite the terms of their contract, there was always the risk that Huang could be involved in "unofficial joint ventures." He knew, for example, that there were some things Huang and his wife simply did not tell him. Tension between the partners, moreover, had recently been exacerbated by Pure Elegance's creation of a new brand, TBF, which targeted a younger clientele interested in a more "international style." This meant that TBF was attempting to appeal to the same market sector as one of Rinaudo's retail chains in China. As a result, while Rinaudo and Pure Elegance had initially cooperated in arranging their location in department stores and shopping malls, they had ceased doing this as they became competitors. Information about where TBF planned to open new stores became sensitive information that Huang expected Politi to keep from Rinaudo, making what had already been a complicated and fraught relation between Politi and the Huangs increasingly tense.

This put Politi in a difficult position. While on the one hand, he was supposed to keep Rinaudo informed of what was going on in the joint venture and maximize their role in it, on the other hand, he did not want to be a spy for Rinaudo. Add to this that Rinaudo, like all the Italian firms involved in joint ventures or subcontracting relations with Chinese firms, was anxious that the latter would use the know-how gained from their collaborations to develop their own fashion collections and merchandising plans and before long go their own way. Politi reported that the only solution he had for the time being was to exercise the "sensibilities" he had acquired to manage communications between Rinaudo and Pure Elegance. The challenge, he said, was figuring out how to make the possibility of competition mutually energizing for each firm.

To complicate matters even further, Rinaudo's business strategy in China was even more complex than its collaborative-yet-competitive arrangement with Pure Elegance. The firm had inserted itself into several allied sectors and phases of the womenswear production and distribution chain in China. It not only produced its own brands but operated as a trading company and a "converter"—importing fabric for other Italian firms manufacturing in China, exporting finished garments for its own brands, and licensing the production of its own brands. Rinaudo was clearly hedging its bets to see which of these activities would be the most profitable in the long run.

In this chapter, I show how the "before China" strategies, structures, and dynamics of Rinaudo and the Italian firms in our study continue to shape their business activities in China. I highlight the histories of four firms to illustrate the ways in which the structure of industrial districts, family firm dynamics, labor conflicts, and state regulation in Italy shaped the goals, strategies, and practices of the Italian firms engaged in outsourcing, joint ventures, and other business collaborations in China. These legacies of capital, labor, and industry are key to understanding the forms of cooperation and the competition forged between the Italians and their Chinese partners.

Together with part I and chapter 5, this chapter shows that the boundary between labor and capital cannot be assumed as fixed and stable but rather is continually remade through particular historical processes. Crucial to capital-labor relations in Italian industrial districts was a fluid process through which labor could be converted into capital through the upward mobility of individuals and families. Unpaid and underpaid labor of family and relatives made possible the accumulation of profits that could be converted into capital and reinvested in productive resources (land, buildings, manufacturing equipment, hiring wage labor) in order to expand the firm. Those firms that were more successful in this expansion process could, in turn, buy the manufacturing services of smaller, less-capitalized family firms that aspired to follow the same path to upward mobility. In short, the conversion of family labor into capital was central to the dynamic structure of Italian industrial manufacturing districts.

When the larger Italian firms in this sector began outsourcing phases of the manufacturing process to China in the 1990s, they were primarily interested in China as a source of cheap labor. As Chinese consumers became increasingly important to the European fashion industry, however, Italian firms reorganized their production and distribution processes to live up to the prestige-value of "Made in Italy." As we saw in part I, this resulted in an ironic twist of the fetishism of commodities in which Italian managers appropriated the immaterial value of *Italian* commodities to constitute their own labor power and affirm the hierarchy of labor in production and distribution. At the same time, the dislocation of Italian managers to China significantly reduced opportunities for them to open new subcontracting firms in their home industrial districts. The Italian managers employed abroad in these transnational ventures enjoyed higher incomes and the benefits of a cosmopolitan lifestyle, but they lacked both family labor on which they could draw to survive the early lean years of a business and local networks to insert themselves in production chains. This has greatly impeded the processes through which Italians are able to convert labor into capital in both Italy and China, hardening the boundary between capital and labor. In chapter 5, "On Generation," the kinship dynamics that are central to the conversion of labor into capital are further spelled out.

Legacies of Expansion: The Rinaudo Production and Distribution Chain

Rinaudo's transformation from a small textile manufacturer in a rural, northern province of Italy into a global fashion business with over one thousand retail outlets has made it a much-touted model of success in the Italian fashion industry. Consumers outside Italy are unlikely to recognize the family name since, in contrast to famous families in the luxury fashion sector such as Prada, Gucci, and Versace, neither its garments nor its retail chain bear its name. In Italy, however, its ubiquitous chain of medium-priced clothing stores targeting young to middle-aged women is well known. A stroll through the central shopping district of major cities and large towns in Italy takes one past several of the firm's retail stores.

As it expanded from textiles to ready-to-wear clothing in the post–World War II era, Rinaudo located production in factories and plants in southern Italy as well as other Mediterranean countries where labor costs were significantly lower than in northern Italy. In the 1970s, it developed a number of women's clothing brands and retail chains, thus creating a fabric-to-apparel production chain in Europe. It then moved production to Eastern Europe, and by 2008 it had developed a far-flung, global network of more than three hundred subcontracted factories located in several low-wage countries, including China, Brazil, Mexico, and Turkey. The firm had also begun to buy local brands and form joint ventures with manufacturers in the same countries to which it had outsourced production. It was considering doing the same in India in 2008 but had put that on hold because of the financial crisis. As it outsourced more of its production to China and other low-wage countries, the firm closed all but five of its factories in Italy.

In China, Rinaudo initiated business in the 1980s, first by purchasing fabric and already finished garments and, subsequently, by subcontracting manufacturing to factories there. It did this at the same time that it was creating its own clothing brands. Indeed, offshore production was critical to its development as a brand and retail chain beyond the borders of Italy. By 2010 China had become the biggest manufacturer of Rinaudo clothing, producing almost half of Rinaudo's global sales. All these garments, except those made for Chinese consumption, were shipped to the company's central warehouse in Italy and from there to retail outlets in other countries. Rinaudo's plan was to eventually have most of the products manufactured in China remain there for domestic consumption, thus saving both transportation time and cost as well as avoiding import taxes. As of 2010, however, this was not yet possible because the firm's sales in China made up only 10 percent of its total global sales. Indeed, some of its stores were yet to show profits in China. Rinaudo's director of distribution in China did not view this as a problem, because the goal was to prepare for the company's future in China. On the other hand, one of the firm's owners expressed the view that even with the increase in Chinese consumption, China would probably never become its principal market. This would continue to be Italy and the rest of Europe, in spite of the increasing number of its retail stores in Japan, India, Turkey, and Brazil.

In 2004 Rinaudo decided it should move beyond subcontracting to Chinese factories and working through Chinese distributors and instead manufacture and sell its clothing in China itself. The idea, as one of the owners put it, was to produce cheaply and sell Chinese fashion to Chinese consumers. To do so, it set about developing a fabric-to-retail production chain in China, just as it had done in Italy. Because Rinaudo felt that it was too risky to go it alone in China, with all its complicated regulations, it formed two joint ventures with Chinese firms to manufacture textiles and a 50–50 joint venture in women's fashion with Huang Huaming's firm, which already had one hundred stores (it owned some of them, and others were franchises). The joint venture with Huang Huaming's firm, Pure Elegance, was created to offer a "Chinese brand with Italian flavor." Because Rinaudo's market research had shown that "Made in Italy" had strong appeal to Chinese consumers, the Italianness of the brand was touted in its retail shops despite being manufactured in China. Indeed, when I browsed in a Pure Elegance store in Shanghai, the first thing the sales clerk told me was that it was an "Italian brand."

For his part, Huang Huaming viewed the partnership with Rinaudo as a way to develop his small clothing manufacturing business into a major fashion retail chain, much as Rinaudo had done in Italy. When we first encountered Pure Elegance in 2002, it was a subcontractor for Italian clothing brands, including Rinaudo, and eager to learn about branding and marketing. Subsequently, Huang traveled to Italy to see Rinaudo's textile and clothing manufacturing and retail chain and returned impressed by its scale and level of organization. He was convinced that this was a golden opportunity to learn about fashion, management, and marketing and, consequently, to elevate the stature of his business. Just how important the prestige of being in a partnership with a well-established Italian firm was for Huang became clear when Rinaudo started looking for other Chinese partners.

The contract negotiations between Rinaudo and Huang took seven months. According to the Rinaudo managers, this was a difficult process, because the Chinese and Italians had different conceptions of a contract. The Italians expected that once they had signed a contract, they would simply adhere to the agreements in it. But, they explained, their Chinese partner changed his mind about what he wanted even after the contract was drawn up. Rinaudo's strategy in the joint venture was to relegate management of the factory to the Chinese partner. To secure their investment, however, Rinaudo placed one of their managers on the administrative board of the joint venture. His job was to assist the Chinese partner in developing a sound business plan. The idea was to allow Huang to operate the joint venture as he wished but to provide him with Rinaudo's administrative and marketing tools.

As we saw in the opening vignette in part I, after three years Pure Elegance was such a great success that Rinaudo decided to replicate this experience by forming joint ventures with other Chinese firms. They asked Massimo Soci, the Italian manager who had led the negotiations to form Pure Elegance, to find other Chinese clothing manufacturers with whom Rinaudo might collaborate. He was to identify promising Chinese manufacturers and convince them that by acquiring Italian investment capital and expertise in branding, advertising, and market positioning, their sales would expand sufficiently to make it worth their while to split half the profits with the Italian firm. This was no easy task, however, as by 2008 most Chinese manufacturers were skeptical that such a deal would benefit them. As they had become more adept at manufacturing, branding, and retailing "Western clothing," Chinese firms were no longer as impressed by what Italian firms would bring to a partnership.

That Politi, the Italian manager who represented Rinaudo in the joint venture, would compare the joint venture to a marriage was all the more fitting in this case as each of the partners was a family firm. Indeed, several of the Italian-Chinese joint ventures in our study could be viewed as transnational alliances between entrepreneurial families. Huang Huaming, after all, had worked alongside his brother and mother in the silk factory his father had opened after directing a state-run clothing factory. Huang's wife also worked in the joint venture, managing the business office, although his children were too young to be involved in the business. Not surprisingly, Rinaudo's owners and managers viewed their Chinese partner as a family firm. Politi went so far as to say it is the "custom" in China to have relatives in the firm. Rinaudo's search for additional firms with which to form joint ventures, moreover, was restricted to family businesses, because these were viewed as more trustworthy and reliable than public enterprises that were owned, even partially, by a unit of the Chinese state. Politi summed up these views of kinship, capital, and the state when he claimed, "In all aspects in studying China, I rediscover Italy—from the public administration to how you move to get ahead of everyone else. It's just as it is in Italy."

As we pointed out in the introduction to part II, and as we shall see in the chapters focused on kinship in part III, these Chinese firms and families emerged from a radically different history than that of Italian family firms. Huang's own experience of taking over the Yufei store in 1997 and his father's history of heading a collective silk clothing factory until the beginning of China's market reforms stand in stark contrast to the Rinaudo family's history of developing a small textile manufacturing firm into a global production and distribution chain based on subcontracting arrangements. Rinaudo's pursuit of multiple joint ventures and its strategy of operating simultaneously in several phases of the manufacturing and distribution chain, thereby making itself a potential competitor of its own business partners, was a legacy of their history. The source of tension and conflict that led to Huang Huaming's outburst of anger in his interview with Rofel was neither new nor peculiar to Rinaudo but, as we shall see in this chapter, one that pervaded the history of Italian family firms in the textile and clothing industry.

Legacies of Italian Industrial Districts

Industrial districts specializing in the manufacture of particular commodities are a well-documented and much-discussed feature of Italian industrial history (Frey 1975; Locke 1995; Piore and Sabel 1984). They have been widely described by economic historians and sociologists as composed of dense networks of small- to medium-sized firms, which provided the organizational structure for Italian manufacturers specializing in products ranging from wine and food to ceramics, machine tools, textiles, and electrical appliances. These networks, moreover, existed side-by-side with larger vertically integrated firms and mass production assembly lines; indeed, the two were dependent on each other. This was especially true of the manufacture of textiles, which was at the forefront of industrialization in Italy, as it has been in many countries.

From the beginning of Italian industrialization around the time of Italian unification (1866), cotton, linen, wool, and silk production were each located in specific districts in the "industrial triangle" of Milan, Turin, and Genoa.

In each of these industrial districts, small, specialized firms that engaged in one or two phases of the manufacturing process were linked in what has been variously referred to as a "decentralized," "dispersed," or "fragmented" system of production. Just as in the wool-producing district where FGS originated, throughout the silk weaving industry of Como there were few vertically integrated firms in which all phases of the production of fabric were done. The vast majority of firms engaged in only one or, at most, two phases of the production process—such as the spinning, twisting, and texturization of yarn; the dyeing, weaving, and printing of fabric; the preparation of screens for printing; and packaging and marketing. The production chain was coordinated by a "converter" firm (called an "impannatore" in Prato) that took orders from textile wholesalers and clothing manufacturers and then set the production process in motion through a series of subcontracting arrangements (Yanagisako 2002, 29). Converters were the industrial-age equivalent of merchant capitalists who, in the previous period, had organized a cottage-based system of production by providing households with the raw materials and equipment to produce yarn and fabric. As we shall see, just as the organization of the industrial production of textiles bore the legacy of the prior period of merchant capitalism, so the current era of transnational production bears the legacy of the prior period of industrial capitalism.

Even in the period between the two world wars, when the Italian fascist state protected and supported large-scale industrialization in sectors such as the chemical industry, small- and medium-sized firms accounted for the bulk of Italian manufacturing (Ginsborg 2003). This continued throughout the "Italian miracle"—the period from the end of World War II to 1973, when state-owned and state-controlled industries focused on steel, iron, and energy took off at the same time that large private companies such as Fiat employed a Fordist mass production model in the manufacture of durable consumer goods. Despite the increase in the number of workers employed in heavy industry and the mean number of workers per firm, Italian manufacturing remained rooted in small firms and light industry (Ginsborg 2003). Firms like this would also be the basis of the "Third Italy," the new industrial districts that emerged in the central and northeastern regions of the country in the 1970s (Piore and Sabel 1984).

A constant throughout these shifts in Italian industrial history has been the country's reliance on external sources of raw material, capital, and energy. This oriented Italian manufacturing toward less capital-intensive production and a focus on the manufacture and export of finished commodities. The clusters of small- and medium-sized firms in these industrial districts commonly emerged out of rural households that had pursued a mix of agriculture and commerce. The success of these spatially concentrated industries has been attributed to a number of factors, among them the low cost of property in rural areas or urban peripheries; the high levels of trust and cooperation among firms, which enabled the rapid diffusion of technological innovation; and favorable tax and labor regulations. In addition, Italian legislation has favored small firms by granting them exceptions to a number of labor regulations.

The vast majority of the small- and medium-sized firms in these industrial districts, moreover, have been owned and managed by families that could draw on unpaid or underpaid family labor, which was often crucial in the early years of the firm. The result was the formation of networks of highly specialized but flexible firms that were rooted in kinship, friendship, and local community relationships. At the same time that these firms were embedded in local production networks, they were far from isolated from transnational supply and distribution networks.

Although some northern industrial districts, such as Como's silk industry, had existed since the nineteenth century, it was only in the 1980s that they attracted considerable international attention from scholars. The economic success in the 1970s of the "Third Italy"—the central and northeast areas of the country—resulted in the lionization of their industrial districts. The flexible specialization and innovation of these firms, it was claimed, enabled them to better weather the economic challenges of the 1970s and 1980s. Indeed, scholars such as Michael Piore and Charles Sabel (1984) went so far as to claim that these Italian districts were ushering in a new period of industrialization that offered a viable alternative to Fordist mass production. Yet, as I have argued earlier (Yanagisako 2002), the rise of the "Third Italy" in the mid-1970s was hardly the first time that small- and medium-sized firms linked in local production networks had predominated in Italy.

In the 1970s, the period just prior to the outsourcing of Italian manufacturing to China, a combination of international and domestic political and economic forces led to the emergence of new industrial districts in northeastern and central Italy and to the reinvigoration of decentralized production in older industrial districts. Among these forces were the increased cost of oil in the wake of the oil crisis of the early 1970s, which led to a decline in energy-intensive mass production and increased demand for human labor, and the intense struggle between labor and capital in Italy and other countries, especially from 1969 to 1974. This led firm owners to decentralize production in order to reduce their vulnerability to labor demands and strikes. In the Como silk industry, for example, firm owners made it clear that decentralization was part of their strategy to undercut the strength of labor unions and regain control of the factory floor (Yanagisako 2002, 120). Dividing the work into separate production units and outsourcing production to small subcontracting firms increased the familial character of the firm and made it more likely that owners could manage the demands from workers. It also enabled firm owners to escape some of the most stringent national labor regulations that were passed in the 1970s.[1]

It was from this history of commodity production in specialized industrial districts of small- to medium-sized firms and the increased pressures on them in the 1970s that Rinaudo and other textile and clothing firms launched their business strategies for China.

From Textile Manufacturing to Luxury Menswear Brand

Like Rinaudo, FGS grew from a small textile manufacturing firm to a global brand and retail chain in the post–World War II era. Unlike Rinaudo, which succeeded in producing and marketing middle-market womenswear, however, FGS created a luxury menswear brand that bears its family name. Furthermore, whereas Rinaudo originated in a semirural area that was known primarily for its agricultural production, FGS came from a semirural, industrial district that specialized in the production of wool.

The FGS firm traces its origins to the textile mill founded in the early twentieth century by the great-grandfather of the youngest generation (see chapter 5 for the kinship history of the firm). Like Rinaudo, after World War II FGS expanded its textile business into clothing to create an integrated manufacturing and distribution chain, thereby increasing its profit margin. By the late 1970s, it was already well established in Italy as a leading menswear luxury brand. The firm's initial activity in China in the early 1980s was limited to purchasing raw wool from state agencies. As the market reforms in China began to be implemented, however, FGS shifted to working with emerging private firms. In the 1990s, it decided to enter into the retail market in China and opened its first store in a luxury hotel in Beijing. Over the next twenty years, it opened more than fifty stores in thirty Chinese cities.

At the firm's headquarters in Milan in 2007, Alessandro Bossi, the CEO of the firm, noted with pride that they were the first Italian luxury brand to open a retail store in China. He was especially proud of the fact they had garnered success without relying on a Hong Kong or Chinese distributor and had instead used their own employees to make their way through a labyrinth of rigid and convoluted laws and import regulations. Later, however, he added that they had hired two Japanese people to work as "explorers" to gain an understanding of the Chinese consumer and figure out how to promote the FGS brand among them. He was also proud that the firm had been bold enough to take on the risk of expanding into China, in contrast to other luxury firms that delayed entering the Chinese market because they viewed it as backward and too unpredictable. On a more humble note, he added that FGS had been fortunate because in the 1990s there were few alternatives on which Chinese consumers could spend their newly acquired money. People had not begun to buy automobiles, the housing market was not yet developed, and travel vacations were still not on Chinese consumers' minds.

By 2003 FGS viewed China as its fastest-growing market and decided to forge a joint venture with a Chinese firm. The aim of this joint venture, Vinimoon, was twofold. The explicit goal was to produce a middle-market version of FGS's menswear line for Chinese customers that was made with Italian fabric. Had they only been interested in manufacturing in China, Bossi explained, they would have created a wholly foreign-owned enterprise. They chose instead to work with an already successful Chinese clothing manufacturer rather than sap the firm's energies dealing with the complex state-private relations and regulations. However, FGS did not appear to recognize how this latter statement was inconsistent with the pride Bossi had expressed in the ability of FGS to market its retail line in China on its own.

The second goal, according to Gianfranco Naldi, the manager of the joint venture, was to prepare a factory ready to produce the FGS luxury line if and when customers were ready to buy FGS made in China. In 2007 he explained to us that Vinimoon was still relatively small in comparison to FGS's worldwide business: "It is peanuts in terms of the global sales of FGS." Hence, the joint venture's importance lay not in its volume of output but rather as a strategic asset for the expansion of FGS into China. In the future, he suggested, Vinimoon could conceivably produce a significant part of FGS's products for China. Whether this would prove feasible would depend not only on the comparative cost of manufacturing in China as opposed to Italy and other countries but in good part on whether Chinese customers were willing to buy an Italian luxury brand made in China. By 2010 it became obvious that they were not.

The formation of this partnership was hardly a new experience for FGS. It was an extension of the way in which the firm had operated in Italy by forming manufacturing partnerships with other firms. Indeed, its transnational expansion replicated the decentralized structure of production with which FGS had operated in Italy. For their part, the Cai brothers, much like the small subcontracting firms in Italian industrial districts that harbored the goal of upward mobility, sought this alliance with an internationally successful company to enable them to expand their reach beyond China. As one of the Italian managers put it, the Cai brothers had come from being welders, so they needed to ally with an Italian company. The fact that their partners were three brothers was considered a plus by FGS, which viewed them as a "family firm" like themselves.

From the beginning of the joint venture, FGS was represented by nonfamily managers whose mission was to bring a "European management structure" to China (see chapter 1 for a discussion of managers and the forging of managerial labor value). According to Bossi, "We had to teach them [the Chinese partners] everything." In order to ensure that this "European approach" to general direction, finance, management, service, and export would be implemented, the joint venture contract stipulated that FGS would appoint the general manager, chief financial officer, and planning director, while their Chinese partners, the Cai brothers, would appoint the president of the board of directors and be directly involved in managing the daily operations of the firm. The eldest Cai brother was the president of the board of directors, the second brother was the head of operations, and the third managed the modeling department. The brothers' wives also held management roles, including director of the purchasing department. In the initial years of the joint venture, FGS sent Italian technicians and technical consultants to the joint venture's factories, but by the fourth year they had left technical matters to their Chinese partners.

When the Italian general manager of the joint venture left in 2010 to take a job with another Italian luxury brand, FGS consented to having one of the Cai brothers take his position. This gave the Chinese partners a bigger voice in both operations and branding. The only remaining Italian manager, the chief financial officer, confided to us that "the last trench in the war between the Italians and Chinese [in the joint venture] is the finance office." This, he explained, "is where the last battle will be fought. If we lose control of the finance office, we lose everything." While this military metaphor signaled that a battle for control of the joint venture was underway, there were stronger indications that FGS's interest in the joint venture had diminished and that they were willingly ceding more of the management to the Cai brothers. This was evidenced by their decreasing physical presence in China. Whereas in the early years of the joint venture, Bossi family members had visited China twice a year, by 2010 they had not come for three years. Instead, they arranged a video conference for the annual meeting of the joint venture's board of directors.

The reasons for the decline in FGS's interest in the joint venture lay in the changing opportunities China offered it. By 2010 China had become the fastest-growing market for FGS's own luxury menswear line and about 10 percent of its global sales. With over seventy retail outlets and more being opened in second- and third-tier cities throughout the country, FGS's sales in China had grown phenomenally while its European and U.S. markets had declined in the wake of the 2008 financial crisis and subsequent recession. This trend was paralleled by growth in the Chinese domestic consumption of Vinimoon's output, which rose from 30 percent to 50 percent over the course of four years. At the same time, it had become increasingly clear that Chinese customers were unwilling to pay the high price of the FGS luxury brand if it was made in China.[2] As a result, FGS realized it had little to fear from competition by Vinimoon or any Chinese brand attempting to compete in the luxury menswear market. Indeed, it wanted to avoid any perception that it was manufacturing its own brand in China. As more wealthy Chinese began to travel to Europe, moreover, FGS and other European luxury brands shifted their retail strategy to selling to them in their stores in Rome, Milan, Paris, and London. The CEO of FGS predicted that there would soon be sixty million Chinese tourists traveling the globe who would be greeted by Chinese-speaking sales clerks who would also understand how to best serve them when they entered a FGS store. The firm became all the more committed to this retail strategy after 2013, as the crackdown on corruption and bribery in China increased.[3]

The willingness of FGS to cede more control of Vinimoon to the Cai brothers made sense, therefore, in light of its diversified investments in both manufacturing and distribution in China. Once it became clear that Vinimoon would not be useful for manufacturing FGS's luxury brand, FGS had less interest in controlling the manufacturing process and the final product. Even when it had initiated the joint venture with the Cai brothers, FGS had been unsure which of Vinimoon's activities would pay off the most in the long run, and so it had arranged for Vinimoon itself to engage in a diversified manufacturing strategy. When we visited Vinimoon's factory, we observed the manufacture of FGS "accessories" (for example, ties and shirts), as well as suits for other European and Chinese menswear brands. In other words, the joint venture was operating in multiple ways: as the manufacturer of its own Chinese brand, as a manufacturer of FGS accessories to be sold in both China and Europe, as a potential future manufacturer of the FGS line itself, and as a subcontractor for other Chinese and European brands, some of whom had the same target clientele as Vinimoon.[4] As in Rinaudo's case, some of these activities were potentially in competition with others. According to FGS's top manager in the joint venture, Vinimoon's production of its own label and its subcontracting work for other labels was not yet a problem in 2008 because Vinimoon's retail chain was still small (only eight stores plus a few franchises). But he acknowledged that this could become a problem if Vinimoon started to open more stores.

The Pursuit of Multiple Partnerships

The diversified manufacturing strategy of FGS, like that of Rinaudo, was far from uncommon among the Italian firms that had gone to China. Many of them were pursuing or planned to establish operations in multiple parts of the production and distribution chain through a combination of joint ventures, franchising, and subcontracting arrangements. In some cases, these various business activities were in direct competition with each other. A striking example of this was the entrepreneurial activity of Vittorio Segalini. Although in Italy he was a converter who arranged production for other brands, when we met him in 2008, Segalini was creating his own menswear brand to sell in China while simultaneously working as a consultant for Chinese brands that were in direct competition with his. His strategy of developing his menswear brand in and of itself showed Segalini to be a master at transcending contradictions. The menswear brand he had created (MB), which was named for him, was marketed as an "Italian brand" despite the fact that it had never existed in Italy but had been invented expressly for China. Segalini's plan was to design the collection in Italy and outsource the manufacturing to Chinese factories, using imported Italian fabric. Only the prototypes would be made in Italy. It would be, as his manager described it, "made in Italy made in China." To promote his brand in China, Segalini had formed a partnership with a Chinese distributor that was working with him to open a chain of MB shops, which they were marketing as a form of "Pure Italian Expression."

At the same time, Segalini had been hired as a consultant for Seripro, one of the largest producers and distributors of menswear in China. In contrast to the Italian firms, Seripro was a vertically organized company with fifteen thousand employees that produced and distributed its own brand. It also distributed European and Chinese brands. Although he spoke openly about his consulting for Seripro when we interviewed him in Milan, Segalini asked us to keep this a secret, especially from his Chinese partner in the MB brand. The reason, he explained, was because Seripro's brand was in direct competition with the MB brand he had created with his Chinese partner. Indeed, these two brands were commonly sold in close proximity to one another in Chinese shopping malls and department stores. Both brands conveyed an "Italian look," although as Segalini pointed out, "ours is really Italian."

Segalini's participation in these two activities turned out to be an even more convoluted strategy of both hedging to see which would be more profitable and, alternatively, engaging in a dual-pronged synergistic investment. Despite his entreaties to us to guard his secret of consulting for Seripro from his Chinese partner, once his manager for China was no longer working for him, she revealed that the Chinese partner knew very well what Segalini was doing. It was just that Segalini did not want to openly acknowledge that he was hedging his investment in the partnership to produce and distribute the MB brand in China. To do so would be to admit a weakness. Moreover, having a brand in his own name enhanced Segalini's credibility as a consultant for Seripro and other Chinese firms.

In spite of the performance of secrecy surrounding Segalini's entrepreneurial activities, his strategy of working simultaneously for competing businesses and brands had much in common with FGS's diversified investment in promoting its own luxury brand while at the same time manufacturing a competing brand through its joint venture in Vinimoon. Segalini and FGS, as well as Rinaudo, were pursuing a strategy of operating in, and attempting to gain control of, multiple phases of the manufacturing and distribution process without investing in a vertically integrated firm that encompassed all these phases. This had been a common strategy in Italian industrial districts throughout the twentieth century. The few large firms and all the medium-sized ones in Como's silk manufacturing district, for example, had engaged in outsourcing some of their production to subcontracting firms while at the same time maintaining some of the manufacturing phases within their own firm. The challenge was to figure out how to best balance their need for reliable and high-quality production that they could control in their own factories with reducing their risk in a volatile and ever-changing fashion market by passing it on to subcontracting firms. For their part, given the difficulty of surviving in the face of competition from other firms, including new ones that were constantly popping up, small subcontracting firms in these industrial districts frequently attempted to broaden both their clientele and the range of manufacturing services they offered (Piore and Sabel 1984, 222; Yanagisako 2002, 132). This meant they were often trying to expand into another phase of production. These expansion strategies were, at the same time, risky because they could place a subcontracting firm in direct competition with its own clients.

Legacies of Betrayal

By 2011 there were clear indications that the partnership between the FGS and Cai family was shaky despite Vinimoon's move to a sparkling new, deluxe headquarters with a showroom in Shanghai. The chief financial officer, Antonio Peroni, joked with us that he had been left by FGS as the sole Italian manager to spy on Vinimoon. Like Politi, the Italian manager in Rinaudo's joint venture, he employed a marriage metaphor to convey the tenuous state of the partnership. As he put it, "a joint venture is like a marriage; when there is a clear division of labor it works." It breaks down, however, "when the husband starts telling the wife how to arrange the house, and the wife starts telling the husband how to manage his career." The Cai-FGS marriage, he offered, was likely to end in a separation. Another FGS manager in the joint venture had earlier commented that entering into a joint venture was "like marrying a woman and then always thinking she is going out with another man."

The uneasy parallel drawn by the Italian managers between marriage and their partnerships with Chinese entrepreneurs did not consistently cast one or the other of the parties as the female or male spouse. The managers did, however, consistently juxtapose intimacy with distrust. In doing so, they echoed the irony of the purported Chinese expression "same bed, different dreams," imparted to us in Shanghai by an Italian attorney who negotiated business contracts between the Chinese and Italians. These conjugal metaphors of intimacy, suspicion, and betrayal were hardly new to the Italians doing business in China. While it might be tempting to attribute them to the intercultural misunderstandings and misperceptions pervading transnational collaborations, to do so would be to ignore their echoes of familiar tensions and conflicts that had been pervasive in Italian industrial districts throughout the twentieth century.

As I explained earlier, the strategies of survival and upward mobility of firms in Italian industrial districts entailed both expanding their range of manufacturing activities and extending their work into adjacent phases of production. By expanding the range of manufacturing services they offered their clients, subcontractors could increase their list of clients, thus decreasing their dependency on one or two firms. This, in turn, enhanced their bargaining power and reduced their vulnerability to the constantly changing fashion market. Manufacturing their own product, moreover, held out the possibility of moving from providing a service to other firms to controlling the sale of their own products and, thereby, increasing their profit margin. For a weaving firm, for example, this might entail shifting from fulfilling subcontracted weaving orders for other firms to producing their own line of fabric and selling it directly to fabric wholesalers or clothing manufacturers. For a printing firm, this might entail designing prints and proposing them to clients for particular clothing styles, thus taking on the role of a converter firm. Some firms moved into adjacent phases of production by investing in joint ventures with their clients. In light of these well-known paths of expansion and upward mobility, firms were constantly concerned that their subcontractors might steal their techniques and designs as well as their business contacts and become their competitors. In the silk industry of Como, this led to a general reluctance to share knowledge about production processes or information about clients and business contacts. Industry observers as well as the owners of larger firms attributed the suspicion and distrust pervading the small- and medium-sized firms, which made up the bulk of the silk industry, to the "closed" and "provincial" character of Como entrepreneurs.

Ambivalent relations of collaboration and competition existed not only between firms who did business with each other. They also existed within firms. In Como, aside from those who inherited their firm from their fathers, most owners of subcontracting firms began their careers working in other firms—either larger ones in which they may have risen to become technical directors or the heads of sections or small ones like the one they would eventually open themselves. These positions not only provided ambitious employees with on-the-job training but also introduced them to clients with whom they could cultivate close ties and collaborative working relations.[5] Once-trusted employees commonly left to open their own subcontracting firms, taking with them both technical knowledge and clients. In some cases, these new firm owners were partially financed by the clients of their former employer. When this occurred, employees (*dipendenti* in Italian) metamorphosed into competitors (*concorrenti* in Italian).

The betrayals in Italian industrial districts were familiar in a second sense. The overwhelming majority of firms—small, medium, and large—in Italian industrial districts were family owned and managed.[6] In the early years of their development, these family firms typically drew on the labor of family and relatives. In my study of the Como silk district, for example, nine of the fifteen subcontracting firms I studied employed relatives, especially in the early years of the firm (Yanagisako 2002, 129). Among these were a wide range of kin of both the owners and their spouses, including siblings, siblings' spouses, nephews, nieces, and cousins. Although some owners were ambivalent about hiring relatives (especially in retrospect), it had distinct advantages. Relatives could be called on to work extra hours without necessarily abiding by state labor regulations, thus increasing the flexibility of the firm and reducing labor costs. They were also viewed as being more reliable and trustworthy than other employees and so were given administrative and managerial jobs. Owners, furthermore, expected relatives to set an example of work discipline and quality standards for other workers (Yanagisako 2002, 125–31).

Despite their greater loyalty, kin were also capable of striking out on their own to start up competing firms. When this occurred, the expression "parenti/ serpenti" (relatives are like snakes) took on additional powerful meaning. The departure of relatives and even close family members to start up their own firms was commonplace in Como's silk district. The timing of these departures was often tied to critical moments in the succession of leadership of the firm. Brothers who were partners in a small firm, for example, could not bring all their children into the firm given its limited capital and productive output. Even if the sons (or, in some cases, the daughters) of the brothers could be brought to work in the firm, in the long run not all of them could be supported by the firm. Moreover, they could not all be managers or heads of the firm. Tensions and even open conflict frequently erupted when the children of more than one brother began working in the firm and competing for leadership. The smaller the firm and the less capital it had, the sooner these conflicts emerged, usually resulting in division of the firm or the departure of some of the relatives. Sons who succeeded to the leadership of the firm usually took steps to consolidate ownership and control, including by sloughing off relatives who had been working in the firm for years. The result was the estrangement of brothers, uncles, nephews, and occasionally nieces, some of whom never spoke to each other again nor acknowledged each other when they passed in the street.[7] As we shall see in chapter 5, the exodus of skilled and knowledgeable technicians and managers—both kin and non-kin—from firms was critical to the continual start-up of new firms and the reproduction of networks of production in industrial districts like Como. Trust and betrayal were, consequently, inherent to the struggles over the ownership and control of firms among people with close bonds of family and marriage.

In extending the geographic range of their decentralized production and distribution networks to China, Italian firms have drawn on some of the same strategies that generated both their success and the fraught sentiments of betrayal that pervaded industrial districts in Italy. Operating simultaneously in different phases of the production and distribution chain, sometimes in direct competition with their clients; forging multiple partnerships, some of which are in competition with each other; and sloughing off employees who were necessary in an earlier phase of the firm were all strategies and practices in which these firms engaged in both Italy and China. In other words, Italian firms brought to their transnational collaborations familiar tensions and conflicts that pervaded their home industrial districts. In China, however, their ambivalent relations of collaboration and competition, trust and betrayal have not been with family or nonfamily partners and employees but with the Chinese.

The diversified strategy pursued by firms in Italian industrial districts—of investing in multiple phases of the production and distribution chain through joint ventures, franchising, and subcontracting—was an alternative to developing a vertically integrated firm that would encompass all these phases. The goal was to gain control over these phases of production and distribution without incorporating them into the firm. As we shall see in the following section, this strategy was reinforced by political and economic events that unfolded in Italy in the late 1960s and early 1970s. Key among these was the conflict between labor and capital.

Legacies of Conflict between Labor and Capital

Luciano Ferrari's personal and career history, among those of all the Italian firm owners we studied, illuminated most clearly the legacies of Italian labor-capital relations that both set the stage for the outsourcing of manufacturing to China by Italian textile and clothing firms and shaped their investment and management strategies there. From the closing of his factory in Italy in the 1970s to his move to China in the 1980s and his subsequent formation of a joint venture in which marriage and business were intertwined, the turning points in Ferrari's life were inextricably linked to shifts in Italian industrial capitalism. His entangled entrepreneurial and conjugal history also poignantly illustrates the tensions between Italian and Chinese business partners through the most intimate of partnerships—in this case, an actual, rather than metaphorical, marriage.

Our first encounter with Luciano Ferrari, which I describe in greater detail in chapter 5, was both off-putting and revealing. While undercurrents of tension and conflict in families commonly emerged over the course of interviews with owners and managers in family firms, in Ferrari's case they were starkly displayed from the moment we met. In our first interview at his office in Milan, Ferrari had no qualms about belittling and humiliating his forty-year-old son in front of us. As uncomfortable as this display of patriarchal abuse made us feel, we also recognized that here was a man who would not hesitate to tell us what he thought. Over the several meetings in which Ferrari recounted his personal and entrepreneurial history, our appreciation of his candor grew.

Ferrari's childhood in the 1930s and early 1940s in the region of Friuli was, in his own words, one of poverty and hardship. At the end of World War II, at the age of fourteen, he left his family home and began working as a sales clerk in Milan. After a decade of employment in a variety of retail shops, he began selling lingerie. By the 1960s, he had opened his own business, including a factory that manufactured lingerie. His firm was, by his account, doing very well and at its peak employed five hundred workers. All this came to an abrupt end in the 1970s, when his business was shut down "because of labor union problems." Ferrari explained that even though he had hired ten disabled people, the union was not satisfied and wanted him to hire another ten. Having done all he felt he could to be a responsible and ethical firm owner, he was angry and deeply disillusioned when his factory was attacked by the unions and suffered millions of dollars of damage. The police did not help him, and his attempts to recover damages through the courts failed. After paying off his debts, he was bankrupt. The long and the short of it was, he recounted, "I lost everything and left for China."

Pioneering Days in China

Ferrari arrived in China in 1982 as the agent of the high-end Italian lingerie brand Meda, which had hired him to find factories that could supply finished garments that would meet their quality standards. In spite of being employed by this firm, Ferrari's account could have easily been interpreted as that of a self-employed entrepreneur. He was, in this pioneering narrative, alone in a strange land, lacking the ability to speak either Chinese or English. Children pulled the hair on his arm because he was the first man with body hair they had set eyes upon. He endured unsanitary conditions, the absence of modern conveniences (there were no hotels), and a landscape so disorienting that he was unable to return to his own residence without a written address. The hardships he faced in those early days in China recalled his childhood in Friuli, which gave him the ability to succeed in spite of them. He identified with the children, many of whom went without shoes as he had in Friuli. Just as American soldiers had given him cigarettes and chocolate in postwar Italy, so he gave Chinese children sweets and candies. His experience raising silkworms as a boy in Friuli, moreover, came in handy in his search for sources of raw silk. He discovered that while many people claimed to know how to raise silkworms and produce raw silk, they were not of sufficiently high quality, so he "had to teach them everything." He found a factory with forty workers who "didn't know how to do anything," but by evening he was able to get them to make three pieces of clothing sufficiently well. In the course of three days he disassembled and reassembled the machinery to organize the manufacturing process to his liking. After transforming the factory, he returned to Italy to rehire his "girls" (the women in Milan who had previously worked with him): "After three years by myself [and hardship] in this unfamiliar place, I calmly conquered all." Despite this imperious, and bordering on imperial, narrative, Ferrari expressed great gratitude to China for the opportunities it offered him. The generosity of the Chinese, who offered him what little they had (although not knowing what the food consisted of, he could not bring himself to eat it), led him to "fall in love" with them: "I owe everything to China. When I went to China, they [other Italians] thought I was crazy, but instead I was right. . . . I love China. It made it possible for me to start a new life. It gave me a wife and a son." As we will see in chapter 5, Ferrari's feelings about China changed dramatically once he came into conflict with his wife.

The enduring resentment Italian firm owners felt toward labor unions in Italy, especially after the 1960s, were palpable in many of our interviews. But Ferrari, whose factory had been shut down by the labor conflict, was especially critical of what he viewed as the decline of the work ethic in Italy. One of the reasons China had offered him a new opportunity, he claimed, was because in contrast to Italians, Chinese are willing to work.

When I was growing up in Italy we raised silkworms. By now in Italy nobody wants to do this. But in China, yes [they do]. The problem with Italy
is that nobody wants to work anymore. They all want to go on vacation,
and they complain about everything. The Chinese instead are willing to do
this; and they have earned millions with silk. . . . It makes me laugh when
people say that Italy is in crisis because of China. They don't work and they
blame the Chinese.

In 1987 Ferrari went from working for Meda to opening his own business.
He worked with three garment factories and a dyeing firm to provide different
phases of production for Italian and French fashion brands, including Meda.
Whereas initially he had been the agent for one firm, he became a converter
who managed the production process linking several firms. This required him
to find more factories to supply timely production, and he grew dissatisfied
with the state corporation with which he had been working. Whether or not
he was predisposed to dislike state corporations because of his experience in
Italy, Ferrari's attitude toward them was unequivocal: "The state corporations,
like everything that is run by the state, don't function."

In order to search for suppliers on his own, Ferrari decided to hire an interpreter. He found a young Chinese woman who was a teacher of Italian language, who went by the first name Maria. She had already worked for several
Italian firms, some of whom had failed to pay her on time, so she asked to be
paid in advance. Ferrari and Maria began traveling around China, selecting
the right suppliers and teaching them how to use new machines. Not long
after they began working together, they married and formed a company in
which each owned 50 percent.

By the early years of the new millennium, the Ferraris were producing
silk and polyester lingerie (plus a small amount of cashmere) for several
well-known brands, Italian department stores, and retailers. Their products
were destined for several levels of the fashion market in multiple countries:
60 percent of it went to Europe, 30 percent to the United States, and 10 percent
to Asia (China, Korea, and Japan). Some of the polyester was imported from
Italy and then mixed with silk in China. The designs for their lingerie continued to be created in the Ferrari office in Milan. So were the prototypes, which
exhibited the particular types of stitches and details that were to be followed
by the manufacturers in China. As converters previously had done in Italy, the
Ferrari firm at times followed the design and construction directions of their
clients and at times made suggestions to their clients about what garments to

produce and how. In either case, the Ferraris taught their Chinese subcontractors how to produce what they wanted. Like converter firms in Italy, they had no interest in developing a vertically integrated firm that incorporated all or most of the phases of production in textile and garment manufacturing. This would have required too much capital investment, entailed less flexibility, and made them more vulnerable to the kinds of forces that had led to the shutdown of the Ferraris' business in Italy. Following the strategy of some of the small- to medium-sized firms in production networks in Italian industrial districts, the Ferraris pursued alliances with the small firms that could conceivably become their competitors.

Same Bed, Different Dreams

It is not clear when Luciano and Maria Ferrari began to disagree about how to run the business, or how this was intertwined with other aspects of their marriage, but their key disagreements, which would eventually lead to the dissolution of their conjugal and business partnership, reveal a good deal about their different ideas and goals for the firm. First among these was their disagreement over firm strategy and its organization of the transnational production process. Maria Ferrari wanted to open factories in China and concentrate several phases of production there. Luciano Ferrari wanted the firm to continue to operate as a converter and trading company that relied on Chinese subcontractors for the manufacturing while retaining the design office in Milan. He was intent on avoiding the replication of the vulnerability he had experienced as a factory owner in Italy. Maria eventually got her way, and by 2007 they had two factories in China.

The disagreement over the organization of the production process was closely tied to the Ferraris' disagreement over the importance of design and the maintenance of the design office in Milan. While Maria felt the office in Milan was not worth the expense, Luciano argued that she simply did not understand the value of the work done there in creating designs and translating them into the manufacture of actual garments. His former manager Leonardo Benini attributed Luciano's commitment to the design office in Milan to his paternalistic attitude toward his long-term employees in the office. He had, after all, been working with these women for many years. Luciano affirmed this in describing how his "ragazze" (girls) in Milan had worked with him for forty-five years. He recounted how he had taken them in when they were babies and sent them to study cutting and sewing with designers at one of Milan's fashion schools. He railed at his wife's "Chinese mentality" of "watching only the price" and trying to cut costs by firing everyone in the Milan office and giving the job to Chinese workers. He accused her of not understanding how to treat workers with respect. In contrast, when he was forced to close the Milan office, he said he "gave" his "ragazze" to a firm that he had worked with.

As the struggle between Luciano and Maria came to a head and the likelihood of the dissolution of their marriage and business partnership grew, control of the firm's patrimony became an issue. Luciano was incensed that Maria wanted to sell the thousands of samples the firm had made over the years. He complained that she did not understand the value of these samples, which constituted a still-useful archive of the translation of design into actual garments. Her idea of opening a small store to sell them seemed to him another example of her shortsighted business strategies and her treatment of an invaluable patrimony as a mere commodity. Above all, Luciano did not want his wife to have the Ferrari name for the firm. Even though Maria had bought out his shares of the firm, he refused to give her the Ferrari name. Benini reported that Ferrari had earlier refused a buy-out offer from the number one producer of bras in the world despite being given assurances that he would be allowed to manage the firm and retain the same structure, because he did not want to sell his name. As Benini put it, "When Italians have a baby they want to keep it."

Transnational Legacies

The history of the industrial manufacture of Italian textiles and clothing belies a popular narrative in which local production and distribution expanded over time into wider geographical space to eventually attain the "global" status it enjoys today. While there has undoubtedly been an increase in the flow of capital, labor, technology, and commodities over time from the second half of the nineteenth century to the first decade of the twenty-first century, this has not entailed a historical transformation from local or even national to transnational capitalism. From its inception in the second half of the nineteenth century, the industrial production of textiles in Italy has always relied on transnational supply and distribution chains. As we mentioned in the introduction, at different times in its history German textile machinery, French dyeing, and Japanese and Chinese raw silk have been crucial to the industrial manufacture of Italian textiles. After World War II, the reliance of Italian textile and clothing manufacturers on transnational supply and distribution chains increased.

The post–World War II success of the Italian fashion industry was largely due to U.S. financing and U.S. consumption (Steele 2003), which were promoted by a U.S. foreign policy that viewed the robustness of Italy's economy as key to the battle against the spread of communism. Simona Segre Reinach's chapter shows how critical the U.S. market was to the development of Italian prêt-à-porter, which subsequently spread to markets in Europe, Japan, and now China. The formation of industrial districts in the Third Italy, likewise, was made possible by transnational chains of supply and distribution.

In the 1990s, the involvement of the Italian fashion industry in transnational supply and production chains became increasingly apparent as Italian firms outsourced phases of manufacturing overseas, especially to China. The importance of transnational distribution chains to the success of Italian fashion increased as sales in China grew rapidly in the first decade of the twenty-first century. In the face of the dramatic upswing in flows of capital, technology, commodities, and sales between Italy and China, earlier—but equally crucial—transnational flows were easily forgotten. The term *delocalizzazione*, which is used widely in Italy by both the popular press and scholars to refer to the outsourcing of manufacturing overseas beginning in the late 1980s, has tended to obscure the transnational connections that had already been integral to the Italian textile and clothing industry. Ownership and management by local families and the employment of a local labor force have been easily misread as signs of an autochthonous era of industrial capitalism. Yet even when the firms in an industrial manufacturing district were owned exclusively by local families, as was the case in Como's silk industry, they had always been reliant on transnational supply and distribution chains. What were viewed as "provincial" manufacturing industries rooted in the local networks of Italian industrial districts were, in fact, already transnational.

This was true not only of silk production in Como but of wool, cotton, and linen manufacturing in Italy. Indeed, the importation of raw material from countries around the Mediterranean was essential to the preindustrial manufacture of cotton and wool fabric as early as the twelfth century (Mazzaoui 1981, 29–30). The technology for textile production, including the spinning wheel used for wool that was taken from Spain's cotton industry (Munro 2012, 53), was also largely imported. In the industrial period, the only time Italian domestic production of raw cotton exceeded imports of raw cotton was during and immediately following the U.S. Civil War (Fenoaltea 2001, 150–51). Italian textile distribution networks, moreover, had been wide-ranging for centuries. Export was essential to the manufacture of Italian cotton, which far exceeded the needs of the domestic market and was distributed to North Africa, the Middle East, France, England, Spain, Germany, and Eastern European countries (Mazzaoui 1981, 64). The Florentine wool industry, likewise, was part of international trade that extended to Syria and Egypt in the fourteenth and fifteenth centuries until it was succeeded by the Venetian woolen industry in the sixteenth century (Munro 2012, 125, 141). By the beginning of the twentieth century, Italian wool and cotton products were being exported as far as South America (Zamagni 1993, 91).

From Silk Merchant to Industrial Manufacturer

The Marini firm, whose history I trace in this section, provides a window into the transnational links that were crucial to the Como silk industry throughout the twentieth century and that long preceded the outsourcing of production to China. The firm's evolution from importer of silk cocoons to industrial manufacturer of silk fabric—first in Como and subsequently in China—is a transnational entrepreneurial tale as much as an Italian one. Hints of this transnational history were present from the moment Simona Segre Reinach and I met with the head of the firm, Luciano Marini, in 1985. Over lunch with his wife, who herself was from a Japanese silk family, in their elegant home in the center of Milan, Marini recounted how his father had come to be a silk merchant by chance in the period between the two world wars. Both Marini's father and his father's brother had originally been cotton merchants who bought and sold cotton from North Africa. At one point, the price of silk fabric dropped precipitously because Como's silk manufacturers had driven the price down by competing with each other. Marini's father organized a meeting of sixteen of these firms that were on the brink of bankruptcy and asked them to give him the exclusive right of sales. He then managed to raise the price of silk fabric eightfold by consolidating the sales of these firms. At the same time, he imported Chinese silk yarn to sell to them as well as to his own texturization firm. His father, whom Marini characterized as a commercial genius, was able to do this because he was attuned to the world market and the supply and demand between Italy, Japan, China, Korea, and the United States.

Over the course of several subsequent meetings between 1985 and 2010, Marini filled in more of the family firm's history, always in rapid-fire monologues that commonly went on for three to four hours and into which he interwove his idiosyncratic version of Italian and Chinese political-economic history. A prominent theme in Marini's detailed narratives was his family firm's knowledge of the global market for both raw materials (cocoons, raw silk) and silk products (silk yarn and fabric), technology (new machinery, processing techniques), its position in relation to both clients and competitors in this market, and its willingness to take calculated risks based on its knowledge and position. China was central in much of this history and had been since 1957, when Luciano Marini started working in the family firm. In 1968, during the Cultural Revolution, his father fell ill, so Marini was left to deal with their Chinese suppliers. This gave him a head start in developing production in China, which was to become indispensable to the silk industry of Como.

As the eldest of three sons, Marini had been trained to take over the family firm in case his father became ill; his brothers, on the other hand, were sent to university. This lack of formal education in comparison to his brothers explained, at least in part, the glee Marini took in recounting how he outfoxed his competitors and, in one instance, even his own father-in-law. He explained how in 1972 he gained his father's respect by using his Japanese father-in-law to make a killing in the silk market. At that time, Japan was the biggest customer of Chinese silk with 70 percent of Chinese raw silk being exported to Japan. Marini convinced his father-in-law, who had a prominent Japanese silk business, to buy futures in Chinese raw silk. This led other firms in Japan to do so as well. In the meantime, Marini loaded a ship in Trieste with cocoons from the Soviet Union and Turkey. When it arrived in Yokohama, flooding the silk market, the price of silk crashed, threatening the Japanese who had invested in silk futures with bankruptcy. Marini and his father-in-law were summoned by the Japanese government to explain the grave situation, and in the end Marini agreed not to lower the price of his silk in exchange for being given an exemption to the import tax.

By 1985, Marini's firm, Jiaxing Style Silk Company, was operating as both silk merchant and silk manufacturer, supplying raw silk to Como's twisting firms, including its own twisting factory, which supplied yarn ready for weaving to Como's weaving firms. Twenty-two years later, in 2007, Marini was selling silk yarn produced by his own factory in China to fabric manufacturers in Italy, England, Germany, India, and Japan.

When we began our research on Italian-Chinese collaborations in fashion, one of the first Como entrepreneurs we were interested in was Marini because of his family firm's long-standing connections to China. Indeed, the idea for undertaking ethnographic research on China-Italy collaborations first occurred to me when I learned of Marini's dealings with Chinese exporters of raw silk while I was conducting my initial research on Como's silk firms in the 1980s. Marini sparked our interest even more when we learned that unlike all the other Italian firm owners operating in China, he actually lived there for several months each year, residing in an apartment above the factory of the firm, Jiaxing Style Silk Company, he had developed in an economic zone one hundred kilometers from Shanghai. Once we began visiting this factory and interviewing its Chinese manager, Italian technical director, and Marini himself between 2004 and 2010, the complex history of ownership and partnerships behind Jiaxing Style Silk Company became a research project in and of itself.

When it first opened in 1994, the factory was owned by a Luxembourg company (35 percent), Marini (10 percent), and the All-China Silk Corporation and the local (Jiaxing) government (55 percent together). In 2006 a Japanese company bought the shares of the All-China Silk Corporation and Jiaxing government, leaving three investors—the Luxembourg firm, Marini's firm, and the Japanese company. In 2010, however, a Hong Kong company bought out all the aforementioned companies, leaving Jiaxing Style Silk Company entirely under its control. This complex history of ownership and changing partnerships puzzled us, especially when the factory manager told us that no representatives of either the Luxembourg company or the Japanese company had ever visited the factory. The puzzle was solved—at least partially—when we learned that the Luxembourg company, the Japanese company, and the Hong Kong company had all been set up by Marini himself with the aim of optimizing his ability to deal with import, tax, and other regulations. Indeed, the silk yarn was sold through the Japanese company (which after 2010 was folded into the Hong Kong company) for tax reasons, shipped directly to Germany, and from there sold to various European countries, including Italy, Germany, and England, as well as to India and Japan.

Marini's reasons for consolidating the ownership of Jiaxing Style Silk Company in the Hong Kong company appeared to stem from two reasons. First, as he approached his seventieth birthday in 2008, he was planning to retire. As he had no children and he did not view his nephews as capable of taking over the family firm, he wanted to consolidate the different parts of Style Company to sell it as one. Second, he had little faith in the guarantees of ownership by the Chinese state and had decided it was safer to have ownership reside in a Hong Kong company rather than one in China.

Two years later, the second reason was still in play, but in spite of Marini's predictions, one of his brother's sons had reentered the firm and was doing pretty much all the administration. While he did not have the technical knowledge of Luciano Marini, this nephew was described by the factory manager as very clever and a quick learner, even though no one could, she said, replace Luciano Marini.

The development of a silk yarn manufacturing factory in China was just the latest chapter in the Marini family's history of involvement in the transnational supply and production chains linking Italy to China as well as to other locations in the global market. Delocalizzazione, for the Marini firm, meant a shift to manufacturing finished products overseas as opposed to purchasing raw materials there. As we shall see in chapter 5, this has had critical consequences for the labor-capital relation and the boundary between them.

4   One Fashion, Two Nations

Italian-Chinese Collaborations

Simona Segre Reinach

That Chinese and Italians would have different sensibilities as regards fashion was inevitable. The issue of taste and the relationship between individual and social needs underpinning the construct of a fashion system is forged out of Eurocentric fantasies that have sedimented over time and resurface in various ways in the present.[1] The resulting monolithic construct, which was clearly visible in the Chinese-Italian collaborations we studied, distinguishes between fashion and garment production, disavowing any possession by

Simona Segre Reinach is a cultural anthropologist and associate professor of fashion studies at the University of Bologna. She has published extensively on fashion from a global perspective. Her books include *Orientalismi: La moda nel mercato globale* (2006), *La moda: Un'introduzione* (2010), *Un mondo di mode* (2011), *Exhibit!* (2017), and *Fashion in Multiple China: Chinese Styles in the Transglobal Landscape* (with Wessie Ling, 2018). Her essays have appeared in the *Berg Encyclopedia of World Dress and Fashion* (2010), *The Fashion History Reader* (2010), and *Fashion Media: Past and Present* (2013). She has also curated fashion exhibitions such as *80s–90s Facing Beauties: Italian Fashion and Japanese Fashion at a Glance* (Rimini Museum 2013) and *Jungle: The Imagery of Animals in Fashion* (Torino, 2017).

the Chinese partners of the very essence of fashion—creativity—and taking for granted the Western monopoly of it.[2] These fantasies surrounding Italian fashion subsume the prerogative of beauty, aesthetic know-how, and artisan skills inherited from the Renaissance workshop into the present-day products of "Made in Italy" and the Italian way of life.[3]

It was the party secretary of Jiaxing's staff who had put us in touch with the firm Pure Elegance, knowing that we were researching Chinese companies working with Italians. The firm was not yet a joint venture but a sort of Janus-faced enterprise. It was simply described by the party secretary's staff as a "store of the Xiuzhou District Silk Corporation." Pure Elegance, as we have seen in the previous chapters, was in fact manufacturing garments for well-known Italian companies such as Giorgio Armani and Max Mara, which outsourced part of their production to China. At the same time, Pure Elegance was a successful fashion company in China with a chain of retail shops. Yet, as was the case with many of the companies in China when we began our research, it yearned for a brand identity. As soon as I met Pure Elegance's design staff, they asked for my advice about their collections. They wanted to know if their brand image and product were in line with current consumer desires in Europe and with major fashion trends. For this reason, they took me from Pure Elegance's factory in Jiaxing to a major fashion fair in Shanghai where the entire brand line was on display. They had already printed a catalog that, for all intents and purposes, presented an image very similar to that of the Italian luxury brand Max Mara. They wanted me to see the full range of the collection to ascertain if it was consistent with their brand image and to advise them on how to improve the design of the garments. I gave them my opinion but wanted to make clear that I could not give any technical advice. The fact that I was not a designer did not faze them: it was enough that I was Italian.

My experience with Pure Elegance—a Sino-Italian joint venture involving a major Italian textile and garment group, Rinaudo—was emblematic of the atmosphere that surrounded Italians in China in 2002. The period in which we conducted fieldwork (2002–10) was marked by a series of important and accelerated changes that transformed China from a country to which to outsource manufacturing into one to which to sell global fashion brands. Only six years elapsed between my first visit to the half-empty luxury mall in Shanghai's Kerry Center in 2002 and the global première in 2008 of the exhibition *Salvatore Ferragamo Evolving Legend* at Shanghai's Museum of Contemporary Art (MOCA), which celebrated the eightieth anniversary of the brand. The latter event attracted a host of celebrities from the global fashion world, attesting to the critical importance of the Chinese market. In this brief time span, Italian-Chinese collaborations in fashion went through a similar radical transformation, inciting, as we shall see, the evolution of the meaning of Italian fashion.

Italian-Chinese Collaborations in Fashion's New World Order

For most fashion theorists, global fashion is not to be read as mere brand circulation or the international expansion of Western fashion (Craik 2009; Crane 2004; Kunz and Garner 2007; Maynard 2004; Riello 2012; Riello and McNeil 2010). According to Sandra Niessen (2010), the expression "expansion of fashion" is misleading and bespeaks an ethnocentric approach. Even the global distribution of jeans and T-shirts, as Margaret Maynard (2004) has demonstrated, is far from being as uniform, widespread, and definitive as it may seem. Each choice of item from the wardrobe of the West by people in places around the world "speaking" different sartorial grammars is embedded in a local context and frame of reference. The concept of "cultural authentication," the process whereby the members of a cultural group incorporate and appropriate foreign cultural elements (Eicher and Evenson 2008), refers to the complexity surrounding the introduction and absorption of garments previously extraneous to local tradition. Fashion, like consumer patterns and advertising, "goes global" through multilocal processes and situated practices. As William Mazzarella (2003, 12) has argued, the globalization of markets occurs "in a piecemeal, contested and multifocal manner."

At the same time, fashion feeds off local sartorial grammars, transforming into fashion what was once categorized as "costume" and introducing it into international circuits of fashion production and reproduction through the mechanism of fashion cities and fashion weeks. Various forms of brand collaboration in which a number of countries are increasingly involved also contribute to these transformations (Breward and Gilbert 2006; Finnane 2008; Tu 2010). The globalization of fashion is thus a heterogeneous process structuring different forms of national subjectivity within an unstable hierarchy (Skov 2011). As noted by Patrizia Calefato (2010), fashion provides both a place of intercultural encounter and a language that is perpetually self-translating. Fashion travels both along channels of global brand communication, catwalks, and shows, and along faster-paced city streets, through exchanges and fusions of taste. This travel is not always harmonious or evenly experienced, as we have already seen in other chapters of this book. Indeed, fashion can be a site of conflict (Hansen 2004, 372). The production of fashion is also critically linked to the industrial manufacture of textile and garments and to the "relationally constituted powers" (Weller 2007, 41) of designers, entrepreneurs, workers, and managers.

China is a crucial site in which to study the conflicts and uneven experiences in fashion's new world order. The reasons for this are multiple. First, it is the country in which the majority of global fashion is manufactured. Second, its vast domestic market is of enormous commercial interest to global brands. Finally, China is very keen to make creativity a distinguishing mark of its post–market reform role in the world, and fashion is a quick route to such global recognition. Italy, small by comparison as both a manufacturer and a market, has a significant role in defining fashion's new world order. Although it is hardly the biggest investor in market transactions with China (among European countries, for example, Germany has a much more substantial role), Italy is of considerable importance in sectors such as design, fashion, and style, because of the international reputation of "Made in Italy."

Despite the myth surrounding the ancient origins of Italian fashion, which places its emergence among the aristocracy in the Italian city-states of the Renaissance, it is difficult to get a fix on an Italian fashion profile for the first half of the twentieth century. It was only from the early 1950s that Italian haute couture of Florence achieved international recognition. The result was the rise of Italian Style, associated with aristocratic elegance, but also with a simplicity of attitude, elegant fabric, and hand-crafted quality. The process of establishing prêt-à-porter (ready-to-wear) fashion in Milan began in 1972, when some fashion designers chose to move their fashion shows from Florence to Milan. It was completed in 1978 with the establishment of Modit, the organization that regulated the scheduling of Milan fashion shows. In the 1980s and 1990s, at the same time that "Made in Italy" was at its peak and was being touted as a vertically integrated system of fashion production, it also started to outsource production to low-wage countries, such as Romania and China.

The global circulation of Italian fashion in China takes various forms. Italian fashion is simultaneously a discourse, a product, and a national brand. As a discourse, it permeates the design, manufacturing, and global sale of "Italian" clothing, including those produced by Italian-Chinese collaborations. As a product, that is, actual garments and accessories, Italian fashion includes a range of objects of different provenance: items may be imported from Italy or made in China. Many, if not all, however, are hybrid products, part-Italian, part-Chinese. Italian fashion also inspires Italian-sounding brands made by non-Italian companies such as the Hong Kong brands Giordano, Bellano, Captaino, and the Swedish brand Vero Moda, all of which are sold in department stores and malls in China. Italian fashion is also an implicit component in Chinese brands produced for the Chinese market by Italian-Chinese joint ventures (see, for example, my discussion of Vinimoon and Pure Elegance and Rofel and Yanagisako's discussion of them throughout the book). For my purposes in this chapter, it is useful to identify three main forms of collaboration between the Italians and Chinese in the textile and clothing sectors: *sourcing*; *fashion production* in both its aspects, material (manufacturing) and immaterial; and *branding*, or the distribution of fashion products through the symbolic index, the brand. All three forms of collaboration were operative from 2002 to 2010. It is not a matter of one form of collaboration replacing another; quite the reverse, these forms of collaboration were superimposed on each other. Over time, however, one or another of these became the dominant focus of Italian-Chinese collaborations. This shift in focus illuminates the evolution of the relations, including the nature of conflict between the Chinese and Italians engaged in these collaborations.

Sourcing

Sourcing is a label subsuming activities that differ considerably from one another. At the same time, it conveys the principal intention behind Italy's initial move to China, namely, to track down sources of inexpensive products and labor. Individual Italians arrived in China's Yangzi delta area, the area covered by our study, by various routes and for various reasons, but were basically intent on utilizing the resources of a country with an abundance of labor, raw materials, and experience in manufacturing (see the pioneering stories in chapter 3 by Sylvia Yanagisako). The majority of these Italians were searching for manufacturers of clothing or components of clothing that were to become, through various means, "Made in Italy." This was true of Meda, the well-known brand of luxury underwear based in Bologna, which was one of the first to profit from Chinese expertise with silk hand-embroidery, for whom Luciano Ferrari was an agent. Likewise, Rinaudo, one of Italy's largest and most important clothing conglomerates (whose history is discussed by Yanagisako in her chapters in parts II and III), which later formed a joint venture with a Chinese firm, started out by purchasing silk from different producers in the late 1990s. Renato Costa was buying cotton in Canton even earlier in 1982 before moving on to silk in 1993, and Molteni, a silk firm in Como, began acquiring raw silk through an office in Hangzhou in 1996.

Sourcing requires knowledge of the territory and companies with the necessary skills to manufacture the desired products at the most competitive prices. Firms prefer to have several sources to rely upon:

> In general the best form of protection is to have a number of competing suppliers, redirecting orders where the need arises. (Gavazza in Barbieri, Gavazza, and Prodi 2011, 125)

> Rather than having a factory or several factories, we prefer to have a network of partners chosen according to the product to be manufactured: from the far north for cashmere to the south for printed Lycra. It is never a good idea to have one foot in only one door. (Elena Corti, Guanzate, 2007)

At our first meeting, Leonardo Benini, an Italian manager, showed me a map of the area around Shanghai where he had circled the location of companies that were supplying his employer, Luciano Ferrari, whose firm, in turn, supplied finished garments to Italian brands. The majority were situated in a small triangle close to Shanghai (Wuxi, Suzhou, and Wujiang) or farther south in Jiaxing. The suppliers marked on the map each had their own specialty and together constituted Ferrari's real treasure trove. Benini explained:

> Ferrari set up his underwear business fifteen years ago, working with three or four garment factories and the same number of dyers, to cover the different phases of production. To know and access these companies is the most precious factor when you're working in China. And knowing the right firm is the most difficult information to obtain. It takes years and years to create a network of firms to work with. (Leonardo Benini, Shanghai, 2002)

The Chinese, for their part, readily grasped and met the demands of individual Italian entrepreneurs, consultants, and companies, without questioning the final destination of the end product—concentrating, according to the Italians, solely on immediate profit. For Chinese and Italians alike, the goal was to manufacture a finished product. The challenge was to identify the best sources of raw material, clothes, and accessories to meet Italian demands for export to Europe. In the absence of a shared conception as to how to transform pieces of cloth into fashion, these early Italian and Chinese collaborations focused on the material properties of the commodities. It could be said that in this initial period of sourcing, the Chinese were predominantly considered allies by the Italians, albeit in an asymmetrical relation between those who are experts in the entire process and those who are said to possess only fragmentary knowledge:

> In many respects the Chinese are like us, have affections and feelings, and wish to be loyal. (Renato Costa, Rome, 2007)

> In our turn we have transmitted to [the Chinese] a way of thinking that for them was completely unknown. We taught them everything. (Alessandro Bossi, Milan, 2007)

Declarations of friendship and affection with the Chinese were in fact commonplace, although there were frequent hints of an unbridgeable distance between different worlds. While recognizing their mutual benefit, the Italians made no attempt to hide their view of their superiority. The differences in the objectives of the two parties were considered fixed in this quasi-colonial exchange. Their respective roles were in no way questioned.

According to this model of sourcing, which never completely disappeared even in later periods when the focus of collaboration shifted to the sale of commodities in situ, the two parties remain separate, constituting two discrete worlds: China is the "primitive" world of resources, and Italy is the "modern" world of refinement. This model of the division of labor between China and Italy was, in part, formed by historical developments in the Como silk industry. In the period after World War I until the 1980s, Italy relied almost exclusively on the import of raw silk from abroad and incorporated a phase of refining silk thread into the manufacturing process in Como. This past binary between the "raw" and the "refined" has become a metaphor and a lens through which Italians view the division of labor with the Chinese. Steeped in this fantasy of a discrete dichotomy between China and Italy, the entrepreneurs who were among the first to seek business opportunities in the early days of the market reforms in China tend to present themselves as pioneers. Unlike the French who went to China in a highly coordinated manner, the Italians arrived virtually one at a time. The big French luxury groups, particularly LVMH (Louis Vuitton Moet Hennessy) and PPR (Pinault Printemps-Redoute) arrived in China to manufacture and, successively, to sell their products with the help of Hong Kong intermediaries. Italian firms rarely worked in groups, and when they did these tended to be much smaller than the French conglomerates. Italian entrepreneurs sought to be autonomous and when they needed assistance turned to state agencies such as the Institute for Foreign Commerce (ICE).

Luciano Ferrari, a self-made man whose biography is recounted in Yanagisako's chapters in parts II and III, fled Italy after his company's bankruptcy, leaving behind his family and debts. He liked to represent himself as an adventurous pioneer on the trail of new opportunities in China.

> I worked for Vestro, and sourced cotton from China for Missoni. I wanted to use mother-of-pearl buttons. We were walking along the beach with my wife. She said they didn't make mother-of-pearl in China. I said, but look, the beach is full of it. So I supplied machines to the factory and we started producing mother-of-pearl buttons. (Luciano Ferrari, San Remo, 2007)

A number of other Italian entrepreneurs, who, like Luciano Ferrari, arrived in China in the early 1990s, attempted to get garments made cheaply for export under their own brand or for third parties. Others, like Renato Costa, who first arrived in China in 1976 immediately after Mao Zedong died, wanted to import exotic Chinese products into Italy. Still others, like the FGS firm that arrived in the early 1980s, were looking for precious raw cashmere. Luciano Marini, on the other hand, who founded a silk throwing and twisting factory that was initially a joint venture, was interested in importing Chinese silk into Europe. All of these early entrepreneurs characterized themselves as willing and able to take on the challenges of finding their way in unknown territory.

> I lived with the peasants, terrible food, dirt. . . . Previously they used rice as softener. They taught me and I taught them. (Luciano Ferrari, Milan, 2007)

> In April 1976, I went to China for the first time. Mao died in September. I found this strange planet, China, and fell in love with it. The factories were the local councils, and everything was done by hand. Hundreds, thousands of workers. Now they have all sorts of festivities, but then there was nothing. I remember one New Year. The workers were given a little bone—perhaps to make broth. This was their present—the equivalent of our Christmas panettone! Something new to wear every four years. The houses had broken windows and it was cold. I remember the first watermelon sold, almost on the sly, then another, then another, then everyone was selling melons on street corners. What had been suffocated inside them was born again—before this there had been only rice paddies. (Renato Costa, Rome, 2007)

In an interview in 2004, Andrea Sanna, a manager of ICE, narrated the curious case of an Italian entrepreneur who, upon returning to China after a brief absence in Italy, was unable to locate the joint venture he had opened in some obscure locale. Disoriented and lacking any points of reference, this entrepreneur came to Sanna with a desperate plea: "Help me find my joint venture!" This apocryphal tale conveys the early arriving Italian entrepreneur's experience of China as a total leap in the dark. Another recurring narrative told by early-day Italian entrepreneurs in China is that of managing to overcome dangers and endless obstacles and at the end emerging happy and victorious, having fallen in love with China.

> In Zhejiang, a peasant woman signaled where the plane should land. This was followed by eight hours of dirt roads. I looked for a hotel. There were none. I found a place to sleep in a house. Dirt, damp, mosquitoes. My childhood came to my rescue. There were children without shoes, as I had been in Friuli. The Chinese looked me over; they stared at my body hair, which they don't have. They shared the little they possessed. I fell in love with this people. I fell in love with them. They brought me food. I ate nothing at all. I couldn't eat those things. I didn't understand what was inside. Rats everywhere. I grabbed my samples and left. One Chinese always came with me. I couldn't find my house again. I walked round and round with my suitcase and my samples. Finally I saw a light and recognized it.
>
> My guide told me that in the factory there were forty people waiting for me. I went, and it was true. Forty workers who didn't know how to do anything, or did everything wrong. By the evening though I had managed to manufacture three decent garments. In three days I'd done everything I wanted to do. I transformed the factory. Disassembled and reassembled the machines to get them as I wanted them. I had one hundred people working for me. (Luciano Ferrari, San Remo, 2007)

These accounts about their early days in China conjure a somewhat embellished, but at the same time intimately experienced, past when Italian-Chinese commercial and industrial relations were developing very rapidly. Although they were recounted in interviews conducted after 2002, the accounts conveyed Italian entrepreneurs' sentiments from the eighties and early nineties, when they were discovering the China of economic reform. The emphasis on the pioneering past can be ascribed both to the Italians' eagerness to communicate their first impression of China and to the challenges of their ongoing collaborations with Chinese. Although far from wholly invented, there was certainly much that was reconstructed to compensate for the less adventurous and more problematic situations, which we shall see in the following section. The reminiscences range from the more colorful, like those above of Ferrari and Costa, to the more pragmatic, like those of Alessandro Bossi, the CEO of FGS. The difference may be due in part to the fact that the latter are not first-person experiences, though, curiously, they were recounted as if they were: "We did it all on our own. We just pulled our sleeves up. No help from either Hong Kong or the Chinese. On our own" (Alessandro Bossi, Milan, 2007).

These pioneering projects were, however, aided by a great number of inter-mediaries, assistants, and collaborators who eased the Italian entrepreneurs' entry into China. In the case of Luciano Ferrari, help came in the form of his Chinese interpreter, who then became his second wife and business partner (see Yanagisako's account in chapter 5). Meanwhile, FGS was assisted by vari-ous state officials, private entities, and, above all, by a "Swiss relative" whose company was already dealing in cashmere in China before FGS arrived. The Swiss relative's company was charged with overseeing relations with sheep farmers and buying wool for other companies as well.

Although solitude and single-handed success may be embellishments of a pioneering myth, there is an important sense in which the Italians were indeed on their own. Absent in this first adventurous phase of collaboration with the Chinese was that faithful ally, namely the "Made in Italy" concept. Though it might have been the objective, fashion was not the issue in this early phase. The claim to the "Made in Italy" national brand was simply not in play at this time. Instead, in the absence of competing claims to its immaterial values, the focus was on manufacturing the product. This may well have been because fashion was hardly a burning issue in the remote areas where sourc-ing took place. More significantly, it may be attributed to the fact that in the 1980s, "Made in Italy" had not yet become the hard currency it represented in the next decade. Although Shanghai already possessed malls and department stores in 2002, the imaginary of fashion—advertising, fashion shows, celebri-ties, models, exhibitions—had barely arrived. Global fashion brands, with few exceptions, did not arrive in China until the 1990s. Among the exceptions were Pierre Cardin, who organized his first show in 1978; Nike, which came in 1971; and Yves Saint Laurent, who arrived in 1985. Ermenegildo Zegna opened his first boutique at the Palace Hotel in Beijing in 1991, and Louis Vuitton arrived in 1992. Valentino's first trip to China followed in 1993. In 2004 Gior-gio Armani opened a boutique in Shanghai, followed by Hugo Boss, Ferré, Ungaro, Gucci, Prada, Dior, Chanel, Versace, Fendi, and many others. These global brands were first seen and sold in the friendship stores, from which Chinese customers were officially excluded, and then in luxury hotels. In the sourcing period, the rare Chinese clients of global luxury brands were far distant in status and income from those with whom the Italians collaborated.

Attachment to a pioneering phase reveals a tension in Italian-Chinese collaborations, relying as it does on a teacher-pupil relation. It is in keeping with the myth of the lone entrepreneur who arrives in the world's great factory, China, chooses his collaborators, and imparts the secret of hand-crafted fashion and with it the recipe for transforming an article of clothing into a fashion statement. In this period, global fashion brands clearly had in mind a linked strategy to create increased demand for their products, on the one hand, and to manufacture them more cheaply through overseas outsourcing, on the other. They did not, however, at this time anticipate that the countries on which they were drawing for cheap labor would become major clients of their global marketing campaign. Consequently, in this sourcing phase in China, fashion was paradoxically absent.

Fashion Production

In 2007 Sylvia Yanagisako and I interviewed Luciano Ferrari again in Milan, reconstructing his entire history in China. At one point the elderly and generally gruff entrepreneur became pensive and with a visionary gaze assured an imaginary Chinese colleague: "If you Chinese had ability, creativity, and good taste, you would own the world" (Luciano Ferrari, Milan, 2007).

Apart from underlining the link between creativity and international appeal, Ferrari's paradoxical statement both recognized and denied that the Chinese could become—indeed, had already become—dangerous rivals of Italian fashion. As manufacturing orders to Chinese factories increased in pace and intensity, fashion started to become a common objective. Beginning around 2005, opportunities for various forms of collaboration in fashion production increased. The result was a significant change in Italian-Chinese relations. Competition became even more direct when the Italians and Chinese began to produce fashion together through more stable and routinized subcontracting relations and joint ventures. The more the production of fashion became a common objective, the more the competing interests of Italian and Chinese entrepreneurs emerged. From unwitting allies, the Chinese had become witting rivals. Where sourcing was concerned, the difficulties for the Italians, as we have seen, mainly regarded coming to grips with a virtually unknown country and selecting the factories best suited for manufacturing their products. As Italian firms developed longer-term relations with Chinese factories, they increasingly counted on them to meet higher-quality demands for both Western and Asian consumption. This entailed greater involvement in the internal processes of manufacturing and a renegotiation of roles in constantly evolving domestic and global markets.

Joint ventures were the next step in these collaborations. In this phase, the Italians did everything they could to improve the quality and efficiency of production, with the long-term objective of possibly acquiring Chinese factories. As Gianfranco Naldi, the manager of the joint venture Vinimoon, stated: "We cede our know-how but in exchange we get the possibility of a well-functioning factory" (Gianfranco Naldi, Shanghai, 2010). Naldi went on to suggest that the firm might concentrate all production in China and close its sites in Mexico, Italy, Switzerland, and Spain. Another motive Italians had for forming joint ventures was to get to know the Chinese market with an eye to eventually buying out their Chinese partner. One of the siblings in an Italian conglomerate in middle-level brands explained: "My brother and cousin wanted a foothold in China because it's such an important end market. They are not interested in selling Italian-brand handbags for thousands of euro but in selling Chinese fashion to the Chinese" (Elisabetta Rinaudo, Milan, 2009).

The risk in this strategy in the long run, however, was that their Chinese partners would, as Naldi put it, "learn everything." Yet even if they went their separate ways, Naldi added, the Chinese partners would still need "Italian contacts, Italian accessories, fabrics, and models" to produce a quality product. What the Chinese said they expect to learn from these Italian companies, however, was not primarily how to produce a quality product. The reason they were handpicked by their Italian partners from among many possible candidates is, they say, because after years of working successfully as subcontractors for Western firms, they already knew how to do this work. What the Chinese expected to learn from these joint ventures was how to develop and manage a firm of growing size and complexity and how to create the required fashion collection. Huang Huaming, partner of Pure Elegance, the joint venture with Rinaudo, explained:

> We were small—not a big business at all. The requirements to become a big business are high. It is very difficult to expand. The benefits for me were that they [Rinaudo] knew fashion and management; they could train

us and advise us. I wanted us to have status in China. They could help me to do this. We negotiated for one year. (Huang Huaming, Jiaxing, 2008, interview by Rofel)

For the Chinese partner, improving quality was a necessary but insufficient step to entering the market with a successful collection. Many of the Chinese companies we studied were far from considering themselves merely factories that manufacture textiles, garments, or accessories. Rather, as Rofel's chapter in part II reveals, they were companies in search of recognition through the creativity of their brand. That the objectives of Italian and Chinese partners often diverge is no mystery to them. The vast improvement in the quality of Chinese manufacturing in a short period of time made it possible for Chinese firms to compete with a range of Italian textiles and clothing firms. As Elisabetta Rinaudo pointed out: "Our Chinese partners react and move fast." This made it increasingly difficult to claim Italian superiority in the production of fashion in China and to warrant the Italian domination of the direction of the joint venture. As one of the Italian managers of Vinimoon told us: "At Vinimoon it was difficult to figure out how to manage things, because there were issues about who had the power, who had the responsibility."

It was in this period that Italian managers emphasized Italian superiority in design, creativity, and taste. As we saw in chapter 1, among the limitations that Italian managers attributed to the Chinese was their inability to create fashion. The Italians characterized the Chinese as being good only at following orders, which is why they could only copy and imitate. Among the many complaints Italian managers had about their Chinese partners, lack of creativity was primary. The Italians also tried to maintain control over the managerial structure of the firm and major strategic decisions. The evolution of joint ventures could go only in the direction of improving the quality of manufacturing, without interfering with the Italian monopoly of management: "We firmly maintain the controls. There are Italian technicians and Chinese technicians, but chosen by us. We have appointed the financial director, the heads of marketing, control, planning, and sales. Only production is left entirely up to the Chinese partner" (Alessandro Bossi, Milan, 2007).

The slogan of the pioneering phase, "we taught and we learned," which characterized an imagined egalitarian relationship of exchange, was no longer in play. "Made in Italy," "taste," and "collections" became the new terms through which the Italians were able to continue to claim their dominance in these collaborations. The Italians can produce style because they live it: "When you look at what people are wearing you can see the difference; the Italians are used to wearing fashionable clothing so they have a feeling for style and fashion; Chinese don't have that feeling yet" (Gianfranco Naldi, Shanghai, 2010).

The lack of creativity among the Chinese and their skill at copying made them, in the eyes of their Italian collaborators, potentially dangerous rivals who would make off with fashion secrets. A story circulating among Italian entrepreneurs and functionaries of the Italian Chamber of Commerce in Shanghai in this period reaffirmed prejudices about the untrustworthiness of Chinese business partners. The story goes more or less as follows: An Italian entrepreneur involved in a joint venture in China—generally a factory—goes to Italy for a short trip. When he returns to China, he discovers to his great surprise that a company identical to his own, but entirely Chinese, has been built across the street from his firm. This Chinese firm makes products identical to his but at a lower price. Faced with this kind of competition, his only option is to close his own factory.

The demon of disloyalty emerged in the early years of the millennium, just as China entered the WTO (2001) and the Textile Agreement ceased (2008). Both of these events took place during the period of our fieldwork, and both reinforced the myth of Chinese noncreativity. However, the rivalry incited by China's WTO membership bears little relationship to the rivalry deplored by our Italian interviewees. In fact, WTO membership brought price competitiveness. Abolishing quotas meant that European and American markets had to open up to cheaper products than those hitherto allowed. This was the so-called invasion of Chinese goods in Europe and America. In the companies we studied, who were producing medium- and high-quality fashion wear, the rivalry was of a different kind. Rather than cut-throat competition, it was a matter of a shift from the sourcing model of complementary roles of suppliers and transformers of raw material to conflict over the claim to the symbolic capital of fashion production.

Branding

In 2007, five years after our first visit to China, Lisa Rofel had the opportunity to accompany Professor Jihong Hu and students from his marketing course to another Chinese company seeking to consolidate its brand, the Ming'er Dress Company Ltd. in Zhejiang province. The company was owned and managed by a young married couple. Their situation was not dissimilar to that of Pure Elegance in 2002, although the couple could only boast of a small store in Jiaxing. They were at pains to make clear to Rofel that they were not merely imitating their clients, Max Mara and Armani, whom, they said, they were supplying with silk fabric. The couple viewed their collaboration with Italian brands above all as an opportunity to expand the sales of their own brand—which they had created four years earlier—beyond China. Rofel learned that the couple worked for foreign companies mainly to learn how to make appealing clothing that they could sell abroad. They had sought professional advice to develop a brand logo that suggested the materiality of silk, and they were eager to hear Professor Hu's and his students' opinions as to its effectiveness and consistency with their brand. In her field notes, Rofel describes the packaging box as having a bright pink round logo with the character of Ming'er inside it. Two different scenes accompanied the logo. One ran along the edge of the box and included an old text and a silk fan with Chinese characters on it. This scene, Hu explained, was an image from the book *The Classics of Poetry* (*Shi Jing*). Along the bottom of the box were smudges of ink from classical Chinese paintings. Hu thought this was very beautiful, and evocative. The second scene was from a classical Chinese scroll painting of women weaving silk. Hu liked this image as well. Like many other small companies that were seeking Hu's advice about developing a brand, Ming'er was still struggling to attain a stable level of quality and an individual identity.

There were many companies that wanted Donghua University's advice on developing a brand. As usual, it was a matter of the relation between style, imitation, and brand identity. The conversation with Rofel and Hu reflected the shared concerns of these aspiring Chinese companies at the time, which was to assert their own brand identity and their independence from their foreign clients. The couple told Rofel that they did not merely copy the styles they made for Armani, because they had added to them (Rofel 2007).

As recounted at the beginning of this chapter, when we first encountered Pure Elegance in 2002, they were very interested in learning about Italian fashion. By 2003 the owner, Huang Huaming, had decided that the best and quickest way to strengthen his brand was to forge a joint venture with the Italian fashion conglomerate Rinaudo (see chapter 3 for the history of this joint venture and its tensions). Huang Huaming had gone to Italy several times to reach this agreement, and on these occasions had come to trust Rinaudo. In turn, Rinaudo had sent managers and designers to Pure Elegance. The exchange of know-how appeared to have been a great success. Since the joint

4.1 Student-designed fashion show at Donghua University, Shanghai, 2008.

venture with Rinaudo began, its sales had increased from eight million to forty-five million euros.

By the time Rofel interviewed Huang Huaming in 2008, Pure Elegance had three hundred stores in various Chinese cities, including Shanghai, Beijing, and other second- and third-tier cities, and had become one of the most important medium- to high-level brands in China aimed at the Chinese market. Unlike other joint ventures, such as Vinimoon, which Huang Huaming said had not benefited from the arrangement with its Italian partner FGS, Pure Elegance had succeeded in quickly becoming a genuine brand. In contrasting Pure Elegance with Vinimoon, Huang Huaming made a fundamental distinction between a factory and a brand. He took pains to emphasize this difference: "We are not just producing for them [Rinaudo], but we have a brand" (Huang Huaming, Jiaxing, 2008, interview by Rofel). He was well aware that Vinimoon did not manufacture clothes exclusively for the Vinimoon brand but for many other brands, which we saw on our visit to their factory. While the Italian managers of Vinimoon did not emphasize it, neither did they attempt to conceal it. It was clear that Vinimoon was acting as a subcontractor, supplying unbranded garments to well-known European brands that would attach their labels to the garments.

Yet Huang Huaming's agreement with Rinaudo had already created friction. We might not have known about this, if Lisa Rofel had not mentioned during her interview with him that she had heard from an Italian manager in the joint venture that Rinaudo was on the lookout for other joint ventures in the same sector. As recounted in chapter 2, when Rofel mentioned this, Huang Huaming exploded in anger. Clearly this was a humiliating "betrayal" for his partner to be looking for other companies with which to form joint ventures, especially in the same geographical area. Huang Huaming felt this would undermine the reputation of his business. Above all, it revealed that Rinaudo did not recognize Pure Elegance as a valuable and autonomous brand. It was as if Pure Elegance were being demoted to being just another manufacturer of garments for foreign companies—that is, a factory. In fact, another Italian firm owner, Luciano Marini, had told us that Pure Elegance was really only a production unit of Rinaudo.

Branding from the Chinese Side

The key word that has defined relations between the Chinese and Italians in fashion production in the most recent phase is certainly "brand." Already in 2002 the general manager of one of the silk corporations in Hangzhou told Rofel that their companies were trying not just to improve the quality of their silk production but also to develop "labels." He explained, "You should also be trying to develop high fashion labels of your own and not just manufacturing for Italian or other fashion companies. The more you can try to produce a high fashion design label, the better." Yet it was only after 2004 that branding became central to Chinese-Italian collaborations.

The meaning of "brand" is still a debatable question. According to Paul Manning, it is a term that "lacks any accepted analytic definition . . . as there is virtually no agreement on what brand is or means. . . . A brand is an intersection of various interested discourses between those who own it, those who produce it, and those who consume it" (2010, 33). There is consensus among scholars of branding that the greater distance a brand has from a commodity, the more it can effectively claim a style. In this period, Chinese firms were caught in the paradox of their ambition to distance themselves from commodities and the necessity of continuing to improve the quality of their production for foreign companies. They recognized that in order to break out of their role as mere subcontractors, they had to develop a brand that communicated immaterial value. Tensions surrounding branding were evident in the different dynamics observed in two of the Italian-Chinese joint ventures we studied. In the case of FGS's joint venture Vinimoon with the Cai brothers, Antonio Peroni explained that the factory of their joint venture was successful while the brand Vinimoon was not because the Chinese partner could not understand the immateriality of the brand: "It's not because they are Chinese but because they are manufacturers, and so they want to see something tangible. Whereas a brand is intangible and you can't see the result of the investment right away. The factory is making good profits but in the brand we are losing" (Antonio Peroni, Shanghai, 2010).

The reason Vinimoon was not as successful in the Chinese market as Pure Elegance, however, was because its Italian partner, FGS, had lost interest in investing in the brand. The Cai brothers, moreover, were not in as strong a position to negotiate with FGS as Pure Elegance was with Rinaudo. In the case of Vinimoon, the aim of FGS was simply to make a product that would combine the advantages of the perceived qualities of "Made in Italy" with the advantage of "Made in China," especially for the feasible costs. In addition, FGS had no interest in developing the Chinese brand because they were using Vinimoon mainly as a manufacturing unit. Rinaudo, however, which occupied an intermediate market level that was of no interest to the famous luxury brands, wanted to sell a Chinese brand with Italian flavor to the Chinese. For both Rinaudo and FGS, the Chinese brand of their joint venture was aimed exclusively at China, where a slight Italian touch was enough to make the product more attractive. In other words, the Italian partners considered their joint venture's brand a local brand for the domestic Chinese market, while the Chinese partners viewed the brand as their first step toward creating a global fashion brand with the promise of international distribution. What the Chinese hoped to acquire more rapidly from collaborations with the Italians was an international quality for their brands. It may seem a contradiction to acquire this through joint ventures because Chinese labels are produced for the Chinese market. Even a small business like Ming'er—which still did not have its own logo—saw, in the relation with foreign clients and, above all, with the Italians, the potential for a future of international sales. This was not only because "'going international' is viewed as vital for Chinese companies to acquire a massive domestic market" (Xiao Lu 2008, 191) but also because their international scope affirmed their move from the manufacturing industry to the cultural industry of fashion.

Although the Chinese in these collaborations viewed themselves as cosmopolitans (see chapter 1), if not yet sufficiently international, the Italians did not recognize this difference. Instead, they construed the production of brands—and conversely the Chinese incapability of grasping the immateriality of fashion—as relying on the cosmopolitanism of Italian fashion. What the brand expresses is the transformation of a supplier and subcontractor into a genuine producer of fashion. As symbol, fashion is subject to the same demands as other cultural practices. But because it operates in both the material and immaterial realms, designers are concerned with both the design and the production of their garments. The inseparability of the immaterial and the material is also governed by other pressures that link these supposedly separate domains. The transformation from supplier to fashion brand was clearly visible on Pure Elegance's website in 2012 when the CEO explained the necessity of being a global brand in order to expand into the markets in Macao, Taiwan, Hong Kong, and Southeast Asia. On more than one occasion, Italian firm owners and managers referred to their Chinese partners' provincialism as a problem. They mentioned, for example, that the Cai brothers and the Zhang couple did not speak English, which meant that relations with international clients of the joint ventures had to be handled by the Italians. This very lack of cosmopolitanism, which as Yanagisako points out is cited by the Italians as a Chinese problem, is what the Italians view as one of their strengths: "The only problem with our Chinese partner is that they don't speak English. Another weak point of the Chinese is that they don't really understand that a brand has to be a coherent whole. They put too many things in it" (Elisabetta Rinaudo, Milan, 2009). Interestingly enough, the Chinese say the same thing about their Italian partners, whom they find parochial and speaking poor English. Cosmopolitanism, in this instance, is usefully regarded as a polysemic word, an imaginary fetish, and a boundary object—"an object which lives in multiple social worlds and which has different identities in it" (Star and Griesemer 1989, 387). It also encapsulates the diverse desires of the Italians and the Chinese and the terrain on which their struggle takes place in this period— that is, the struggle between the Chinese aspiration to replace the materiality of production with the immateriality of the brand and the Italian wish to maintain control of the immateriality of "Made in Italy."

Branding from the Italian Side

"I don't know any brand that *isn't* made in China" (emphasis added), Leonardo Benini told us during one of the conversations we had in Shanghai. As someone who had worked with several Italian fashion firms in China over the last decade, Benini was very familiar with issues surrounding the relocation of production. His remark referred explicitly to the fact that whatever advertising claims were made about "Made in Italy" and however Italian law attempted to regulate the use of this label, outsourcing abroad would continue to be a widespread practice (Segre Reinach 2010a). Benini's statement takes on an even more interesting meaning when we consider the importance of China in the creation of Italian brands. There are various ways in which China contributes to *producing* Italian fashion. It can, for example, be an opportunity for firms that are only converters or subcontractors in Italy, supplying garments to a recognized brand, to become brands in their own right and so strengthen their market position.

Vittorio Segalini did just this. We met him in his showroom in the center of Milan, where he began by recounting his long career in fashion. He told us that like Giorgio Armani, he started off at La Rinascente department stores in the 1970s. Armani, as is well known, enjoyed extraordinary international success as a designer and entrepreneur. Segalini, on the other hand, was successful in developing a converter firm that supplied menswear clothing to various "Made in Italy" brands. In 2005 he and his Chinese partner created the Vittorio Segalini brand Pure Italian Expression in China for the Chinese market. The photos in the catalog made ample use of clichés of Italian lifestyle: Tuscan landscapes, olive oil, elegantly dressed managers in professional attire or equally elegant casual wear. By 2007 his brand could be found in malls and department stores in Beijing, Shanghai, Hangzhou, Chengdu, and several other Chinese cities. The aim of Segalini's joint venture was not to produce goods but simply to market and distribute them in China. At the same time, he developed a consultation service offering advice to Chinese brands. As his aide Monica Campani explained: "Having a brand gives him more credibility to consult about style in the Chinese market for consultancies" (Monica Campani, Milan, 2009). Meanwhile, in Italy, Segalini continued his work as a converter.

Marco Azzali (Gruppo Forall) is also an Italian brand made in China for the Chinese market. Another was created by Renato Costa, a Roman businessman who imported into Italy unbranded garments in silk, cashmere, and cotton made in China by a joint venture company of which he was a minority partner. In 1989, after some years of success, he decided to make it into the brand Affinity. Affinity then became Vela, a brand with many outlets in Italy. From being an importer of unbranded products in silk, cashmere, and cotton that were resold with low profit margins, it became a middle-level brand and retailer in Italy.

Another way in which China contributes to the identity of Italian brands is through negotiations to obtain a suitable location in department stores. The image and prestige of brands derive from both the neighboring brands and the floor of the department stores. Brand position in Europe can easily be overturned in China, given Chinese consumers' relative lack of familiarity with what can be called the European "luxury map": "So many international brands have entered the market that the Chinese have problems recognizing the status brand hierarchy. While some European and American brands are well known, most are not. This results in what we would think of as incongruous placements of brands" (Welters and Mead 2012, 30).

The fame of international brands in China derives from their entry into the Chinese fashion market in the 1980s. Until very recently, writes Juanjuan Wu (2009), the Chinese did not distinguish between American brands of sportswear, which were the first to enter China in the 1980s, and the luxury European ones.

> Brand names were too vague a concept for most Chinese to connect with company image or meaning. . . . But the effective ad campaigns and promotional events of global brands started to make wearers aware of the hierarchy of brand names, which were differentiated not only by price but also by brand image. It was only then that the Chinese consumers separated casual brands from luxury brands like Louis Vuitton, Armani, YSL, Prada, Chanel, Burberry, Gucci, Versace, and Hugo Boss. (J. Wu 2009, 168–71)

In China, far and away the most significant element for creating brand image is distribution. "Brand" and "retail" are terms that are, for the most part, interchangeable and, in any case, closely linked. The contribution of the Chinese in obtaining the desired position in malls or department stores is vital. It is the Chinese "developer" who negotiates where a brand will be located. Global luxury brands use established Chinese distributors who are often from Hong Kong and often powerful enough to require the formation of a joint venture as a condition of receiving their services. A case in point is Salvatore Ferragamo's joint venture with ImagineX.

Cai Farong, who had worked in real estate for several years, mentioned that luxury brands have to re-create their map in China. Before he opened his own firm, he had worked on a project to construct in Hangzhou a street inspired by Milan's via Montenapoleone and New York's Park Avenue. His first port of call was Prada, which would participate only on condition that a precise list of twenty other luxury brands, including Armani, Zegna, and Ferragamo, would be on the street. "No Kentucky Fried Chicken" was the clear message (Cai Farong, Hangzhou, April 9, 2008). Likewise Bulgari, an Italian luxury brand in the watch and jewelry sector, could count on a thick web of relations to position it in department stores among the other big names that are its peers, even though it had not long been in China. Gianfranco Naldi, the manager of Bulgari in China, said that while retail in China is difficult, "if the brand is very well known, then it is not difficult, at least in the most important cities. Sometimes it's the builders (of the malls) who come looking for me, as anywhere Bulgari opens, Zegna, Vuitton, and all the others open too, so they all have to be there." Most of the Italian brands in China, however, cannot count on the fame of brands such as Bulgari, Armani, and Prada. For brands with less symbolic capital, the relation with the Chinese developer requires lengthy negotiation. As Timothy Coghlan maintains:

> For developers, the leasing process for a luxury mall in China takes from 18 months to three years on average to complete. Creating an appropriate trade mix in a mall where all brands are satisfied with their locations and neighbors is a complicated and arduous affair. Each brand has very strong opinions of where they belong and which brands they should and shouldn't be next to. It's like creating a seating plan for a wedding, only much, much, harder. (Coghlan 2012)

Unlike the French luxury brands that have organized themselves in large multinationals, the Italian brands are often small- or medium-sized family businesses (Segre Reinach 2005). These brands are very different from the mythologized creative superiority of "Made in Italy." They consist of many different small companies that are looking to China for an opportunity to develop in ways that they cannot in Europe. If they are expensive but not well-known luxury brands, it is a struggle for them to avoid being confused with less prestigious ones. If they are in the medium-low level market, they struggle to acquire their desired position in China by making the right choices in distribution and communication. Collaborating with a Chinese developer is vital for this kind of company. Without this, it is difficult to win "a place in the sun." If a brand's initial place is not a prestigious one, moreover, it is very difficult to recover. In the words of Silvana Salvianti, general manager of the Italian brand Reporter: "At the level of positioning if there are problems in the department stores, it's difficult to reposition yourself afterward on the basis of choices you made and the change in the market. You're there and you stay there" (Silvana Salvianti, Shanghai 2008).

Successful collaboration with the Chinese developers, who are sometimes called facilitators, also determines the success of the brand. Franco Mollona, whom Rinaudo put in charge of opening stores for the Targa brand without using the services of Chinese facilitators, had the target of opening ten new stores a year. Targa is an Italian brand, made in various parts of the world where labor costs are lower, which targets a young clientele in the medium-low level of the market. It is competing with local Chinese labels and foreign fast-fashion brands, such as Only, Vero Moda, and others. It is not able to count on advertising investment and cannot use Chinese distributors directly. The decision to "go it alone" imposed by Rinaudo left Mollona with a difficult job. According to him:

> Being in China is not easy for a company. You waste a year, perhaps two, and companies leave. In our sector only the large groups remain: FGS, Rinaudo. China is big, but it's a big prison. If they want to close your store, they'll do it straightaway. They look at the labels, these guards turn up . . . they're scary, they force you to close without reason. Every test costs 10,000 yuan. I've done two or three now, they give me the OK. But it's just a formality, for two or three products. They always need this paperwork. Obstructionism. But the department stores now don't let us open if we don't have a quality test that isn't even required by law. I follow international standards. But they don't let us open. So I have to do these tests, which cost money. (Franco Mollona, Shanghai, 2007)

Finally, due to its role as the "workshop of the world," China plays an important role in consolidating "minor" Italian fashion. Many Chinese companies manufacturing garments for all brands, large and small, famous and little-known, become a repository for ideas and solutions to production problems. Knowing them is a way of discovering the latest trends, the newest processes, and quickly adding them to one's own collection. In an interview with Splendid China, a Chinese manufacturer for Italian fashion companies, the manager's assistant explained to Rofel how it was not only the owners of large international brands who visited them. In addition, little-known Italian designers came to view the factory's production of internationally known Italian brands to "get ideas," pick up tips, and often simply to copy, perhaps altering a detail, in order to gain access to the international elite of brands.

These designers like to come here because they like to go to the factories and have a look at what the others are doing. Then they can copy what the others are doing. These designers are not the most famous. They are not from Milan, at the top. They are middle level. They do not make clothing tailored for one person. If the garment has already been on the market in Europe, then it is OK for them to copy. But if it is a "sample," then we tell them to be careful. We do talk with our customers, and tell them to be careful about what they see. Some of the highest-level clothing has this issue in the contract. Meda, for example—we make lingerie for them. They write in the contract that it can't be copied. But with the middle-level production, there is not so much conflict. They copy a detail, a pocket or a sleeve style. (Luo Huayan, Hangzhou, 2008)

For most Italian brands, then, the Chinese market provides an opportunity to create, develop, and increase the value of a brand. Depending on strategic choices and negotiations, it can also result in losing the value of a brand.

Italian Fashion Now

Since the end of the 1990s, Italian fashion has been suffering from a profound identity crisis (Mora 2009), which has undermined its very foundations in the alliance between *stilismo* and large-scale industrial manufacturing: "The prospect is serious, it's undeniable: many actually consider the life cycle of the 'Made in Italy' label to be over" (Corbellini and Saviolo 2004, 137).

During the golden years of "Made in Italy," fashion research moved in parallel with experimental manufacturing technology made possible by industrial districts (see chapter 3 regarding Italian industrial districts). As Emanuela Mora writes (2009), the innovative and dynamic charge of "Made in Italy" has become entrenched and almost stagnant in its famous brands, including the new generation of the 1980s and 1990s (Dolce and Gabbana, Roberto Cavalli, Miuccia Prada, etc.) that were its offspring. From the 1990s onward these famous brands no longer searched for new sources of inspiration in experiments in fabric and techniques of manufacturing. Instead, they concentrated their creative energies on marketing by developing lines of accessories, often produced under license in China. Fast fashion further extended the market, which was once exclusively Italian prêt-à-porter. The family origins of Italian companies, which had been an advantage in the 1970s and 1980s, allowing the necessary flexibility for experimenting with new production processes, began to inhibit development and prevent stock market quotation of Italian brands. In terms of production, beginning in the later 1990s, the integrated production chain in Italy represented only a minimal part of Italian fashion production. The manufacture of fashion abroad (particularly in China and Romania), the extension of the consumer "catchment area," and the entry of finance into the fashion industry modified the character of "Made in Italy." This marked a radical move from the profile it had acquired between the 1950s and 1980s. According to Miuccia Prada:

> "Made in Italy" is no longer enough: it's a retro concept that can only partly add to a product's success. Plus there's the impression abroad that the country's whole system is on the wane, and has fewer resources, less vitality, less money. If a country loses its edge, its attraction, fashion goes elsewhere, looks for something better, where it knows it can flaunt success in front of all the people who count. (Aspesi 2012)

The entry of finance into fashion, as we know, created the phenomenon of luxury brands.

> The pull of luxury is proposed as a transcultural concept: the luxury brand can be sold to everyone and the luxury market has gone global (Louis Vuitton bags and wallets are bought and sold practically everywhere). The dimensions of this market are considerable: in 2004 the turnover was estimated at some 40 billion euro with a more than 10 percent increase per year. Italy, on the strength of the success of its stylists and its prêt-à-porter, covers approximately one-third of the luxury sector. (Riello 2012, 153)

Financial investment has become a new differentiator among the big fashion brands, which have enormous capital to invest in communication. According to Sonnet Stanfill, "the survival of Italian fashion companies in the twenty-first century is not just a question of geographic authenticity but also one of finance" (2014, 28). Although Italian fashion companies largely remained family owned, they had to compete with a more complex system known as the luxury industry in which French conglomerates, such as LVMH and Kering, were major actors. Despite the prominence of Italian luxury brands, moreover, Italy has no luxury conglomerate of any prominence. The top two luxury conglomerates are French and the third is Swiss. Today many industry observers insist that Italy is undergoing a creativity crisis and while its level of production remains high at the luxury level, it is put to completely different purposes. Miuccia Prada comments:

> Italy is the top producer of excellence, including for the French and other international markets, but with the sales of our luxury brands, our whole fashion system risks being relegated to the second division, having probably been the very top, and transforming our workforce and our companies into subsidiary, third-party producers, albeit of quality. When brands cross borders [i.e., are bought by conglomerates], all the praise and glamour and fame and vital decisions go to someone else, and we are ignored and downgraded. And already the great creators coming from the most important schools have started to snub us and choose Paris instead. (Aspesi 2012)

The purchase of Italian brands by the big luxury groups is still ongoing. In 2001 Bottega Veneta was bought by Gucci, which is itself part of the French group Kering. Kering handed off the brand relaunch to Tomas Mayer, a German designer living in the United States. Only the actual manufacture remains Italian—in Vicenza, its historic place of origin. The Vicenza factory, which uses the distinctive technique of *intrecciato* for which Bottega Veneta is known, is its only manufacturing site. Sergio Rossi's shoe manufacturing company also belongs to Kering, as does Brioni, a luxury menswear brand. In other words, the globalization of "Made in Italy" dismantled the original fashion production model that created its success.

If the first two characteristic elements of Italian fashion, the 1950s fashion boutique and the 1980s prêt-à-porter, were principally backed and endorsed by the United States, in the present phase China has become the main interlocutor of Italian fashion. Statements on the importance of China to European fashion are heard every day. "If you don't get [China], I think you go backward," the CEO of FGS told a Chinese newspaper. The chief designer of FGS agreed: "Milan is where we were born and Shanghai is where our future lies."[4]

What the Chinese partners in the Italian-Chinese joint ventures want from their Italian partners is precisely the international dimension that Italy has gained by sacrificing localization, product specificity, and the power to act autonomously in the international markets. This localization was the key to Italian fashion's initial success, which it is now seeking to reconstruct in China. In Florentia Village, the luxury discount outlet created in 2011 in Wuqing, the Italian stereotype reaches its most spectacular form. Its shopping streets include all the great architectural symbols of Italian Renaissance cities:

Venice's narrow streets, the Tower of Pisa, Florence Cathedral, Bernini's fountains in Rome, and the Colosseum. Among the many symbols of an Italy synonymous with craftsmanship, taste, pleasure, and lifestyle is the restaurant Bella Vita, with hints at the famous "dolce vita." Modeling the clothes on sale in the shops are full-scale reproductions of Michelangelo's David and Botticelli's Venus. Italian fashion, as we have seen, however, no longer corresponds to the image it projects of itself in China: a contemporary whole, drawing on its romanticized origins (the Renaissance of the small artisan's shop) and on the period (between the 1950s and the 1980s) when "Made in Italy" took on shape and identity. As the entrepreneur Renato Costa lamented, "The artisan's golden hands are lost forever."

Renato Costa's misplaced nostalgia obscures the historical fact that it was precisely the move beyond the artisan phase that allowed Italian fashion to become "Made in Italy." Yet this yearning for the handmade is crucial to the "Made in Italy" mythology. Luigi Maramotti from Max Mara, a pioneer in industrially produced clothing, clearly feels the need to defend the industrial origins of Italian fashion success: "I believe that reality and creativity go very well together," said Mr. Maramotti, who has another mission: to sing the praises of a fine factory-made product in an era when "handcraft" has become a catchphrase for luxury. "We are in luxury but not afraid to show industrial elements," he continued. "I want to show people that 'handmade' does not necessarily become quality" (Menkes 2011).

Italians today are indeed artisans in the shop window rather than artisans in the workshop. After appearing in Salvatore Ferragamo's sixtieth anniversary celebration at MOCA in Shanghai, the shoemakers went on to the Triennale Design Museum in Milan, where they met with the same huge public success, no doubt thanks to their performance in Shanghai. The belated re-evocation of an ersatz "Made in Italy" has obscured the true state of an Italian fashion that is in search of a new identity in the global context. Rather than the export of Italian fashion to China, the very identity of Italian fashion has been resituated in China's global fashion. Whether this will lead to the relocation of high-end fashion production in Italy remains to be seen. What is evident is that the European luxury map has not been merely superimposed on China. Rather, along with "Made in Italy," it is a continually evolving, complex cultural construct that is reconfiguring the dynamics of fashion production, distribution, and consumption.

III Kinship and Transnational Capitalism

As inconspicuous as it appears at times, kinship pervades the Chinese-Italian business collaborations in our study. The two chapters in this section reveal the centrality of kinship in the transnational relations through which the Chinese and Italians in our study generate and transform material, personal, and social resources in their pursuit of financial gain. They demonstrate that conversions among financial, cultural, and social capital are not only crucial to the reproduction of social class, as Pierre Bourdieu (1984) argued, but that kinship is an inextricable part of these processes. Given the very different historical legacies that brought the Chinese and Italians to their transnational collaborations in textiles and apparel, the forms and values through which relations of kinship and capital have played out are not the same. Neither are the ways in which Chinese and Italians construe the proper connections between kinship, profit-making enterprises, and the state. These differences include how they define a "family firm" and whether they identify their businesses as such. As we shall see, the absence of a universal definition of "family firm" or "family business" in both scholarly and popular parlance contributes to the variation in Italian and Chinese usages of these terms. Yet much more than the lack of a standard definition lies behind this variation. More significant are the different political and social connotations and implications attached to the nexus of family, business, and state. Where Italian entrepreneurs tout the family ownership and management of firms as a sign of stability, authenticity and trustworthiness, Chinese entrepreneurs struggle with it as an index of corruption.

In spite of these differences in Chinese and Italian conceptions and valuations of links between kinship and profit-seeking enterprises, their transnational collaborations challenge models of capitalist modernity that purport the separation of kinship and economy. As both of the following chapters show, the aspirations, sentiments, and practices of both the Italians and the Chinese engaged in these transnational enterprises are shaped by crosscutting currents of kinship. Yanagisako (2013) has noted that kinship rarely makes more than a fleeting appearance in both popular and scholarly models of transnational capitalism, global capitalism, and postindustrial society. She points out that if it appears at all, it is commonly as a metonym for the distinctive local cultures that are being transformed into standardized sites of capitalist production and consumption. Both neoliberal celebrations of the global triumph of capitalism and antiglobalization critiques of its dehumanizing consequences tend to portray capitalism as a relentless and overpowering force that converts actors with culturally specific goals, including kinship, into universal rational actors driven solely by the pursuit of profit and accumulation.

Once central to anthropological models of social structure, kinship fell to the margins of theory as anthropology broadened the scope of its inquiry to include modern capitalist societies. Having turned our attention to what we viewed as the future of cultural and social transformation rather than its past, anthropologists too readily embraced social theories of modernity that posited a decline in the importance of kinship as its functions were taken over by other institutions such as the corporation, the market, the judiciary, and the state. Our once powerful engagement with kinship turned quickly into neglect. As Susan McKinnon (2013) has pointed out, there has been a puzzling absence of both studies of and theorizing about the constitutive power of kinship and marriage in the literature on transnationalism and globalization.[1] Our lack of curiosity about the connections between kinship and corporations, for example, persists despite the fact that many leading corporations in the U.S. and elsewhere are both publicly traded and family corporations.

An unintended consequence of the inattention to kinship in research on transnational economic ventures is the endowment of capitalism with reproductive powers independent of kinship sentiments and bonds (Yanagisako 2013). In this account, firm owners, investors, and professional managers emerge as rational seekers of profit in corporate capitalism. Family businesses, in contrast, are treated as archaic survivals of an earlier stage of capitalism. As is the case in social evolutionary models, a narrative of lag discounts and marginalizes social forms that diverge from the "modern firm," which is construed as a multiunit, professionally managed corporation in which ownership is separated from control (Chandler 1980; Daems 1980). The thesis of the inexorable decline in the significance of kinship and its displacement by modern institutions of governance and an unfettered, rational market is allied to a functionalist theory of the inefficiency of economic action fettered by sentimental (and thereby irrational) bonds of kinship rather than focused exclusively on the rational pursuit of profit. The mixing of kinship and the state, on the other hand, undermines the rational institutions of governance and leads to corruption.

This model of modern capitalism persists despite overwhelming evidence of the prevalence of family business in a wide swath of societies around the world. There are, admittedly, serious limitations to the comparative data and analysis of family firms since there is no standard definition of a "family firm" among scholars and researchers.[2] Problems of definition aside, the data demonstrate without a doubt that family ownership and control of firms prevail in Europe as well as in other regions of the world. In Italy, at the turn of the twentieth century, family firms constituted 75–95 percent of all registered firms.[3] Italy is by no means an outlier in Europe. The comparable percentages were 70–80 percent in Spain, 75 percent in the United Kingdom, more than 90 percent in Sweden, 85 percent in Switzerland, and 80 percent in Germany (Colli, Pérez, and Rose 2003; Neubauer and Lank 1998, 10). Family firms, moreover, prevail not only among small- and medium-sized businesses but also large businesses (Colli 2003, 16). In Italy, almost 50 percent of the top one hundred corporations are family controlled, and family ownership prevails at all levels, sectors, and dimensions of business.[4] At the end of his history of family business in the U.S. and Europe from 1850 to 2000, Colli (2003) concludes that the family firm is not merely a "transient state on the way to more developed and sophisticated organizational forms." Rather, it has proved to be resilient and capable of adapting to rapid shifts and changes in the market (Colli 2003, 65).

Celebrations and Denials of Kinship

Yanagisako's chapter in part III shows that kinship has been a key productive force in Italian industrial districts such as Como and is no less so after two decades of outsourcing manufacturing to China and other countries in spite of the contraction of the industry. Indeed, kinship is so central to Italian firms that rather than categorize them as a type of "business" or "economic" enterprise whose persistence can be explained by assessing their profitability, she argues for treating them as kinship enterprises whose persistence is rooted in their pursuit of kinship sentiments and commitments. These kinship enterprises are projects whose goals and strategies are constantly being reassessed and reformulated by people who construe themselves to be connected by bonds of relatedness and whose relations are shaped by a dense assemblage of beliefs, sentiments, and commitments attached to these bonds.

Yanagisako focuses on the interplay between two interlinked but different processes of generation that are critical to understanding both the histories of individual family firms and the historical persistence of family firms in Italy. These include, first, the generation of new family firms, and second, the succession of generations in family firms. The sentiments, tensions, conflicts, and uncertainties that emerge in the period of transition from one generation to the next are simultaneously forces for the demise of firms and the creation of new ones. Family firms that end in the second or third generation because of disagreements or lack of sufficient capital to incorporate the next generation frequently spawn new family firms as fractions of the family hive off to initiate their own firms. Other family firms are constantly being created by enterprising technicians and managers who have gained invaluable experience and social contacts through their employment.

The transnational expansion of the Italian textile and clothing industry has had different consequences for these two crucial processes of generation and, consequently, for family firms in Italy. On the one hand, transnational expansion has reinforced the succession of generations in those family firms that have successfully expanded production and distribution to China—whether by outsourcing manufacturing to Chinese factories, opening their own factories in China, forging joint ventures with Chinese firms, setting up distribution chains in China for their products, or some combination of these activities. Although there have been increasing opportunities for nonfamily managers in these firms, this has not brought about a "managerial revolution" in which professionally trained, nonfamily managers have taken control of the firm. To the contrary, increased profits and capital accumulation have enabled these firms to incorporate more generations and branches of the family and, consequently, to postpone division of the patrimony.

On the other hand, transnational outsourcing has severely undermined the generation of new family firms in industrial districts such as Como. The number of medium and small firms that once serviced the manufacturing needs of larger firms in industrial districts such as Como has been drastically reduced as larger firms have sent manufacturing phases overseas, thus reducing their need for local subcontractors. Hence, the very success of expansionary family firms in relocating manufacturing to China and other low-wage countries has undermined the generation of new subcontracting family firms in their home industrial districts. This has made it much more difficult for managers and technicians in Como and other industrial districts to open their own firms, which had been a key path of social mobility. Kinship continues to be central to those family firms that have not expanded transnationally, including management succession, tensions, and conflicts over the division of property, the dissolution of bonds, and the demise of firms. Whether they have downsized or closed, reinvested in new firms, or shifted their investments to enable the next generation to move into the professions, kinship has been central in the conversion of capital.

The celebration of the family origins and character of Italian family firms as signs of authenticity, integrity, and distinction brings in sharp relief the ambiguity and ambivalence regarding the family character of Chinese firms. While Chinese firm owners asserted to their Italian partners and collaborators that they are family firms, they vehemently denied this to Rofel and others. Some justified the family character of their firms by pointing out that this facilitated their working with prominent Italian family firms in the fashion industry, and, indeed, Italian firm owners and managers confirmed that they feel more confident working with Chinese family firms than with state-owned enterprises (although, as Rofel's chapter reveals, the distinction between these is not as clear as they may assume). Key to this ambiguity and ambivalence among the Chinese are concerns about the corruption indexed by family involvement in business enterprises.

While Rofel's chapter in part II reveals how largely the socialist past looms in the ways in which Chinese firm owners, managers, and workers view their current profit-seeking projects, her chapter in part III demonstrates how critical it is to the ways in which they construe the relations among family, business, and the state. As she shows, many seemingly private firms are in fact complex private/public business enterprises. Because profit-making enterprises in China developed out of a history of socialism and continue to be supported by, and in many cases are a part of, the state, the boundary between private and public enterprise is blurred. Even those that are viewed as models of privatization are situated within what Rofel calls pyramid schemes, in which small firms nestle themselves within state-owned import-export companies. The involvement of family members in firms that have developed out of formerly state-run enterprises treads dangerously closely to prohibited connections between family and state. Indeed, a "family firm" is easily read as a sign of corruption. Hence, Chinese firms either deny that they are family firms or deny that they have evolved out of state-run enterprises. Sensitivities and anxieties about the corruption of family involvement in business can taint even family firms that originated within the market economy. People from various positions both within and without the commodity chain of fashion clothing told cautionary tales of family involvement in companies.

Whether intergenerational succession of ownership and management of Chinese firms of the sort that prevails among Italian family firms will emerge in China remains to be seen. After all, the shift to the market economy in China is recent enough that the children of firm owners are too young for any emergent pattern to be discernible. The taint of corruption associated with family firms may be a serious impediment, but there are also indications that parents may try to have their children succeed them. The cultural mediator/translator for Vinimoon, for example, has brought his eldest daughter into the small family firm he has established, in part because her fluency in English is vital for their work with foreign firms. There are also father-son successions. One is Pure Elegance, in which the current owner, Huang Huaming, took over the firm from his father, though at that time it was not a "family firm" but had only recently been converted from a collective neighborhood factory into a private one. Similarly, the son of the former manager-then-owner of Zhenfu factory inherited the factory when his father died suddenly. The board of directors appointed him, though he was ill-suited to the job. Neither of these two latter examples clearly delineate "family firm" succession, though they do indicate family succession.

Kinship ties are also central to the recruitment of managerial personnel in Chinese firms. While Italian firm owners hire and groom their own children for succession, in China, at least up until now, the children of government cadres are frequently hired in managerial positions where they can be instrumental in helping the firm.

States of Exception

Given the promotion of profit-making enterprises by the Chinese state, family firms that are not linked to state officials are commonly viewed as cultural exceptions in need of explanation. A frequent explanation of family firms in China is that they are the product of exceptional regional cultures. Wenzhou, a city in the southern part of coastal Zhejiang province, is held up as the quintessential exception. The "Wenzhou model of development" is based on small family firms as opposed to the "Shanghai model," which is based on government investment. At the same time, it is said to require a specific kind of entrepreneurial actor—namely, a "Wenzhou person," who is characterized as having a different psychological attitude, different philosophy, and perhaps even a different genetic makeup than other people in China. As demonstrated by the Cai brothers, who comprise the Chinese side of the joint venture Vinimoon with FGS, however, the Wenzhou model of development can still be driven by family conflicts and animosities that challenge the success of entrepreneurial projects.

The exceptional character of the "Wenzhou person" resonates with the way Italian entrepreneurs describe themselves in contrast to the Chinese in general. As we saw in the first section of the book, Italian firm owners and managers fault their Chinese partners and workers for depending too much on the state and lacking in risk-taking entrepreneurial creativity. Like the "Wenzhou person," moreover, Italian firm owners view themselves as self-made men whose success was built on their own hard work, inventiveness, and innovation, even as they may have drawn on the help of family members. This self-image is displayed even by firm owners who took over firms that had been handed on to them by their fathers—thus conjuring up the seeming oxymoron of the second-generation self-made man (Yanagisako 2002). Whether Chinese or Italian, however, the ideal type of the entrepreneurial person and the ideal type of the entrepreneurial family play out in more tension-ridden relations and ambivalence in the actual cases we recount.

Wenzhou as an exception reveals the historically variable meaning of "corruption" and "immorality" of economic practices in China. In the early 1980s, Wenzhou's "special characteristics" were targeted in anticorruption campaigns against speculation and profiteering. After 1984, however, when central officials in favor of greater economic reform gained power, these characteristics were promoted. Aside from a brief hiatus after the Tiananmen protests of 1989, they have continued to be promoted in China. Depending on whether they emerged through the privatization of state resources or developed independently of the state, family firms may be held up as models of deviant or proper behavior. The various privatization stories recounted by Rofel convey not only anxiety about the family/state connection and corruption but reveal that there are multiple routes to creating firms. The variable judgment of family involvement in business, moreover, reveals a fundamental paradox. In China it is taken for granted that one should help family members to advance. Yet in the context of the market economy and inequality in people's means to help their children, accusations of corruption are deployed to account for the different outcomes of children. In short, talk of family as corruption is at the same time talk of hierarchy and inequality and debate about the particular kinds of inequalities that have emerged in the shift to a market economy. This talk does not reject the existence of hierarchies in favor of radical egalitarianism. Rather, discourses about family, business, and state are about legitimating certain hierarchies and delegitimating others.

The Italian families engaged in these transnational collaborations are concerned about different challenges arising from the dominant model of capitalist modernity and the separation of kinship, economy, and the state. Their sense of vulnerability lies less in the link between kinship and the state and more in the link between kinship and business and the supposed inefficiencies the mixing of sentiment and rationality is purported to bring. The loyalties and commitments among family members and the difficulties of succession have been criticized for decades by business schools and consultants in Italy who have been influenced by ideologies of capitalist modernity that have been dominant in U.S. business schools. Yet, given the predominance of family firms in Italy, the funding they have provided to business schools, and their hiring of business consultants, the argument that family and business do not mix well is much less dominant in Italy than in the United States.

In China, too, concerns about being viewed as inefficient or not sufficiently geared toward making a profit also fuel denials that one's firm is a family firm. The Zhejiang New Dawn Group Ltd. that Rofel discusses in her chapter is one such example. Portraying himself as a self-made man, the firm owner, Zhang Hualiang, told Rofel unequivocally that he had no family in his firm. But several of his staff casually complained to her about the family members working in the company. Zhang's denial, while perhaps technically correct in that his family members did not share ownership with him, reveals the anxiety about being viewed as a firm that does not make profit its primary and overriding concern. Again, however, this connection of family firm and inefficiency contains echoes of the concern with corruption.

Concerns about the corruption entailed in connections between family and the state, of course, are also present in Italy as in China. It is, after all, widely recognized in Italy that wealthy capitalist families such as Agnelli, Pirelli, Falck, and others have been powerful in shaping the state and its policies. In the twentieth century, the strong ties between the Italian state, banks, and family-controlled joint-stock companies were especially pronounced in heavy industry, including iron and steel (Colli, Pérez, and Rose 2003, 50). The formation of the Istituto di Ricostruzione Industriale (IRI) as a publicly owned holding company in 1933 meant that the state has controlled a considerable part of big business in capital-intensive industries since the interwar period. The textile and clothing manufacturing sector, however, has had considerably less involvement with the state. Indeed, Italian firm owners in this sector pride themselves on operating independently of the state.

Finally, the chapters in part III reveal that while the possibilities for starting new textile and clothing firms in Italy have decreased, they have expanded in China. Yanagisako's chapter describes the rare cases in which Italian managers and technicians working in China have developed the kinship and friendship networks that make it possible for them to start new firms there. The rest of their colleagues with desires for social mobility plan to move up through the ranks of their employer's business rather than strike out on their own. Isolated from the kinship resources in their home districts, these transplanted Italians have little hope of following the path of class mobility that had been more open to their predecessors. It is among the Chinese that the promise of moving from worker to subcontractor to entrepreneur is most alive. Hence, the boundary between labor and capital has become more fluid and permeable in China while it has hardened in Italy. For the Chinese, the ability to open one's own business is held out as a promise for all, even as those with the most expansive networks—familial and state—have the greatest possibility of succeeding in this regard.

5   On Generation

Sylvia J. Yanagisako

A great family makes a great company, a great company
makes a great family. —GILDO ZEGNA

In 2009 a friend working in the Italian fashion industry received a request from a Chinese entrepreneur who was planning to launch
a new clothing line with an Italian name. Having done his homework on
the promotional campaigns of prestigious Italian brands, he asked that she
construct a convincing narrative that would trace the proprietary family's
roots to a specific Italian locale. As we saw in chapter 1 on managerial labor in
transnational Italian firms, Italian family firms in the global fashion industry
tout the global distinction of their brand while at the same time celebrating
the family's enduring commitment to its provincial origins. The enterprising
Chinese businessman figured that a similarly compelling story of his brand's
development by several generations of a fictive Italian family would both enhance its distinction and authenticate its Italianness.

Claims of provincial origins and multigenerational continuity are, however, much more than a mere marketing strategy of Italian family firms.
They are also genuine expressions of pride in enduring family ownership

and management and people's deep commitments to the intergenerational succession through which this is achieved. Just as Chinese entrepreneurs like the one described here have come to appreciate the marketing benefits of an esteemed family history, so they are beginning to recognize the affective sentiments that have shaped these histories. Young Chinese managers and entrepreneurs who work for Italian family firms are increasingly discovering that the principles of capitalist rationality they were taught in business school do not necessarily hold in practice. As we saw in part II, these young Chinese managers and entrepreneurs are critical of the Communist Party's management of state-owned businesses and the nepotism they view as rife within them. Many are attracted to business because they view it as an opportunity to escape the constraints of the state and the burdensome social obligations required to work within it. They are learning, however, that far from conforming to a model of the liberal free market, Italian capitalism is itself fettered by "communistic" bonds of family and kinship. Some have learned this the hard way.

Lou Jingxiao/Maggi is one of them (see chapter 1). Lou worked for several years with an Italian entrepreneur to locate Chinese factories to manufacture apparel for European designer brands. Educated at Donghua University in international business at a time when Western economics and business models had replaced Marxist economics, Lou drew on her training and her network of former classmates, professors, and friends to develop her own middleman business in the transnational production chain. Donghua had been a textile school, so although it had broadened its range, many of its alumni had gone into careers in textiles, clothing, and fashion. Much like the "converters" of Como and the "impannatore" of Prato who linked specialized factories in production chains in their industrial districts, Lou and her Italian colleague and mentor, Eduardo Fieramosca, sought Chinese manufacturing firms that could be relied on to meet the production needs of their European clients. Lou had expected that once Fieramosca retired, he would pick someone to succeed him with whom she would continue to work. As all her clients initially came from Fieramosca, this would have a significant impact on her business. To her dismay, Fieramosca handed over his clients to his son, despite having described him as a playboy lacking in the requisite discipline, work ethic, and experience to take over the business. Lou's disappointment was familiar not only to the Chinese who had been employed by or worked with Italian family firms in China but also to the Italians who had worked in family firms in Italy.

Modernity and Transnational Family Capitalism

As we noted in the introduction to this part of the book, the Italian-Chinese transnational business ventures and the respective firms that collaborate in them are shaped by deep kinship commitments. Yet, even in the face of empirical evidence that family business is the predominant form of capitalist enterprise in most areas of the world, the hypothesized decline of kinship in modern capitalism continues to shape the way many economic sociologists and economic historians approach research on family firms.[1] Above all, they feel compelled to explain the "survival" of family firms in contemporary capitalism. Attempts to answer the question of why it is that family firms continue to be found in a particular society or a particular business sector are rooted in the idea that the family firm is an anomaly destined to be supplanted by a more efficient and rational "managerial capitalism." Hence, inquiries into the persistence of family firms commonly focus on the efficiencies and inefficiencies that the familial character of these firms pose for economic actors, including the probability of financial loss and economic damage.

Along these lines, economic historian Andrea Colli (2003) concludes that family firms by their very nature both reduce and increase uncertainty and risk at different times and in different ways. By adopting a longitudinal view of the balance between positive and negative effects of the family character of these firms, Colli brings a much-needed temporal perspective to what is too often a static approach to family firms. At the same time, while he considers both the family dynamics and business dynamics of these firms over time, Colli's evaluation of "final outcomes" is based exclusively on the success of the firm as a profit-making entity. In basing his assessment of the survival and growth of family firms on their financial performance, Colli treats them as profit-seeking enterprises located squarely in the domain of the "economy." He states that "the presence of the family firm inside a certain economic system is largely—if not completely—due to asymmetric information, a turbulent environment, and a legal system unable to secure and enforce property rights" (Colli 2003, 8–9). Colli's attribution of the presence of family firms to insecure, unstable environments is a consequence of his assumption that managerial capitalism is a more suitable form of business in a well-functioning modern economy. Hence, for Colli what determines the presence of family firms is a social-political-economic environment *lacking* in the institutional characteristics of modern capitalist society.[2]

Marianne Bertrand and Antoinette Schoar (2006) likewise locate family firms in the domain of the "economic" even as they discuss both "efficiency-based theories" and "cultural theories" used to explain the persistence of family firms in a range of societies. While the former theories consider family firms as optimal adaptations to the economic environment, the latter treat them as the outcome of family norms and values. This serious consideration of family norms and values as "a first-order determinant of economic outcomes" (Bertrand and Schoar 2006, 82) would seem to be a welcome exception to the adaptationist approach to family firms in many sociological studies. At the same time, however, Bertrand and Schoar state that "family values can create efficiency distortions if they introduce nonmonetary objectives into the founder's utility maximization that run counter to the optimal decisions for the business" (2006, 78). In other words, for them the success and viability of firms rests solely on financial outcomes even when these are not the priority of the firm owners. The authors' comparisons of the "underperformance" of family firms relative to nonfamily firms are based on "economic performance" criteria such as wealth maximization. It does not appear to occur to these authors, and to many others studying family firms, that the owners of these firms are employing "noneconomic" criteria as well as "economic" ones to assess the performance and success of their enterprise.

To their credit, Bertrand and Schoar recognize that "the observed low performance of family firms is not inconsistent with high financial benefits for the families themselves" (2006, 81). They are aware of the possibility that, for example, low performance may reflect a tunneling of capital out of the firms by the controlling families. Yet, even with this caveat, they restrict their assessment of performance to financial benefits, never bothering to consider the affective and social benefits of family ownership and control.

If family sentiments and commitments are to be taken seriously as "first-order determinants of economic outcomes," however, we need to consider the possibility that people's assessments of the relative success of family firms may depend on the attainment of "kinship outcomes" as well as "economic" ones. In other words, the persistence of family firms may depend less on their performance as wealth-maximizing enterprises than their performance as kinship enterprises. My research on Italian family firms (Yanagisako 2002) has shown that for many capitalist families, providing jobs for family members and keeping them engaged in a collective project is at least as high, if not higher, a priority than maximizing wealth. Many view the two goals as mutually enhancing. Hence, rather than assessing solely how well family firms perform in comparison to nonfamily firms based on financial criteria, we should also consider how well families with firms perform in comparison to families that do not have firms based on kinship criteria.

Family Firms as Kinship Enterprises

In this chapter, I pursue a different analytic strategy than the prevailing one in economic sociology. Rather than treat family firms as a type of "business" or "economic" enterprise whose persistence can be explained by assessing their profitability, I treat them as kinship enterprises whose persistence must be understood by their meaningful pursuit of kinship sentiments and commitments. By enterprise, I mean a project whose goals and strategies are constantly being reassessed and reformulated by the people engaged in it. By kinship, I mean the dense assemblage of beliefs, sentiments, and commitments that motivate and shape relations among people who construe themselves to be connected by enduring bonds of relatedness.[3] A kinship enterprise is, accordingly, a project whose goals and strategies are constantly being reassessed and reformulated by people who construe themselves to be connected by enduring bonds of relatedness and whose relations are shaped by a dense assemblage of beliefs, sentiments, and commitments attached to these bonds. This admittedly unwieldy definition is not intended to operate as a fixed component of a theory of kinship but rather as a heuristic strategy for a cultural and social analysis. Having suffered the pitfalls of employing universal definitions of kinship (as well as of other institutions), anthropologists are understandably wary of offering up yet another one. Indeed, as I note above, the social science and business literature on family firms is shot through with definitional problems that plague attempts to understand the dynamics of family firms and assess their success and persistence.

I approach transnational Italian family firms as a type of kinship enterprise, not because I believe that they are fundamentally more structured by goals, sentiments, and norms of kinship than by the financial goals, sentiments, and norms that are assumed to structure capitalist firms. Rather, I employ this alternative framework, which is rooted in a history of anthropological research and critical scholarship on family, gender, and kinship, to move beyond the recognition that "economic action" is embedded in structures of social relations (Granovetter 1985) to the recognition that what is narrowly construed as "economic action" is a more complex form of social action in which kinship as well as other cultural meanings, sentiments, and commitments are at play. In short, "economic action" construed as a purely utility-driven Weberian ideal-type is both nonexistent and a distortion. Like all human social action, what has been deemed "economic action" is always shaped by multiple goals and multiple sentiments.

My inquiry in this chapter is also informed by unpacking two meanings of "generation" whose interplay is crucial to understanding the dynamics of the firms I have studied. These include (1) the succession of generations in family firms, and (2) the generation of new family firms. Both the scholarly literature on family firms and commentaries by business consultants focus primarily on the first of these meanings. Both engage in extensive discussion of the challenges that generational succession presents to family firms, identifying succession as the phase of greatest uncertainty in the developmental cycle of family firms. Considerably less attention is paid to the second meaning of generation—namely, the creation of new family firms.

The near-exclusive focus by family firm scholars on the first of these meanings of generation is a collateral product of the theory of modernity discussed above that asserts that kinship and business do not mix well in modern capitalism. The assumption is that family firms are not efficient enough to survive in competition with professionally managed firms guided by rational decision-making. This focus on survival draws on an evolutionary metaphor in which business "efficiency" is treated as a form of "economic fitness" that parallels "reproductive fitness" in Darwinian theory. The social forms that can survive and reproduce themselves over time are deemed to have greater reproductive fitness than the social forms that do not. In other words, for family firms, intergenerational succession constitutes reproductive fitness.

The focus on the reproductive fitness and survival of the firm through intergenerational transmission, however, obscures another meaning of "generation," which I suggest is equally, if not more, critical to the persistence of family firms in any society. This is the generation—the creation—of new family firms. This process of generation is incited, enabled, and shaped by social, cultural, and political processes and by institutions and structures, just as are all business and kinship enterprises. Yet because the enterprises they create are identified as "family firms," thereby implicating reproductive processes associated with the families, scholars have tended to employ a model of biological reproduction in studying their persistence. In doing so they have conflated the persistence of family firms over time (that is, their prevalence as a business form) with the rate of intergenerational transmission of family firms. Paradoxically, family firms are treated as kinship (reproductive) enterprises in assessments of their persistence but not sufficiently recognized as enterprises motivated by kinship sentiments and goals when it comes to explaining why it is that they keep popping up.

Although, as I have been arguing, the processes signified by these two meanings of generation should be analytically differentiated, at the same time, the interplay between them must be investigated if we are to understand family firms. Comparative studies of family firms commonly conflate these two processes of generation by assuming that a low rate of intergenerational transmission of family firms in a particular setting indicates that it is an unsustainable business form in that setting. In short, a low rate of survival of particular firms over successive generations is equated with a low rate of survival of the family firm as a social phenomenon in the society as a whole. The error in this conflation is obvious when we consider the parallel of equating the low rate of survival of particular families over successive generations with the low rate of survival of the family in general. The conceptual error in doing so is even clearer if we consider equating the survival over time of individual capitalist firms with the demise of capitalism writ large. These are clearly different things.[4] We know that new capitalist businesses are constantly being produced, even though the high rate of failure of new businesses is common knowledge. Likewise, new families are constantly being formed, including by individuals and couples who consider their families of origin to have been dysfunctional disasters.

Family firms are no different. New ones are constantly being created in Italy as well as in other countries (e.g., Germany, Japan, and France) in which family ownership and management is a prevailing form of capitalist enterprise. New family firms, moreover, frequently rise out of the ashes of previous ones. The prevalent practice of labeling family firms that cease to exist as "failures" unfortunately obscures the ways in which these firms may have served the family very well. The demise of a family firm, in other words, does not necessarily mean the demise of the kinship enterprise.

My earlier ethnographic study of family firms in the silk industry of Como, Italy, revealed that the interplay between these two processes of generation is key to understanding both the histories of individual family firms and the historical persistence of family firms in this industry as well as others in Italy (Yanagisako 2002). In that study, I show that the sentiments, tensions, conflicts, uncertainties, and actions that emerge in the period of transition from one generation to the next are simultaneously forces for the demise of firms and the creation of new ones. Family firms that end in the second or third generation because of disagreements or lack of sufficient capital to incorporate the next generation frequently spawn new family firms as fractions of the family hive off to initiate their own firms. Other family firms are constantly being created by enterprising technicians and managers who have gained invaluable experience and social contacts through their employment.

In this chapter, I show that the transnational expansion of the Italian textile and clothing industry has had a different impact on these two processes of generation. On the one hand, transnational expansion has strengthened generational succession in those family firms that have successfully developed production and distribution in China—whether by outsourcing manufacturing to Chinese factories, opening factories in China, forging joint ventures with Chinese firms, or a combination of these activities. Although there have been increased opportunities for nonfamily managers in these firms, this has not resulted in a "managerial revolution" in which professionally trained, nonfamily managers have taken control of the firm.[5] To the contrary, increased profits and capital accumulation have enabled these firms to incorporate more generations and branches of the family and, consequently, to postpone division of the patrimony.[6] Family firms that have not successfully made the shift to transnational expansion, however, have had a more mixed experience. Some, especially those specializing in the luxury market, have been able to survive, but many others have not (see the section below on the decline in Italian textile districts).

On the other hand, transnational expansion has severely undermined the generation of new family firms in the textile and clothing industries in Italy. The very success of expansionary family firms in relocating manufacturing to China and other low-wage countries has stifled the creation and continuation of subcontractor family firms in their home industrial districts. As we shall see, for example, the number of small and medium firms that once serviced the manufacturing needs of larger firms in Como has decreased drastically as larger firms have sent manufacturing phases overseas, thus reducing their need for local subcontractors.

A few Italian managers who have been employed in Italian overseas production units have gained the knowledge and experience that their earlier counterparts in Italian industrial districts drew on to initiate their own firms. But the linguistic, social, and bureaucratic barriers to developing in China the networks that are necessary to successfully start up a small subcontracting firm have, thus far, been too great to overcome. Thus, although, as we saw in chapter 1, the Italian managers in these transnational ventures enjoy higher incomes and the benefits of a cosmopolitan lifestyle, they lack access to the family labor they need to survive the early lean years of a new firm and the local kinship and friendship networks to successfully insert themselves in production chains. This has greatly impeded the processes through which managers are able to convert labor into capital in both Italy and China, hardening the boundary between capital and labor.

As we saw in chapter 3, two Italian family firms that have been successful in the global fashion industry are the Rinaudo and FGS firms. Both relocated manufacturing to China—initially by outsourcing phases of production and later by forming joint ventures with Chinese firms. Both also developed a chain of retail stores in China, where they sell their fashion brand, as well as retail stores that sell the brand of their joint venture. We saw in that chapter that both these family firms originated in small towns in northern Italy, which had been early sites of industrial development. After World War II, the most successful of these textile firms expanded into clothing manufacturing, thus moving up the commodity value chain. The most successful of these, in turn, developed their own fashion brands and retail chains.

Transnational Expansion and Generational Succession

The Rinaudo firm's history of growth, expansion, and generational succession traced in chapter 3 exemplifies the trajectory of those Italian family firms that have transformed themselves from small manufacturers of textiles firmly rooted in localized industrial networks to global fashion businesses. Although the family traces the founding of the firm to the retail store started by Stefano Rinaudo in the late nineteenth century, it was not until the end of World War II that his son Marco Rinaudo transformed the family business into a large-scale industrial manufacturer of textiles that were sold throughout Italy. In the next (third) generation, two of Marco's sons, Paolo and Claudio, expanded the business to encompass all phases of production of women's clothing, from fabric to finished garments. In 2006 Paolo's and Claudio's sons (cousins in the fourth generation) became coheads of the firm, taking on the offices of president and vice president of the firm's administrative council. The other ten members of the council included Paolo's and Claudio's daughters and four nonfamily members. Three executive committees—each headed by a general director who was not a family member—rounded out the governance structure of the firm. In 2009 the firm was further restructured into three divisions, including a holding company that controlled financial strategy; a clothing division that managed its multiple fashion brands, factories, and retail outlets; and a textile division with plants both inside and outside Italy.

The transnational expansion of the firm made possible not only the transmission of the firm to the fourth generation of the family; it also reproduced the gender division of labor and hierarchy in the family and the firm. Elisabetta Rinaudo, Paolo's daughter and the sister of one of the coheads of the firm, minced few words with us about what she called the "culture of male chauvinism" in the family. When we met with her in the firm's elegant showroom in a trendy zone of Milan, Elisabetta, who was in charge of coordinating brand publicity with the firm's general business strategy, broached this subject candidly. She explained that although as a young girl she had been interested in architecture, her father strongly encouraged all three of his children to get college degrees in Economia e Commercio (Economy and Business). Despite having been included in the management of the firm, Elisabetta was critical of the "masculinista" (male chauvinist) culture of the family reflected both in its history and its present. Her father's sister, she noted, had not received shares in the firm, but instead had been given money (how much was unclear) to resolve her claim to inheritance.

The denial of daughters' legal rights to their share of patrimony has been a common practice among Italian bourgeois families, especially those with family firms (Yanagisako 2002). Since the beginning of the nineteenth century when it adopted the Napoleonic code, Italian law has prescribed that all children—whether male or female, offspring of a legal marriage or not—are entitled to inherit an equal share of their parents' property (Yanagisako 2002, 168).[7] In contrast to U.S. and British inheritance law, moreover, Italian inheritance law dictates that the majority of an individual's property goes to his or her family members, specifying the precise portions that each family member is to receive depending on the configuration of the family at the time of the individual's death.[8]

Firm owners have frequently avoided equal division, however, motivated by a combination of the financial threat that this division posed to the firm and the "masculinista" sentiments cited by Elisabetta Rinaudo. Division of the patrimony at the time of a parent's (usually the father's) death can be a crippling, if not fatal, blow to the family firm by forcing the sale of the firm if some of the children demand to be bought out. At the very least, it can place great strain on the firm's capital and ability to reinvest in itself. Daughters were often asked to waive their inheritance rights and accept in its place a premortem inheritance when they married. These premortem payments commonly were far less than the amount to which they had a legal claim. Fathers describe this as "liquidating" their daughters' shares in the firm, and justify it on the grounds that daughters are "marrying out" of the family. The idea that daughters are lost to the family upon marriage is predicated on the expectation that wives are controlled by their husbands. Alternatively, daughters were asked to keep their shares in the firm and to be satisfied with annual earnings doled out by their brothers.

When daughters who did not participate in the management of the firm were given less than their brothers, the equation of the family with the firm was clear. Elisabetta's father's explanation that he was giving his daughters less than his sons since they were going to be married reflected this rationale. Yet both Elisabetta and her sister were given half the shares allotted to their brother in spite of working in the firm. As their brother also married, the inequality could no longer be justified on the basis of whether a child worked in the firm or not. Gender was what clearly made the difference.

Elisabetta's mother had never worked in the firm but instead helped manage the family's charitable foundation—a role frequently occupied by women in wealthy bourgeois families (see the discussion of the Bossi family foundation later in this chapter). Yet she had insisted that her daughters be given managerial positions in the firm. Neither Elisabetta nor her sister, nor their two female cousins, however, had top-tier management roles comparable to those of their brothers. Despite the firm's focus on women's clothing, moreover, there were few nonfamily women managers in the firm, and none were at the higher levels. For Elisabetta, the "patriarchal" culture of the firm had been a continual problem, and she was openly critical of the ways in which the older generation of both family and nonfamily managers had persisted in their "old style" of running the firm. This did not mean that she was ready to cash in her shares of the firm or cede control of the firm to her brother and male cousins. The question that loomed before the firm, she stated, is how to bring in professional management without losing the firm's family identity. In other words, the challenge was to transform it into a "modern family firm."

The FGS Family Firm

Like Rinaudo, the FGS firm traces its origins to the nineteenth-century textile mill founded in northern Italy by the great-grandfather of the current generation. Like Rinaudo, the family expanded its business over the course of three generations to manufacturing its own clothing brand and, eventually, to developing a chain of retail stores. Whereas Rinaudo focused on middle-priced womenswear, FGS's success lay in luxury menswear. In spite of this difference in market sector, FGS's history of succession and its managerial division of labor in the fourth generation parallel that of Rinaudo in several ways. First, the family members in the fourth generation who are the top executives of the firm are both men. These male cousins rotate between the positions of CEO and president of the board of directors. Second, the only female family member with a management role has, like Elisabetta Rinaudo, been relegated largely to a public relations role as head of communications. Like Elisabetta's mother, she heads the family's philanthropic foundation. Finally, nonfamily managers lead various divisions of the firm, including its overseas operations. None are at the highest executive level. In the fourth generation, therefore, male consanguinity remains a crucial qualification of leadership.

As we saw in chapter 3, from the beginning of its joint venture with the Chinese firm Vinimoon, FGS was represented by nonfamily managers who viewed their mission as importing a "European management structure" to China. Hence, while the Bossi family managed the joint venture from a distance, their Chinese partners, the Cai brothers, were directly involved in managing the daily operations of the firm. Their wives also held management roles. An ironic tension in this partnership between two family firms was that FGS's Italian managers attributed some of their difficulties in working in the joint venture to the fact that their Chinese partner was a family firm. One expressed his exasperation by lamenting that working with them required dealing with "family, family, family!" Another complained that the Chinese partners treat the firm like it is their family, guarding secrets and engaging in power struggles, which in turn creates confusion about who is responsible for certain decisions. The eldest Cai brother appeared to agree with them to some extent, because he welcomed, at least initially, the creation of a formal management structure. This enabled him to consolidate his executive position and power, rather than having to negotiate constantly with his brothers. He also decided that once the joint venture was formed, no more relatives could be hired. (See chapter 6 for a further discussion of the Cai brothers' family struggles.)

Family Brand, Family Bonds, and Provincial Origins

Although FGS and Rinaudo were represented by nonfamily managers in both their own brands and their joint ventures with Chinese, their success in China strengthened the family's ownership and control of the firm. Contrary to Alfred D. Chandler's (1977, 13–14) widely accepted thesis of the separation of ownership from control in large, multiunit business enterprises, transnational expansion did not result in the takeover of management by nonfamily, "professional" managers. According to Chandler, in such modern businesses, salaried managers first replace family members in middle management and then eventually in top positions. As salaried managers develop specialized knowledge and generate funds for expansion, family members come to view their enterprise, like stockholders, from the point of view of rentiers whose interests are focused not on management but on the income derived from profits. This has certainly not been the case for FGS or Rinaudo.

For decades, Italian business schools, like their counterparts in the U.S., have been advocating the professionalization of business management and financial strategies using business models informed by the social sciences, especially economics. A continual stream of warnings about the limitations and perils of family management appear in Italian business magazines and the popular press. In the U.S., professional management became hegemonic in the first half of the twentieth century with the increasing concentration of capital in corporations (itself a product of capitalists' strategies to reduce uncertainty by reducing competition) and the incorporation of business education into research universities (Khurana 2007). In Italy, by comparison, the continuation of family ownership and control of small, medium, and even large firms throughout the twentieth century has checked the power of professional managers, muting their challenge to owners' authority and the legitimacy of owners' rights to control firms. The growth and transnational expansion of the Rinaudo and FGS firms have brought ample profits to family members, including those who are not actively engaged in management. These latter family members are content to cede control to others and be satisfied with the income from their shares in the firm. But the others to whom they cede control are family members.

Large- and medium-sized family firms are generally incorporated as joint-stock companies (*società per azioni*) in which equal shares are distributed among the children, who, in turn, distribute shares to their children. Children and grandchildren who are dissatisfied with the annual earnings from their shares, especially if they see a significant disparity between their incomes and those of their siblings and cousins working in the firm, can bring down a firm by demanding that their shares be bought out. This has been particularly the case with daughters who were excluded from managerial positions or even from working in the firm but who hold the same inheritance rights as their brothers. In the past and still today, as in the case of the Rinaudo family, daughters were commonly given a smaller inheritance than their brothers, whether in the form of a premortem payment at the time they married or at the time of their father's death. Daughters (and their children) are less likely these days to be satisfied with these settlements. Consequently, family firms are under greater pressure to increase the earnings paid out to family shareholders or face the division of the firm.

Firms like Rinaudo and FGS, which have been successful in transnational expansion, are able to satisfy these demands for earnings from family shareholders, thus bolstering the continuity of the family firm. In addition to the financial rewards to family members, there is the reward of social distinction. Both the Rinaudo and Bossi families are highly esteemed and admired in Italy, although the Bossi name carries more prestige because of its association with a luxury brand. Like other families in luxury fashion, the Bossi are among the new aristocracy of Italy. Rinaudo as well is widely known and respected. To be a member of such a family, even if one is not actively involved in managing its business, is to be a member of bourgeois royalty.

As the global expansion and fame of these family firms was achieved over the course of three to four generations, their provincial origins are also widely known and celebrated. As recounted in chapter 1, proprietary families maintain homes and reside for at least part of the year in the small cities and towns where the family's business originated. This reinforces public perception of the family's enduring connection to its provincial and artisanal origins and counterbalances the resentment and anger fueled by the loss of jobs as manufacturing has been outsourced to China and other countries. Provincial origins are integral to the narrative that makes them a global brand and at the same time quintessentially Italian. In addition to maintaining homes in their home provinces, the owners of both Rinaudo and FGS have funded philanthropic foundations that contribute to a range of health, education, social welfare, and environmental projects there. More recently, they have funded environmental and health projects in China.

The Decline of Italian Manufacturing

In this section, I discuss the impact of the decline in manufacturing for both forms of generation—intergenerational succession and the generation of new firms—in the textile industrial districts of northern Italy in which firms like

FGS and Rinaudo originated. I focus on the silk industry of Como because my previous research on family firms in that industrial district (Yanagisako 2002) enables me to trace the histories of specific families in my earlier study from the boom decades of the 1970s and 1980s to the crisis decades of the 1990s and into the following decade to the present. The industrial districts in which FGS and Rinaudo originated have a great deal in common with the silk district of Como. Like the silk industry, these districts were characterized by the overwhelming predominance of locally owned family firms.[9] Local ownership, of course, did not mean that these industrial districts were isolated from national and international flows of capital, technology, labor, and raw materials or from international markets. As we explained in the introduction and as the history of the Marini family firm in part II showed, interregional and international links were critical to the Como silk industry for the acquisition of raw materials, technology, machinery, and clients of its products.

Como's silk industry, like other northern Italian textile industries, supported an extensive network of subcontracting firms that provided manufacturing services for both larger firms and "converter" firms, which coordinated production chains. Some of these firms worked exclusively as subcontractors (*per conto terzi*), while others worked simultaneously as subcontractors and producers of their own goods (*per conto proprio*) (Yanagisako 2002). Throughout the history of silk production in Como, moreover, firms relied on outworkers, some of whom worked as subcontractors using their own equipment, while others used equipment provided by the firm. What was mistakenly characterized by some scholars (Piore and Sabel 1984) as the "decentralization" of Como's silk industry during the 1970s was merely an adjustment in an industry that had a long history of decentralized production. The national and international forces of political economy in the 1970s merely reinvigorated a system of dispersed production that had long been rooted in family capitalism.

By 2010 the combination of competition from textile manufacturers in China and other low-wage countries and the outsourcing of production to the same countries had reduced the Como silk industry to half of what it was in 1990. Overseas production had transformed an Italian industrial district into a node in a transnational production and distribution chain linking Como with cities and economic zones in China, Romania, and other low-wage countries.[10] Como's silk industry was not alone in experiencing this decline in textile and clothing manufacturing. The wool industry of Biella along with other textile and apparel industries saw similar declines in manufacturing. For example, in 1991 the knitwear giant Benetton manufactured almost 90 percent of its clothing in Italy. By 2006 it was manufacturing only 30 percent in Italy and had become heavily reliant on Chinese suppliers ("Material Fitness" 2006). The cotton industrial cluster that was centered near Malpensa airport in Lombardy likewise shrank from 4,900 to 2,900 firms in the two decades between 1981 and 2001 ("Material Fitness" 2006).[11]

The reduction in Como's silk industry is reflected in the histories of the thirty-eight family firms that I began studying in 1985. In 2012 I was able to track down thirty-one of the thirty-eight family firms in my earlier sample through a combination of ethnographic and archival research at the Camera di Commercio, the Italian state regulatory agency that compiles information on commercial, industrial, and agricultural enterprises at the provincial level. In my 2002 book, I divided the owners of these thirty-eight firms into three fractions of the Como bourgeoisie—upper, middle, and lower—based on a combination of firm and family characteristics that indicated the extent of their control of the means of production, their past social trajectories, and their strategies for reproduction and mobility (Yanagisako 2002, 100–109).[12] The text below summarizes what happened to these firms in the intervening twenty-seven years.

Change in Status of Family Firms from 1985 to 2012

UPPER FRACTION (9 IN INITIAL SAMPLE)

Active: 5
Liquidated: 3 (year of liquidation: 2001, 2004, 2011)
Closed to merge with other firm: 1 (1989)[13]

MIDDLE FRACTION (18 IN INITIAL SAMPLE)

Active: 6
Liquidated: 3 (1992, 2000, 2009)
Closed to merge with other firm: 3 (1989, 1994, 1994)
Unknown status: 6

LOWER FRACTION (11 IN INITIAL SAMPLE)

Active: 3
Liquidated: 5 (1992, 1993, 2003, 2006, 2007)
Closed to merge with other firm: 2 (1999, 2001)
Unknown status: 1

TOTAL (ALL FRACTIONS)

Active: 14
Liquidated: 11
Closed to merge with other firms: 6
Unknown: 7

If we assume that the seven firms that were not traceable through the Camera di Commercio had closed, then fourteen of thirty-eight (37 percent) of the firms in the initial sample were still in business in 2012. If we assume, on the other hand, that those seven firms that were not traceable had a range of outcomes and exclude them from the sample, then fourteen of thirty-one (45 percent) of the firms were still active. Since industry reports do not track the survival rate of firms over time, I cannot tell if the fate of the firms in my initial sample over the past twenty-five years is representative of the totality of Como silk firms. In any case, the Camera di Commercio files show that at least eleven of the thirty-eight firms (30 percent) had closed in this period, and another six (15 percent) had merged with other firms.

The Camera di Commercio records, of course, do not tell the whole story of what happened to these family firms from 1985 to 2012. Indeed, exclusive reliance on these records can be misleading if one assumes that closure of the firm means the end of the family's entrepreneurial activity in the industry. One must be careful not to equate the demise of a family firm as a legal entity with the demise of the kinship project or projects entailed. My ethnographic research revealed that some firms whose files indicate they were liquidated became the basis of the start-up of new firms by one or more of the owners of the original firm—sometimes with only a minor change in the firm name. In the case of the liquidation of the Casati firm, for example, one of the daughters of the original founder founded a new firm with only a minor change in the name. On the other hand, firms whose files indicate the original firm is still active are sometimes owned and managed by only a small part of the original family (e.g., Cattaneo, Molteni). In short, the Camera di Commercio records may indicate very different outcomes for firms that have undergone similar processes of family division with some appearing as "liquidated" and others as "active." Conversely, they may indicate similar outcomes for firms whose family outcomes are very different. The histories of firms whose files indicate that they "closed to merge with other firms" are even more ambiguous. Some were absorbed by firms owned by other families, and, therefore, essentially liquidated. Others were incorporated into firms owned by the same family.

The firms still active in 2012 included large firms that had survived by downsizing drastically and medium and small firms that had survived by specializing in niches of the luxury fashion industry. Most of the former had been losing money for several years and were barely hanging on. These once leading firms, whose proprietary families were once considered dynasties in the province, were most frequently mentioned when people in Como talked about the crisis in the silk industry. One of these, the Molteni firm, which I had studied in the 1980s and 1990s, had shrunk to a third of its former size. Like the other large family firms in Como's silk industry, it had not been successful in meeting the challenges that China posed to the Italian fashion industry in the new millennium. It was not for lack of trying.

Molteni: An Upper Bourgeois Family Firm

The Molteni firm was founded in 1902 by Riccardo Molteni, who had started out as a textile merchant and later became a "converter" who bought thread, had it woven, and then sold the woven fabric to shops. He brought his two sons into the business and eventually six of his grandsons managed the firm. Over the course of the twentieth century, especially after World War II, the firm expanded to include six other firms that, in turn, owned factories that specialized in weaving, printing, and dyeing. They also owned several converter firms. By the 1980s, they were among the few firms in the industry that had control of the complete production cycle.

As the firm's sales and profits began to decline in the late 1990s, the Molteni family undertook a series of strategies to adapt to shifts in the U.S. clothing industry, which was their major client and in which China was gaining an increasing market share. They began manufacturing ties and clothing in China, and they opened a weaving firm there to produce their own fabric. They even initiated a joint venture in fabric printing with a Chinese partner. None of these except the tie manufacturing succeeded. According to the Italian technical manager who was sent to regulate the looms in the weaving firm in China, it was too difficult to manage. The workers spoke only Chinese, he did not, and the details and nuances of production were lost in translation. In 2001 Molteni opened an office in Hangzhou to manage the procurement of raw silk, thread, and fabric and to buy accessories in China. A second nonfamily manager who was hired in 2002 to oversee their operations in China described to us how he traveled around the country for two weeks every three months buying raw silk, thread, fabric, and accessories. Twelve Chinese employees worked under him in what he called a converter firm that arranged for the manufacture of unfinished fabric, printed fabric, and ties by ten different factories, which Molteni then sold directly to U.S. and German clothing makers. In short, they coordinated a production chain among Chinese subcontractors just as the firm's founder and his heirs had done in Como over the course of the twentieth century. In this instance, however, the industrial district was spread among several Chinese provinces rather than concentrated in the province of Como.

Despite these efforts to shift from manufacturing in Como to manufacturing in China, the firm continued to decline. By 2012 Molteni's workforce had shrunk to a third of its size in the halcyon years of the 1980s. When we met with him on several occasions from 2007 to 2010, Sebastiani Molteni, the grandson of the nineteenth-century founder of the firm, who had remained in the firm even as his siblings cashed in their shares in the 1990s, offered various reasons for the firm's lack of success. Among these was the difficulty of establishing their own brand, because of the firm's structural position in the fashion industry. Since their clients were famous designer brands, any attempt to develop a Molteni brand would have been viewed as competing with their own clientele. When I pointed out that some other Italian textile firms had succeeded in developing their own brands and retail outlets in spite of their similar structural position in the fashion industry, he countered that it was one thing for wool manufacturers to design men's suits and for cotton manufacturers to develop men's shirts. These, he explained, were relatively simple, stable fashion sectors. The difficulty of developing a women's fashion brand for silk fabric was another thing.

The extent of the firm's efforts to turn around its downhill slide is no better indicated than by two moves it made in the first decade of the new millennium. Both of these, according to industry watchers, veered strongly from "Como tradition." The first was the hiring of a CEO external to the family. In 2000 the firm hired a nonfamily member to lead the firm for the first time in its hundred-year history. When, after a couple of years, he had failed to turn around the company's decline, Sebastiani returned to take command of the firm. Then in 2006 another nonfamily CEO, Giorgio Menghi, was hired to lead the firm. Menghi was not from the textile sector but was an expert in restructuring firms. As he put it, "a fat body not only doesn't perform but also tires out the vital organs." Once Menghi was in place, Sebastiani's role in the firm was limited to relations with clients and suppliers. Menghi made all operational decisions. Once again things did not go as hoped for, and by 2010 there was yet another new nonfamily CEO.

The second move taken by Molteni that deviated from Como tradition was the plan to merge with another firm in the industry. The story in a national paper about the planned fusion of Molteni with the Tessuto Marangoni firm cast it as the alliance between two longtime rivals in order to surpass the leading silk firm in Como. The merger was, more accurately, a desperate move by two firms to survive. The newspaper story declared that this was the first time such a merger of Como family firms had been proposed. Both Sebastiani Molteni and the head of Tessuto Marangoni emphasized that the new firm would be managed by "professionals," although the presidency of the board would alternate between the heads of the two family firms. Both acknowledged that they were embarking on an unknown path with many challenges, including integrating the cultures of the two firms. The alternative, they argued, was the death of Como's silk industry. On the positive side of this unconventional venture was the promise of not only surviving but forging alliances with firms in other manufacturing sectors (e.g., wool, linen), thus enabling Como to become a new hub of the Italian textile industry.

Despite veering from tradition in these two moves, it was clear that Sebastiani Molteni's hopes for intergenerational succession were far from dead. After his siblings had left the firm, Sebastiani owned 90 percent of the shares. Only one other brother had retained a small minority share in the firm. Both Sebastiani and the brother had brought their children into the firm, and while Sebastiani was aware of the difficulties that faced the firm, he had not abandoned the hope that he would be able to hand down the firm to his children. His son, who had studied economics in college, was involved in the sales of middle-level products. His daughter, who had studied foreign languages and communications, was in charge of obtaining and managing licenses to make and distribute accessories for a number of luxury fashion brands. Both children had studied abroad and together had the language and cultural knowledge to operate in England and France. His two nephews, who had also studied economics and communication, were involved in research, technical production, and sales.

Each spring or summer that we met between 2007 and 2010, Sebastiani expressed hope that the firm would break even the following year. He did not, however, exclude the possibility that his son would eventually become the CEO of the firm. His grandfather, after all, had faced the challenges of a different era, and so had his father, who had initiated the firm's ventures in China. His children would face different challenges, including the decline of industrial manufacturing in Italy and the expansion of the firm's business in China.

He explained, "It's not just about the money. I could have opted out like my brothers awhile back instead of continuing to lose money. When push comes to shove, it's more about protecting and saving the patrimony than your own ego." His daughter Patrizia, for her part, explained that she had not decided to enter the firm until she did some work on its centennial celebration while she was in college. It was then, she said, that she "fell in love with the firm."

Sebastiani and Patrizia Molteni's deep commitment to the patrimony had, by the end of 2010, placed them in the awkward position of having to compromise it in order to save it. Since his father's death, Sebastiani and his brothers had kept their mother informed of what was going on in the family firm. As the daughter of a family that had a firm with a long history in the industry, she was well steeped in the kinship, social, and business networks of the Como bourgeoisie. Sebastiani, however, did not tell her about the negotiations to merge with their former rival. This was just as well, as a year later the negotiations had fallen apart. As another firm owner put it, "It was the union of two weak firms and couldn't work."

The Molteni firm was far from alone in suffering the fate of those who had not found a way to either compete with or work with the Chinese textile industry. They had a lot of company among the larger firms in Como—many of which had made forays into China. The four upper bourgeois firms in my 1985 sample on which I was able to gather post-1990s histories had all tried to do so. At the very least, they had hired agents to seek out sources of raw materials or finished products in China. Others had looked into or launched joint ventures with Chinese partners. None of these joint ventures had survived, and by 2010 the original firms were still losing money. One had been bought by and absorbed into a large multifirm conglomerate from outside Como that was itself family owned and managed. The others were still not ready to abandon their hopes of survival and intergenerational succession.

Contracting Firms, Contracting Families

The last decade of the twentieth century was one of continuing crises for the Molteni family. As the firm's profits plummeted, it became obvious that it would not be able to absorb even a small number of the children who were coming of age in the fourth generation. Over the course of the 1990s, four of the six brothers who had been managing the firm together for three decades left the firm. Although the brothers, along with their sisters, still held shares in the family's holding company and real estate business, each successive departure was a blow to the firm and the family. Sebastiani admitted that this had soured his relations with his brothers. Their children, at least, had been able to maintain better relations among themselves.

In 1985, when we had met with Sebastiani's mother at her home on the northern shore of Lake Como, she spoke proudly of their good fortune in being "una famiglia molto unita" (a very united family). She later went on to say: "Yes. We are very united and we are very envied and resented by other people. There's another family in Como that wanted to be like us, but they didn't succeed because the children went their own ways."

By the beginning of the new millennium, Signora Molteni's children had also gone their own ways.

The breaking of family bonds accompanying the crisis in Como's silk industry at the end of the twentieth century was hardly a novel phenomenon. It had been a regular occurrence in the developmental cycle of family firms in Como and the rest of Italy. Less predictable was that several of the families who owned the largest firms in Como would be shattered as much as those who owned medium and small firms. In the post–World War II period of growth in the Italian textile and garment industry, upper bourgeois families were able to postpone division of the firm longer than middle and lower bourgeois families (Yanagisako 2002, 175). Their financial and social assets enabled them to diversify by expanding into new areas of production and by creating allied firms headed by children. By financing the futures of the next generation—whether by absorbing them into management or by settling inheritance claims—they were able to avoid pressures for division of the firm (Yanagisako 2002, 176). When the industry crisis hit in the 1990s, however, their greater generational depth meant that they had more branches of the family and more shareholders to satisfy. Molteni, for example, had eight family shareholders in the third generation and eighteen in the fourth generation. The drastic reduction in the firm's profits meant that even though the firm was able to survive—in greatly reduced size—the family was not.

Barbieri: Firm Continuity, Family Dissolution

While Sebastiani Molteni's relations with his brothers had soured, Mario Barbieri's relations with his cousins, he told us in 2010, had been "permanently broken." Along with the Molteni family, the Barbieri family was one of the most prominent in Como throughout the twentieth century. Like Molteni, its prestige derived not only from owning one of the largest firms in the industry but from its history of generational succession. When I first studied the Barbieri firm in 1985, it was being managed by three cousins in the third generation and anticipating the entrance of members of the fourth generation. Like the Molteni firm, it was one of the few in the industry that had escaped the demise predicted by the local adage: "The grandfather founded the firm, the sons develop it, the grandsons destroy it."[14] In 2010 the Barbieri firm was still in business. But, like Molteni, it was greatly reduced.

In 1985, as the firm was riding high, Mario Barbieri explained to me that their secret to success was the accord between himself and his two cousins who comanaged the firm. In 1999, however, one year after they had celebrated the firm's centennial, a struggle over the control of the firm and its direction broke out. Mario left the firm, taking his son with him. The break was absolute. In 2009 Mario reported that since he had left the firm, he and his children had had no contact with his cousins and their children. After a century of working together, he said, "the patriarchal family is finished."

The firm had been founded by Mario Barbieri's grandfather, Renzo Barbieri, who was himself from a Milanese textile family that had several factories in the region.[15] Renzo had been set up by his family to take over a small weaving factory in Como to manufacture fabric using thread produced by the family's spinning firm. As in the *système Motte*, named after the cotton textile manufacturer Alfred Motte, the Barbieri family had used family ties to build a confederation of medium- to small-sized firms, each specializing in one of the component phases of production.[16] In Como, confederations like these were limited to only the wealthiest industrial families, all of whom traced their industrial roots to the late nineteenth century. Renzo's brothers and sisters were nonactive shareholders in the firm. Over the years he slowly bought them out, so that by 1950, he had complete ownership of the firm.

Three of Renzo's sons took on management roles in the firm, although the eldest died shortly after entering the firm. After World War II, Renzo began ceding his shares to his four remaining children and the children of his deceased son. This was divided in equal parts per stirpes. In the 1960s, three of Renzo's grandsons—including Mario—entered the firm, and by the 1980s, they were managing the firm together. One was the president and general manager, one was the technical manager, and one the commercial manager.

Until the 1960s, the Barbieris had only a weaving factory—albeit one of the largest in Como. As the third generation ascended to head the firm, they invested heavily in machinery and technological renovation. They built a new factory and began to verticalize production so that by the mid-1980s, they had control over all phases of silk fabric production. In 1969 they opened a retail outlet that was managed by a couple of the sisters of the managers, but they did not invest much into it and after several years it closed. Whether this was a missed opportunity to create a retail brand like Rinaudo and FGS is difficult to say. In 1987 one of the three cousins died suddenly, and the remaining brother and Mario took over his role.

When I interviewed numerous family members in the 1980s and early 1990s, I wondered how the firm would make the transition to the next generation, as by then it had a large number of shareholders. The three male cousins managing the firm had a total of eight children (five of them sons), all of whom were in high school or university at the time. But there were thirty-six grandchildren of Renzo, each with equal shares and each a potential contender for management of the firm. The eldest daughter of one of the cousins managing the firm expressed resentment at not being invited into management because of her gender. She was adamant that she would not settle for what her aunts had—being set up in a retail outlet rather than managing the firm.

As I later learned, however, the discontent that was to lead to the breakup of the family came not from this great-granddaughter of the founder or her female cousins but from a coalition of great-grandsons who disagreed with Mario over the direction of the firm. In a poignant meeting with us in 2010, Mario recounted how he had been pushed out of the firm in 1999. He noted that by coincidence it was the tenth anniversary to the day of his last day at the firm, and he added that this was the first time he had told anyone outside the firm the story of what really happened. The long and the short of it was that a coalition of his cousins and their children had outvoted him and his children. This was the culmination of a decade of generational transition in which the remaining members of the second generation died and in which four great-grandsons, one of them Mario's son, entered the firm. In Mario's view, the demise of the second generation eliminated the moral restraints on the usurpation of leadership by the younger generation. Two years after Mario and his son left the firm, the remaining manager from the third generation was fired.

Mario Barbieri's account of the breakup of the family and what he saw as the beginning of the demise of the firm centered on both disagreements over the firm's business strategies and the demographic pressures on the family. On the latter score, he recognized that by the fourth generation there were simply too many people to manage. The interests of some members of the family were different from the interests of others, and the appetites of the shareholders had prevailed. Because he had distributed little of the profits but instead plowed them back into the firm, Mario was considered an impediment by many of the shareholders—especially those who were not involved in managing the firm. They had turned into the rentier family shareholders identified by Chandler who treat the firm merely as a source of income. They allied with their kin who were engaged in managing the firm to oust Mario and his son.

Andrea Barbieri, one of the cousins who had been involved in this challenge to Mario's leadership, mentioned none of this when he was interviewed in 2005. Nor did he mention the historical continuity (and irony) that the firm was again being managed by a troika of cousins. Once again there were two brothers and their cousin—as there had been in the third generation. Only this time they were members of the fourth generation, and they were second cousins.[17]

Similar stories abounded in Como about other upper bourgeois families that had broken up as firms underwent the crisis years of the 1990s and the following decade. In some of these cases, like Molteni and Barbieri, the firm had survived but the family had not. In others, like the Casati family, neither had. In the latter case, one of the sisters, Elisabetta, among the five siblings who had managed the firm, forced out her brother, who then went on to take over another firm in the industry. Eventually the Casati firm closed. But very shortly thereafter, Elisabetta opened a new firm bearing almost the identical family name.

Middle and Lower Bourgeois Families

While several of the upper bourgeois family firms in Como struggled to find a way to gain a foothold for their business in China, middle- and lower-level bourgeois family firms lacked the resources to even try. Despite sharing the same desires for firm continuity and intergenerational succession as the upper bourgeois families, middle and lower bourgeois families lacked sufficient capital to expand enough to satisfy the demands of both firm and family beyond the second generation. As the siblings who managed the firm pushed to reinvest profits back into the firm to strengthen it for their children, those who did not pressed for the distribution of profits to invest in their children's educations and careers. This led middle and lower bourgeois firms and families to break apart sooner than those of the upper bourgeoisie—commonly, as the third generation came of age and began to work.

The Galbiati Family: From Entrepreneurial to Professional

The Galbiati family history illustrates a well-known process of firm and family division among the middle bourgeoisie of Como. At the same time, it reveals how the decline in the silk industry has led industrial-entrepreneurial families to increasingly pursue what Pierre Bourdieu has called "reconversion strategies"—the conversion of one form of capital into another (1984, 125).

When I had last spoken to family members in the late 1980s, the Galbiatis were still struggling to recover from a dispute that had emerged when their father, who had founded the family's weaving firm in 1925, died intestate in 1982 (see Yanagisako 2002, 145–50). After the revision of family law that accompanied the legalization of divorce in 1975, widows as well as children had inheritance rights that were clearly laid forth in rules for the division of the patrimony in the case of intestacy. In this case, however, the application of the law was complicated by the fact that in the 1960s and 1970s, the father had worked out an agreement with the three sons who managed the firm (whom the family referred to as the "inside" siblings) to "buy" the shares of their five siblings who did not work in the firm (the "outside" siblings). The outside siblings were only told of this agreement by their father, however, shortly before he died. The terms of the agreement were that the inside siblings would compensate the outside siblings by paying them a fair interest rate for keeping their shares of the inheritance in the firm. The inside siblings would also provide their mother a regular stipend.

A year after their father's death, the inside siblings announced that the firm could not afford to pay the promised interest rate, and they asked for their siblings' forbearance. Their mother and the outside siblings were upset and disappointed as they had been planning to use the interest to renovate the family home in town where several of them resided. Their dismay at being asked to be patient was undoubtedly aggravated by the fact that while the family home was badly in need of repair, the brothers who managed the firm lived in elegant villas and plush condominiums in the most prestigious residential areas outside Como. Their children, moreover, had educational and cultural opportunities, such as travel and study abroad, that were not available to the children of the outside siblings.

Twenty years later, the family home in the center of Como was almost unrecognizable even though the neighborhood itself had hardly changed. I walked past it two or three times before I realized I had found it. The older building had been demolished and had been replaced by a new building that housed seven apartments that sat above several small shops facing the street. It struck me only later that the commercial rents the family collected from these shops paralleled, albeit on a smaller scale, the real estate investments of the upper bourgeois families.[18] Andreina Balzareti, who continued to live with her husband in one of the family apartments, was more reluctant to recapitulate the difficult experience of the family than she had been when they were in the thick of the struggle. She referred me instead to one of her younger brothers, who remembered well what both of them acknowledged was an "ugly period" of the family's history.

The renovation of the family home, which was paid for by the three brothers who managed the firm, yielded apartments for each of the outside siblings. But this came about only after a period of considerable conflict. Their mother had wanted to leave the house to only the five outside children, but the inside sons insisted that it be divided into nine apartments—one for each of the children, including them, and their mother. Eventually, the siblings who took up residence in the apartments paid those who did not, so the house ended up in the hands of the five outside siblings. Throughout the dispute, the inside brothers felt they had been more than generous to their outside siblings. The feeling was mutual.

The struggle over the renovation of the family home was only one of the conflicts that erupted among the siblings during the later years of the firm. By the time the firm was liquidated, it became apparent that tensions and conflicts were not limited to those outside versus those inside the firm. The aftermath of the "ugly period" of family conflict was the estrangement of the inside siblings from the outside siblings and from each other. The "family" that continued to see each other frequently consisted of the outside siblings—especially those who maintained apartments in the family building. The two sisters, moreover, had become central in bringing the family together. It was they who now organized family gatherings, including weddings, funerals, and baptisms. The inside brothers participated only infrequently in these gatherings. In short, a male-centered bourgeois family tied together by capital, management, and sentiments of patriarchal desire had transformed into a female-centered bourgeois family held together by property and sentiments of affective solidarity.

At the same time, what had been an industrial bourgeois family was transformed into a family of professionals. Through the conversion of financial capital into cultural capital, many families like the Galbiatis who owned middle-level firms moved into the *liberi professionisti* (independent professionals) sector of the bourgeoisie. Even before it was clear that the firm was not going to survive, the siblings had supported the education of their children. The outside siblings were especially aware of the need to invest in their children's education. Indeed, this had been one of the sources of conflict between them and the inside siblings, who wanted to use the firm's profits to pay for their children's education.

The investments in their children's education by both inside and outside children were especially timely "reconversion strategies" for turning financial capital into cultural capital given the decline in the silk industry (Bourdieu 1984, 125). For Bourdieu, the different practices that individuals or families pursue to maintain or improve their position in the class structure depend on the volume and composition of the capital to be reproduced and the state of the instruments of reproduction (e.g., inheritance law and custom, labor market, the educational system). A change in the instruments of reproduction or the state of the capital to be reproduced "leads to the restructuring of the system of reproduction strategies. The reconversion of capital held in one form to another, more accessible, more profitable or more legitimate form tends to induce a transformation of asset structure" (Bourdieu 1984, 125, 131).

As Bourdieu's model would predict, throughout the twentieth century and increasingly after World War II, sons in Como's middle bourgeois families who did not plan to enter the firm pursued professional careers as lawyers, engineers, scientists, and university professors. These were commonly the younger sons in large sibships. Their older brothers, in contrast, prepared to manage the firm by studying for a laurea (equivalent to a bachelor's degree) in economics and business. Daughters commonly studied languages that would be useful in either the commercial and marketing departments of the firm or as cultural capital that enhanced their marriage prospects and the family's social prestige.

As the silk industry contracted and the prospects of class reproduction through the inheritance of firms and capital decreased, more children pursued higher education and professional careers. In the end, the education and career trajectories of the inside and outside siblings' children in the Galbiati family were remarkably similar. They became professionals, teachers, social workers, employees of business firms, and business consultants. Most significantly, none of them owned and managed their own firm. In 2010, when I asked one of the outside siblings who is a successful professional how his family's ownership of a firm when he was growing up affected his life, he said, "We had more money than I have now. We went on more vacations."

The Borsani Family: In Praise of Specialization

Not all firms owned by the middle bourgeoisie of Como shut down. Those that weathered the crisis in manufacturing are, for the most part, those specializing in producing fabric in small batches for the high end of the fashion industry. Camisca Tessitura Serica, a weaving firm founded in 1925, is one such firm. When I first studied it in 1985, the firm had successfully made the transition of management and ownership from its founder to his sons (Yanagisako 2002, 70–73). The two sons had continued the weaving firm but also diversified their investments by opening a converter firm. This enabled them to expand into a sector of the industry that was becoming increasingly important for the successful marketing of textiles.

When I returned to find out what had happened in the intervening twenty-five years, the firm appeared to be in the midst of the transition to the next generation. Ettore Borsani, who at the time I interviewed him in 1985 had been one of the middle-aged sons managing the firm, was now the about-to-retire father of the son who was taking over active management. He recounted how, after his father's death, he and his brother, Franco, had each inherited 42 percent, while his mother and sister together had inherited 16 percent. He did not explain how this had been brought about, but given Italian inheritance law, it must have been with the consent (whether happy or grudging) of his mother and sister. Franco had only one child—a daughter—who was not interested in taking over the firm; nor was Ettore's daughter. Hence, the path to succession was clear for Ettore's only son.

The firm responded to the decline in manufacturing and reduced demand for their products in the 1990s by closing the converter firm and absorbing some of its employees into the weaving firm. Ettore explained that they had never considered initiating business in China, because they specialize in producing luxury fabrics in small quantities. This enabled them to avoid competition from manufacturers at lower levels. Ettore was in the middle of telling us how his son, Lorenzo, had worked in their converter firm for four years and then gone to work for other firms after it closed, when Lorenzo arrived to join the conversation. Like his father, Lorenzo was congenial and gracious—if quite a bit more ebullient. He jumped into the conversation to recount the firms he had worked for before returning to take his uncle's place in the commercial end of the firm. As often occurred in such interviews with fathers and sons, Ettore almost immediately interrupted Lorenzo to correct his statements or add details. When Lorenzo left, Ettore gave a surprisingly candid assessment of his son's strengths (having good taste, being exacting) and weaknesses (being too difficult to please, being a bit naïve). He explained that they have a difficult relationship and disagree on a number of issues, including how to hold down costs. His relationship with his own father had been easier, he reflected, perhaps because Carlo had left the management of the firm to Ettore and Franco when they were in their early thirties. It was also, he acknowledged, an easier time in the industry and the clients were more loyal.

Contentious as the relationship between father and son may have been, intergenerational succession appeared to be underway once again at Camisca Tessitura Serica. If the firm was not in a phase of expansion as it had been in the 1980s, the Borsani family could still count itself among the chosen few that had been successful enough to survive the transition to the next generation.

The Lost Generation of Firms

Family members have not been the only source of the generation of firms in industrial districts like Como. This was especially the case for small, subcontracting firms. In my 1985 sample, among the eleven firms in the lower bourgeoisie who worked as subcontractors for larger firms, only two had parents in the industry. The other nine had working-class, technical, or white-collar fathers who had never owned firms (Yanagisako 2002, 108–9). Many of the owners of subcontracting firms, moreover, began their careers working as technical directors or managers in other firms, often with the clear intention of learning their employers' techniques and acquiring the practical training that would prepare them to open their own firms. As was noted in both parts I and II of this book, throughout the nineteenth century, family firms were the breeding grounds for managers and technicians who left to open their own firms. Some of these were relatives who were not in the line of succession; others were nonrelatives.

The transformation of technical directors and managers into the owners of subcontracting firms was a well-established pattern of upward mobility in industrial districts such as Como and an integral part of the process of the reproduction of subcontracting firms (Yanagisako 2002). It has also meant that a firm's employees, especially its managers, could become its competitors. The thin line between on-the-job training and industrial espionage reinforced owners' disinclination to place nonfamily members in upper-level management positions, creating a "kinship glass ceiling" beyond which nonfamily members did not rise (Yanagisako 2002, 138). This cap on advancement, in turn, fueled the frustrations of ambitious managers who would leave to start their own firms. The continual exodus of skilled technical managers from Como firms generated a constant supply of potential founders of new subcontracting firms. These men had not only knowledge and experience but also indispensable social ties to other firms in the industrial network. Their ambitions were spurred by both the demand for their services from larger firms during the robust growth of the industry in the 1960s and 1970s and by masculine sentiments and desires to be their own boss.

With the overseas outsourcing of all the phases of production except design, the impetus for opening new firms was drastically reduced. Not only was the number of large- and medium-sized firms reduced, but those that continued were being supplied by weaving, printing, and dyeing subcontracting firms in China or Romania. At the same time, as we saw in chapter 1, the vast majority of Italian technicians and managers who are employed in Italian or Italian-Chinese joint ventures in China have neither the Chinese-language skills nor the knowledge of local industrial networks to draw on. Neither do they have access to the labor of family members, which was critical in the early years of small and medium firms in Como. In short, outsourcing has impeded the generation of new firms by Italian managers and technicians in both Italy and China.

Among the twenty Italian technicians and managers we encountered in China, only two had learned Mandarin or the local dialect, developed local friendships and networks, and appeared to have any interest in starting a firm in China. Both had recently married local Chinese women. Consequently, in addition to having local social networks, these men had wives and in-laws who were potential collaborators in a family firm.

The Promise of Transnational Start-Ups

In contrast to some other managers who appeared to have been chosen as visual representations of their Italian fashion brand, Antonio Peroni seemed more like the friendly corner grocer. His wrinkled suit and jovial banter were uncharacteristic and refreshing, and he seemed to be enjoying himself more than the others. As the chief financial officer in the Vinimoon joint venture, he was one of two managers appointed by the Italian firm to work with their Chinese partners. Peroni had joined the firm in Italy after obtaining his laurea in business management and working in management control for another company. When we first met him at the joint venture's factory in Wenzhou, he had been working there for five years. Two years later, we met with him in the joint venture's main office in Shanghai, which he had been traveling to weekly. Most of the time, he lived with his Chinese wife and young son in her home city, where the factory was located and where he appeared to have more ties to the Chinese than did his colleagues. As his son approached school age, he became interested in moving to Shanghai, where his son would have access to a better education.

In contrast to the other managers, moreover, Peroni had made some effort to learn Mandarin. He had enrolled in some classes and also learned, as he put it, "from the street." He met his wife, who worked at a travel agency, through friends in the city where the factory was located. He joked that he was waiting for his child to start school so that he could learn Chinese with him. While he expected to return to Italy one day, he did not know when, and he was content with his life in China for the time being. He reported that he and his wife had made a verbal agreement that she would one day move to Italy with him. Yet he said that he was aware that when Chinese people get old they just want to go back home, and he expected that this would happen to his wife. Peroni had no immediate plans to start a firm in China, but he had the managerial experience, cultural knowledge, and social networks to make this a distinct possibility.

Carlo Stella, on the other hand, had already begun to lay the groundwork for his future in China after his work in the Jiaxing Style Silk Company ended. His career and family history, moreover, resembled that of technicians in Como who worked as employees for years before starting up their own firms. At the age of forty, he had more than twenty years of on-the-job training as a technician in silk production. After completing two years of technical school, Stella had begun working in his current employer's factory in Italy when he was sixteen years old. This was the same factory where his mother had worked before he was born. Although he was, above all, an electrician, over the years he has learned just about every aspect of production in a silk weaving factory, and he was now the head technician at his employer's factory in Jiaxing. As he gave us a guided tour of the factory, in which he took great pleasure in describing the details of the manufacturing process, he recounted how he had agreed to be transferred to China in 2001. As we later learned, this was just after he and his first wife had divorced.

Like Antonio Peroni, Carlo Stella stood out among the Italian managers and technicians in China. Like Peroni, he had spent several of his early years in China living the late-night, bachelor life with Chinese friends. He had, moreover, learned the local Jiaxing dialect through his night-time social life and weekend fishing trips with local friends, as well as through daily communication with the workers he supervised. When he took us for lunch at a local restaurant, he brought along a close Chinese friend with whom he spoke the local dialect. At another lunch with the Chinese manager of the factory, he spoke a mix of the local dialect, Mandarin, and English, which he had learned from his girlfriend and the manager. Stella also expressed more positive attitudes toward Chinese workers, whom he described as good people who were more reliable and hard-working than Italian workers—in spite of what he viewed as their racist attitude toward those with darker skin from other regions of the country. He was content with his life in China and had returned to Italy only three times over ten years—once for his father's funeral and then to visit his widowed mother. Ever since a German supermarket had opened in town and he could get all his favorite Italian foods, the only things he missed were horseback riding and skiing. The absence of other Italians in the area was of little consequence to him.

Stella's marriage to his girlfriend, which he said was at the insistence of her parents, brought him not only in-laws with local social networks but a wife whose work skills complemented his. She drew on her English speaking and writing skills in her job handling client relations with a clothing manufacturer, which we later discovered was one of the other joint ventures we were studying. Together he and his wife combined two skill sets indispensable to initiating a silk weaving firm: a skilled and experienced technician and a multilingual commercial agent with knowledge of client networks. When rumors began circulating that the firm he was working for might be sold any day to a Hong Kong company, Stella mused that he might accept a friend's offer to work as a consultant in quality control or he might find another job as a technician. In any event, he planned to continue working in China for another dozen years and return to Italy only after retiring. Returning to work in Italy was not a serious consideration since the textile sector was doing very badly there. The factory where he used to work, for example, had reduced its workforce from five hundred to thirty employees. But, he said lightheartedly, the real reason he could not return to Italy was because he was very attached to his dog.

Neither Antonio Peroni nor Carlo Stella had immediate plans to open their own firms in China. To do so would require both substantial financial investment and a leap of faith. But both men had the knowledge, skills, and access to local social networks to be the transnational counterparts to the ambitious technicians and managers who generated new firms in Italian industrial districts. Luciano Ferrari, whose entrepreneurial history was discussed in chapter 3 and whose marital history I discuss below, had drawn on a similar combination of experience and kinship resources to do just that.

A Promising Transnational Marriage

After owning and managing a firm near Milan that had been shut down during a period of intense labor conflict, Luciano Ferrari took a job in China working for one of the leading Italian brands in women's intimate clothing. He was in his late fifties and, by his own account, struggling to remake himself and his career after a devastating end to his business and his marriage. His search for garment factories that could meet the quality demanded by the Italian luxury brands during these early days of outsourcing production to China led him on the pioneering adventures described in chapter 3. It also led him to set up his own independent trading company, which contracted with a number of Italian and French fashion brands, including his former employer, to arrange production in China. Expanding production to meet the needs of his new clients required finding the right factories to hire as subcontractors. This was proving difficult because the state corporation with which he had worked was not meeting these needs, so he decided to hire an interpreter and track down sources on his own. He found a young Chinese woman with a university degree in Italian language who proved very adept at leading him to the right factories. He subsequently married her. Ferrari was then in his early sixties; his wife—who took on the name Patrizia— was twenty-five to thirty years younger than him.

By the time Simona Segre Reinach and I met him in Milan in 2005, Luciano Ferrari was seventy-three years old. A son from his first marriage, Paolo, who worked in the firm, was about to turn forty. Leonardo Benini, who managed the Ferrari firm in Shanghai, had told us Paolo and his stepmother, Maria, did not always agree, and sometimes they had verbal disagreements in front of clients. Neither was the relationship between father and son unproblematic. If we were a bit surprised that Benini would be so indiscreet as to reveal the tensions within the family, we began to appreciate what an understatement this was when we met with father and son in their Milan office. Luciano Ferrari openly belittled his son, complaining that he did not know how to sell anything, contradicting his answers to our questions, and, in the end, telling him to shut up. Paolo made a weak attempt to curb his father's performance of patriarchal power. Simona and I, having gotten most of the information we were seeking, withdrew.

By winter 2007, the firm's office in Milan had closed. Luciano Ferrari, however, was far from ready to give up and was searching for a new office site in Milan. He reported that the business in China was going strong and that they had opened a new factory thirty kilometers from Shanghai. His wife, he said, continued to manage the business in China, and his son Paolo handled their clients in Europe. Yet there were clear indications that all was not well in either the firm or the family. Whereas in the earlier meeting, Luciano had told us it was thanks to his wife that he had been able to find the right suppliers, he now complained that Maria did not know how to keep employees happy, was too brusque and curt, and was making bad decisions about where to locate the factory. Whereas he had said he loved China because it had given him the possibility to remake his life and had given him a wife and son, he now said that he had made a mistake in setting up a 50–50 partnership with a "Chinese woman." Toward the end of our meeting, he asked if I was Chinese. When I told him I was not, he launched into a litany of complaints of how difficult it was to work with Chinese people.

When we asked whether we could speak to his wife when we were in China, Ferrari was ambivalent. He first told us not to, then reversed himself and told us to go ahead and contact her but not to mention that we had spoken to him; otherwise she would think that he had spoken badly of her. We never did get to speak to Maria Ferrari, who proved to be quite elusive. When I finally got her on the phone, she was clearly wary of us and declined to meet. This was not surprising, as she and Luciano were by that time on the verge of an acrimonious divorce.

Four months after our last meeting with him in Milan, Segre Reinach and I spoke with Luciano Ferrari at his vacation home on the coast near San Remo. Meeting at the bright sunny port where he moored his boat only heightened the gloom of our conversation. While earlier he had been hesitant to fully disclose the crisis in the firm and family, he no longer held back. The complaints about his wife were now accusations and condemnations. In short, he rued the day he had married his wife and gave her 50 percent of the business. He revealed that she had fired the staff in the Milan design office without his permission because she decided they cost too much. She threw out all the designs and estimates of his architect for the factory in Shanghai and tried to save money by giving the job to Chinese architects. The result, he said, was doors that do not close, silk awnings that do not open, and dirty bathrooms. At their last meeting, it became clear that she had been planning to push him out of the firm, because she had laid out several options for him—all of which gave her control of the firm. He was livid. They were having dinner at his sister's house, and he was seated at an antique table. He wanted to throw the table at her, but his son stopped him. Luciano explained, "She has the houses, the estates, the factories. She has everything. What does she want? She wants to become the *padrona del mondo* [boss of the world]." As for himself, Luciano said, "I will never leave. I will die inside [the business]. I would like to continue it for the son we have in common." At the end of our lunch in the sunny port, he invited Segre Reinach and me to see the photos of his family in his condominium on the hill overlooking the port. Our tour of the family photos that lined the white walls and stood on the white shelves of his contemporary, spacious condominium had the tone of a memorial service. Among the photos were several childhood photos of his two sons from his first marriage, and some that appeared to be of his older son, this son's wife, and their children. The majority of the photos, however, were of himself and Maria, and their son. The photos had been taken in various sites in China, and they showed a family that appeared to be happy. Maria was indeed a beautiful woman.

A year later in Shanghai, Leonardo Benini, who had been working in a different firm since 2005, told us that Luciano and Maria had divorced. According to him, Luciano had wanted to continue as a converter and keep the design office in Italy. He had, after all, worked with many of the women in the Milan office for forty years and felt a paternalist commitment to them. But Maria felt it cost too much and wanted instead to move all the work to China. She won and opened two factories in China. How she had succeeded in buying out Luciano was unclear, but she was now the sole owner of the firm. She and Luciano continued fighting even after they had separated and she had bought him out, because he did not want her to have the Ferrari name for the company. Benini said he understood how painful it was for Luciano to let her continue with the Ferrari name because of his Italian pride of being a self-made man.

Three years later, in 2010, Benini reported that her business was doing very well. Maria had renamed it. It was now called "Maria Intimates."

Conclusion

Kinship has always been a key productive force in industrial capitalism in Italy. It is no less so after two decades of outsourcing manufacturing overseas and the decline in manufacturing in many Italian industrial districts. In this chapter, I have shown how the transnational expansion of some family firms, such as FGS and Rinaudo, strengthened intergenerational succession, enabling these families to bind together multiple generations and branches of the family. At the same time, kinship has been central in the division and the demise of firms that have not succeeded in transnational expansion. Whether bourgeois families have continued their firms in constricted form, as in the case of Molteni and Barbieri, or have closed them and moved the next generation into the professions, as in the case of Galbiati, kinship has been central in shaping their investments and the conversion of financial capital into other forms of social and cultural capital. It continues, as well, to be key to generational succession in small firms like Borsani, whose specialization in luxury production has enabled it to survive, and in the emergence of new firms out of the ashes of old ones, as in the case of Casati.

These family and industrial histories reveal that kinship continues to be crucial in yet another way to the generative potentialities of Como and other Italian textile and clothing districts. The reduction of manufacturing, employment, and gross output in these industrial districts has been accompanied by a reduction in the creation of new firms. Given the outsourcing to China, greater potential for the generation of new firms lies in developing industrial networks in China. Whether the few Italian-Chinese marriages described in this chapter presage the forging of new kinship enterprises and new family firms remains to be seen. Luciano and Maria Ferrari's marriage attests to the challenges of such transnational collaborations. As in all kinship enterprises, not all family members share the same goals and vision.

Finally, in this chapter I have argued for the analytic benefits of a dynamic approach to the relation between labor and capital, which investigates how the boundary between them is made and remade through historically specific processes and relations. Rather than assume that this boundary is a stable structure of capitalism, my analysis has shown how its rigidity and permeability changes in relation to the shifting opportunities and availability of not only financial but also social and cultural capital. With the outsourcing of manufacturing to overseas locations, Italian managers and technicians have been blocked from their main path of social mobility in Italian industrial districts—namely, opening a firm of their own. The outsourcing of manufacturing to China has largely closed off this avenue of career advancement and class mobility to managers who have neither family labor on which to draw or local networks that would provide them with sufficient social capital to open a firm. In short, the boundary between labor and capital has hardened.

6 The Reappearance and Elusiveness of Chinese Family Firms

Lisa Rofel

With economic reform in China, "family firms" have once again reappeared in the market economy. Family firms are scattered throughout the textile and garment industries. My argument in this chapter is that in order to appreciate the meanings and practices of "family firms" in China today, we need to examine how interpretations of the socialist past inform the discussions and debates about what family firms stand for and how they should—and should not—do business. The whole nexus of relations between family, business, and the state, in other words, is shaped by these historical legacies and revisionist histories. Rather than simply assert that family firms have arisen in China, my argument is that in fact it is not entirely clear what counts as a legitimate "family firm."[1] In contrast with Italy, where there has long existed a hegemonic ideal type of the family firm (which many deviate from, as shown in Yanagisako's chapter in part III), China is in the midst of a heated debate with different and ambivalent valences surrounding this question. There does not yet exist a single, dominant notion of the "family firm," as ideas about the relations of family/private enterprise/the state/guanxi (networking) have not settled into a single ideal. Instead, there are multiple, emergent discourses that are all fraught. These complicated negotiations over the meanings and practices of family firms are in turn shaped by negotiations over what constitutes a proper capitalist market economy: what counts as fair and unfair profit-seeking practices, and what counts as truly "private" and separate from the state. Italian firms in the fashion industry play a key role in the ideological shifts in China enabling more family firms. Those who collaborate with Italian firms know that the latter prefer to work with family firms in China, thus legitimizing their operation, at least in the textile and apparel industries. Moreover, as we shall see, several Chinese firms that work with Italians actually got their start in Italy. Their sense of themselves as personally connected to both China and Italy enables them to step outside the ambivalence about family firms in China. Finally, one Chinese family firm I discuss wanted to work with an Italian firm in order to prevent family feuds about the business and possibly its dissolution.

This chapter outlines how family firms take some unexpected forms as a result of socialist historical legacies. First, family firms are often seen as an index of corruption and therefore, rather than touted, are usually hidden or denied. Second, family firms are equated with "privatization." Depending on how the process of privatization has occurred—whether through a state-owned enterprise or the development of the firm wholly within the market economy—these firms are held up as the model of deviant or proper economic behavior. Third, family firms that are not those of officials' families, especially large family firms, are often viewed as cultural exceptions within China and therefore in need of explanation. Fourth, although family firms are often equated with privatization, in fact for them to exist and thrive, they often need to be nestled within what we might call pyramid schemes linked to the state. This situation leads to the hiring of children in family firms—not necessarily the children of the firm owners, but rather the children of government officials who are instrumental to helping the firm. Finally, to reiterate, within the fashion industry in particular, the family firms that exist find some of their justification from the fact that they work with Italian family firms that are so prominent in the industry. That is, those who have worked closely with Italian firms or who have lived in Italy feel less concerned about displaying the fact that they are a family firm.

These variations not just in the form but in the valuation of family firms are tied to the effective evacuation of socialism. Corruption is blamed on socialism rather than the capitalist pursuit of wealth, thus enabling people to fantasize an ideal market economy that would be fair and equal, allowing family firms not tied to the families of officials to thrive. Yet talk of family as corruption is simultaneously a discussion of hierarchies and inequalities that are both a continuation of previous inequalities as well as the appearance of new ones. There exists a fundamental paradox in these discussions: everyone takes for granted that one should help family members advance, yet in the context of the market economy and unequal means for helping one's children, accusations of corruption account for different abilities to do so.[2]

Family Guanxi (Connections) as an Index of Corruption

Kinship plays an important role in the transnational managerial class. Yet family firms in contemporary mainland China (as distinct from Hong Kong, Taiwan, and Southeast Asia) have a different valence than among Italian entrepreneurial families. Most striking from our research is the dichotomy in the self-presentation of many firms in China's textile, garment, and fashion industries. To their Italian counterparts, they asserted that they are family firms because the Italians were looking for family firms to work with, as they believed them to be more trustworthy than government firms. But to me or anyone in China who asked, they just as vehemently denied they are family firms.

For example, I was able to interview the owner of a conglomerate of textile/garment/dyeing factories, Zhejiang New Dawn Group Ltd., located along the historic Grand Canal in one of the former villages that had been transformed into a highly polluted industrial town. Zhang Hualiang was a young man around thirty-five years old at the time I met him in 2008. We spoke in his office on the spacious company grounds. The President's Office (so named on the prominent door sign) was of huge proportions. There were also tasteful pieces of traditional Chinoiserie placed around the room.

Zhang Hualiang was casually dressed with a white sports shirt and highly designed jeans. He wore several silver rings and sported a very long fingernail on the pinkie, a recovery of a presocialist elite practice signifying a male who does not need to labor with his hands. In his own narrative, he had risen up from an ordinary farmer family to become the owner of a highly profitable business that produced for Italians and other foreigners. He had bought out state-run factories that had gone bankrupt. When I asked if he had family members involved in the business, he categorically answered in the negative. But the very next day, one of his administrative staff casually commented on his sisters who worked in the firm. He complained that these sisters felt entitled to treat the staff badly and therefore had a bad effect on business.

In contemporary China, having family manage or own a business together is often seen as an index of corruption and inefficiency rather than a sign of trustworthiness, good business sense, or even proper morality. This is especially true if the firm has evolved out of a state-run enterprise. People from various positions both within and without the commodity chain of fashion clothing told cautionary tales of family involvement in companies. We heard one of these cautionary tales when we visited Fashion Power, a large, casual-wear firm that started in Wenzhou (a city in southern Zhejiang province discussed below) but then moved its headquarters to Pudong, Shanghai. Fashion Power's headquarters looked like a cross between Soviet-style architecture, once popular all over China, and European medieval grandiosity.[3] The vice president who met us was a young man in his midthirties. He spoke excellent English, having studied at a U.S. business school. He had perfect public relations skills. He explained the firm's history:

> Fashion Power was started as a factory in Wenzhou but the owner quickly tried to move away from production and into branding and retailing. They really began this business in 1995, though he started the factory in 1991. It is not public—not on the stock exchange. It is fully private but it is not a family firm either. Family firms can be a lot of trouble; they bring a lot of emotions and are not just a business relationship. The owner keeps his family out of the business.

Sylvia Yanagisako then remarked that she had studied family firms in Italy and yes, they are complicated in that way.

Although the vice president did not directly reference corruption, it need not always be explicitly invoked. Yet there is a wide and general discourse about it. Netizens in China delight in detailing the enormous wealth amassed by family members of top party/state officials. The scandal about former premier Wen Jiabao's family wealth is merely one of the most prominent of these narrative events.[4]

That family involvement indexes corruption goes back to the Cultural Revolution (1966–76).[5] During the Cultural Revolution, urban youth were sent to the countryside to learn from peasants.[6] Many youth went willingly and with political passion. But what they had not realized at first is that they would never be allowed to return to the cities. Gradually, only those whose parents had political connections, or those with worker parents who resigned their factory positions by retiring early in order to have their child replace them, managed to leave the countryside. Since the Cultural Revolution, it has become commonplace to believe that only family connections—particularly political connections—allow someone to get anywhere in life. This view has its corollary assumption: that someone who advances in any way owing to family members is not a qualified, capable individual but is only filling a position owing to what is commonly called guanxi.[7]

A young woman who had recently graduated from Donghua University's business school talked to us about how young graduates find jobs in Shanghai, which is a coveted place to work.

LISA   Do students not want to work for the government?

CELIA   It depends. Often those who have family guanxi will work for the government or in a state-owned enterprise. They get a secure job and don't have to worry.

LISA   Is this the case for students who come from Shanghai?

CELIA   Yes, of course, they have guanxi here in Shanghai. Those students from other places, they sometimes go back to those places to work because of their family guanxi. But here in Shanghai they go to work for foreign companies.

LISA   Does this family guanxi extend to private businesses, like Chinese businesses?

CELIA   Of course, the family will know someone who will hire their child. In foreign businesses, too.

LISA   How does that work?

CELIA   The parent might be a government official and the foreign company needs a favor from the government, so they hire their child. It might be for a job that does not require much and many people could do it, so they hire that person's child over someone else.

Celia's comments demonstrate how kinship is important to the transnational managerial class. Yet the valence Celia gives to that importance is ambiguous. The fact that kinship is central to acquiring jobs in firms proves, in Celia's view, that they are not hiring qualified people. Moreover, this family guanxi depends on location. Celia prides herself on not relying on family guanxi in Shanghai, as her family is in Xian, thus implying that she earned her position through her own personal qualifications.

At the same time, everyone knows they have to rely on their kin—and on their kin's guanxi—to get anywhere, even though they make a negative evaluation of this need, at least when it pertains to others. If Celia had family connections in Shanghai, presumably she would have been happy to use them. Thus, the line between "corrupt" and "proper" familial support is not always clear. One person's understandable desire to help a family member or be helped by them is another person's corruption. Indeed, it would seem unnatural to most people in China if family members were unwilling to help one another. Such a refusal would be interpreted as a refusal to recognize one another as kin. Hence the paradoxical condemnation of family involvement in a business. People condemn this state of affairs as yet another example of government corruption. Yet they assume everyone—not just already privileged elites—use family relations or guanxi to help their children get ahead.

A young female sales representative for Zhang Hualiang's company explained to me:

> Now, it's hard to find work in China, even for college graduates. You have to know how to handle relationships between people [meaning you have to be able to pull strings to get a job]. This is really too strong in China. In our factory workshop, there is a university graduate working as an ordinary worker. That means he didn't have anybody he knew who could help him get a job, no relatives who could help him.

This comment exemplifies my argument that discourse about family connections and corruption is simultaneously a discussion about new hierarchies and inequalities.

Li Linfeng, whom I introduced in chapter 1 as the manager of Hui Hua Yi/Silk Nouvelle, spoke about his own son one day over lunch at the company headquarters. His son is the head of a silk factory in a small city not far from Hangzhou. As Li explained, when his son graduated from college, he asked his father for advice about whether he should work in the international trade office or in a factory. Li advised him to work in the factory because, he reasoned, with the lower profits in the silk industry, the role of the international trade offices was going to shrink because foreign customers want to go directly to the factories. But he let his son choose, he said. His son chose to head up the factory. Li emphasized that he does not give his son any special advantage because he believes that family members should prove their worth.

This conversation only makes sense if what is implied is made explicit: that the factory where his son works is owned by Li's corporation, Splendid

China. The fact that his son could choose which place to work is entirely due to Li's position and ability to provide his son with a job. To become head of a factory right out of college is nearly impossible without family connections. Li did not need to spell out these facts to me in this conversation. When Li says he does not give his son any special advantage, he means that he does not use Splendid China's funds to supplement any losses at his son's factory, nor does he skew contracts entirely in his son's direction. From Li's point of view, he has done the right thing by his son and has done no more nor less than others who help their family members. But others might readily use this example as proving the point about the corruption rampant in government entities, for only children of government officials would be able to rise so quickly in this manner.

Yet even among party cadres, there exists a critique of corruption through family guanxi. Recall from chapter 2 that what we conventionally consider to be privatization had indeed occurred at the lower end of the textile industry's hierarchy, that is, with the factories themselves. In that chapter, I described how my friend Tang Shan, an upright party cadre, had described the privatization process for me in the Zhenfu factory, the one I had written about in my first book: the state had handed over the factory and its resources to the factory's state-appointed manager and had given him a loan from a state-owned bank to buy the majority of shares.

I then asked about the current owner. Tang Shan explained that the former manager/owner had died of a sudden heart attack and the board of directors had appointed his son to take over. We continued.

> LR   I have to ask an impolite question. I have been sensing that something is wrong with Zhenfu. It doesn't feel right. No one told me anything but I could feel it. What is going on?

This question finally allowed Tang Shan's characteristic bluntness to burst forth.

> TS   Ah, you sense it too. This son has no ability [*mei nengli*]. He's uncultivated [*mei wenhua*]. He's just like we were talking about the other day. Parents who are better off end up with children who don't want to make an effort to study, while the children of workers, these workers push their children to go to university.
>
> LR   Then why did they make him owner of this factory?

TS   The silk corporation was trying to honor "the face" of his dad [*ta babade mianzi*].

LR   But if he's so incapable, why doesn't the board of directors gently push him to one side?

TS   Because they are all older and about to retire, and they don't want to insult [*dezui*] him.

LR   But in this way, Zhenfu will eventually have to close. Why don't they hire someone younger?

TS   This son is only in his early thirties. He's just lazy and doesn't want to use his brain. I've gone and yelled at him. Just the other day I yelled at him. I said to him, you don't move your brain. If you and I are both on the job market, I'd like to see which one of us gets the better job, me, an old lady with gray hair, or you. I'm sure it will be me.

What upset Tang Shan was not just the inability of the current owner to be agile in making profits. She was angry that Zhenfu, which had once been a renowned factory, was ignominiously losing its former glory.[8] This extended conversation with Tang Shan perfectly captures a widespread narrative about the corruption associated with establishing a family firm out of state resources. Discourses about family firms as an index of corruption are simultaneously debates about the particular kinds of social inequalities that have arisen out of the market economy in China. This discourse does not reject the existence of hierarchies in favor of radical egalitarianism. The latter has been discredited along with the rejection of most of the socialist past. Rather, discourses about corruption are a discussion about legitimating certain hierarchies and delegitimating others. This, in turn, depends on an ideal notion of a market economy that could work well for everyone if only one could get rid of corruption. This notion, of course, begs the question of whether capitalism itself produces corruption and inefficiencies or the kinds of inequalities and exploitations that could be labeled corruption.[9] Discourses of corruption place the root cause of that corruption in the socialist past. They indicate the difficulty of making clear distinctions between the desire to help family members to advance, which is taken for granted as cultural common sense, and the reality that certain families are better positioned to help their members than others.

Wenzhou as (Exception and) Exceptional

There are, of course, numerous family firms throughout China and in different sectors of the economy. When "corruption" is not used as the explanation for their success, scholars, economic researchers, and popular media search for other explanations. One frequent explanation they turn to are the differences in regional cultures. One popular example is the city of Wenzhou. Wenzhou is in the southern part of coastal Zhejiang province, which is adjacent to and just south of Shanghai. Wenzhou is often held up as the quintessential exception to the dominant form of economic success in China, which depends on official involvement. Professor Jihong Hu of Donghua University business school, for example, once invoked what is often called "the Wenzhou model of development" to contrast it with the Shanghai model of development. The former, he averred, is based on small family firms, while the latter is based on government investment.

A great deal has been written about what makes Wenzhou special. One popular Chinese book (H. Yang 2007) attributes Wenzhou's seemingly special economic vitality to essential cultural traits. The book's title already sets out the clear cultural differences between Wenzhou and the rest of China: *Wenzhou People Think Differently Than You: How Wenzhou People Become Rich* (*Wenzhou ren xiangde he ni buyiyang: Wenzhou ren weishenma hui chengwei furen*). The book starts out with a short aphorism, meant to represent the archetypes of "poor person" and "Wenzhou person."

POOR PERSON I think about starting my own business, but setting up business doesn't suit everyone and there are a lot of risks. It's better to be a worker and have some security.

WENZHOU PERSON Why should I work for someone else? Even with little capital it's important to set up one's own business, to work for oneself. To be one's own boss is the proper goal in life. To fail is also a life experience. Someone who doesn't want to be a boss is definitely not from Wenzhou. (Wu 2004, 3)

In this aphorism, a "poor person" is someone who eats the "iron rice bowl" of a steady job, presumably in a state-owned company. A "Wenzhou person" is the opposite. A Wenzhou person demonstrates a willingness to take risks in order to be one's own boss. Interestingly, the figure of the "poor person" is not necessarily a factory worker; he or she could just as easily be a government employee. Indeed, secure jobs in China today are mostly found in government, not in factories, and they are highly desirable (see Tang and Tomba 2013).

The book is filled with anecdotal stories about successful entrepreneurs from Wenzhou. One story goes as follows: Hu Xucang graduated from Wenzhou University. His father, who worked in the municipal commerce bureau, asked him what he wanted to do after he graduated. Without hesitation, he said, "I want to open a company, even if I fail I want to work in business, I don't want to have a lifetime's iron rice bowl." All of his relatives were entrepreneurs; Hu went to work for his third uncle, who had a plastic tubing business. Hu then made the company a success by forming a joint venture with an international company; he became board chairman and eventually a representative of Wenzhou in the People's Congress. His father praised him as having daring, vision, and courage as well as maturity.

While *Wenzhou People Think Differently Than You* purports to describe essential traits of all who hail from Wenzhou, the story of Hu Xucang sounds exactly like those family businesses that are accused of corruption—with the important exception that Hu's family, and implicitly Wenzhou people more broadly, do not build their businesses out of state resources but rather from their own capital. (Although Hu's father is a government official and presumably used his connections to help the family businesses.)

Strikingly, this book argues that it is precisely reliance on the family and the formation of family businesses that make Wenzhou quintessentially distinct.

> Because family members not only have a relationship of mutual benefit, but even more, a relationship of blood ties, which strengthens the feeling of responsibility and togetherness, it leads them to develop boundless capabilities, to produce a cooperation that means one plus one is greater than two. (Wu 2004, 95)

Building on this familial mutuality of benefits, Wenzhou people are also willing to sacrifice for the sake of the family business.

> When they first start going into business, the majority of Wenzhou people choose family workshops as their form of business. . . . Within these businesses, some are husband/wife, some are brothers, some are sisters, and some are partners from the same village. Their family strength continues to grow. In the end, the small workshops turn into family businesses. (Wu 2004, 95)

Here one finds language very similar to that of the Maoist socialist period. Though the object or goal of one's sacrifice and hard work is obviously quite different, the manner in which one reaches it is quite similar—what used to be termed "eating bitterness." Moreover, one finds a blurring between those ties built on "blood" and those ties built on native-place affiliation, that is, partners from the same village.

One story praises the daughter of a company founder who was first chosen to be a "red hat" company (that is, one of the first to become a private company). After the 1989 Tiananmen demonstrations, when private enterprises were attacked in the Chinese media, the founders fled to Spain. In the interim, the daughter, who had stayed behind, stepped in.

> Family members' self-constraint and self-sacrificing spirit strengthen the cohesiveness of the firm. At the same time because management and the possession of property rights are all in the family, there can be unanimity throughout the management, and decision-making is very simple. (Wu 2004, 98)

Here one must point out the gendered subtext: although the father actually fled and left the firm to others who might have been the object of a serious political campaign, and although his eldest daughter actually saved the company, the father is still head of the firm, not simply because of property rights but because of his position as family patriarch. There is in fact a chapter in the book on how the women of Wenzhou are just as successful as the men at becoming entrepreneurs. In that chapter, the language again echoes Maoist socialism in praising women for being the same as men, on the one hand, and using men as the standard, on the other.[10]

In sum, Wenzhou people are said to have a different psychological attitude, philosophy, and perhaps even biology than other people in China. But even with the text's attempts to explain how Wenzhou is exceptional in terms of entrepreneurship and family firms, we are still left with a major question: Why is Wenzhou proffered as exceptional? Here we must turn to more structural histories for an answer. Kristen Parris (1993), for example, points out that what she calls Wenzhou's "lively unofficial economy" began in the 1960s and 1970s, well before official economic reform that began in the 1980s. This unofficial, or illegal, economy, she explains, was encouraged by several different factors. These include geographic factors, in that Wenzhou is located in mountainous terrain, with little viable agricultural land. But far more significant were political factors. Wenzhou was considered a strategically vulnerable frontline against nationalist forces in Taiwan and thus received little investment from the central government.[11] Thus, prior to the 1990s, Wenzhou was far poorer than the rest of Zhejiang province and forced to rely on its own resources and expand activities that were at the time considered illegal. In contrast to the central government, however, local Wenzhou officials recognized that they could benefit from this economic activity, and therefore decided to protect it. Thus, the combination of the increased political autonomy of local officials with economic reform and the lack of infrastructure to overcome Wenzhou's geographical isolation from the more economically developed northern part of Zhejiang province enabled a productive collusion between Wenzhou officials and entrepreneurs.

What has been called the Wenzhou model of development—a model that has, since the early 1990s, spread throughout the country—includes widespread household industry and commerce, private wage labor, and labor, commodity, credit, and financial markets. According to Parris, household industry began in Wenzhou during the Cultural Revolution, when basic consumer goods were scarce and the public economy was barely functioning. By the late 1970s, there were several institutional aspects to these household workshops that were already in place. Parris highlights *guahu*, or "hang-on households," in which an independent enterprise became associated with a public enterprise.[12] A second, related institution was known as "wearing a red hat," in which an independent operator registered as a collective with a government neighborhood committee or village office and paid a management fee.[13]

Indeed, much of the "Wenzhou model" is striking for its reflection of the historically variable meanings of "corruption" and "immorality" in economic practices. For example, before the full range of marketing activities were sanctioned by the central government, Wenzhou's commodity markets were already relying on numerous "private marketing agents" (*gongxiao yuan*) who brought information as well as materials and goods to and from Wenzhou and many other areas of China. According to Parris, they were once considered smugglers and profiteers but in the later 1980s were touted as the "backbone of the Wenzhou model." Further, private banks emerged early on in Wenzhou since it was and still is difficult for individual entrepreneurs to obtain loans from state banks. These institutions were also first viewed as illegal by the central government and then legally sanctioned later.

In the early 1980s, debates about Wenzhou rose to the level of national attention, because the central government made Wenzhou into a target in one of its early campaigns against economic corruption. Wenzhou's "special characteristics" were attacked as speculation and profiteering; some private entrepreneurs were imprisoned (Parris 1993, 252). In the mid-1980s, these debates continued: should Wenzhou be a model for the rest of the country or should its practices be considered exploitative? After 1984, when central officials in favor of an expanded market economy gained power, Wenzhou was no longer considered to be a primary exemplar of immoral economic behavior. To the contrary, Wenzhou's "special characteristics" were promoted and have been ever since, with a brief hiatus after the 1989 Tiananmen protests.

Parris (1993) reminds us, however, not to homogenize Wenzhou citizens. There are vast inequalities in wealth in Wenzhou as elsewhere in China. There are many who did not become entrepreneurs but who became workers for others. There is also an increase in school dropouts among the poor and consequently in child labor.

Wenzhou-Italian Joint Venture

We had one major case study of a joint venture between Chinese and Italians in which the Chinese partners in the joint venture were a family firm from Wenzhou. The headquarters of this joint venture, Vinimoon, are located in Wenzhou. This case resonates with some of the descriptions of the Wenzhou model but also departs rather far from it, and certainly far from the paeans discussed above. (See also Yanagisako's discussion of the Italian partner in chapter 5.) I learned about the complications of this joint venture mainly from Jiang Li/Nico, whom we discussed in chapter 1. Recall that Jiang had lived in Italy and then decided to come back to China to work for this joint venture. He was also an ideal informant for us, as he knew a great deal of the intimate details of the firm's problems. I had met with him several times to discuss the firm, but it was not until 2013, when he had left the firm altogether, that he was willing to tell me the following story.

The Chinese partners in the joint venture were the three Cai brothers, all born in the 1960s, thus close to one another in age. The oldest brother began working by selling clothing made at a factory in Wenzhou. But many of the stores threw out the clothing and told him it was junk. That humiliating experience led him to start his own clothing factory. He asked his brothers to join in with him.

This narrative is quite distinct from the paeans to Wenzhou people's seemingly natural business abilities. With his first failures, the oldest brother experienced a sense not of expressing his natural Wenzhou instincts but rather of humiliation that he was not a capable entrepreneur. In addition, these brothers opened their factory in the late 1980s, when it was quite widespread to do so in many rural areas and small towns throughout China, not just Wenzhou.

The second oldest brother had been a carpenter, while the third oldest was a welder. None of them had more than a junior high school education. The oldest brother hired an experienced master worker (*shifu*) from Shanghai to help them make clothing. The oldest brother named the factory after his oldest daughter. As Jiang explained, when you name a business after your child, people know they can trust you to do a good business because you do not want to bring shame to your child.

They had only a few machines in the beginning but gradually they expanded. The business did well because in the 1980s, as Jiang explained, people did not pay that much attention to fashion; they just wanted nice clothes. The brothers had borrowed money from friends and family and eventually paid them back with interest. It is important to note here that the rest of the family, including the parents of these brothers, were not considered to be owners of the business or even long-term investors or shareholders. They enabled the business through their loans but did not have any role in it, either formal or informal. Paying them back in full indicates as much. The oldest brother was the general manager/CEO (*zong jingli*) and managed the finances and investment, the second oldest learned how to make the patterns for the clothing, and the youngest oversaw the actual production.

As the business grew, the Cai brothers started to have problems with each other. The two younger brothers did not like the way their oldest brother acted like the boss. He often made decisions without consulting them. Jiang gave as an example the fact that the oldest brother would invite local government officials to lunch, without inviting his brothers or telling them about it. Some of these officials had no direct relationship to the business. At the end of the year, the two younger brothers would find out that these expenses were charged to the business. They did not know at first because the oldest brother's wife was in charge of accounting. They did not like that he used the money from the business to entertain people. The brother argued that this activity was important for building his reputation and thereby the reputation of the business. And indeed, everyone in China who does business must interact with officials in this manner (see Osburg 2013).[14]

But the two younger brothers were not satisfied. In their view, the oldest brother acted like an authoritarian. He took it upon himself to make decisions about how to invest the money in the business, or how much should be divided among the brothers at the end of the year. Finally, the younger brothers asked the elders among their kinship network to come and settle the matter. They had never made it clear in the beginning who owned what portion of the business. It was a family, so they had not made a contract. But now the parents and other elders made them draw up a contract: the oldest brother would own 45 percent of the business and the two youngest together would own 55 percent. That way, if the two of them did not like something the oldest did, they could oppose him.

It was at this point that the oldest brother went in search of an Italian partner and found FGS, the well-known Italian fashion firm. His ostensible purpose was to expand the business and to learn from an Italian partner how to make fashion clothing. His other purpose, in the view of Jiang, was to have the Italians help keep his brothers from fighting with him or eventually to ease them out of the firm. This aspect of creating a joint venture again runs counter to the popular tale of Wenzhou success. According to the mythology, the key to Wenzhou people's entrepreneurial prowess is precisely the ability of the family to sacrifice for the business and thus the family's advancement. Here, of course, we have a much more tension-ridden process that could potentially tear apart not only the family but also the firm.

Once the joint venture with FGS was established, the Cai brothers indeed set aside their problems for a time, feeling they were facing another entity they had to deal with together. The oldest was still the general manager and was part of the board, the second oldest was still in charge of patterns, and the third was still in charge of production. On the Italian side, they put someone in charge of accounts and also hired an executive director, Paolo Rinaldi (see Yanagisako's chapter 3). The three brothers then began to give Rinaldi a hard time about how much money he was spending. They would tell him he should take the subway from the airport instead of a taxi. He had an apartment in Wenzhou but he liked to go to Shanghai on weekends. They did not like spending the money on his Shanghai apartment. Eventually, Rinaldi got fed up and decided to take a job with another Italian firm, to be in charge of their operations all over Asia. Although the brothers had given him a hard time, they regretted that he had left.

After Rinaldi's departure, the Italian-appointed manager in charge of accounts tried to be executive director but was not up to the job so he stepped down. Then the oldest Cai brother took on the job. The Italian firm decided to send just one person to be the general overseer. He looked over everything that happened but did not really have any other position. The fact that the oldest brother became executive director, without an Italian to balance his power, eventually led to conflicts once again among the brothers. (Again, see chapter 3 for an explanation from the Italian firm owner's point of view.)

These conflicts were aggravated by the fact that FGS changed its production plans. While FGS had owned a factory in Mexico before it established this joint venture, the firm began to use the Mexican factory more extensively to make clothing for the U.S. market. In that way, it did not need to pay taxes for importing into the U.S., whereas it had to pay high taxes for importing from China. The joint venture tried to have its own label for the Chinese market, but it did poorly. The Italian firm owners discovered that Chinese people will buy their clothing if it says "Made in Italy" but not if it says "Made in China." Also, the Cai brothers felt that the Italian manager was wasting a lot of money on this latter venture, so they pulled out. When FGS decided that label was not worth the continuing losses, the firm closed it down.

As of December 2013, when I last spoke with Jiang, FGS was thinking of pulling out of the joint venture. According to Chinese government regulations, they have to stay in the joint venture for ten years, which is how much time had passed by 2013. According to Jiang, FGS does not need to produce clothing in China anymore. The second oldest brother had already pulled out. He fought with the eldest brother, even punching him. He sold his shares to the eldest and left to set up his own clothing factory. The youngest was also thinking of pulling out. Now the eldest brother can do as he likes.

This story of the Wenzhou-based joint venture reveals several important aspects of family firms in China: contrary to the mythology about Wenzhou, the brothers needed the Italians to keep them from tearing apart their family firm. That is, rather than first developing a successful family firm and only then turning to foreign partners, the reverse was the case. In addition, the brothers could not agree on what many have assumed as essential to the way Chinese carry out their business: currying the favor of officials. Here, we see an ambiguity where the line between corruption and successful business strategy is difficult to draw. Third, as with many firms that have evolved out of the market economy in China, it is the children rather than the parents who establish the business. Most entrepreneurs we encountered were young—no more than thirty-five years old—and they all treated their parents as sources of financial support but not at all as a source of knowledge about how to maneuver in the market economy. Fourth, the constant changes in the joint venture were not solely due to the difficulties of Chinese and Italians working together to manage a transnational business but rather to the difficulties among the Cai brothers. They were also due to the particularities of international tariffs, the ability of the Italian firm to locate its production facilities in multiple locations, and the desires of an emerging middle class in China for European fashion—not made in China. Finally, as we will learn later in this chapter, according to Jiang, their difficulties also stemmed from the ethnic nationalism of the Italians. That is, FGS only wanted to hire managers to represent it whom the firm believed were "truly" Italian, not Chinese who had lived in Italy for however long a period of time.

Privatization and Family Firms

As I argue in chapter 2, "privatization" has multiple meanings in relation to the market economy and the introduction of capitalist modes of profit-seeking. This section addresses those multiple meanings in relation to private family firms. I offer three examples. As I argue earlier in this chapter, those firms that have developed out of formerly state-run enterprises often deny that they are family firms, even when their employees clearly state otherwise, because family business is one key index of corruption. But there is also the opposite phenomenon: certain Chinese firms that have evolved out of the state-run system deny they have done so to emphasize that they are a private, family firm, especially for the purpose of finding foreign joint venture partners. This is the case with the first privatization story about Pure Elegance, whose owner, Huang Huaming, we discuss in chapter 1. Huang readily acknowledged his is a family firm but denied that it grew out of a state-owned enterprise. The second example, briefly alluded to at the beginning of this chapter, is an example of multiple meanings of "family firm." Zhejiang New Dawn Group Ltd's Zhang Hualiang stated categorically his is not a family firm. I argue that while he does in fact hire family members to work in his company, his meaning is that no members of his family "own" the firm with him. This second privatization story exemplifies how those whose firms did not devolve out of the state-owned economy nonetheless feel hesitant about acknowledging the involvement of family members in their firm. The third privatization story is yet a different example of the creation of a small firm where family relations enabled it to develop and thrive, even as it is not a "family firm" in any sense of the term. It has grown out of the state system, and while I could place this example in the next section on pyramid schemes, since it still nestles within the state system, I discuss it here as a contrast with the first two examples. The final privatization story, Ming'er Dress Company, is quite distinct from the others. This fourth case is of a firm that was developed not from the top of the industry hierarchy but out of the bottom of the industry by former workers in state-run factories who were laid off when their factories closed.

Privatization Story 1

To recall, Pure Elegance is a joint venture between the Chinese firm Yufei and the Italian Rinaudo firm. Recall also Huang Huaming's furious outburst about the perfidy of his Italian partners. But before his outburst, I began with an open-ended question: "Could you tell me the history of this firm?" This question seemed to surprise and relieve him. He then proceeded to summarize for me: "From 1982 to 1988, my father was the head of a collective factory [*jiti qiye*]." Collective enterprises were part of the socialist state system but smaller than state-run factories and managed by neighborhood committees rather than government bureaus. They did not have the economic backing of the latter. Collective enterprises had begun in order to encourage women to work outside the home and were often precarious ventures, opening and closing depending on central government policies about economic development.

According to Huang, in 1988 his father left that factory and started a *getihu*. *Getihu* literally means "individual household business," because most of these very small businesses started in people's homes in the 1980s with the beginning of economic reform. At that time, they were viewed as small sideline ventures that supplemented people's wages from work in state-run work units. Huang emphasized the private aspect of his father's venture by stating: "It was privately run. That was really before privately owned businesses were allowed but it was basically privately owned. They called it 'collective' but it was actually private." In 1994 his father formally opened a private business, registering it as a "limited company." Huang said that his father had built this business on top of that previous one. It was called the Yufei Clothing Store. His father was the president. Then in 1997, Huang took over as the "head [*lingdao*]." *Lingdao* is the term used for government cadre/officials who run state-owned enterprises.

I asked for a bit more elaboration about how his father became head of the factory. Huang explained that his father used to be a doctor in one of the factories and with economic reform, they were looking for someone "who had a little bit of intelligence [*siwei*]," so they asked his father to become the head. (This story is plausible, though it leaves out a lot of details, such as whether his father had important connections, or whether he was a party member, which I never had the opportunity to follow up on.) Then his father died young, so

Huang took over. But Huang offered that he had been going into the factory since he was small, because his mother worked in a silk factory, and therefore he knew a great deal about how silk factories operate.

Huang's story is straightforward. His father first ran a collective factory and then opened a private one. Huang had no trouble telling me that he and his wife both own the firm. But that evening, I had dinner with the interpreter for the joint venture Huang had formed with the Italian Rinaudo firm. To recall from chapter 1, Shu Hailun/Antonio announced that he had just resigned from his job that day and had complained about the new Italian manager, Andrea Politi. It was almost in passing that Shu mentioned something about the history of Yufei/Pure Elegance. When he described his possible future plans, they were related to continuing to do business with Yufei. He had been making these plans with the *laobanniang* (the owner's wife), whom he described as the assistant manager of the firm. Then he casually added: "Yufei used to be a state-run company, then it became private and belonged to his father. Then he passed it on to his son. So family still matters a lot."

This description was counter to Huang's in one critical respect: the evolution of Yufei out of a state-run company versus Huang's narrative that Yufei had been established separately as a private company from the beginning. I stopped Shu there and asked him to clarify.

SH   Yes, Yufei developed out of a state-run company that was handed over to the father.

LR   Didn't the father leave and establish his own private company?

SH   He set up the private company out of the previous one.

Thus, although in the majority of cases firm owners were reluctant to admit theirs was a family firm, especially if it had evolved out of a state-owned enterprise, in the case of Yufei/Pure Elegance, we see the opposite: Huang's reluctance to trace a history of the firm back to the state. In his—and many other people's—views, that kind of history might have led people to believe that the firm was both corrupt and incompetent.

Privatization Story 2

While Huang denied that his family firm had devolved out of a state-run enterprise, the majority of situations we encountered involved owners of firms that have devolved from state-run enterprises who denied the fact that they are family firms, in order to deflect the widespread criticism of corruption.

I would now like to complicate that argument by turning to Zhejiang New Dawn Group Ltd.

In my interview with Zhang Laoban (Boss Zhang), I asked him to tell me the history of the firm. He began by telling me that he had grown up in this canal town. His father and mother are from the countryside (*nongcun*). They planted rice and chrysanthemum tea and raised silkworms. He used to help them when he was young. He said he was always "full of ideas [*xiangfa*]" but just needed to save up the capital (*zijin*). After he graduated from high school (a noted accomplishment for a young man from the countryside), he worked for three years in a local township enterprise that sold household goods.

I asked him how he came to think about starting his own business. He said that his wages were very low, only seventy-five yuan per month as a temporary worker. He borrowed money from a friend and in 1993 started a small workshop, with six workers. He did not need to explain that the workers only got paid if Zhang found customers who would give him orders. Since his town is a center for manufacturing sweaters, they made sweaters, selling them wholesale.

The first year they made a lot of profit because supply could not meet the demand. In the second year, they expanded to thirty workers (*gongren*). At that time, the demand was high but there was not a big emphasis on design. He first figured out the design of the sweaters by looking through magazines and looking at other stores. Later he began to develop his own brand, hiring a French designer and fifty Chinese employees from Shanghai. Then he expanded to other aspects of the textile industry, such as dyeing. In 1996 he opened a dyeing factory, which now has over one hundred workers. He also began placing orders with yarn spinning factories, rather than open his own. He chose the ones that enabled him to make distinctive sweaters. In 2006 he started a clothing factory. He currently has six hundred people working there. He bought the factory from the previous owners. Here, I might add that I had learned from my friend, the former manager of this clothing factory, that this factory had been a state-owned factory that had been "privatized." It had not been owned by Zhang but by the former managers, who then later declared bankruptcy.[15]

In 2003 he started his real estate business. Several years after the government had begun selling the land in 2001, Zhang bought land from the local government and built homes, which he sold. He also opened a restaurant. His company gradually became a group (*jituan*). He currently has eight people on his board of directors. They represent the branch companies (*fengongsi*) of the group, plus the accountant, the personnel office, and the planning department (*jihuabu*). They meet once a month to discuss management issues. He has two assistant directors (*fuzhong*), in charge of production and sales. Zhang stated that he borrowed money from the bank to expand his business—10 percent of his net assets. He has expanded his profit by 25 percent. He now has thirty shops, in Hangzhou, Shanghai, Chongqing, Nanjing, and Suzhou.

Zhang was categorical in stating he does not have any of his family in the business. They are all from the countryside, he emphasized, so they are not capable of working in his business. His wife does not work in his business either, he asserted. In response to my question about his children, he said he has two daughters, one twelve years old and the other seven. He will not necessarily make them work in the business in the future; he will respect their choice of what they want to do.

Later that afternoon, I went to talk with Xiao Hu, the manager of Zhejiang New Dawn Group Ltd.'s dyeing factory.[16] He told a very different story than that of Zhang. Xiao Hu began by saying that the economy was not as good as before and thus their profit was smaller.[17] He said it was hard to guarantee the labor because workers constantly move around to other factories in search of better wages and working conditions. They lose about 20 percent of their workers every year. I then asked him the key question: Are any of the owner's family involved in the company? Xiao Hu replied without hesitation: Yes, the owner's wife is the accountant. The older sister's son is one of the sales representatives (*yewu yuan*), the older sister and her husband are buyers (*caigou*)— they buy the yarn. They do jobs that are not disruptive of the business, not the main part of the business, he emphasized.

This last sentence is key. Xiao Hu also implicitly responded to the widespread critique of having family in one's business: it spells both corruption and inefficiency. The accusation of corruption means the business will suffer, will not be focused on supposedly the only raison d'être of a business: to produce profit. Yet Xiao Hu's listing of the family members who work in Zhang's company does not actually contradict Zhang's assertion that he does not have his family involved in the business. While Zhang was not willing to tell me which family members work in the company, I take his assertion to mean that his family did not start the business with him, did not put up the capital to begin or expand the business, do not legally own the company with him, and do not make major decisions about investments or the future direction of the company. I take his assertion to mean, in other words, that his is not a "family business" in the sense we saw with the paeans to Wenzhou family firms: that several family members together can claim ownership, investment, managerial, and decision-making powers to run the business. Rather, here we have a situation in which Zhang views himself as having hired his family members, of having honored the strong prescription to take care of one's family.

Certainly, an accusation of corruption could be lodged against him. But he can state unequivocally that his is not a family firm. The fact that he desires to do so reflects a complication of the argument that those whose family firms devolved from state-owned enterprises tend to make this assertion. It indicates that indeed, the concern that a family firm will be seen as both corrupt and incompetent, as not caring about profit but only self-interest, is widespread even among those who began their firms in the market economy. In the case of Zhang, his unequivocal statement that his is not a family firm is meant to clarify that his is a business geared to making profit rather than to dissipating those profits in supporting various family members. Hence his claim to exclusive ownership. As Yanagisako discusses in chapter 5, many Italian family firms begin in the same way, with only one person such as Zhang investing the capital and legally owning the company, hiring other family members as employees. Yanagisako points out how this situation has often generated conflict about management and succession of the firm. The difference is that in the cases of Italian firms, owners do not deny it is a family firm but rather deny that collateral and affinal kin are part of the "family" that owns the firm.

Privatization Story 3

In the case of Zhejiang Yafeng Fashion Co. Ltd., the fact that it is not a family firm has more to do with the generational divide, in which young people might rely on their parents for financial help or connections but do not look to their parents for guidance in a market economy, since their parents' generation has had little experience in this regard.

Liu Shufeng was general manager of Zhejiang Yafeng Fashion Co. Ltd., located in Hangzhou, when I met him in the spring of 2008. He was thirty-one years old. The person who made this connection for me explained that Liu's family has a long history in the silk industry; his mother was an accountant in one of the state-run factories. Liu's family history in the silk industry indicated a high status within factory labor in two senses: the silk industry was the most prestigious of the local industries; and his family had moved from being workers to cadres, as indicated by his mother's position as accountant. Thus, Liu clearly had enough family support to set up his own firm—not by getting loans from his family but by having the connections within the silk industry to get customers, especially foreign customers, through state bureaus and thus to enter the import-export business.

Liu had initially been reluctant to talk to me.[18] His wife, Jiang Tian, accompanied him, as the meeting had been set up through her. We met at an ice cream parlor. Both were dressed very casually, down to the sneakers. Liu sat with his arms tensely folded across his chest. Contrary to the usual politeness in China, he did not offer me his business card. I began by asking him to tell me the history of his firm. His factory is a joint venture. He is the manager, or "CEO" (said in English). There are four main shareholders (*gudong*): a Hong Kong company; a big brand-name mainland China company, privately owned by a friend; a private individual; and a state-owned import-export company. Liu represents the import-export company, which exports clothing to Japan, Europe, and the United States. He had worked in clothing for ten years, six and a half years in import-export. He had been managing this factory for the past ten years. He got the job in import-export because he knew someone there. Here Liu indirectly refers to family connections. Jiang chimed in: "In those days, ten years ago, it was much easier to get a job than now. Now, you have to really look." By that, she meant that previously family connections could help one get a job. Now, even family connections do not guarantee a decent job.

His factory has two hundred workers. They make cotton sports clothing. They used to make silk clothing. But then his partner—whom he did not name or describe—was the one who knew silk, and they separated. They had differences over management issues. Currently, he was looking for a European company to establish a joint venture with him, to focus on the Chinese domestic market. He wanted to use their brand name to sell in China.

Contrary to his body language, Liu Shufeng averred he would be happy to answer any of my questions. I asked him about his experiences of economic reform. He said he could answer this question because his experiences were an epitome (*suoying*) of this whole process. He had turned from export to the domestic market. Export was not easy for several reasons: the currency exchange rate, the fact that there are other Third World countries that can make clothing more cheaply than China, the end of government support for the textile industry—as evidenced by the end of the favorable tax policy—and finally, the falling profits. Before, they used to make clothing for popular Italian brands, among others. They did not have their own brand or their own market. Nor did he ever have direct contact with foreign customers. The state-owned import-export company handled all the foreign customers. They now make clothing for the domestic brand of one of the shareholders.[19] They make one 100 million Chinese yuan per year or US$15 million in sales (at that time).

Liu Shufeng also explained that the other reason for switching to focus on the domestic market was the difficulty in keeping workers. With production for foreigners, the schedule—and wages—are erratic. With production for a domestic market, he could have stable customers, more time to fill the orders, and hence a stable labor force, with a stable time schedule and stable wages. I said I knew that the workers were suffering (*xinku*) but I also thought that you managers have a tough time (*xinku*). My remark finally led him to relax a bit more. He said yes, in fact the workers can leave, even if they have signed a contract, but he, on the other hand, cannot leave them; he has to take care of them. Since they were a small company, he planned to subcontract orders to others, another direction in which he and other factories were heading. He also planned to expand his business by buying up other brands—much like Zara and H&M do—rather than relying on a single top brand to make money.

I asked him if he really likes working in the textile industry and if he, like the workers, thought of changing to another type of job. He said he already had the social resources in the textile industry, meaning his family connections. He said he had been married to the textile industry longer than he was married to his wife. An American had once said to him that if God loves you, he has you work in the textile industry, and if God hates you, he has you work in the textile industry.

Liu Shufeng and Jiang Tian then offered a spontaneous invitation to dinner at their home—a luxurious home, not an apartment—in western Hangzhou in an area that looked similar to an American suburb. They had two domestic servants (*ayi*), one looking after the baby and the other preparing the meal. Over dinner, we chatted about his plans for the future. He was taking a class once a month on doing business. He then proudly stated that his younger brother was at Cambridge, getting his PhD in business and management. Without needing to be explicit, it was clear that Liu had financially helped his younger brother follow this path. Later, when he drove me back, he said that he encouraged his younger brother to work in Hong Kong after he finished his studies. It was clear he has no intention of pressuring his brother to come into his own business.

Liu Shufeng thus established Zhejiang Yafeng Fashion Co. Ltd. through his family lineage in the silk industry, without which he would not have had the necessary guanxi, or connections, to jump into the garment industry. Family was absolutely key to his ability to be successful in his firm. His parents had smoothed the way for him to work in one of Hangzhou's import-export corporations. His parents helped him find the necessary people to establish his own factory and firm. Yet he was not planning to make it a "family firm." He did not want his brother to enter into this firm in the textile industry, which he clearly imagined was only for people who could not succeed at other more lucrative business.

Privatization Story 4

Ming'er Dress Company Ltd. is located in a small town in northern Zhejiang province that is another well-known historical site of silk production. I had met Shi Qian, who owns Ming'er (named after her daughter) with her husband, Zhao Houming, in Shanghai at a fashion exhibit set up by the Italian town of Prato. She had taken a seminar offered by Professor Hu of the Donghua University business school, who was seated next to me and who introduced us. She agreed to speak with me about her business but urged Hu to accompany me. She wanted his advice. He brought two of his students along for a field study.

That town had not changed much from when I had visited there in the 1980s. It was a small, pretty, and rather sleepy town. As Shi drove us from the bus station, she explained that the silk industry in her town had declined a great deal in recent years. The basis of the local economy was now construction.

Ming'er was located in a building that used to house the former neighborhood committee.[20] This visual detail indexes the relationship between commerce and government in China: on the one hand, commerce seems to have taken over from government; on the other, the neighborhood committee still owns the building and Ming'er pays them rent. Real estate is one of the primary means by which local government entities have thrived in the market economy. This issue of real estate has also fueled the widespread discourse about corruption in government.

Her husband, Zhao Houming, was waiting for us at the firm. They were both dressed casually, as if they were working at home. And indeed, they had started this company as a workshop in their home. Ming'er had two rooms, a reception and a production room. The reception area was quite elegant, with a large print image hung on the wall of footprints in the sand. Shi explained that this image symbolized the Silk Road.

In the production area, we saw samples of their clothing, made from 100 percent silk, with designs aimed at an older clientele. Shi explained they were trying to reach a target audience of twenty to forty year olds, but they could only sell to the local, conservative market at the moment. They also made bed quilt covers, a popular marriage dowry item. The visual and spatial design of Ming'er reflected how the company sat on the cusp between socialist and postsocialist production relations.

Prior to opening Ming'er four years earlier, they had both worked in the silk industry for fifteen years. Shi had worked in a textile factory, eventually managing to transfer within the factory from the production line to an office job in which she traveled around sourcing fabric. Zhao had worked in a silk dyeing factory. All of his family, including his grandparents and great-grandparents, had worked in silk. Through the 1990s, all the state-run silk factories in their town had closed. When I asked what happened to the workers, the husband replied, *xiagang*—laid off.[21] The leaders of the factories just lost their seats, he said, but workers lost everything.

They started the business by taking in piecework. When they formally started Ming'er, an import-export company owned by a friend of theirs subcontracted out to them. Thus, they needed very little capital to begin. At the time we visited them, they had thirty people working for them. They were making lingerie for Armani and shirts for Max Mara. Zhao emphasized that they do not work for these international companies to make a profit but mainly to learn from them how to make good clothing and also what foreigners like because they hope to be able to sell their clothes abroad. He said they do not exactly copy the styles they make for Armani because then they add to them.

By 2007, when we visited, it was unusual to find pure silk clothing still being manufactured. But Shi explained that their town has a rich history in silk and it was a shame to lose it. They started this company because they wanted to preserve the silk. Silk, her husband said, is important and it is a wonderful material.

Shi Qian and Zhao Houming actually began our discussion not with details about production or management or the history of silk fabric. Rather, they turned to Professor Hu and his students for advice on how to improve their brand image. Branding had become all the rage in China at the time we were doing this research. It seemed like it would provide the holy grail to a successful business. The logo they had designed had a bright pink circle with the character for Ming written inside it and two images of silk from classical Chinese painting. Professor Hu agreed with them that developing their logo was very important and not just the logo but the whole image to go with the logo. (See Simona Segre Reinach's chapter for a further discussion of this company in relation to branding.)

After that brief comment, he passed all the images to one of his students who was studying branding and asked her to think about it. She stared very hard at the logo for a time, and finally said that she thought Ming'er sounded very nice for Chinese people, but foreigners would have a difficult time pronouncing it. She suggested M&E as an English logo, the two romanized letters for Ming'er.

After a break for lunch, Shi showed us around the production room. It was extremely tiny, like the size of a large living room. Women workers were cutting out patterns, sewing garments, and ironing the finished product. The women were all between eighteen and twenty years old and were all locals from the town.

One could definitely label Ming'er a "family firm." Shi Qian and Zhao Houming were proud of being a family firm, one with a history of deep roots in the silk industry. Their firm had devolved indirectly from several state-owned enterprises. Yet the contrast between Ming'er and a company like Pure Elegance or Zhejiang Yafeng Fashion Co. Ltd. could not be more stark. Ming'er sits at the bottom of the food chain. The husband and wife who own it did not gain any capital resources from their relationship to the silk factories they had worked in. As workers, they had experience. But they did not have the kinds of social or familial connections that enabled both Pure Elegance and Yafeng to thrive. They had one connection to an import-export firm in Hangzhou, through a friend. But they did not have any way to connect to foreign customers directly, nor to figure out how to succeed in this new world of subcontracting. Their firm was reminiscent of the early reform years in all senses: its location in the neighborhood committee building, the type of fashions they produced, and the kinds of advertising posters they hung. Yet they were no longer of that world, having been permanently laid off. And they were only partly in the new world. As workers yearning to become entrepreneurs, they embraced the idea of brands, store positioning, and marketing. But they were far from the successful family firms that were the object of so many accusations of corruption. (See also Segre Reinach's discussion of Ming'er in relation to Italian fashion in chapter 4.)

Pyramid Schemes

Most small companies in China that have not developed out of state-run enterprises have a difficult time establishing themselves because of the need for start-up capital and the fact that banks in China generally make loans only to state-owned enterprises (Tsai 2004). Thus, most small firms turn to family members for financial support; conversely, most family firms are small. This financial challenge to establish a firm is compounded for companies that are involved in export related to textiles and garments, especially during the period we conducted our research. In place until 2008, at the urging of the United States but also countries in the Global South competing with China to produce textiles, the World Trade Organization established import quotas for China's textile and garment sector. The central Chinese government bureaus in turn awarded quota amounts to central, provincial, and municipal state-owned import-export corporations. These corporations found it impossible to use up their annual quota, and since each annual quota was based on the previous year's usage, they were eager to find other companies to whom they could "subcontract" their quota allotments. Conversely, small companies found it impossible to obtain on their own an import quota allowance from the central government. Hence the pyramid scheme.

By pyramid scheme, I mean the way in which small firms nestle themselves within state-owned import-export companies. The latter not only offer them a quota allowance; they also take care of all the bureaucratic hassles involved in export. These include dealing with the customs bureau, the tax bureau, the labor bureau, the inspection bureau, and the import/export company itself. Small firms pay a fee to the import-export corporation for this service.

Throughout the book, I have already discussed several firms that participate in pyramid schemes: Lou Jingxiao's Xiaoyu Ltd., and in this chapter, Zhejiang Yafeng Fashion Co. Ltd. Lou placed her company under the aegis of Three Swords, the Shanghai import-export corporation at which her classmate Wang Shiyao worked. Only after the end of the import quotas did Lou turn her business into a fully independent enterprise, though she continued to pay the state corporation a fee to deal with what she called the headache of guanxi (connections) with all the bureaus one needs to interact with. As she once commented, "You have to gao guanxi [engage in a lot of networking] in a state-owned enterprise. I don't want to do that."

Liu Shufeng, head of the Yafeng Fashion Co. Ltd., talked about "his boss" several times, meaning the head of one of the provincial import-export companies who steered customers his way and for whom he produced clothing. I placed this company in the previous section to emphasize the importance of family in the way this firm was established and able to thrive. Recall also that Li Linfeng, manager of Splendid China, discussed the "children companies" that Splendid China sponsors under its aegis. They are managed by employees. It is not coincidental that they use kinship terms for these companies, as Splendid China wants to continue claiming rights to a portion of their profits.

In this section, I focus on two additional examples to highlight pyramid schemes. These two firms are run by young people, all around thirty to thirty-five years old when we met them. As with other young entrepreneurs, they do not involve their parents in the business for the same reason stated previously: although their parents lend them money, they view their parents as having come of age in the old socialist system and therefore "timid" and lacking knowledge of how to maneuver in a market economy. Instead they rely on their school classmates to help them. The connections these firms have with state-owned import-export corporations tend to be through these school classmates, whom they trust because of their classmate relationships. In contrast to views about the incompetence and corruption associated with family firms and family guanxi, young entrepreneurs were more than willing to explain to me the importance of guanxi through their classmates. These were portrayed as noble sentiments, in direct contrast to discourses about kinship guanxi. Individual entrepreneurs were proud of their classmate guanxi because, in their view, it indexed their own reliability and principled manner of doing business. Wang Shiyao talked about his job at Three Swords as relying on classmates. One key aspect of his job is to shepherd business contracts for independent companies that are under the aegis of his corporation, many of which are owned and managed by his classmates. He further explained that all his subcontracting partners who make the garments are classmates. "I can trust them because they are classmates. I have to go to Customs and say to Customs that everything is fine with their products. But actually I don't have time to look at their products and see if they are making a fraudulent claim [xubao]. But because they are my classmates, I can relax about that and not worry."

Dai Jiangyuan, in his midthirties, who is the owner of the Shanghai Sun Garments Co. Ltd., is one of those classmates. I was introduced to him through Lou Jingxiao, who was helping me find people in the textile and garment industries. Lou had taken me to meet him at a designer studio of someone who does interior design and in whose business Dai had recently invested. We sat on one of the sofas there to chat. Simona Segre Reinach had also come to speak with the designer.

Dai Jiangyuan had graduated from Donghua University's fashion institute. Within the fashion institute there are two majors—one that emphasizes design and the other that emphasizes management. Although he likes design, Dai decided it would be safer for him to choose the management major. Dai worked for several years in the government textile import-export bureau, from 1994 to 1997. Then in 1999 he opened Shanghai Sun Garments Co. Ltd. He managed to open a factory of his own at such a young age because, as he said, he has a "background" (*beijing*): his mother used to work in a textile factory. When Dai decided to set up his own factory, she gave him a lot of important advice and recommended people he should hire and other factories he should make links with. His mother also lent him the start-up capital. She said "lent" but she did not expect him to pay it back. Still, he had just paid it all back.

When he began, he had a very tiny factory, basically three managerial personnel and one small workshop. He got orders from his classmates who work at Shanghai's several import-export corporations. He also got orders from Lou, who at that time worked for an import-export corporation. Currently, he continues to get orders from her, through her independent mediator firm.

When Dai first set up his factory, the orders he received were often bigger than he could handle. He outsourced (*waibao*) to other factories. Slowly he built up his factory, to about thirty people working for him. Another problem he had at that time was the unevenness of the orders. It is important to try to guarantee to workers a steady income. But his customers were mostly from Japan and they ordered during the fall and winter months and then in the spring and summer he would not have any orders, so that is when he started turning to European customers, because they order in the spring and summer. Now he has about 120 employees, with about 13 managerial personnel. But his factory has actually shrunk. It is more difficult to get workers, who would rather work in the electronics industry because it looks cleaner, the working conditions seem better to them—the hours are steady—and they feel more pride in telling people they work in an electronics factory. Echoing Liu Shufeng, Dai plans to outsource his subcontracting orders to factories in smaller towns outside Shanghai.

Thus, Dai Jiangyuan's company is part of a pyramid scheme built through his classmates. He has classmates in the import-export corporations, as well as independent firms like Lou's, who send orders to him, knowing full well his factory is not large enough to handle them but trusting him, as a classmate, to find other reliable factories for further outsourcing.

In response to my query about where he thinks his business is headed in the near future, Dai said his factory will continue to get smaller and he will outsource most of the contracts. He cannot really get rid of some people because they are relatives.

LR   Oh, who is working in your factory who are relatives?

DJ   My sister is working there and also some cousins. They do things like work in the office but also drive the trucks. It's not really a family business, but I do have family working there.

By insisting that his firm is "not really a family business," Dai Jiangyuan was being technically correct insofar as he meant that his family did not make business decisions about the company, nor apparently did they own any shares in the business. Or so I thought. Yet the next time I saw Lou, I asked her to clarify for me whether Dai's firm was a family firm. She said yes, it was because his mother gave him money and his younger sister works there. I asked if they also had shares in the company or he holds all the shares. She said that the family members also hold shares but she does not know how much because that is something only family members discuss with each other and would not tell someone outside the family. Clearly, however, Dai Jiangyuan felt that the major factor in leading to his thriving business was his guanxi with his classmates, not with his family.

My second example of a pyramid scheme is slightly different, in that this business is nestled within a former state-owned enterprise that is now a privatized family firm, namely Pure Elegance. Recall that Pure Elegance was an example of how the owner, rather than hide that his is a family firm, wanted to hide that his firm morphed out of a state-run enterprise. It was the translator, Shu Hailun/Antonio, who unexpectedly alerted me to this history. I first met Shu the previous year, before I had spoken with the Chinese owner of Pure Elegance. We met one morning in the offices of Rinaudo in Shanghai. No one else was around that day except the secretary.

I asked Shu to explain concretely what he does. He said that most of the work he does is to be an assistant to Massimo Soci. He does all the translation for him. He goes with him on all his business trips. He also translates documents, contracts, and business statements about the firm's sales and finances. Finally, he goes with Soci to look over locations for shops that they might want to open.

Shu had studied Italian at Nanjing Normal College. He had just graduated from college the previous year. He first started out at another Italian company outside Shanghai that made electrical parts. The Italian head of that company did not come to China very often, maybe once or twice a year, so he did not have much to do. A classmate of his mentioned that Rinaudo was looking for someone, so he quickly went on the internet and looked them up and called them. Thus, neither his previous work experience nor his college education had anything to do with textiles, garments, or fashion.

When Shu first came to work at Pure Elegance, he was working in the sales office. He worked there for several months and then the person doing the job of translator for Soci left, so they asked him to do it. "To be honest," he said, "I like the other job in the sales office better. This job is more appropriate for women to do." By this he meant that the other job was more challenging and he could learn more about becoming an entrepreneur. The job of translation was, in his words, "just back and forth and back and forth": mundane and repetitive. Hence his gendering of the job as feminine.

Although Shu averred that he was not learning much as a translator, it became clear that one key aspect of doing business he learned was how to open up a shop. When I asked him if there are ways that Chinese and Italians in his company do business differently, he answered immediately.

Italians have a hard time understanding why Chinese do business a certain way here. You know, with Chinese people you have to take care of relationships [guanxi]. In order to make things smooth and successful [shunli], you have to, you know, offer a lot of money. The Italians don't understand why Chinese have to spend all this money. They think, opening a new shop, for example, should be a very simple thing. It should be straightforward. But actually, for Chinese, it is hard, because they have to take care of these kinds of relationships. And of course, when they offer over this money, they are not going to get a receipt.

From the other way around, that is, the Chinese managers' views, Shu asserted:

Foreigners like to spell out every little detail. Chinese don't like things to be this clear. And also, foreigners are very strict. Chinese feel, why should I do 100 percent when 98 percent is good enough? Chinese like to have many different ways of doing things [i.e., leave things more open-ended].

An example he gave about conflicts in business strategy involved the location of a store. The Chinese owner of Yufei/Pure Elegance wanted to open a store in Yiwu, a small town famous for specializing in the small goods market. But the Italians were opposed. They thought Yiwu was not an appropriate place for their brand. Shu explained: "You know, Chinese like to move up from the countryside to the city. First, they like to set up business in small towns and then gradually move up to the big city. But Italians, they want to set up right away in the big city. It is difficult to enter these shopping malls in the big cities. Even if you try to offer money, it is still difficult."

Thus, in his "feminine" job as translator, Shu learned three important skills that he could later put to use: the management of social relationships to set up shops, the need to keep things open-ended to leave room for maneuverability on both sides, and the possibility of setting up shops in small towns.[22]

Indeed, he had already begun putting them to use. Through our conversations over that year and the next, I learned that Shu Hailun had set up several of his own shops. When I first met Shu, he had been hesitant to tell me where he was from, clearly not wanting to say he was not from a major city or that he was from the countryside. So he responded by saying he was from Jiangsu province (the province in which Shanghai is located). Thus, when I asked him near the end of our conversation about his future plans, he responded immediately that he had already opened several small clothes stores in Jiangsu province, along with a friend from Hangzhou. "I want to try to make something of myself [zuo yidian shiqing]."

As I learned a year later in one of our conversations, Shu had family working with him in his stores—a sister and a cousin. But, as with other young entrepreneurs, he did not consider his business to be a "family firm." Indeed, in his case, he did not even tell his parents that he quit his job and was solely focused on his stores. He did not want to worry them. And as with many young entrepreneurs, Shu did not rely on his parents' money but the reverse. "You see, I have always been a very well-behaved child. I helped them by giving them money to build a nicer home and fix it up. Now I don't have to give them money anymore. You see, I am rather famous in my hometown because I have been the most successful. Anyway, I will live closer because I am getting married."

When we talked about his impending marriage, he casually mentioned that his fiancée's father had invested Y20,000 (US$2881 in 2008) in his business. Her father, he explained, ran a good business in bedwares, a very successful business in the countryside. Shu saw this investment as just that. It did not turn his business into a "family firm," in his view.

Shu saw himself as nestled within Pure Elegance, which gave him all of his business for his stores. He thus felt he could maintain the fiction of working for them, which, for his parents' generation, sounded more permanent and reliable. That is, he sold clothing from Pure Elegance in his two stores. Thus, though he was relatively new at this kind of entrepreneurial activity, he was willing to dive in and try it out.

> I don't want to work for anyone else. I don't want to have a boss anymore. I want to relax a little more. This work was getting too hard. It used to be my friends envied me. They saw that my work wasn't too hard. But then it changed with this new guy [Politi]. Anyway, it is important to try new things every few years. After a few years, you should change what you are doing. Everyone does that now. And you should always try to become independent. Even if you don't succeed, at least you chose your own path. And you can feel a sense that you struggled to do something on your own.

Here, Shu echoes the mythologies about Wenzhou people, which by this time had become a broad discourse of paeans about becoming an independent entrepreneur. Later, when he was saying he felt a bit upset about leaving the job, he then mused: "I guess it's for the best. And now I can get on and make something of myself. Or at least try to. You always have to try. Otherwise, you don't know what you are capable of. And if I hadn't done this job, I wouldn't have known how to enter into the garment business."

But Shu did not really want his fiancée working in his stores. His fiancée used to work in Beijing, as a buyer for a Japanese company. But when I asked if she would work in his business, he replied: "I don't know yet. Because in China, a woman is supposed to have a family and a child and not worry about work. And in China, a woman as a buyer is not so good. People think it is not good for a woman to be running around like that."

These two examples of pyramid schemes illuminate several aspects of "family firms" in China: (1) Reliance on, or guanxi with, classmates was seen as the epitome of good business sense. By contrast, family and kinship guanxi was something one had to endure or accept but not something that these young entrepreneurs aspired to have define their business success. (2) Nestling within the state, in one case, and a joint venture, in the other case, was absolutely essential for any hope of having one's business thrive. (3) Even those who have no direct involvement with the state, that is, they do not work for or represent the state, categorically refuse to describe their firm as a family firm. Thus among these young entrepreneurs, there also exists a widespread sense of the negative evaluation of family firms.

Chinese-Italian Chinese Firms

In this final section, I offer two examples of firms in China that were formed by Chinese couples who had lived in Italy for some time and have legal residence in Italy but who chose to return to China to live. My argument, in brief, is that these firm owners have no difficulty asserting that they are family firms and feel no need to defend or explain the fact that they are family firms because they are following a common model they learned in Italy—in the context of working with Italian customers in the textile, garment, and fashion industries.

I met Li Yue, introduced in chapter 1, through a very old friend of mine from Hangzhou, whom I got to know when we were both graduate students in the 1980s. We met in one of the new, upscale hotels in Hangzhou, on the northwest side of the famous West Lake. I waited in the spacious lobby for a bit and then was approached by a nice-looking tall man. As I was the only foreigner in the hotel lobby, he could not mistake me. He was elegantly dressed in casual but clearly expensive clothes in a European style, all black: a nicely styled shirt with no collar, nice-fitting pants, and casual shoes that were stylishly like sneakers. When I later asked him where he buys his clothes, he explained that he and my old classmate were the ones to introduce the concept of small boutiques to Hangzhou by setting up the Italian stores alongside West Lake—an extremely desirable location. We sat down in the area at the back of the lobby where they serve tea and exchanged cards. Li had just returned from Beijing, where, I later learned, he works closely with the Italian embassy.

Li Yue had studied travel and hotel management in college. He first worked for the provincial government travel bureau. But he left that job after five years. At that time, it was quite unusual to leave such a secure job. As Li put it, "Everyone's ideal at that time was to become a civil servant." The government was just beginning to encourage citizens to start small businesses, and Li felt he wanted a new challenge. So he abandoned what others envied and went to work in the travel business in Hainan Island and Shenzhen. At the time, those were the two main places being developed for tourism. In effect, Li still worked for the government, but in their commercial wing. But after only a year, he left because he felt the company he worked for, as he described it, "still had too much government involvement."

When Li Yue returned to Hangzhou, he got married. He met his wife through friends. (He never told me her name.) She had been living in Italy since 1983 but was originally from Hangzhou. She had a factory and a restaurant in Rome at the time they met. Li returned with her to Italy, where she gave birth to their two children.[23] After living in Italy for several years, they decided to return to China. They both have permanent residency in Italy and have maintained a home there.

In China, Li Yue and his wife started out with a business helping Italian companies transport goods to and from Italy and China. In 1993 they set up a consulting company (*zixun gongsi*), helping Italians find companies in China they could work with. They worked with all sorts of companies, including those who wanted to sell textile machines, make Italian furniture, or sell equipment. As mentioned in chapter 1, in 1994 Li became the consultant for the top fashion companies in Italy, to be in charge of quality control. He got these customers through the Italian embassy. He took responsibility for overseeing the different factories that made their clothing. They were working with an international trading company in China (*waimao gongsi*), but Li was overseeing whether the international trading company was getting the right quality

In 1999 they decided to open their own factory, Molto Bene Ltd., as Li Yue said, "not to make money but to be able to control the quality. We wanted to be able to guarantee the quality. We had been feeling out these problems for four or five years and decided to open our own factory." They used only their own savings from their previous business; they did not borrow from their parents, who, as farmers in the countryside, would not have had much to give them. The factory is on the outskirts of Hangzhou. They have two hundred workers and thirty office personnel. According to Li, "By European standards, ours is a large factory." They produce Y5,000,000 (US$770,000) worth of products in one year. They make only high-end Italian clothing for the top Italian companies. These companies deal directly with them; they do not go through anyone else. Li asserted that "this is a direction that all businesses would like to go in [i.e., deal directly with the factory]. It involves less money and you can get a better price." They started out just doing the sewing, but then, because it is difficult to find other factories that know how to do the other processes for high-end fashion, they began to take on more of it themselves, including the embroidery, knitting, and printing.

Having experienced a great deal of reluctance by owners to tell me whether and in what ways their companies were family firms, I waited until this point in the conversation to ask Li Yue whether he owned the business together with his wife. He readily replied that they each own 50 percent of the shares. I then asked if they had other relatives working there. Li's response was as follows:

"We did in the beginning but now we don't anymore. We want professional management [zhiye jingying]."

My second example of a Chinese family firm formed through having lived in Italy is Jiang Li/Nico (introduced in chapter 1), the translator/cultural mediator for Vinimoon. As with many others from Wenzhou, in the early 1990s, Jiang migrated out. He went to Italy. He had been a teacher in Wenzhou, as had his parents, but he worked in various capacities in Italy, starting with restaurant work. He picked up the Italian language quickly and was eager to absorb Italian culture. By the time the oldest Cai brother of Vinimoon (see the earlier discussion in this chapter) came to find him in Italy in the late 1990s to help him sell things in China, Jiang already had his own tie factory in Italy. Indeed, Cai was willing to sell Jiang's ties in China, among other goods that Jiang helped him find and take back. At that time, Jiang had a small factory in Italy, only ten people. He did not have a shop to sell his ties; he made ties for Italian companies. I asked if it was difficult to set up a business in Italy. Jiang replied: "It wasn't that difficult. Friends helped me set it up and gave me business. We would give each other business. There were only about twenty such factories in all of Milan. But yes, my business did not develop very quickly and never became very big. Because if you are sincere and honest [chengxin, laoshi] then you can't develop your business very well." This, he averred, was even more true in China.

Jiang Li moved back to China when FGS's manager in China and the Cai brothers were having conflicts. When FGS asked Jiang Li how much money he was making with his factory, the firm said it would give him the same amount of money if he went back to live in China. He decided it was a good idea to move back to China because of the children, so that they could study Chinese. They did not know much Chinese then, he explained: "We spoke Chinese with them at home but they couldn't really read or write Chinese." At the time we spoke in April 2008, he had been back in China for four years.

Although he closed the factory in Italy, Jiang Li has continued the tie business in China. Indeed, I could have discussed Jiang's firm in the section on pyramid schemes, as his tie business, Angelina (named after his daughter), is literally tucked into the Vinimoon building in Shanghai and into the Vinimoon business. In our first interview, Jiang very easily mentioned that he has a tie business in Shanghai. I had asked him about his children and their education and he said his wife has a photo she can show me, and that she is in the building because she manages their tie business.

At the end of our interview about Vinimoon, we stepped out the door of the Vinimoon office, turned left, walked five feet or so, and entered an office that did not have a sign on the door. I assumed that the office still belonged to Vinimoon. But then Jiang walked over to a desk and handed me a catalog of ties that his business Angelina makes. In reply to my question, he confirmed that they sell their ties to Vinimoon. Then he walked into the back office and introduced his wife. She was petite and very pretty, with curled hair falling to her shoulders. She showed me a photo of her daughters on her computer screen. They had named their business after their eldest daughter.

Jiang Li brought in two examples of their ties. He said that the Italian wholesale company he used to work for designs the ties for them but they have them made in China, in a factory outside Shanghai. They buy all the materials in China. They are made entirely of silk.

Jiang Li, his wife, Yu Hui, and I met several times during the next several years, always in the same office. But the last time we met, in December 2013, they had moved their business office to an entirely different part of town, to the Xujiahui district on the west side of Shanghai. They had expanded their business. They still have the silk ties but now they have expanded to import cloth from Italy for companies to use in China to make clothing. They do not bother with making the clothing themselves. They sell to both foreign and domestic companies in China. Their daughter now also works in the business. She had studied abroad in Australia but found it unrealistic to find work there. "They don't really hire foreigners there," she said. So she came back and joined her parents in their business. They had also severed ties with Vinimoon. Jiang Li told me the following:

> I decided to leave a few years ago. I left in 2011. They didn't need me anymore, once there was no more executive director from FGS. But also, they passed over me. They promoted Pizzoli. When he first came, he was making less than me. But then they promoted him and he was making more than me. And I told FGS they should raise my salary or promote me but they said they wanted to have an Italian in that position. I said I am Italian but they said no, someone who is really Italian. They still looked at me as foreign. So I left. I want to build something that I can hand on to my children. Now we have customers who come to us because their previous supplier is not working out anymore. So we are doing well.

Conclusion

"Family firms" in China, as I have argued in this chapter, have an ambivalent valence, because the family firms that have arisen in China since the beginning of economic reform have done so in relationship to China's socialist past. This socialist past is evident in the way in which family firms index corruption in public discourse; the fact that most family firms are established by a younger generation without their parents' active involvement, even if the latter offer loans; the contrast these entrepreneurs make between guanxi among classmates versus kinship guanxi; the way in which pyramid schemes operate; and the regular denial that one's firm is indeed a family firm. The one major exception to this denial are those who operated family firms in Italy before returning to China to do the same. These firms, what I have called Chinese-Italian Chinese firms, reach beyond China for a sense of justification for establishing a family firm that could index successful entrepreneurship rather than corruption. Thus, "family firm" has not congealed into a normative ideal, business model, or praiseworthy endeavor. To the contrary, it is yet one more site that highlights the contradictions of postsocialist entrepreneurship. Doing business with the Italian firms, as demonstrated in this chapter, has multiple effects: to reinforce the possibility of having a family firm, to help ease tensions within Chinese family firms, and finally, to produce new problems that a "family firm" does not necessarily resolve.

Conclusion

This ethnography of transnational capitalism would not have been possible without the collaboration that underscores it. Our collaborative methodology has enabled us to move beyond a comparative study of two different countries or national cultures. Rather than merely compare Chinese and Italian engagements in the transnational commodity chain of the global garment and fashion industry, we have analyzed the dynamic and shifting character of their interaction. This has led to our insights about the unstable nature of transnational capitalism. Our collaboration has also enabled us to move beyond the constraints of fieldwork by one ethnographer, which tends to result in an ethnographic focus on one of the parties in a commodity chain. Neither have we pursued parallel analyses of cultural problematics, such as "corruption" in China and Italy. Such an approach would have inaccurately equated the different historically constituted concerns, hopes, and actions of the parties engaged in these transnational collaborations. Our goal instead has been to pursue a shared theoretical perspective and an integrated analysis without speaking in one voice. Our collaborative ethnography has led us to challenge the idea of a unified perspective—whether among our interlocutors or ourselves—and the formation of a unified transnational capitalist mindset or the formation of a transnational managerial class. Our ability to hear and bring together multiple perspectives meant we could avoid the tendency to homogenize the Italians, on the one side, and the Chinese, on the other. We argue instead that the encounters among them produced an emphasis on the differential value of their varied capacities both in relation to one another and in relation to other Italians and Chinese with whom they contrasted themselves. We have thus argued that the different histories of the Chinese and Italians in these collaborations and their shifting location and relations in the global fashion industry yielded different experiences, perceptions, and ideas about labor, commodities, and identities. Furthermore, these different histories, concerns, and anxieties, which emerged in the interactional negotiation of labor value, shaped their capitalist goals and strategies, producing new forms of value and generating new projects.

Our collaborative methodology has led us to new insights about transnational capitalism involving historical legacies, privatization, the negotiation over labor value, the rearrangement of accumulation, the reconfiguration of kinship, and the outsourcing of inequality. Contrary to the idea that capitalism operates in neatly divided eras, we found that historical legacies and revisionist histories continue to play a vital role in shaping the kinds of interdependent capitalist practices that the various Italian and Chinese entrepreneurs sought in their transnational relations of production and distribution. The Italian firms brought to their interactions with their Chinese counterparts their historical experiences with the decentralized structure of Italian industrial districts rooted in kinship, friendship, and local community networks, which entailed trust and betrayal, family succession and dissolution, class mobility and labor conflict. The relative lack of involvement of the Italian state in the textile and clothing industry except through labor and banking regulations—despite a history of state investment and ownership in other economic sectors—was also a part of the historical legacy that shaped the way Italian firms engaged in outsourcing, subcontracting, joint ventures, and other business collaborations in China.

The Chinese entrepreneurs brought to their interactions with the Italians their struggles with overcoming the socialist past, a broad discourse on corruption, complex relations with the Chinese state, and historical questions of inequality, including a long colonial history. These respective historical legacies led to some of the tensions in joint ventures, like those in Vinimoon, between the FGS firm, with its global brand, and the Cai brothers, who aspired to have a global reach. Historical legacies also engendered the conflict in Pure Elegance, between the Rinaudo and Huang family firms over the acceptability of pursuing multiple partnerships. Both Vinimoon and Pure Elegance evidenced variations of the complex relations of collaboration and competition that were already present in Italian industrial districts and a continuation of the ever-present Chinese memories of colonial encounters with foreigners.

Yet these diverse historical legacies could also lead to smooth cooperation, such as that between the state import-export corporation and the Italian firm of Renato Costa in the "privatized" joint venture Splendid China; or the relation of mediator firms like Lou Jingxiao's Xiaoyu Ltd. with her Italian clients. In all these cases, our collaborative ethnography has enabled us to avoid the pitfalls of arguments about a clash of different "cultures of capitalism" or the widespread notion that the cross-cultural character of transnational collaborations is in itself the source of the conflict they frequently entail.

We have demonstrated, moreover, that these histories also led to divergent experiences among Italians and among Chinese. Those Italian family firms that had an earlier history of national expansion and capital accumulation were able to expand into China and develop as global fashion brands, while smaller firms with less capital declined. Yet even among firms that had expanded to China, the opportunities for nonfamily managers and technicians to create their own firms declined, thus hardening the boundary between capital and labor. Yet some small firms, like Luciano Ferrari's, were able to thrive in the Chinese market—at least for a time. Others, like Segalini, were able to transform from being a converter firm in Italy to producing its own brand in China.

Among the Chinese engaged in these transnational relations, private entrepreneurs, state import-export officials, and workers all had different interpretations of the socialist past that motivated different affective engagements with their labor as well as different strategies for overcoming what they viewed as the main structural constraints on their lives. Private entrepreneurs like Lou Jingxiao/Maggi, Li Yue, Jiang Li/Nico, the assistant to the manager at Vinimoon, and even Wang Shiyao/George, who was in charge of an office in a Shanghai import-export corporation (but who distanced himself from being viewed as a state bureaucrat), were motivated to engage with their Italian clients and managerial counterparts in order to prove their cosmopolitan transcendence of the socialist past. State corporations like Hui Hua Yi/Silk Nouvelle pursued "privatization" to prove their trustworthiness to their foreign collaborators. Migrant factory workers, by contrast, held a sense of continuity between the socialist past and present in terms of their experiences of social inequality between rural and urban citizens and aimed their criticisms more at Chinese firms and the whole labor regime of textile and garment production than at foreign clients.

Our ethnography has further emphasized that both China and Italy have had long histories of transnational relations of production and distribution that lie at the heart of the fashion industry. The Marini family (of the Jiaxing Style Silk Company joint venture in China) is a case in point. Chinese state bureaus also had long histories of textile export under socialism. At the same time, we argued that these historical legacies did not lead to a reproduction of the same transnational relations. Rather, for the Italians, these recent collaborations enabled some new firms to expand distribution to a global fashion market, and for Chinese entrepreneurs, the ability to move beyond the socialist past depended, in part, on the success of their interactions with foreign investors from capitalist economies.

Understanding the multiple historical legacies that Italians and Chinese brought to their interactions has also enabled us to have a better grasp of the ongoing, contested processes of negotiations over the value of their respective labors. A comparative or primarily one-sided focus would have inadvertently led to the assumption that Italian and Chinese owners, managers, technicians, consultants, translators, and workers brought the value of their labor power and thus their contribution to these processes already formed prior to their encounters. Instead, we were able to show how these various social actors negotiated the value of their labor power through their encounters. These negotiations were not always smooth. The ongoing tensions over the relative values of the various contributions of Italian and Chinese managers and others led joint ventures like Vinimoon and Pure Elegance to the brink of dissolution. Our collaborative methodology has thus enabled us to move beyond the theoretical separation of the production and reproduction of labor power. We have shown instead how capitalist processes are not merely embedded in those aspects of social life—such as kinship, gender, nationalism, sentiments, and belief—considered to be "noneconomic" but are in fact constituted by them. Our ability to gather multiple perspectives meant we could trace the dynamic collaborations and negotiations *in the workplace* to kinship within and across Italian and Chinese family firms. We were able to show how the desire of Italians to work with nonstate firms could lead state corporations to "privatize" in order to prove they had moved beyond the socialist past.

Negotiations over the value of the capacities that Italians and Chinese brought to the production and distribution of textiles and garments did not lead to the enactment of a singular logic of value. To the contrary, we have shown that what gets to count as "value" reflects ongoing processes that bring together different historically and culturally informed knowledges into these negotiations. The asymmetry between the Chinese and Italians in the collaborations we studied have been shaped, among other things, by the specific history and structure of the fashion industry, with its emphasis on design. As Simona Segre Reinach argued in her chapter, the three main forms of collaboration between the Italians and Chinese in the textile and clothing sectors—sourcing, fashion production in its material and immaterial aspects, and branding—led to different emphases on complementary roles (e.g., sourcing) versus conflicts over claims to the symbolic capital of fashion production.

Italian managers—some of whom, like Gianfranco Naldi, had little experience in the fashion industry prior to working in China—emphasized the value of their labor power as Italianità, an intuitive feeling for design, fashion, and, more broadly, aesthetics that they construe as having acquired by growing up in Italy. This self-perception of embodying Italianità, as we have argued, was actually formed through their work experiences in these transnational production relations, by contrasting themselves with their Chinese counterparts, whom they viewed as lacking this aesthetic sensibility. In affirming the claims of Italianità, moreover, Italian managers appropriated the fetishized powers of the commodity to constitute their own labor power.

Chinese managers, mediators, and translators, on the other hand, had to demonstrate that they had transcended their national culture by becoming cosmopolitan. This cosmopolitanism, they emphasized, allowed them to understand the universals of transnational business while also being able to grasp the cultural peculiarities and provincialism of their Italian and other foreign partners and clients. This cosmopolitanism also led them to point out that production and distribution processes require many steps that were often downplayed and that went well beyond a narrow focus on design and brand. These steps included translation, both linguistic and cultural; the sourcing of raw materials and fabric; the choice of appropriate fabrics to realize the designer's initial design; the choice of trustworthy and capable factories; the shepherding of Italians and other foreigners through the landscape of China, both physically and metaphorically; the constant need to oversee quality control in the factories; and navigation of the Chinese state. Chinese entrepreneurs thus viewed their cosmopolitanism as both necessary to the success of their transnational collaborations and strengthened by them. Our research has thus led us to revise an assumption about labor power and value in capitalist production: namely, that the process of negotiating the value of labor power is a direct effect of capitalist investments or the result of a global stage of capitalism in which the presumed stable core of the production of value has become unhinged. We have concluded instead that labor power and value are an outcome of how people in relations of interdependence assert the value of their cultural capital, including their identities, knowledge, and habitus. That is, the Italians and Chinese involved in the production and distribution of Italian fashion made in China come to know themselves and the character and value of their labor through their hierarchically structured relations of production.

We further challenge the singularity of another common argument about capitalist expansion: that the domination of the pursuit of wealth over other goals leads to the rearrangement of social life. In counterpoint to this view, we have emphasized that "economic action" is always shaped by multiple goals and sentiments. Thus, we have highlighted instead how the accumulation of wealth is rearranged to pursue culturally meaningful goals. We have discussed three main aspects of the transnational Italian fashion commodity chain in this regard: the process of privatization, the critical role of kinship, and the role of the state.

Drawing on the long-standing feminist critique of the ideological division between domestic and public, we have argued that what counts as private and what counts as public in the formation of transnational capitalist projects are forged by historically specific processes. The way in which Chinese state-owned firms prove themselves worthy of foreign partners is to "privatize." As Rofel has argued, this process did not simply lead to hybrid public/private enterprises but to a blurring of the distinction between the two. The meanings of "public" and "private" were thus transformed in light of attempts to overcome the socialist past. The extended case study of Splendid China revealed a firm that asserted it had "privatized," but the meaning of "privatization" was diffuse and included an ongoing, close relationship with the state import-export corporation that had spawned it. This analysis thus offers a challenge to the common assumption that neoliberalism has led to increased "privatization."

The formation and regeneration of family firms was another culturally meaningful project that shaped the pursuit of profit and capital accumulation. This kinship project had long constituted the way family firms operated in Italian industrial districts. Transnational expansion to China meant that the firms such as Rinaudo and FGS that had been successful in pursuing this project could simultaneously expand and reproduce both family and firm. Those less successful with transnational expansion, such as Molteni and Cappechi, experienced the constriction of both their firm and their family. Those family firms that did not pursue transnational expansion, like the Galbiatis, converted their financial capital into cultural capital, moving their children into the independent professional sector of the bourgeoisie. At the same time, as opportunities for subcontractors in Italian industrial districts decreased with the outsourcing of manufacture to China and other countries, the generation of new family firms by technicians and managers employed in other people's family firms declined. With a few exceptions, those who worked for Italian family firms in China lacked the capital, family labor, and industrial networks required to open new firms in China.

China also witnessed the appearance of family firms in the textile and garment industries. Indeed, these firms were, in part, spurred on by the desire of Italian firms to work with nonstate Chinese family firms. Yet, in China, the widespread discourse on corruption in relation to the state and to new relations of inequality meant that "family firm" had a more ambivalent valence than in Italy. Thus, the rearrangement of the pursuit of wealth on the Chinese side meant the need to either deny that one's firm was a family firm—as Zhang Hualiang did about his Zhejiang New Dawn Group Ltd.—or to deny involvement with the state, as Huang Huaming did with Pure Elegance. Only in the case of those firms that had a more intimate experience of Italian family firms was there no need to obscure the family nature of the firm.

We have further emphasized that the role of the state is always present in the pursuit of wealth and shapes the kind of accumulation strategies pursued. We have pointed out that the involvement of the Italian state with private enterprises long predates neoliberalism. Although Italian state investment and ownership of firms did not extend to the textile and clothing sector, as it did to energy, steel, and automobiles, it was in part the reaction against the state's role in regulating labor relations that led firms in Italian textile districts to reinvigorate their decentralized structure of production in the 1970s and 1980s and then to outsource production to China in the 1990s. Similarly, the desire to prove one had distanced oneself from the Chinese state (as nearly impossible as that might be), whether on the part of a small mediator firm like Lou Jingxiao's Xiaoyu company or a large state-owned corporation like the one that oversaw Splendid China, led to the ambivalent valences of "private" and "family" firms.

Finally, we have argued that the outsourcing of inequality, like privatization, has multiple meanings and instantiations. Most obviously, the Italian firms that outsourced production to China did so to escape the labor conflicts and union demands in Italy, thus creating a commodity chain in which the inequality between capital and labor became largely the relationship of Italian capital to Chinese labor, even though some phases of production such as design and branding remained in Italy. Yet Chinese managers also played an important part in constructing this commodity chain, thus facilitating the outsourcing of inequality to workers in China. The Chinese state outsourced inequality in another way as state-owned corporations forced factories formerly under their aegis to "privatize." This meant that the factories themselves had to take on all the risks of profit-seeking activities and find their own way to fund workers' wages. This put factory owners and managers in a quite different position with the state-owned import-export corporations. In the past, not only did the latter serve as their hierarchical superiors who organized their production relations, but there was also an explicit recognition of the social relations of interdependence—and responsibility—involved in these relationships. That is, the state bureau (now corporation) recognized their responsibility for the social and economic welfare of urban factory workers. Now, however, the state not only forces the risk onto individual factories but also disavows any responsibility for the social welfare of those still in relations of social interdependence with them, relations that have been recast as individual firm responsibilities. Yet these factories cannot survive unless the state corporations offer them contracts with foreign firms.

Our ethnography has enabled us to further demonstrate yet another meaning of "outsourcing of inequality." In constituting themselves as the guardians of a legacy of artisanal production and claiming its productive powers for themselves, Italian managers obscured the industrial labor of Chinese workers through what Yanagisako terms "transnational industrial drag." This echoes an earlier historical moment in which the abstraction of labor in the Italian fashion industry had entailed disguising the gender of workers. Chinese managers thus accused Italian firm owners and managers of failing to acknowledge the value of the former's labor in the production of Italian commodities made in China. As Rofel argues, however, Chinese managers also occluded Chinese workers in this critique: when Chinese managers criticized the asymmetrical relations with Italians, they usually referred to themselves, not to Chinese workers, thus contributing to disguising the labor of Chinese workers.

Chinese workers, for their part, experienced the outsourcing of inequality in several senses. As migrant workers from the countryside, they shouldered the burden of the costs of being a worker, without any of the benefits that had accrued to urban workers in the previous socialist era. Moreover, they were forced to take it upon themselves to be "entrepreneurial" about their own labor, as factories producing for export only paid them when there were production orders and offered them erratic work hours, thus preventing other kinds of entrepreneurial pursuits workers might undertake.

Much has transpired since we completed the research for this collaborative ethnography. There is less talk these days—either in China or in Western media—about China being the workshop of the world. Instead, we hear a great deal about "the rise of China." In the last decade, China has certainly dramatically expanded its transnational economic activities, mainly in the search for energy and natural resources to fuel its economic growth. It has also sought to establish international networks, with banks such as the Asian Infrastructure Investment Bank (AIIB) and trading organizations such as BRICS (Brazil, Russia, India, China, South Africa) and the One Belt, One Road initiative, all of which are offered in place of the World Bank, IMF, and Wall Street. Economic growth—and the emphasis on consumerism—is one of the main means by which the Communist Party in China hopes to remain in power. China's average annual GDP growth from 1979 until 2010 was a phenomenal 9.91 percent. Recently, this growth rate has slowed to 6.7 percent, which is still substantially higher than that of the U.S. (1.6 percent) or many European countries. This slowdown, however, has led to even more emphasis on foreign investment by China into other areas of the world, as the Chinese government seeks to displace potential domestic social tensions elsewhere—a familiar dynamic from colonial and neocolonial histories.

Currently, China's foreign direct investment (FDI) outside China has soared to US$222 billion. But we should not assume that China's growing transnational presence, along with its growing middle class, has erased the substantial social inequality within China. The difference since we finished our research is not one of less inequality in China but one in which China's factories that are part of transnational commodity chains coexist with production that has shifted to address itself more to the Chinese domestic market, alongside China's rising national wealth.

We had seen the beginnings of these trends in the period in which we conducted our research. Nearly all of the Chinese owners, managers, and translators/assistants who had collaborated with Italian textile, garment, and fashion firms have either supplemented their mediator roles or left those positions entirely to establish their own companies, and in some cases brands, to focus on Chinese consumers. Lou Jingxiao/Maggi closed her mediator firm and developed a unique web company targeting professional Chinese women to help them buy fashionable clothing. Her popular web-based fashion advice has been bought and installed in major foreign retail stores in Shanghai. Li Yue developed his own brand, while Jiang Li/Nico left Vinimoon to open his own small clothing company.

Italians in the fashion industry today, like those who sponsored the Prato Excellence fashion show that we describe in the beginning of this book, are both hopeful and anxious about these changes. On the one hand, they are even more worried that as the Chinese gain more knowledge of Western tastes, design, branding, and marketing, they will take over more of the fashion market—both in China and the West. These anxieties, of course, were already present in the "Made in Italy" campaigns of the past twenty years. Fears that Italy would suffer with the "rise of China" and other developments in the global economy have only been reinforced by the further decline in manufacturing in Italy, the stagnation of the Italian economy, which has contracted or shown very weak growth since 2009, and the stubbornly high unemployment rate that has hovered around 10–12 percent. On the other hand, the Italian fashion industry, especially the luxury brands, view the Chinese market as the salvation of "Made in Italy." The rise in consumption of Italian brands in clothing as well as other commodities by China's expanding middle class has made China the fastest-growing market for Italian luxury brands—so much so that these firms now depend heavily on it for growth in their total global sales.

As greater numbers of wealthy Chinese people began to travel to Europe, Italian and other European luxury brands shifted their retail strategy to selling to Chinese customers (as well as Russians and other newly emerging elites) in their stores in Rome, Milan, Paris, and London. In 2010 the CEO of one of the Italian luxury firms we studied had informed us that there would soon be sixty million Chinese tourists traveling the globe whom his firm planned to have greeted by Chinese-speaking sales clerks at their retail stores in Europe. Since then, as the crackdown on corruption and bribery increased in China, Italian luxury brands became all the more committed to this retail strategy. As gifts of luxury items had been one of the ways to establish guanxi with government and party officials, Chinese consumers became increasingly wary of being seen entering luxury stores in China. Buying such goods while traveling overseas was more discreet. Thus, whereas the former "Made in Italy" campaign touted the "Italianness" captured in commodities by evoking Italian artisanal and craft traditions that could be traced back to the Renaissance, marketing campaigns more recently tout the experience of traveling and shopping for luxury items in Italy, which has become a living museum of an elegant Italian lifestyle.

These recent shifts reinforce one of our arguments in this book—that transnational capitalism is an unstable process constituted in a dynamic and uneven field of power. If there is one prediction we are confident in making, it is that transnational capitalist relations between Chinese and Italians will continue to change in the coming decade.

Appendix

Four Types of Collaboration between Chinese and Italian Firms

Our study includes four types of collaboration between Chinese and Italian firms. We have listed the names (pseudonyms) of the firms in each type that we studied so they can be easily followed in the chapters.

1. JOINT VENTURES WITH ACTIVE MANAGEMENT COLLABORATION: In these joint ventures, both Italian and Chinese investors make major decisions together about production, management, and marketing. This first type of collaboration includes both joint ventures between private Italian firms and various levels of the Chinese government and also joint ventures between private Italian firms and private Chinese firms. The former is exemplified by the Jiaxing Style Silk Company, which, when we first began this research, was a joint venture in Jiaxing between the central Chinese government Import-Export Bureau, the municipal government of Jiaxing, and the Italian silk entrepreneur Luciano Marini, whose family firm has been one of the three biggest importers of raw silk from China to Europe over the past three decades (see chapter 3 for a discussion of the Marini firm's legacy of transnational capitalism). Marini is unusual in that he lives in the factory half the year and is actively engaged in its management. He and the representatives of the Chinese government together made all decisions, through a board of directors, about production, the workforce, and marketing. The division of management responsibility and hierarchy between

the Chinese technical manager hired and groomed by Marini and the Chinese cadre-manager appointed by the central government Import-Export Bureau is common in joint ventures between foreign investors and Chinese government entities. As an example of how collaborative relations are continuously changing, however, constant friction and disagreements eventually led Marini to buy out his Chinese partners with the help of capital from Japanese and Hong Kong partners, while keeping his Chinese technical manager.

An example of a joint venture between a private Italian firm and a private Chinese firm is Vinimoon, which produces expensive menswear. Both the Italian (FGS) and Chinese partners (Cai brothers) in Vinimoon are family firms, although the Italian family is in its fourth generation of owner-managers while the Chinese family is in its first. In 2005 the firm's management committee was composed of the three Cai brothers, who were the 50 percent owners of the firm, and three Italian managers from FGS. The management committee reported to the board of directors, which was composed of the shareholding families, with the chair appointed by the Cai brothers. The CEO who was in charge of overall direction was an Italian from FGS, as was the general manager and the chief financial officer, but the Cai brothers were in charge of factory operations, preparing the models and patterns, acquisitions, and personnel. In the early years of the joint venture, the Cai brothers and Italian managers actively collaborated to make decisions together about production, distribution, and marketing. After the departure of the Italian general manager (who was recruited to direct another Italian luxury brand in China), however, one of the Cai brothers stepped into the role of general manager. The resulting management structure, with four deputy general managers (two appointed by the Cai brothers and two by FGS), reflected the increasing separation between the two divisions of the business: operations and the factory (managed by the Cai brothers) and branding and distribution (managed by FGS). As with the Jiaxing Style Silk Company, this joint venture continually faced organizational challenges. In this case, however, the problems were due as much to the conflicts among the Cai brothers as to disagreements with FGS management decisions. As of 2018, the joint venture was still operating with FGS firmly in charge of branding and distribution.

Other firms that are joint ventures with active management collaboration: two private firms, Pure Elegance and Rinaudo.

2. JOINT VENTURES WITH DIVISION OF MANAGEMENT LABOR: These firms are jointly owned by the Italian and Chinese partners but leave each other to take full responsibility for their respective domains. The Italian cap-

italists and their managers are generally in charge of design and marketing while the Chinese entrepreneurs and managers are in charge of the production process. Silk Nouvelle, located in one of Hangzhou's townships, is an example of this second type of collaboration. Established in the late 1990s, this joint venture, when we first began our research, was run by the Zhejiang Fu-Hua Silk Corporation, which held 50 percent of the investment, along with the Italian-owned Float, which held 40 percent; the remaining 10 percent was owned by the firm itself. Recall that Zhejiang FuHua Silk Corporation started as a rebranded, "profitized" version of the Zhejiang provincial silk bureau. The owner-manager of Float is in charge of design and marketing, including relations with European and U.S. apparel retailers, but leaves the production process to the Chinese managers. He rarely comes to China, instead faxing specifications for fabric production to the Chinese managers, who, in turn, send him samples to review at his firm headquarters in Rome. Again, however, as our research proceeded, the Chinese side of this collaboration "privatized," so that it is now a joint venture between Splendid China and Float. The Chinese personnel have all remained the same.

Other firms that are joint ventures with division of management labor: Molteni and its Chinese partners in the 1990s.

3. WHOLLY CHINESE-OWNED ENTERPRISES THAT PROVIDE SUBCONTRACTING FOR ITALIANS: In these collaborations, a Chinese-owned firm is subcontracted to provide manufacturing services to an Italian-owned firm. This reproduces the subcontracting arrangements that characterized Italian industrial districts, except that now the subcontracting firms are owned by the Chinese. An example is the Zhejiang New Dawn Group Ltd. This group of companies includes fabric, garment, and dyeing factories. It also includes businesses unrelated to the textile industry, specifically a restaurant and a real estate firm. New Dawn is privately owned, the owner having bought a bankrupt formerly state-run enterprise. It subcontracts for Italian companies through one of the Zhejiang provincial import-export companies. The import-export company is responsible for guaranteeing the entire production process. Yet other examples of this type include Chinese state-owned import-export companies that handle the entire process through their own factories (although they might also subcontract to other factories), as well as private "mediator" firms and Italian "converter" firms located in China that do not own any factories but organize production networks. The Italian converter firms usually work through the Chinese mediator firms. These

firms take orders from European and U.S. designers and apparel makers and send detailed prototypes to the Chinese factories. They are also proactive about visiting the factories at least weekly to ensure that proper production is taking place. In the case of the Chinese companies, they buy from the factories and sell to the European and U.S. firms, thus putting their own capital at risk. They also collect a commission from the foreign firms. Again, as our research proceeded, these relations shifted subtly: the Italian converter firms seemed to become less important as the Chinese mediator firms gained in experience and began to work more directly with Italian and other foreign clients.

Chinese state-owned firms

Three Swords

Chinese private firms

Angelina
FuHua Co. Ltd.
Ming'er Dress Company Ltd.
Molto Bene Ltd.
Shanghai Sun Garments Co. Ltd.
Xiaoyu Ltd.
Zhejiang Yafeng Fashion Co. Ltd.
Zhenfu

4. WHOLLY ITALIAN-OWNED FIRMS IN CHINA: When we first began our research, there were no wholly Italian-owned enterprises in textile or clothing manufacturing in the Lower Yangzi River region. As our research proceeded, however, this type of firm increasingly emerged. Not only had the Chinese state begun to allow wholly foreign-owned enterprises (WFOE) in accordance with China's entrance into the WTO, but both Italian capitalists and Chinese entrepreneurs expressed dissatisfaction with joint ventures. The wholly foreign-owned option is attractive to Italian firm owners because they do not have to share management with Chinese government entities. Although these enterprises are owned entirely by Italians, they employ Chinese entrepreneurs in managerial positions. Moreover, they rely heavily on Chinese managers to negotiate relations with Chinese workers and Chinese government offi-

cials, as well as to take a leading role in opening the Chinese market to Italian products.

Firms that are wholly Italian-owned firms operating in China: Jiaxing Style Silk Company (after Luciano Marini bought out the Chinese partner), Eduardo Fieramosca, Molteni after 2001, Vittorio Segalini, and Luciano Ferrari. Ferrari is included as wholly Italian-owned although his Chinese wife later became part-owner of the firm.

Notes

Introduction

1 The names of individuals, firms, and brands that we studied and write about in this book are pseudonyms. We use real names only when we write about well-known individuals, firms, and brands about whom there is information in the public domain.

2 Until the 1950s, Prato's textile production relied primarily on recovered wool from old clothing and industrial scraps. After the 1950s, the incorporation of nylon and other synthetics enabled the production of lighter fabrics, and Prato became known for its innovative textiles. In describing Prato's success, Italians jokingly pointed out that it had gone literally "from rags to riches."

3 We define transnational capitalism as a form of capitalism in which relations between capital and wage labor cross national boundaries. Transnational relations of production involve individuals and groups whose actions are enabled and constrained by more than one nation-state.

4 Wallerstein (1989, 141–51) gives successive examples of places where indigenous manufacturing declines and raw material exports increase after "incorporation" into the world-system (e.g., India and the Ottoman Empire, where cotton became a primary export while textile exports declined; Russia, where 95 percent of their exports became primary products after increasing trade with Western Europe; and West Africa, where metal smithing was ruined by cheap European imports).

5 For a prominent exception, see Choy et al. 2009 on the Matsutake collaborative research group.

6 While David Graeber's (2001) approach is also useful for bringing together cultural and economic values, he tends to treat these processes as bounded and unified within one culture and thus loses sight of questions of hierarchy and inequality. Our study, in contrast, treats them as inextricable to the formation of capitalist relations of production and distribution.

7 These studies have ranged in focus from urban development and infrastructure (Linder 1999; Shatkin 2008; Siemiaticki 2015), to "resources" such as water, transportation, and energy (Bakker 2010; Bear 2015; Pírez 2002), medical care (McLafferty 1998; Smith-Nonini 1998), social welfare (J. Song 2009), plant self-cloning (Hodges 2012), NGOs (Kamat 2004), and information technologies (Kuriyan and Ray 2009).

8 Stephen Linder (1999) identifies six distinct types of private-public partnerships: management reform, problem conversion, moral regeneration, risk shifting, power-sharing, and restructuring public service.

9 Yingyao Wang offers a wonderfully insightful study of the "historical and institutional process in which the Chinese state refashioned itself as a shareholder and institutional investor in the economy," arguing that this has involved a shift in management, state bodies, and investment vehicles (2015, 603). Wang posits the emergence in China of a "mutually leveraging effect" between state power and finance.

10 Although Michelle Rosaldo (1974) initially hypothesized that the division between "domestic" and "public" structured gender inequality in all societies, she later (1980) argued that what counts as "domestic" and "public" varies a great deal across cultures and through time.

11 The distinction called out for strict scrutiny because it was an "encompassing framework for a cluster of notions which pervade[d] anthropological studies of the family and household," including "the conviction that the core of domestic relations is the mother-child bond" (Yanagisako 1979, 189). This bond was viewed as universal and derived from the biological acts of procreation and nurturance.

12 Feminist activism in relation to domestic violence, for example, drew attention to both the way in which this violence had been naturalized in the context of assumptions about male dominance and masculine nature and the need for changes in the law to protect female victims rather than male perpetrators. One could make the same argument about pro-life activists who, as Faye Ginsburg (1989) pointed out, also changed what counts as private or public in relation to birthing and abortion. Theorists of sexuality have long argued that the state and the church, as well as social norms that become subjectivized, regulate the seemingly intimate realm of sexual desire and activity (Butler 2011; Rubin 1993). See also critical legal studies scholars on similar points (D'Emilio and Freedman 1988; Wiesner-Hanks 2014).

13 See Collins 2000; Crenshaw 1989; Williams 1991.

14 Linda Kerber (1988) traced a genealogy of changes in the development of this metaphor, from efforts to identify these spheres as central to women's historical experience, to the identification of complexities within these spheres, to finally unpacking the metaphor itself and its development as an ideology to address contradictory tensions in nineteenth-century American republican politics and values (see also Kerber et al. 1989).

15 More recently, Kathi Weeks (2011) has elaborated on this earlier movement to challenge the very category of labor. Neferti Tadiar (2009) has also elaborated on the gendering of the category of labor, arguing that Marx's definition of the unnatural condition of alienated labor under capitalism depends on a gendered distinction

from corporeal labor, which is debased as the "mere being for something or someone else" and mere service for the satisfaction of immediate needs.

16 Laura Bear's (2015) study of the shift away from an earlier period of state socialism toward "neoliberal" economic policies on the Hooghly River and the Kolkata Port Trust of West Bengal is a stellar example of a fine-grained historical and ethnographic study of how specific forms of "privatization" are implemented by different categories of social actors to create new practices of governance. She presents a compelling processual analysis of how bureaucrats both suspend and generate boundaries between the state and the market through the medium of useful friendships. The invisibility of these friendships helps support the illusion that the state and the market are distinct spheres characterized by different ethics and productive powers.

17 Needless to say, the authors cited here do not agree with one another on how to assess the role of the Chinese state in fostering a market economy. They have differing evaluations on whether the Chinese state hinders or fosters the development of capitalism.

18 This debate depends, in part, on which indicators one examines: the capital markets (e.g., Shanghai stock exchange), contribution to gross domestic product (GDP), debt holdings, or number of legally registered firms (although in whose name they are registered often obscures rather than clarifies the complex relations of ownership).

19 Ritu Birla's (2009) historical study of indigenous merchant-capitalists in India highlights the ongoing debates over the "fair" and "unfair" ways to conduct profit-seeking activities between British colonialists and indigenous merchant-capitalists in India. She demonstrates how these negotiations took place through specific histories and cultural practices, especially those of gender and kinship.

20 Anthropologists have shown how "value" has multiple valences based in the culturally normative goals people strive for (Graeber 2001; Guyer 2004; Munn 1976). With the exception of Jane Guyer (2004), who examines traders as they move through various African communities, these studies tend to focus on the values of one culture or use a comparative approach to bounded cultures.

21 See Bairati 1988; Colli and Rose 2002.

22 Prominent analysts of migrant workers' lives in China (Lee 2007; Pun 2005; Pun and Lu 2010; Sun 2014) have demonstrated how migrant workers have developed both implicit and explicit critiques of the capitalist exploitation of their labor, though their critiques have been marginalized. Wanning Sun (2014) further argues that in some cases, migrant workers fold their critique into hopes of gaining wealth themselves. Leftist intellectuals in China have also developed a robust discussion and critique of capitalism. See Dai Jinhua, forthcoming; Wang Hui 2003, 2009. Lin Chun (2006, 2013) has directly challenged the displacement of this critique onto the socialist past.

23 Italian firms, especially those located in the northeast of the country, have been attracted to Romania. In 2006 there were about 1,500 Italian-owned textile and clothing factories in Romania ("Material Fitness" 2006, 7).

24 "Socialist world economy" refers to the well-developed international networks of production, distribution, and trade among socialist countries, dominated by the Soviet Union. These networks also included aid and interest-free loans as well as gifts of equipment and expertise.

25 Nicholas Lardy (2012) argues, however, that private firms are the most important driver of economic growth in China today.

26 Nicholas Lardy implicitly demonstrates the central role of government bureaus in his discussion of what he calls "imbalanced growth," in which export-import industries, coastal provinces, real estate, and construction industries and commercial banks dominate economic policy in China (2012, 137–54). These industries have some private firms, but they are dominated by state corporations.

27 Unlike Russia or some of the Eastern European nations, China never engaged in wholesale "spontaneous privatization" under the direction of U.S. economists. Indeed, an experimental and gradual approach has defined the direction of China's reforms, highlighting the nondeterministic content and direction of the reforms (Naughton 2007).

28 Along with the commodification of labor and the end of guaranteed social welfare (Lee 2005, 2007), these transformations have led to increased social differentiation, including regional disparities, and heated debates about social inequality based on the pursuit of wealth (Sun and Guo 2013; Wang and Hu 1999; L. Zhang 2001, 2010). The transfer of resources in the process of privatization reorganized social relations, advantages, and interests. The most prominent beneficiaries were a small minority, including some managers but also diverse government cadres who have led the formation of a new capitalist class.

29 Mary Gallagher (2005) has insightfully argued that the central government used the liberalization of foreign direct investment to encourage greater economic competitiveness within China. As a result, FDI became a driving force that pressured the eventual demise of the majority of China's state-owned enterprises, while simultaneously keeping an incipient domestic entrepreneurial class weak, thus managing to enhance its staying power and keep labor unrest from destabilizing the government. She emphasizes, however, that FDI liberalization was dynamic and gradual, reflecting practices on the ground. Indeed, she argues that its momentum was often from below, especially the convergence of the interests of foreign investors and local officials. Nonetheless, she argues that FDI liberalization played three crucial roles in this process: (1) it placed competitive pressures on regions and firms to reconceptualize labor practices and regulations, pressuring the eventual demise of the majority of China's state-owned enterprises; (2) it served as a laboratory for politically sensitive reforms; and (3) it shifted the debate from public ownership to national ownership. That is, the CCP successfully redirected the debate about socialism and state-owned industry away from the public/private dichotomy and toward a debate over the need for Chinese national industry amid foreign competition, even as the government continued to depend on foreign investment to develop China's economy. She concludes that this ideological transition has shaped

the content and form of labor protests in China. In the textile and garment sectors, the demise of state-owned enterprises is apparent in the lower-level factories that state bureaucracies have sloughed off. But the reverse is true for the import-export corporations that are as tightly controlled by the state as before.

30 Yasheng Huang (2003) argues that foreign direct investment in China has certain characteristics not shared by FDI in other countries: China's dependence on FDI relative to domestic investments is high; foreign-invested enterprises have replaced contractual alliances between foreign and domestic firms; the dominance of foreign-invested enterprises in labor-intensive and export-oriented industries is far more substantial than their presence in other Asian economies; they are spread throughout many industries and regions, in contrast to other countries, where FDI is usually concentrated in a few industries; and finally, most FDI projects in China are investments by small- and medium-sized foreign companies rather than by multinational corporations. See Ye (2010) for an extension of this discussion with a focus on Chinese diasporic investments in China.

31 The 1997 "Asian" financial crisis did not affect China directly, mainly because China's financial system was not open to foreign financial speculation at that time. It did, however, lead to the realization that globalization was not external to China but internal to it because China's economy was affected by the ties it had built with Southeast and East Asian nations. This crisis played a large role in moving China more quickly to join the WTO.

32 While the WTO's Multi-Fiber Agreement ended in 2005, sections of it were extended in the case of China until 2008.

33 According to the 2014 and 2015 China Statistics Yearbook, foreign investment projects in 2014 experienced a growth of 4.4 percent and in 2015 a growth of 11.8 percent. In the garment and textile industries, there was a slight drop in foreign investment projects, from 4,631 in 2013 to 4,023 in 2014 (garments), and from 3,152 in 2013 to 2,841 in 2014 (textiles).

34 In 1985, out of the approximately four hundred firms in the province of Como, which employed about thirteen thousand workers, there was only one joint-stock company that was owned by investors from outside Como.

35 Como's silk industry was not the only to experience a 50 percent decline in its number of firms between 1981 and 2001. In the cotton industry in the neighboring province of Varese, the number of firms dropped from 4,900 to 2,900, and the number of workers was halved ("Material Fitness" 2006, 3).

36 The focus on designer creativity in the marketing of clothing has also gained force with the shift in emphasis in Europe and the United States over the last thirty years to "creative" knowledge (Van Eekelen 2010). Indeed, Bregje Van Eekelen (2010) shows how governments are now moving to figure out how to measure this "creative" knowledge and include it in the GDP. This shift coincided historically with the outsourcing of industrial labor to the Global South. While on the one hand, it is a clear extension of the cultural division between mental and manual labor, on the other hand, it builds on the proliferation of intellectual property laws. This shift to

measure and value "creative" labor, then, is part of the ongoing attempt to maintain European and U.S. hegemony in the world economy. Hence, the specific asymmetry in the fashion sector cautions against an assertion of China's uniform "rise" in the world economy.

37 We thank one of the anonymous readers of our initial book manuscript for encouraging us to do this.

38 Corruption in relation to family firms is salient in Italy only when Italian capitalist families attempt to influence the Italian state.

Part I. The Negotiation of Value

1 We concur with Robert Foster that "mapping commodity networks and following things in motion are not ends in themselves" and that an "emphasis on discrete things must give way to an emphasis on relations" (2006, 296). Tracking a global supply chain is only the first step toward understanding how "value—quantitative as well as qualitative—is variably created and unequally distributed in and through contingent relations or assemblages of persons and things" (296).

2 Marx (1965, 1976) was quite clear that culture makes a difference in what counts as adequate reproduction of labor power, that there are historical transformations in people's needs and capacities, and that they differ along national-cultural lines. As feminist theorists have long pointed out, the reproduction of labor power outside the workplace is the unremunerated part of labor in capitalism. As cultural studies theorists have argued as well, class production occurs in numerous realms of social life. Our approach overlaps with that of Jason Moore (2015), especially his critique of the legacies of Cartesian dualism that privilege substance over relations and his emphasis on the importance of science, power, and culture as co-constitutive of what he calls "value's gravitational field" (2015, 54). We part ways from Moore, however, as he ends up accepting the substance of value as lying in socially necessary abstract labor. In contrast, we take a processual approach to production relations that treats them, as well as labor power, as contingent and historically formed.

Chapter 1. Negotiating Labor Power and Value

1 In keeping with the residential practices of the Italian entrepreneurs and managers we were studying, Yanagisako lived in what is called a "serviced apartment" while conducting research in Shanghai. These furnished apartments provide a range of amenities, including maid and concierge service, which make them especially convenient for foreigners who do not speak Chinese. Although they are located in several parts of the city, the one Yanagisako chose was in the French concession, one of the former colonial areas of the city, which is a favorite of many European and American businesspeople.

2 There is an obvious bias to our sample (in addition to self-selection bias affected by the firms that were willing to be studied)—namely, that our study includes more

firms that have been successful in forging joint ventures or other forms of collaboration in China than those that have not. We do not have good figures on the percentage of textile and clothing firms that fail in these transnational ventures in China, but one of the directors of the Italian Trade Commission in Shanghai estimated that 75 percent fail. Yanagisako's chapter in part III discusses the histories of Como firms and families that have not been successful in transnational expansion.

3 Two managers initially came to China to continue their study of Chinese language and literature and only later began working in business, and a couple of the women came to China because they were engaged or married to another worker in the firm.

4 All quotations from the Italian and Chinese have been translated into English by the chapter's author(s) unless otherwise noted.

5 See Zhang 2012 for the importance of private home ownership in the construction and display of middle-class status in China.

6 For debates and discussions on the category of "entrepreneur," see Carland, Hoy, and Carland 1988; Gartner 1988; Granovetter 2005; Schumpeter [1911] 1934, 1961.

7 Schumpeter argued, moreover, that entrepreneurial motivation lies not in the search for profits nor in the satisfaction of wants and needs but rather in the "will to found a private kingdom," the impulse to "prove oneself superior to others," and the joy of "exercising one's ingenuity" (Schumpeter [1911] 1934, 93, as quoted in Medearis 2013, 44). Scholars have argued for over a century about the extent to which entrepreneurs propel economic development as well as the salient features of an entrepreneur and entrepreneurial activity, emphasizing variously individual creativity, rationality, and psychology; social networks; innovation; and the ability to break from tradition.

8 In Chinese, people mostly say *zuo shengyi*, meaning "to do business," when they talk about being or becoming an entrepreneur. They rarely use the term *laoban*, or boss, when referring to themselves, although one of the main goals of becoming an entrepreneur is to become one's own boss. (Workers and employees, however, readily use the term *laoban* to refer to the company owner.) *Zuo shengyi* has semiotic flexibility.

9 See N. Chu 2014; Hsu 2007; Krug 2004; Ong 2006; and Tsai 2007 for further discussion of the wide array of entrepreneurial practices in contemporary China. Nellie Chu (2014) offers an especially rich ethnographic analysis of the precarity of migrant entrepreneurs in southern China who are positioned within fast fashion supply chains. The temporality and insecurity of landing contracts means these entrepreneurs constantly teeter on the ambiguous edge of the worker/entrepreneur divide.

10 As Rofel addresses in more detail in chapter 2, the expansiveness of this dream of becoming an entrepreneur derives from people's desires to move away from the previous socialist categories of labor and personhood, including both the positive and negative ones, namely worker, peasant, cadre, as well as landlord, capitalist, manager, and intellectual, respectively. To become an entrepreneur currently has a prestige analogous to that of a worker or peasant under Maoist socialism.

11 The imprimatur of this status is signified by the fact that wealthy entrepreneurs have been offered membership in the Communist Party.

12 Among entrepreneurs in Shanghai, even those who "own" their own company often list it as a subcontracted company with a larger state-owned enterprise, in part to ease the bureaucratic maneuvers one has to perform to do business in China. Conversely, as Rofel discusses in more detail in part II of the book, state-owned enterprises can appear as both public and private. Some entrepreneurs are involved in marketing and distribution, while others own a small shop or several shops. Some are entrepreneurs full-time but others hold multiple positions: some are employees in private firms and in addition engage in their own entrepreneurial activity. Yet others are managers in state-owned companies but also view themselves as entrepreneurs because they are responsible for seeking out clients and creating profits for their particular office. Tracing individuals' class/work trajectories further highlights the multiple valences of being and becoming an entrepreneur.

13 Recently, there is indication that this situation might be changing a bit. A few private banks that offer loans to non-state-owned firms have opened.

14 In 2012, according to the World Bank, China's GINI coefficient (the standard measure of income inequality) was 42.16 (0 represents perfect equality) (World Bank n.d.c).

15 Debates about corruption signal varying interpretations of how capitalism should be enacted in China. For more, see Rofel's chapters in parts II and III.

16 This was partly due to the fact that very few Chinese consumers had the kind of wealth necessary to buy luxury goods such as fashion clothing and partly due to the fact that state-owned companies still tended to dominate the domestic market, although that was changing by the time we finished our research.

17 Italians add Italian suffixes to the names of Chinese cities to indicate the people from there. People from Hong Kong are Hong Kongesi, those from Shanghai are Shanghainesi, and those from Wenzhou are Wenzhounesi.

18 In addition, during the time we did our research, what actually constituted "Chinese culture" was widely debated in China, as people searched for a satisfying replacement to socialist ideology.

19 In making comparisons among foreigners and how they conduct transnational business, Chinese entrepreneurs echoed a broader public discourse that invoked the categories of "foreigner," "Westerner," "European," "American," "Japanese," "Korean," and "Hong Kong, Taiwan, and other overseas Chinese." They viewed Korean and Japanese companies as having "small country consciousness" (*xiaoguo yishi*), while Americans, on the other hand, often acted like they have all the answers. Still, they felt that Americans and Europeans tried to ensure their Chinese counterparts were able to survive.

20 As Rofel has argued in her previous work (1999), in addition to the pressures of time, "quality" is one of the main sources of pressure in Chinese factories and one of the main disciplinary techniques that shapes the experience of labor (and pay) for Chinese workers in the textile and garment industries. "Quality" is a variable

measure; indeed, it can be the site on which Chinese entrepreneurs and their Italian counterparts struggle with one another when they disagree whether the "quality" of any particular batch of fabric or clothing is sufficiently high. Chinese entrepreneurs therefore spend a great deal of their time going to the factories to oversee quality as well as other aspects of production.

21 This practice has been in evidence in Hong Kong for a much longer period of time, owing to British colonial rule. It also existed in Shanghai prior to the 1949 socialist revolution. It is quite possible that this contemporary practice in Shanghai was borrowed from Hong Kong.

22 In the production of higher-end designer labels and even of middle-high brands, the garments are exported to Italy, where they are "finished," labeled, and organized for distribution to the brand's stores or other retailers. Finishing may entail a wide range of work—from assembling pieces of the garment, to sewing on buttons, to sewing on the label. If the garments are to be sold in China, the "finished" garments are then reimported into China.

23 Global annual sales of luxury goods are estimated to be between $130 billion to $200 billion. Until 2007 Japan was responsible for one-third of sales, Europe and the U.S. about one-fourth each. Although two-fifths of sales are now in Europe, much of this is to tourists. Some industry analysts predict that by 2014, Chinese consumers will be responsible for one-fourth of the luxury industry's profits ("Tutto in Famiglia" 2007).

24 Indeed, this history leads them to emphasize how they are able to transcend their own culture in dealing with foreigners.

25 For an analysis of class-based segregated communities in Chinese cities, see L. Zhang 2010. For an overview of contemporary urban life in China, see Logan 2008; Ren 2013; Solinger 1999. For a discussion of real estate in China, see Des Forges 2016.

26 Far from having an overarching state that regulates all market activity, the state-promoted market economy lets one thousand state-derived entrepreneurial firms blossom. Ministries and bureaus can no longer rely on the government for financial subventions. They must seek their funds from their own entrepreneurial activity. One of the major debates among scholars in China today is the dilemma of having massive state-supported firms able to create monopolies in various markets. These are mainly focused in natural resources, high technology, and finance. State involvement in the textile and garment industries is mainly through import-export trading companies run by various levels of government (i.e., China has central, provincial, municipal, and country import-export trading companies, all competing with one another). Thus navigating the Chinese state entails building social relationships with officials in numerous offices, even ostensibly within the same ministry.

27 The matter of who controls (and profits from) collective rural land is more contentious (Smith 2013).

28 As stated above, this is due to the fact that the banks, almost all state-owned, give loans only to state-owned companies.

29 Until World War II, the main source of labor in these areas were peasant households that engaged in a mix of farming, petty entrepreneurship, and wage labor.

30 While Koreans, Japanese, Hong Kongese, and Taiwanese have also established resident communities in Shanghai, they tend to roam more widely in China.

31 Regional dialects such as Shanghai dialect persist, though people complain that rural migration to the cities is forcing everyone to speak *putonghua* (Mandarin), thus losing regional, especially urban, languages.

32 For studies of regional identities in China not just as holdovers from the past but as reinventions in the present, see Friedman 1994; Oakes 2000. See also Honig 1992 on regional discriminations within Shanghai both prior to and during the socialist period.

33 The misleading characterization of the manufacturing process of luxury brands is not unique to Italian ones. For example, in 2010 two Louis Vuitton ads were banned by Britain's Advertising Standards Agency (ASA) for misleading customers. One of the ads depicts a seamstress sewing a handbag with text that reads, "The seamstress with linen thread and beeswax. A needle, linen thread, beeswax and infinite patience protect each over-stitch from humidity and the passage of time." A second ad shows a woman making a wallet accompanied by the text "What secret little gestures do our craftsmen discretely pass on? How do we blend innate skill and inherent prowess?" The ASA concluded that Louis Vuitton's luxury handbags are actually made by machine. Although the company admitted that sewing machines are used in the production process, they also argued that the "production of the bags was 'not automated' and that there were over 100 stages in the making of each bag." Yet they failed to document the proportion of the manufacturing process that is carried out by hand or by machine, leading the ASA to conclude that the ads were misleading. "Louis Vuitton Ads Banned after Design House Misled Customers by Suggesting Its Bags Were Hand-Stitched," *Mail Online*, 26 May 2010, http://www.dailymail.co.uk/femail/article-1281443/Louis-Vuitton-ads-banned-suggesting-bags-hand-stitched.html.

34 I thank Dan Segal for this insight.

35 "Made in Italy" clothing is also manufactured by Chinese living in Italy, including the Chinese community in Prato (next to Florence), which is estimated to number around twenty thousand, and others in the area of Naples.

36 The gendered character of the concept of "affective labor," moreover, lends itself toward a characterization of men's work as "instrumental" and "economically productive," while women's "affective" work produces forms of sociality. The failure to fully recognize the gender dimension of these distinctions overlooks an important critique by feminist scholars of such distinctions, namely, that it is in the making of such categorical distinctions about human social action that inequality is constituted.

37 All managers' notions of Italianità are not necessarily forged exclusively through their work in China. Paolo Rinaldi and his wife, who also worked in Mexico and Turkey for the Italian firm, integrate their experiences at these sites as well into

their concept of Italianità. The vast majority of the managers in our study, however, have worked overseas only in China.

38 The naturalizing and embodying of productive powers and knowledge that congeal in situated engagements within specific labor processes is hardly unique to Italian transnational managers. It appears to be a widespread way to both objectify and claim the value of one's labor and resist estrangement. See, for example, Karen Ho's (2009) ethnography of Wall Street in which investment bankers acquire social powers and knowledge they did not have previously but are able to claim these as inherent capacities and abilities because of the selection process through which they are recruited. The highly selective process of recruitment (only the top students from Ivy League colleges are chosen) makes it appear that only a small percentage of people (the best and the brightest) have the intelligence and skill to generate profit for shareholders, thus rationalizing their high pay. What is obscured is that it is the situated experience of working in Wall Street firms that endows these bankers with the knowledge and skill needed to generate shareholder profit.

Part II. Historical Legacies and Revisionist Histories

1 The Bretton Woods agreements (crafted in 1944 at a conference held in Bretton Woods, New Hampshire, and signed at the end of World War II by a small number of states from North America and Western Europe), were intended to reorder the world economy, under U.S. leadership and domination, in an effort to ensure peace. These agreements established the International Monetary Fund (IMF) to regulate international control over exchange rates among national currencies. The IMF also became a source of loans for development. The Bretton Woods agreements essentially collapsed after 1971 when the U.S. unilaterally terminated the convertibility of the U.S. dollar to gold. See Peet 2003.

2 David Harvey (2005), for example, has emphasized the importance of these economic crises in shaping what he calls the "politics of neoliberalisation." However, in his classical Marxist approach, neoliberalism resolved these crises to produce a new era of capitalism. We disagree with this approach.

Chapter 2. Entrepreneurialism in Postsocialist China

1 Dorothy Solinger (2013) has also recently emphasized temporality, in contradistinction to spatiality, as an important measure of inequality in China. Focusing on the vast disparity in material standards of living among urban residents, Solinger argues that the new urban elite have seen significant improvements in their lives while the urban poor have regressed to the poverty common among everyone in the Maoist era. Moreover, official discourse represents the former as signifying progress while the latter signifies backwardness.

2 See Dai Jinhua's most recent collection of translated essays (2018) for a discussion of this historical revisionism in relation to public culture in China. Her argument is

that Chinese citizens are encouraged not just to reject the socialist past but to erase it from history altogether.

3 In his distinctive analysis, Yurchak argues that the last generation of those who lived under Soviet socialism experienced a paradox in which their understanding of "'socialism' as a system of human values . . . was not necessarily equivalent to 'the state' or 'ideology'" (2006, 8). It was this paradox, what Yurchak calls the "internal displacement" (283) of a seemingly immutable system, that made the end of the Soviet Union both expected and unexpected among its citizens.

4 A prevalent colonial myth that continues to circulate in the West is that China was an inward-looking, closed society prior to the West's ability to pry it open in the nineteenth century. One often hears, both in China and elsewhere, that China once again became a closed country under socialism and only now is opening up to the world. This myth ignores the fact that throughout its long history, China has been engaged in several distinctive "worlding" projects, to borrow a term from Mei Zhan (2009, 23). The revisionist histories centering on Shanghai, which I discuss in this chapter, invoke one of those long-term encounters that resulted in a specific world, that of colonial cosmopolitanism. See Rofel 2012.

5 I use the term "encounter" to refer to engagements across difference. Attention to how culture-making occurs through everyday encounters among members of two or more groups with different cultural backgrounds and histories and unequally positioned stakes in their relationships helps us understand how "the cultural" is made and remade in everyday life. Encounters prompt unexpected responses and improvised actions, as well as long-term negotiations with unforeseen outcomes. See Faier and Rofel 2014.

6 For this reason, David Goodman (2014) argues that China has a socialist market economy.

7 There is a voluminous literature on affective labor. In Michael Hardt (1999) and Hardt and Negri (2000), the emphasis is on affect as the product of one's labor. Others emphasize affective attachments to one's job, as fostered by corporate employers, especially in the knowledge economy (see Boltanski and Chiapello 2005; Clough 2007; Ditmor 2007; Donzelot 1991; Ducey 2007; Gilbert 2007; Gregg and Seigworth 2010; Kao 2014, 2016; Moreton, 2009; Rose 1999; Sanchez 2012, Staples 2007, Wissenger 2007). In the situations in China I describe in this chapter, affective engagements are not with the products of one's labor nor with the job itself but with temporality. The affective engagements I highlight here are with revisionist histories and imagined futures.

8 See Andrew Wedeman's (2005, 2012) empirical studies of corruption in China that analyze their effects on state integrity.

9 Anthropologists eschew the Orientalist view that corruption is particular to the non-West or the neoliberal view that it is endemic in public institutions alone. The latter view produces the idea that deregulation, privatization, and market economic activity will resolve problems of corruption in government.

10 They have traced how people make sense of politics and their state through these discourses. Capitalist anthropologists have argued that corruption is a fundamental element in the workings of capitalism (Schneider and Schneider 2003). Rather than treat corruption in the narrow sense, they have elaborated on corruption as a set of rituals, beliefs, and practices for getting by as well as a site through which to understand inequality.

11 On behalf of small companies that work under their aegis, the import-export corporation deals with regulations from the following bureaus: export, customs, numerous tax bureaus, foreign trade, and labor.

12 One of the biggest complaints I heard from both Chinese and foreign entrepreneurs about doing export business in China is the need to cultivate these kinds of connections—which usually also involved various extra payments or gifts to individual officials. Many called these payments bribes. In addition to these payments, it is the time and effort involved in cultivating the relationships—including meals and entertainment together—that is so demanding (see Osburg 2013). And in the case of a woman entrepreneur, like Lou, it is not always easy, as the entertainment can often involve bringing young women into the mix.

13 The WTO quotas ended in 2008. Lou then severed her relationship with this municipal textile corporation, established an independent name for her company, but continued to pay a fee to the state corporation to take care of numerous bureaucratic regulations.

14 Since this import-export corporation is also a subbranch of the municipal government, it is unlikely they will ever have to give up their claims to this real estate.

15 There was a wide public discourse on reinvigorating Confucian principles as the basis for social relations, such as *xiushen, jijia, zhiguo, pingtianxia* (cultivate one's moral character, put one's family in order, put one's country in order, strive for world peace). Indeed, both Lou Jingxiao and Wang Shiyao had gifted me recently published books that popularize Confucian ethics for everyday life. China's central government eventually also got into the business of promoting Confucianism.

16 Nostalgia, as I have previously argued (1999), is not just a sentiment but also a strategy of representation that yearns for both the clarity of beginnings and the certitude of endings. As I argue in that earlier work, nostalgia for the early and putatively purer period of socialism longs for the very ways of life that the political struggles under socialism destroyed. Neofeudal nostalgia, by contrast, longs for a way of life prior to the socialist period, which this longing yearns to regain.

17 Needless to say, this cosmopolitanism based in colonialism is quite distinct from socialist internationalism.

18 Corner food and drink stores were run by the neighborhood or resident committees, which were linked to the municipal public safety bureau. See Z. Wang 2005.

19 See Koga 2016 for a similar description of the recuperation of the remainders of Japanese colonial history in northeast China, what she brilliantly calls the capitalization of history and the political economy of redemption.

20 Some of them had been *cohong* merchants under the old system. Cohongs were merchant guilds that had operated the import-export business in Canton (Guangzhou) in the Qing dynasty (1644–1911).

21 But Yen-p'ing Hao (1970) also describes the decline of the comprador system in the early twentieth century, owing to the decline in foreign imports during World War I, foreign and Chinese firms starting to deal directly with one another, and the rise of modern Chinese banks that put traditional native banks out of business. In addition, Howard Cox and Kai Yiu Chan (2000) discuss how foreign firms began to replace semiautonomous compradors as they set up joint ventures with Chinese firms, which were characterized by a parent/subsidiary rather than a principal/ agent relationship.

22 For histories of Shanghai's presocialist commercial life, see Bergère 1989, 2009; Coble 1986; Cochran 1980, 1999; Hershatter 1997; Ji 2003. For Shanghai's presocialist labor conditions, see Perry 1993; Honig 1986. For descriptions of the lives of ordinary Chinese residents of presocialist Shanghai, see B. Goodman 1995; Lu 1999. For a discussion of the importance of an international presence to the formation of Shanghai, see Wasserstrom 2008.

23 In the period of New Democracy (1949–1953), the state permitted the national bourgeoisie (e.g., entrepreneurs, shopkeepers, owners of small factories and workshops) to continue private-sector operations in the cities to support the nation's economic recovery and provide for the needs of the Korean War. In 1952, however, more than 450,000 private industrial and commercial enterprises in the nine biggest cities became targets in the five-anti (*wufan*) campaign. By 1956 all private enterprises were nationalized or converted into joint public-private enterprises in which capital assets and shares would be held by private owners and government organs (Brown and Pickowicz 2007; Eckstein 1977, 75–76; Meisner 1999, 84–87; Riskin 1987, 45–48). Following the failure of the Great Leap Forward (1958–1960), individual small businesses reemerged and employed about 1.04 million people before being attacked and suppressed again during the Cultural Revolution. At the start of reforms, there were 140,000 individual businesses employing 150,000 people (Kraus 1991, 59, 62–63).

24 The vast numbers of Chinese people living in the downtown area were pushed out by municipal officials who took advantage of the emergent real estate market with its skyrocketing values, combined with the fact that the urban land, now property, was still held publicly by the government, to force Chinese citizens to accept a fraction of the newly calculated value of their homes and move to the distant outskirts of Shanghai. For an analysis of class-based segregated communities in Chinese cities, see L. Zhang 2010. For an overview of contemporary urban life in China, see Logan 2008; Ren 2013; Solinger 1999. For a discussion of real estate in China, see Des Forges 2016. See Greenspan 2014 for a provocative analysis of imaginings of the future embedded in the makeover of Shanghai today. See Zhan 2009 for descriptions of the medical colleges that had moved from downtown Shanghai to Pudong.

25 This neofeudal nostalgia is pervasive in other realms as well. A historian from the Shanghai Social Sciences Institute waxed eloquent to me about Shanghai's glorious

history of prewar cosmopolitanism, before the CCP, in an obscurantist manner, in her view, closed it off. A friend took me to a restaurant on a street in Shanghai that is entirely retro 1930s. The restaurant patrons, most of them young men and women, were dressed in 1930s-style clothing. This dream is further fostered by the outpouring of soap operas about prewar elite entrepreneurs. Since the mid-1990s, there have been at least twelve long, multi-episode television dramas celebrating merchants. They go by titles such as *Confucian Commerce* (*Rushang*), *The Mansion* (*Dazhaimen*), *Imperial Business* (*Longpiao*), *Qiao Family Courtyard* (*Qiaojia dayuan*), *Oriental Merchants* (*Dongfang shangren*), and *The Dyeing Mill* (*Da ranfang*). Even Isaac Julien, in his recent nine-screen video installation, *Ten Thousand Waves*, at New York's Museum of Modern Art (MOMA), inspired by several recent tragedies involving Chinese migrants to England, repeatedly invoked these nostalgic images of prewar Shanghai. One could mention other films as well, such as Ang Lee's *Lust, Caution*.

26 While private firms are rapidly increasing in number, firms that might start out as private seek a close linkage with the state, most often local or regional bureaucracies, in order to flourish. Without the imprimatur of a particular state bureaucracy, it is difficult to do business. Conversely, as I argue later in this chapter, some pieces of state firms, especially factories at the bottom of the state hierarchy, have "privatized," meaning the state no longer "owns" them. Still, these firms continue to have a close relationship with the bureaucracy within which they were formed. Often, this problem is related not simply to Chinese state regulations. Global neoliberal strategies to develop post–Cold War capitalism, as embodied in the WTO and more recently in various transnational trade agreements, also have been influential in the transformations that China currently experiences. Mimicking U.S. trade strategies, China has also been developing transnational trade agreements and institutions, such as the Silk Road Economic Belt and the 21st Century Maritime Silk Road (also known as "One Belt, One Road" or OBOR), and the new Asian Infrastructure Investment Bank.

27 The socialist past was certainly a contradictory endeavor of ideological commitments to equality along with a drive to achieve wealth and power in a modernist, developmentalist mode (Lin 2006). This latter technocratic mode, combatted by Maoism and utopian socialist thought, became triumphant in the reform era. Current inequality is thus a continuation of prior developmentalist practices combined with novel forms bred out of the specific mode of capitalist accumulation China has embraced (Lin 2013).

28 They did so through Shenzhen, located on the border with Hong Kong. Shenzhen was then a new city wholly created by the state in the mid-1980s to experiment with foreign investment. It was the first special economic zone (SEZ). The SEZs followed in the footsteps of export processing zones (EPZS), established in Asia during the 1970s, which encouraged foreign investment with lower tax rates, streamlined administrative procedures, the duty-free import of components and raw materials, and no export or sales tax on exports (Naughton 2007, 406–7; W. Wu 1999, 16–17).

However, sezs serve primarily as conduits for foreign investment and only second-arily as a source of employment generation (K. Wong and Chu 1985, 6–7; W. Wu 1999, 18–19).

29 Huang is intent on proving the assumption that only privatization produces real economic productivity and growth and equitable distribution of wealth. His focus is therefore on finding out whether a corporation is actually privately or state owned, which is not always easy to answer. He never deeply follows through on the question of why this difficulty persists.

30 My favorite example is the massage parlor that used to exist around the corner from the Women's Federation hostel where I stay in Beijing. It clearly fronted as a sex parlor—confirmed by what friends told me—with beautiful women standing out front trying to lure customers. I was told it was owned by the Beijing Retired Cadres Bureau.

31 Yasheng Huang (2008) argues that securitizing a firm does not index its priva-tization. Instead, it merely means the superficial appearance of a capitalist mar-ket. Huang implies here, however, that these firms, whether state or privately owned, are geared toward producing profit.

32 The manner in which losses are dealt with can be more revealing of an entity's relationship to the state than the manner in which profits are dealt with. This is not to say that these entities are necessarily "inefficient" or not truly capitalist. As we witnessed in the 2008 financial crisis in the U.S. and Europe, the actions of the state to bail out certain sectors of the economy and certain companies is not self-evident from free market ideology.

33 The majority of the companies listed on the Shanghai Stock Exchange that have gone "public" and are listed as selling stock are state owned. Thus, they are both "public" and "state owned," again blending the meaning of "public," "private," and "state."

34 Moreover, the range of entrepreneurial activities and the wide range of foreign joint venture customers that comprise Splendid China point strongly toward an intimate relationship with the state. The textile and garment industries in the Shanghai and Hangzhou areas, especially those geared toward export, are clearly divided between large state-owned companies and independent companies that focus on sourcing for foreign firms but do not engage in large-scale buying of yarn or fabrics, nor do they tend to own factories, instead subcontracting with factories that have been privatized or that have been established as wholly new entities since the beginning of economic reform. Splendid China, like Wang Shiyao's state-owned corporation, also has its own brand of clothing, which it markets through branch stores mainly in northern China.

35 This might have been especially true after the 2003 tax reform that put greater pres-sure on local governments to find their own profits.

36 Upon entry into the wto, China had to partially eliminate subsidies to state-owned enterprises and let them operate on a commercial basis, making them responsible for their own profits and losses. Banks also reduced lending to nonperforming state-owned enterprises (soes). Consequently, soes were restructured and unprof-

itable ones were closed (L. Song 2015, 192–93). In 2003 the State Asset Supervision and Administration Commission (SASAC) was established to exercise ownership over 196 state firms. Its leaders sought to restructure them into listed corporations, marked by corporate governance and disclosure regulations, and subject to capital markets. Local governments assumed ownership over the thousands of other state-owned companies, establishing local SASACs at the provincial level. Local governments gained the right to restructure and privatize firms regardless of national policy, frequently shutting down or selling off firms that were unprofitable (see Naughton 2015, 48, 55, 62).

37 The entire working-class neighborhood that used to surround Zhenfu has been given a facelift. It has been razed to the ground and rebuilt, with fancy stores, newly built apartment buildings, and wide, even roads for cars replacing the winding, narrow alleyways where most workers used to live.

38 In the 1980s, workers used to explain how difficult this shift system was—from the problems it produced for their bodily rhythms and disruptive sleep patterns, to the challenges of arranging their family lives, including childrearing.

39 Moreover, the bank loans; the board of directors, all of whom are party cadres; and the owner, who is the son of the former manager and who was appointed by the Zhejiang FuHua Silk Corporation, point toward an ongoing intimate relationship with the state.

40 This was in part due to Soviet advice and to military threats from the United States. See Lin 2006, 2013.

41 Much has been written on the general contours of the exploitative working conditions in supply chain factories in China. See Chan and Lüthje 2015; Jacka 2005; Kuruvilla et al. 2011; Lee 1998, 2007; Litzinger 2013b; Pringle 2013; Pun 2005, 2016; Pun and Chan 2013.

42 Yan Hairong (2008) similarly argues that in official discourse, migrant workers from the countryside represent a backward spatial dimension but also a forward-looking life when compared to older urban workers, most of whom have been laid off. My argument in this chapter builds on this work by focusing on how migrant workers grapple with these contradictory temporal representations.

43 This vision of themselves as entrepreneurs of their own labor displaces previous notions of class identification as a proletariat and disrupts, though not entirely, a view of themselves as part of a working class in the present.

44 As often happens with fieldwork, I fortuitously found my way into this factory by way of a friend of a friend. My connection at the factory, who later became a friend, is a young woman who was then finishing her PhD on French views of China through cinema and literature. She held a managerial position, which she treated as temporary. When I arrived at the factory, we spent most of our conversation on her thesis and her various translations of well-known French authors into Chinese. While most factory owners and managers are leery of having foreigners view factory conditions or talk with workers, this person threw open the doors for me to talk with as many workers as I wanted to.

45 As Gail Hershatter has alerted us in *The Gender of Memory* (2011), her book about rural women's lives under Maoist socialism in China, the oral histories of China's rural citizens do not subvert so much as transverse official histories.

46 Prior to the socialist revolution, large-scale textile factories were found mainly in Shanghai, where workers were women. By contrast, in the Hangzhou area, textile production, especially of silk, took place largely in household workshops, where men did the weaving, while women prepared the thread. Once the socialist government pulled these household workshops into large-scale factories in the 1950s, they instituted a gendered division of labor that increasingly made silk weaving into women's work. By the 1980s, when I had conducted my research on the silk industry in Hangzhou, there were no men—none whatsoever—doing either the thread production or the weaving. Men fixed machines, did the dyeing, and, of course, were managers/cadres.

47 Authors in Litzinger's (2013a) *South Atlantic Quarterly* special issue, for instance, have pointed out that China's new generation of workers is better educated and therefore can give voice to a range of insights about their living and laboring conditions.

48 Ching Kwan Lee (2007) describes the labor protests by migrant workers in southern Guangdong province who work in production factories for export. They protest unpaid wages and illegal wage rates, disciplinary violence and humiliation, and industrial injuries. They turn largely to the legal system in hopes of redress from the state. But they also engage in street protests. Pun Ngai (2005), who also did research in Guangdong, points to more submerged but nonetheless evident forms of "transgression," as she calls them, in which incipient subaltern resistance has the potential to form. These transgressions include speaking to one another about their working conditions, daring to voice criticisms, or covering for one another at work. Pun Ngai and Jenny Chan (2013) more recently have documented the activism of workers in transnational supply chain factories, such as sharing organizing skills and disseminating protest strategies, bringing specific issues to management, and presenting demands to the local government. They emphasize the central role of what they call the "dormitory labor regime," in which factory owners house and feed workers at minimal levels in order to better exploit their labor. This dormitory labor regime fosters the discontents—as well as organizing abilities—that fuel workers' protests. Ho-fung Hung (2013) further argues that the protests by migrant workers in the export-oriented sector have also played a role in helping the central government pressure local governments to accept labor reform.

49 Yan (2008) and Pun and Chan (2013) have pointed out how the production of labor power in China depends on the social reproduction of migrant workers, most of whom eventually return to the rural areas from which they come.

50 Ching Kwan Lee has similarly argued that migrant workers want to leave behind their "vivid memories of and aversion to poverty associated with collectivized agriculture" (2007, 206). Moreover, she argues, "Bereft of an alternative vision of the social order," migrant workers in Guangdong, like migrant workers in the lower Yangzi delta, "aspire to rural entrepreneurialism" (206).

51 See Yan 2008 for a description of how domestic servants who have started their own businesses are lauded for their success at self-development.

52 In my 2013 visit to China, even former workers at Zhenfu, who had worked under the old socialist system, were all scrambling to open their own small businesses. My friend Tang Shan, former head of the Youth League, for example, had opened a restaurant. Another former worker in the spinning workshop had opened a real estate business.

53 In this sense, their futuristic aspirations resemble those who hope to migrate to various elsewheres—especially Europe or North America. As Julie Chu (2010) has so eloquently shown, those from China who hope to migrate to these elsewheres often construe their preparations for such often unrealized dreams as in themselves a form of mobility. Here we find a very close resonance with the migrant workers I met in the factories. For their various preparations—fantasizing possible entrepreneurial paths, saving for that dream, enlisting others to dream with them—resemble these rural Fujian residents Chu writes about.

54 Yan (2008) further emphasizes what she calls the "emaciation" of the rural, by which she means that the countryside has been eviscerated of state investment, sociality, people, and even production, as more and more people are encouraged to migrate to urban areas. Starting with Hu Jintao and continuing into the present, the central state leadership has begun to encourage more investment in rural areas, but their goal is to urbanize much of the countryside.

55 This is not to discount real differences between life under socialism and under post-socialism for those in the countryside (see Yan 2008). However, it is also important to acknowledge that, from the beginning, the socialist state had extracted resources from the countryside to focus on urban industrial development and offered full socialist welfare only to those living in the cities. The hukou system implemented under socialism hardened these differentiations.

Chapter 3. Italian Legacies of Capital and Labor

1 For example, artisan firms with a maximum of ten employees and ten apprentices had been granted tax concessions and lighter contributions for worker social insurance and family allowances since the 1950s (Blim 1990). The new labor regulations passed in the 1970s exempted artisan firms from many of their provisions, enabling them to pay less for social welfare benefits, fire workers more easily, and schedule work hours more flexibly (Piore and Sabel 1984, 228).

2 Judging by the behavior of the managers at the joint venture, neither were some customers in Europe and the U.S. willing to pay high prices for Italian luxury menswear made in China. They were hesitant to reveal the names of the European "private labels" for which the joint venture manufactured suits. When we toured the factory floors, however, we saw the labels of several prestigious Italian brands on the suits.

3 In the autumn of 2013, one of the ex-managers of FGS who had gone to work for an Italian luxury jewelry brand reported that sales of luxury brands had plummeted in

China over the past year as wealthy Chinese customers, especially those with Communist Party ties, had become nervous about even being seen entering a luxury brand store. Foreign luxury consumer goods had been common gifts from those seeking favor from party officials.

4 In 2010 the Vinimoon factory's production was 15 percent for the Vinimoon label, 40 percent for other Chinese brands, and 45 percent for other European brands.

5 For histories of several subcontractors who rose from being employees to starting a competing firm, see Yanagisako 2002, 124–31.

6 Throughout the twentieth century, 75–95 percent of all registered firms in Italy were family firms (Amatori and Colli 2000; Bairati 1988; Chiesi 1986).

7 For an account of specific cases, see Yanagisako 2002, 139–42.

Chapter 4. Italian-Chinese Collaborations

1 The construct of a fashion system is an ideology articulated since the late nineteenth century in Europe, in line with the "invention" of haute couture and the connection between fashion, civilization, taste, and social class (Bourdieu 1984). This construct is shared by not only the Italians but the majority of foreigners in the fashion business in China and by many Chinese entrepreneurs themselves.

2 See, for example, the anecdote about The Chinese Tailor: "There once was a European who wanted a new suit. Since there were no European tailors in China, he called in a Chinese tailor and asked him if he was able to copy and sew a European suit. The tailor said he could make it up, if he provided him with a model. The European found an old, worn-out suit and gave it to him. After a few days the tailor brought the new suit. The European examined it and found it perfect. The only thing was that on the shoulders of the suit the tailor had made a hole, and mended it with a patch. The European asked him why. The tailor replied, 'I followed the model exactly.' Today, the narrator comments, 'China seeks to imitate the West in everything, without understanding the reason why.'" The episode is included in a book by André Chih, *The Christian Occident Seen by the Chinese in the Late 19th Century* (1961), which he "discovered" in the diary (published in Taipei in 1954) of Ku Hung Ming (1857–1928).

3 A Eurocentric vision considers fashion a Western product, predicated on the cult of individualism from the Renaissance and consolidated by the Industrial Revolution. "Made in Italy" is seen as a modern development of the same concept linking the Italian artisanal past to the economic boom after World War II, down to its present-day global expansion.

4 "Zegna's Tale of Two Cities," *China Daily*, 2 August 2010, Chinadaily.com.cn.

Part III. Kinship and Transnational Capitalism

1 McKinnon 2013 argues convincingly that underpinning the absence of kinship in metanarratives of transnational and global capitalism is an evolutionary model of

modernity that posits a steady global march away from the importance of family and kinship bonds.

2 There is a large body of literature on family business to which economic historians, economists, sociologists, psychologists, management specialists, and a few anthropologists have contributed. Comparative figures on the prevalence of family businesses must be carefully qualified, however, since there is no standard definition of a family firm (Colli 2003, 16). For example, depending on whether a broad definition (some degree of family control) or a restrictive definition (multiple generations directly involved, direct family involvement in strategic decisions, more than one family member having managerial responsibilities employed) is used, the estimated number of family firms present in U.S. industry varies from 4 million to 20 million. For useful reviews of the interdisciplinary scholarship on family business, see Colli 2003; Colli and Rose 2002.

3 See also Amatori and Colli 2000; Bairati 1988; and Chiesi 1986, 434, on family shareholding and control of firms in Italy.

4 At the end of the twentieth century, 17 percent of the top one hundred corporations, both in the United States and in Germany, were family firms. Among the top five thousand major Dutch corporations, 46 percent were family-run companies, while one-third of the top one hundred Swiss corporations were entrepreneurial or family firms (Colli 2003, 16).

Chapter 5. On Generation

Epigraph: Former website of Ermenegildo Zegna.

1 For an extended critique of Weber's model of "modern" capitalism and its contrast to premodern capitalism rooted in the "communal" bonds of family, see Yanagisako 2002, 2013.

2 In addition, in spite of recognizing that family businesses come in a wide variety of types, Colli treats them as a "particular form of business organization" whose "historical evolution" and reasons for decline and persistence can be studied by drawing on data on family business from a wide range of "cultural and institutional environments" (Colli 2003, 5).

3 Ever since anthropologists (Carsten 2000; Collier and Yanagisako 1987; Delaney 1986; Franklin and McKinnon 2001; Schneider 1964, 1984) called into question the "biological" basis of kinship and argued that the supposedly universal "biological facts" of conception, parturition, and consanguinity are themselves constructed through culturally specific symbols and meanings, anthropologists have reconceptualized kinship as rooted in cultural models of relatedness that must be empirically investigated rather than assumed.

4 As Meyer Fortes (1949) pointed out nearly seven decades ago, families, households, and other "domestic groups" are not static structural units but change over the course of their developmental cycle. Depending on when in the developmental cycle a family or household is observed, it will have a different composition, organization, and

social dynamic and may be classified by researchers as different types of "domestic groups." Fortes's key point is still valuable, although his definition of "domestic group" is flawed. For a critique of Fortes's and other anthropologists' use of the term "domestic," see Yanagisako 1979.

5　I use the term "nonfamily manager" rather than the term "professional manager" because the latter implies that managers who are not members of the proprietary family are professionally trained, while those who are members of the proprietary family are not. This is not the case in the family firms in this study, nor has it been throughout their histories. Most of the family members with an active role in management of the firm have formal educations relevant to their positions. Many have the equivalent of a bachelor's degree (laurea) in Economia e Commercio (economy and business), which is the degree of choice among those preparing for managerial positions in business in Italy.

6　According to Colli, who specializes in family business, the medium-sized Italian enterprises that are expanding into certain global market niches—such as clothing, luxury goods, machine goods, and the various branches of "Made in Italy" enterprises—have been "managed by the creation of hierarchical structures based upon a multi-subsidiary system" that remains firmly in the control of the family (2003, 62).

7　The Civil Code of unified Italy, which was modeled on the Napoleonic code, governed Italian inheritance from 1865 until the enactment of the new family laws of 1975.

8　For a detailed description of the proportioning of inheritance claims before the passage of the new family laws in 1975, see Davis 1973, 174–86. For a discussion of how widows' inheritance rights were strengthened by the revision of the Civil Code of 1975, see Yanagisako 2002, 169–72.

9　When I initiated my study of Como family firms, out of approximately four hundred firms in the industry there was only one joint-stock company that had been started by investors from outside the province.

10　In 1990 there were 1,131 textile firms and 1,082 clothing firms in Como for a total of 2,213 firms, which employed 29,215 workers. In 2005 there were 853 textile firms and 593 clothing firms for a total of 1,446 firms, which employed 19,035 workers—a 65 percent decline in the number of firms and workers. Note that the clothing firms had declined more than the textile firms, and the mean number of workers per firm had remained stable at 13 workers per firm (Luraschi 2010).

　　Between 2005 and 2009, Como's silk industry again experienced a dramatic decline. The annual drop in exports of textiles and clothing was 22.4 percent. This was similar to the decline in Beilla's wool district (−21.2 percent) and close to the national median (−20.6 percent) (Centro Tessile Serico 2010, 4).

11　This decline in the number of firms and employees, however, did not mean a decline in Italy's textile exports. The latter actually rose 10.4 percent in 2010 because fashion brands paid a premium for "Made in Italy" fabric (Greta and Lewandowski 2010, 20).

12 My division of the Como families that owned firms in the silk industry into three fractions—upper, middle, and lower—was based on a combination of firm and family characteristics. Firm characteristics included annual gross revenue, number of employees, the extent to which they sold their own products or worked as subcontractors for other firms, and their ownership of other firms. Family characteristics included indicators of past and present social class, including the education and occupation of the founder's parents, the founder's spouse and parents, the founder's children, and their spouses and children (Yanagisako 2002, 100). For the firm and family characteristics of the thirty-eight family firms in my sample, see tables 3.2 and 3.3 in Yanagisako 2002, 102–5.

13 I was unable to track down what happened to the firms into which these firms merged through archival research. Therefore, I only know what happened to those that I was able to follow through ethnographic research. See my discussion later in this chapter regarding the limitations of relying solely on the Camera di Commercio files.

14 The vast majority of family firms in Como do not survive long enough for grandsons to take over their management. Few even survive long enough for grandsons to begin working in them (Yanagisako 2002, 38). Only two of the thirty-eight firms in my sample had been founded by the grandfather of the current generation of owner-managers, and in only two more had grandsons even begun working in the firm (see table 2.1 in Yanagisako 2002, 38).

15 For a discussion of the history of the Barbieri family, see Yanagisako 2002, 35–38, 150–53.

16 The cotton textile manufacturer Alfred Motte is reported to have conceived this system after other strategies had failed in competition with more established mass producers. In the système Motte, each family member who had come of age was paired with an experienced technician from one of the family's firms. The pair was provided with startup capital to initiate a firm that specialized in one of the phases of production needed by the confederation (Piore and Sabel 1984, 34).

17 The other cousins in the fourth generation had mostly become professionals: lawyers, scientists, engineers, bankers. Only two had entered the textile industry.

18 As the Como silk industry declined, many families with firms—whether in the middle or upper bourgeoisie—had shifted their investments to real estate. Whether they did it on a small scale, as the Galbiati family had done by building apartments and shops on the site of the old family home, or by setting up real estate holding companies, as the Molteni siblings had, these bourgeois families had shifted their capital from industrial production to rents.

Chapter 6. Chinese Family Firms

1 Susan Greenhalgh (1994) has provided the classic deconstruction of the Orientalist approach to Chinese family firms (viz, they succeed because they are based on collectivist Confucian traditions).

2 David Pistrui et al. (2001) argue that family is a key factor in the growth of small private firms in China. Yet they tend to blur the distinction between whether firms that are family-owned and firms that rely on family members for finance and as a source of employment. Panikkos Poutziouris, Yong Wang, and Sally Chan (2002) argue that the small family firm is essential to the development of the private sector in China. But as I argue here and in chapter 2, what counts as "private sector" is not always so clear-cut.

3 The company's English name is an alliteration from Chinese, translated as "beautiful, special, powerful country." To solidify this connection between the grandeur of firm, product, and nation, the firm headquarters had a permanent exhibit of ancient clothing, making the visual connection with China's imperial history.

4 For recent articles in English about Wen Jiabao's family wealth, see Barboza 2012; Gates 2012. For a general description of the family wealth of various political leaders, see Barboza and LaFraniere 2012. In response to Chinese citizens' discussions of political leaders' corruption, the current president Xi Jinping has made a number of rulings restricting the involvement of political leaders' family members in state-owned businesses as well as numerous other rulings on bribery, graft, and administrative and moral discipline. For a recent evaluation of the effectiveness of President Xi's anticorruption campaign, see Keliher and Wu 2016. He has also restricted having government officials sit on the boards of private or public firms. For the latter, see Fan 2016. For a discussion of the importance of political connections to the corporate valuation of Chinese family firms, see Tang, Ye, and Zhou 2013.

5 Although the link between kinship and corruption emerged out of the Cultural Revolution, the idea that kinship and social inequality are wrapped up in one another goes back much further. Prior to the socialist revolution, the Chinese Communist Party's initial critique of and attack on the power of kinship within villages in turn developed out of the earlier May Fourth Movement of 1919, a period that shaped the ideological outlook of many of the first Communist Party leaders. See Evans 1997; Hershatter 2007, 2011.

6 Mao had ordered this policy for two reasons: to stop the violent fighting that had erupted in the cities and to further his ideological commitment to end the new bureaucratic privileges of party-state officials.

7 On guanxi, see Kipnis 1997; M. Yang 1994. For an insightful recent ethnography of the importance of guanxi in the success of entrepreneurial ventures, see Osburg 2013.

8 In the 1980s, Zhenfu had been famous for its beautiful multicolored and elaborately designed silk quilt covers. It was difficult then to even get a job at Zhenfu. Tang explained with evident pride how she had to go through a thorough interview process before she was chosen to work there. Zhenfu had also been an elaborate state-run *danwei*, or work unit, that had supplied workers with benefits and also many items they could not get on the then just emerging "free markets."

9 In the early 1990s in China, many were accused of corruption for practices that today are de rigueur for creating wealth. Similarly, in the United States we have seen

the increased acceptance of profit-seeking practices that a few decades ago landed people in jail.

10 "They are the same as men, they do not fear hardship, do not fear exhaustion, do not fear setbacks, they are brave and strong in facing the ups and downs of doing business" (Wu 2004, 9).

11 Julie Chu (2010) makes a similar argument for Fujian, the province just to the south of Wenzhou.

12 The independent enterprise paid fees to the public enterprise and in return could use its name and bank account and pay taxes through them. Parris points out that one needed personal ties to make this work, since no legal procedures were in place. At the time, central authorities considered guahu a form of illegal speculation and profiteering. As we saw in chapter 2 on privatization in China, however, it is now a central means through which state-owned corporations develop their own profit.

13 Wenzhou was also one of the earliest locations to develop "shareholding firms" that were often new hybrid forms of ownership between public and private enterprises. According to Parris 1993, Wenzhou also had a very large number of privately hired wage laborers at a time when it was against socialist policies.

14 Though again, as noted in note 4, this situation may be changing under President Xi Jinping.

15 They specialize in women's clothing, often with leather in it because there is a large wholesale leather market in this town. The clothing they make is for both the domestic and international markets. Their foreign customers include Europe, the U.S., Russia, and Spain. As for Italy, they mostly work with Chinese customers who are already in Italy. He said he did not know of any Italian companies that they dealt with directly. Later that afternoon, however, I learned from the manager of their dyeing factory that they were in the middle of negotiating with several Italian customers with offices or branch companies located in China who wanted to contract for clothing production. To do so, they go through import-export agents in Hangzhou and Shanghai.

16 We had become friendly the year before through my friend who was in charge of the garment factory.

17 The competition was stiffer. In addition, the price of raw materials, like that of the chemicals they put in the dyeing process, had gone up.

18 I eventually realized Liu's reluctance was owing to the fact that the person who connected us had told him I wanted to talk with workers. Though I had no trouble speaking with workers when I did ethnographic research for my first book, by 2008 there had been a great deal of international attention and criticism of the treatment of workers in factories for export in China.

19 He described this arrangement as *xuni jingying*—which could be translated as "fictitious business" or "virtual business." By that he meant the Nike model: that the domestic company they produced for only marketed their brand and subcontracted to others to produce the actual product.

20 Neighborhood committees were run by volunteers, mostly older women, who were literally street-level socialist government representatives, keeping track of problems in the neighborhood, including domestic disputes, factory collectives, and so on.

21 *Xiagang* literally means "step down from your position"; it is the term used for those with positions in state-owned enterprises who are laid off. Zhao laughed and said, "They became unemployed but we Chinese have flowery ways of saying things, like xiagang."

22 Ritu Birla (2009) discusses analogous differences between British colonial and Indian entrepreneurs and the issue of maneuverability that the British interpreted as irregular, underhanded and dishonest.

23 The dominant gendered narratives about people overseas coming home to find spouses entails a man coming back to China to find a woman. But here we find the reverse, and Li seemed to have no trouble telling me this narrative in part, I assume, because his wife had succeeded in her Italian businesses.

References

Abu-Lughod, Janet. 1989. *Before European Hegemony: The World System* A.D. *1250–1350*. New York: Oxford University Press.

Alexievich, Svetlana. [2013] 2016. *Secondhand Time: The Last of the Soviets*. Translated by Bela Shayevich. New York: Random House.

Anagnost, Ann. 1997. *National Past-Times: Narrative, Representation, and Power in Modern China*. Durham, NC: Duke University Press.

Arrighi, Giovanni, Beverly J. Silver, and Benjamin D. Brewer. 2003. "Industrial Convergence, Globalization, and the Persistence of the North-South Divide." *Studies in Comparative International Development* 38 (1): 3–31.

Aspesi, Natalia. 2012. "Miuccia Prada: La moda glamour dice addio a Milano e trasloca a Parigi." *La Repubblica*, July 27.

Atanasoski, Neda, and Kalindi Vora. 2017. "Introduction: Postsocialist Politics and the Ends of Revolution," special issue, *Social Identities* 24 (2): 1–15. DOI: 10.1080 /13504630.2017.1321712.

Ayling, Joe. 2011. "'Made in Italy' Survives without EU Label." *Just-Style.com*, May 13. http://www.just-style.com/analysis/made-in-italy-thrives-without-eu-label-law _id111078.aspx.

Bairati, Piero. 1988. *La Famiglia italiana dal'ottocento a oggi*. Rome: Laterza.

Bakker, Karen. 2010. *Privatizing Water: Governance Failure and the World's Urban Water Crisis*. Ithaca, NY: Cornell University Press.

Barbieri, Paolo, Lelio Gavazza, and Giorgio Prodi, eds. 2011. *Supply China Management: Strategia, approvvigionamenti e produzione: Opportunità e sfide per le imprese italiane nel paese del dragone*. Bologna: Il Mulino.

Barboza, David. 2012. "Billions in Hidden Riches for Family of Chinese Leader." *New York Times*, October 25.

Barboza, David, and Sharon LaFraniere. 2012. "'Princelings' in China Use Family Ties to Gain Riches." *New York Times*, May 17.

Bear, Laura. 2007. *Lines of the Nation: Indian Railway Workers, Bureaucracy, and the Intimate Historical Self*. New York: Columbia University Press.

Bear, Laura. 2015. *Navigating Austerity: Currents of Debt along a South Asian River*. Stanford, CA: Stanford University Press.

Bear, Laura, Karen Ho, Anna Tsing, and Sylvia Yanagisako. 2015. "Gens: A Feminist Manifesto for the Study of Capitalism." Theorizing the Contemporary, *Cultural Anthropology* website, March 30. https://culanth.org/fieldsights/652-gens-a -feminist-manifesto-for-the-study-of-capitalism.

Berdahl, Daphne. 2010. *On the Social Life of Post-Socialism: Memory, Consumption, Germany*. Bloomington: Indiana University Press.

Bergère, Marie-Claire. 1989. *Golden Age of the Chinese Bourgeoisie, 1911–1937*. Cambridge: Cambridge University Press.

Bergère, Marie-Claire. 2009. *Shanghai: China's Gateway to Modernity*. Stanford: Stanford University Press.

Bertrand, Marianne, and Antoinette Schoar. 2006. "The Role of Family in Family Firms." *Journal of Economic Perspectives* 20 (2): 73–96.

Birla, Ritu. 2009. *Stages of Capital: Law, Culture, and Market Governance in Late Colonial India*. Durham, NC: Duke University Press.

Blim, Michael. 1990. *Made in Italy: Small-Scale Industrialization and Its Consequences*. New York: Praeger.

Bourdieu, Pierre. 1984. *Distinction: A Social Critique of the Judgement of Taste*. Cambridge, MA: Harvard University Press.

Boyle, James. 2003. "The Second Enclosure Movement and the Construction of the Public Domain." *Law and Contemporary Problems* 66 (1/2): 33–74.

Breward, Christopher, and David Gilbert. 2006. *Fashion's World Cities*. New York: Berg.

Brown, Jacqueline Nassy. 2017. "Making New York Great Again: Race, Place, and Nation in the Empire City." Lecture, Department of Geography, University of California, Berkeley, April 19.

Brown, Jeremy, and Paul G. Pickowicz. 2007. "The Early Years of the People's Republic of China: An Introduction." In *Dilemmas of Victory: The Early Years of the People's Republic of China*, edited by Jeremy Brown and Paul G. Pickowicz, 1–18. Cambridge, MA: Harvard University Press.

Brown, Wendy. 2001. *Politics Out of History*. Princeton, NJ: Princeton University Press.

Brown, Wendy. 2015. *Undoing the Demos: Neoliberalism's Stealth Revolution*. Cambridge, MA: MIT Press.

Burton, Antoinette. 1998. *At the Heart of the Empire: Indians and the Colonial Encounter in Late-Victorian Britain*. Berkeley: University of California Press.

Butler, Judith. 2011. *Gender Trouble: Feminism and the Subversion of Identity*. New York: Routledge.

Caldwell, Melissa. 2011. *Dacha Idylls: Living Organically in Russia's Countryside*. Berkeley: University of California Press.

Calefato, Patrizia. 2010. "Fashion as Cultural Translation: Knowledge, Constrictions and Transgressions on/of the Female Body." *Social Semiotics* 20 (4): 343–55.

Callon, Michel. 1998. "Introduction: The Embeddedness of Economic Markets in Economics." In *The Laws of the Markets*, edited by M. Callon, 1–68. Oxford: Blackwell.

Caratozzolo, Vittoria Caterina. 2014. "Reorienting Fashion: Italy's Wayfinding." In *The Glamour of Italian Fashion since 1945*, edited by Sonnet Stanfill, 46–57. London: V and A Publishing.

Carland, James W., Frank Hoy, and Jo Ann C. Carland. 1988. "Who Is an Entrepreneur? Is a Question Worth Asking." *American Journal of Small Business* 12 (4): 33–39.

Carsten, Janet. 2000. *Cultures of Relatedness: New Approaches to the Study of Kinship.* Cambridge: Cambridge University Press.

Centro, Tessile Serico. 2010. " 'Cosa cambia per Il Tessile Comasco?': Riflessioni a partire dall'analisi dei risultati distrettuali 2009." 3 June 2010. Report prepared by Prometeia.

Chan, Anita Boy Lüthje. 2015. *Chinese Workers in Comparative Perspective.* Ithaca, NY: ILR Press.

Chandler, Alfred D. 1977. *The Visible Hand: The Managerial Revolution in American Business.* Cambridge, MA: Harvard University Press.

Chelcea, Liviu, and Oana Druta. 2016. "Zombie Socialism and the Rise of Neoliberalism in Post-socialist Central and Eastern Europe." *Eurasian Geography and Economics.* DOI: 10.1080/15387216.2016.1266273.

Chiesi, Antonio. 1986. "Fattori di persistenza del capitalismo familiare." *Stato e Mercato* 18 (3): 433–53.

Choy, Timothy K., Lieba Faier, Michael J. Hathaway, Miyako Inoue, Shiho Satsuka, and Anna Tsing. 2009. "A New Form of Collaboration in Cultural Anthropology: Matsutake Worlds." *American Ethnologist* 36 (2): 380–403.

Chu, Julie Y. 2010. *Cosmologies of Credit: Transnational Mobility and the Politics of Destination in China.* Durham, NC: Duke University Press.

Chu, Nellie. 2014. "Global Supply Chains of Desires and Risks: The Crafting of Migrant Entrepreneurship in Guangzhou, China." PhD diss., University of California, Santa Cruz.

Clough, Patricia Ticineto. 2007. "Introduction." In *The Affective Turn: Theorizing the Social*, edited by Patricia Ticineto Clough and Jean Halley, 1–33. Durham, NC: Duke University Press.

Coble, Parks M. 1986. *The Shanghai Capitalists and the Nationalist Government, 1927–1937.* Cambridge, MA: Harvard University Asia Center.

Cochran, Sherman. 1980. *Big Business in China: Sino-Foreign Rivalry in the Cigarette Industry, 1890–1930.* Cambridge, MA: Harvard University Press.

Cochran, Sherman. 1999. *Inventing Nanjing Road: Commercial Culture in Shanghai, 1900–1945.* Cornell East Asia 103. Ithaca, NY: East Asia Program, Cornell University.

Coghlan, Timothy. 2012. "China's Best Designed Luxury Mall." *MAOSUIT*, July 13. http://maosuit.com/retail-2/real-estate/chinas-best-designed-luxury-mall/.

Colli, Andrea. 2003. *The History of Family Business, 1850–2000*. Cambridge: Cambridge University Press.

Colli, Andrea, Paloma Fernández Pérez, and Mary B. Rose. 2003. "National Determinants of Family Firm Development? Family Firms in Britain, Spain, and Italy in the Nineteenth and Twentieth Centuries." *Enterprise and Society* 4 (1): 28–64.

Collier, Jane Fishburne, and Sylvia Junko Yanagisako, eds. 1987. *Gender and Kinship: Essays toward a Unified Analysis*. Stanford: Stanford University Press.

Collins, Patricia Hill. 2000. *Black Feminist Thought: Knowledge, Consciousness, and the Politics of Empowerment*. New York: Routledge.

Comaroff, John L. 1987. "Sui Genderis: Feminism, Kinship Theory, and Structural Domains." In *Gender and Kinship: Essays toward a Unified Analysis*, edited by Jane Fishburne Collier and Sylvia Junko Yanagisako, 53–85. Stanford: Stanford University Press, 53–85.

Conaghan, Joanne, ed. 2009. *Feminist Legal Studies: Critical Concepts in Law*. London: Routledge.

Corbellini, Erica, and Stefania Saviolo. 2004. *La scommessa del Made in Italy e il futuro della moda italiana*. Milan: Etas.

Cox, Howard, and Kai Yiu Chan. 2000. "The Changing Nature of Sino-Foreign Business Relationships, 1842–1941." *Asia Pacific Business Review* 7 (2): 93–110.

Craik, Jennifer. 2009. *Fashion: The Key Concepts*. New York: Berg.

Crane, Diane. 2004. "The Globalization of Culture: The Fashion Industry as a Case Study." Paper presented at Convegno Internazionale Questioni Di Moda. Milan.

Crenshaw, Kimberle. 1989. "Demarginalizing the Intersection of Race and Sex: A Black Feminist Critique of Antidiscrimination Doctrine, Feminist Theory and Antiracist Politics." *University of Chicago Legal Forum* 1989 (1): 139–67.

Daems, Herman. 1980. *The Determinants of the Hierarchical Organization of Industry*. Brussels: European Institute for Advanced Studies in Management.

Dai, Jinhua. 2018. *After the Post–Cold War: The Future of Chinese History*. Durham, NC: Duke University Press.

Davis, John. 1973. *Land and Family in Pisticci*. London: Burns and Oates.

D'Emilio, John, and Estelle B. Freedman. 1988. *Intimate Matters: A History of Sexuality in America*. Chicago: University of Chicago Press.

Des Forges, Alexander. 2016. "Hegel's Portfolio: Real Estate and Consciousness in Contemporary Shanghai." In *Ghost Protocol: Development and Displacement in Global China*, edited by Carlos Rojas and Ralph A. Litzinger, 62–83. Durham, NC: Duke University Press.

Ditmor, Melissa. 2007. "In Calcutta, Sex Workers Organize." In *The Affective Turn: Theorizing the Social*, edited by Patricia Ticineto Clough and Jean Halley, 170–86. Durham, NC: Duke University Press.

Donzelot, Jacques. 1991. "Pleasure in Work." In *The Foucault Effect: Studies in Govern-mentality*, edited by Graham Burchell, Colin Gordon, and Peter Miller, 251–80. Chicago: University of Chicago Press.

Ducey, Ariel. 2007. "More Than a Job: Meaning, Affect, and Training Health Care Workers." In *The Affective Turn: Theorizing the Social*, edited by Patricia Ticineto Clough and Jean Halley, 187–208. Durham, NC: Duke University Press.

Eckstein, Alexander. 1966. *Communist China's Economic Growth and Foreign Trade: Implications for U.S. Policy*. New York: McGraw-Hill.

Eckstein, Alexander. 1977. *China's Economic Revolution*. Cambridge: Cambridge University Press.

Eicher, Joanne B., and Sandra Lee Evenson. 2008. *The Visible Self: Global Perspectives on Dress, Culture, and Society*. New York: Fairchild.

Ernst, Dieter, and Barry J. Naughton. 2008. "China's Emergent Political Economy: Insights from the IT Industry." In *China's Emergent Political Economy: Capitalism in the Dragon's Lair*, edited by Christopher McNally, 39–59. London: Routledge.

Evans, Harriet. 1997. *Women and Sexuality in China: Dominant Discourses of Female Sexuality and Gender since 1949*. Cambridge: Polity Press.

Faier, Lieba, and Lisa Rofel. 2014. "Ethnographies of Encounter." *Annual Review of Anthropology* 43 (October): 363–77.

Fan, Jijian. 2016. "The Value of Political Connections in China: Government Officials on the Board of Directors." https://papers.ssrn.com/sol3/papers.cfm?abstract_id =2866559.

Fenoaltea, Stefano. 2001. "The Growth of Italy's Cotton Industry, 1861–1913: A Statisti-cal Reconstruction." *Rivista Di Storia Economica* 17 (2): 139–72.

Fewsmith, Joseph, and Xiang Gao. 2014. "Local Governance in China: Incentives and Tensions." *Daedalus* 143 (2): 170–83.

Finnane, Antonia. 2008. *Changing Clothes in China: Fashion, History, Nation*. New York: Columbia University Press.

Fortes, Meyer. 1949. *Time and Social Structure: An Ashanti Case Study*. Indianapolis: Bobbs-Merrill.

Foster, Robert J. 2006. "Tracking Globalization: Commodities and Value in Motion." In *Handbook of Material Culture*, edited by Chris Tilley, Webb Keane, Susanne Küchler, Mike Rowlands, and Patricia Spyer, 285–302. London: SAGE.

Foucault, Michel. 1986. *The History of Sexuality*. Vol. 3, *The Care of the Self*. New York: Vintage Books.

Franklin, Sarah, and Susan McKinnon. 2001. *Relative Values: Reconfiguring Kinship Studies*. Durham, NC: Duke University Press.

Frey, Luigi, ed. 1975. *Lavoro a domicilio e decentramento dell'attività produttiva nei settori tessile e dell'abbiqliamento in Italia*. Milan: Franco Angeli.

Friedman, Edward. 1994. "Reconstructing China's National Identity: A Southern Alternative to Mao-Era Anti-Imperialist Nationalism." *Journal of Asian Studies* 53 (1): 67–91.

Gallagher, Mary Elizabeth. 2005. *Contagious Capitalism: Globalization and the Politics of Labor in China*. Princeton, NJ: Princeton University Press.

Gartner, William B. 1988. "Who Is an Entrepreneur? Is the Wrong Question." *American Journal of Small Business* 12 (4): 11–32.

Gates, Guilbert. 2012. "The Wen Family Empire." *New York Times*, October 25.

Gilbert, Karen Wendy. 2007. "Slowness: Notes toward an Economy of Differential Rates of Being." In *The Affective Turn: Theorizing the Social*, edited by Patricia Ticineto Clough and Jean Halley, 77–105. Durham, NC: Duke University Press.

Ginsborg, Paul. 2003. *A History of Contemporary Italy: Society and Politics, 1943–1988*. New York: Palgrave Macmillan.

Ginsborg, Paul. 2013. "Civil Society in Contemporary Italy: Theory, History and Practice." *Journal of Modern Italian Studies* 18 (3): 283–95.

Ginsburg, Faye. 1989. *Contested Lives: The Abortion Debate in an American Community*. Berkeley: University of California Press.

Goodman, Bryna. 1995. *Native Place, City, and Nation: Regional Networks and Identities in Shanghai, 1853–1937*. Berkeley: University of California Press.

Goodman, David S. 2014 *Class in Contemporary China*. Malden, MA: Polity Press.

Graeber, David. 2001. *Toward an Anthropological Theory of Value: The False Coin of Our Own Dreams*. New York: Palgrave Macmillan.

Granovetter, Mark. 1985. "Economic Action and Social Structure: The Problem of Embeddedness." *American Journal of Sociology* 91 (3): 481–510.

Granovetter, Mark. 2005. "The Impact of Social Structure on Economic Outcomes." *Journal of Economic Perspectives* 19 (1): 33–50.

Green, Stephen Paul, and Guy Shaojia Liu. 2005. *Exit the Dragon? Privatization and State Control in China*. London: Wiley-Blackwell.

Greenhalgh, Susan. 1994. "De-Orientalizing the Chinese Family Firm." *American Ethnologist* 21 (4): 746–75.

Greenspan, Anna. 2014. *Shanghai Future: Modernity Remade*. Oxford: Oxford University Press.

Gregg, Melissa, and Gregory J. Seigworth, eds. 2010. *The Affect Theory Reader*. Durham, NC: Duke University Press.

Greta, Marianna, and Krzysztof Lewandowski. 2010. "The Textile and Apparel Industry in Italy: Current State and Challenges to Further Growth." *Fibres and Textiles in Eastern Europe* 18 (6): 20–25.

Gupta, Akhil. 1995. "Blurred Boundaries: The Discourse of Corruption, the Culture of Politics, and the Blurred State." *American Ethnologist* 22 (2): 375–402.

Gupta, Akhil. 2005. Narratives of Corruption: Anthropological and Fictional Accounts of the Indian State. *Ethnography* 6 (1): 5–34.

Gupta, Akhil. 2012. *Red Tape: Bureaucracy, Structural Violence, and Poverty in India*. Durham, NC: Duke University Press.

Guthrie, Douglas. 1999. *Dragon in a Three-Piece Suit: The Emergence of Capitalism in China*. Princeton, NJ: Princeton University Press.

Guyer, Jane I. 1984. "Naturalism in Models of African Production." *Man*, n.s. 19 (3): 371–88.

Guyer, Jane I. 2004. *Marginal Gains: Monetary Transactions in Atlantic Africa*. Chicago: University of Chicago Press.

Haller, Dieter, and Chris Shore. 2005. *Corruption: Anthropological Perspectives*. Ann Arbor, MI: Pluto Press.

Hansen, Karen Tranberg. 2004. "The World in Dress: Anthropological Perspectives on Clothing, Fashion, and Culture." *Annual Review of Anthropology* 33: 369–92.

Hao, Yen-p'ing. 1970. *The Comprador in Nineteenth Century China: Bridge between East and West*. Cambridge, MA: Harvard University Press.

Hardt, Michael. 1999. "Affective Labor." *Boundary 2* 26 (2): 89–100.

Hardt, Michael, and Antonio Negri. 2000. *Empire*. Cambridge, MA: Harvard University Press.

Hardt, Michael, and Antonio Negri. 2004. *Multitude: War and Democracy in the Age of Empire*. New York: Penguin.

Harvey, David. 2005. *A Brief History of Neoliberalism*. Oxford: Oxford University Press.

Hershatter, Gail. 1997. *Dangerous Pleasures: Prostitution and Modernity in Twentieth-Century Shanghai*. Berkeley: University of California Press.

Hershatter, Gail. 2007. *Women in China's Long Twentieth Century*. Berkeley: University of California Press.

Hershatter, Gail. 2011. *The Gender of Memory: Rural Women and China's Collective Past*. Berkeley: University of California Press.

Heynen, Nik, James McCarthy, Scott Prudham, and Paul Robbins. 2007. *Neoliberal Environments: False Promises and Unnatural Consequences*. New York: Routledge.

Ho, Karen. 2009. *Liquidated: An Ethnography of Wall Street*. Durham, NC: Duke University Press.

Hodges, Matt. 2012. "The Politics of Emergence: Public-Private Partnerships and the Conflictive Timescapes of Apomixis Technology Development." *BioSocieties* 7 (1): 23–49.

Holland, Kateryna. 2012. "The Wealth Effects of Government Investment in Publicly Traded Firms." Working paper, University of Oklahoma, Norman.

Holland, Stuart. 1972. "Introduction." In *The State as Entrepreneur: New Dimensions for Public Enterprise*, edited by Stuart Holland, 1–4. London: Weidenfeld and Nicolson.

Honig, Emily. 1986. *Sisters and Strangers: Women in the Shanghai Cotton Mills, 1919–1949*. Stanford: Stanford University Press.

Honig, Emily. 1992. *Creating Chinese Ethnicity: Subei People in Shanghai, 1850–1980*. New Haven, CT: Yale University Press.

Horvat, Srećko, and Igor Štiks, eds. 2015. *Welcome to the Desert of Post-Socialism: Radical Politics after Yugoslavia*. New York: Verso.

Hsiao, Gene T. 1977. *The Foreign Trade of China: Policy, Law, and Practice*. Berkeley: University of California Press.

Hsing, You-tien. 2010. *The Great Urban Transformation: Politics of Land and Property in China*. Oxford: Oxford University Press.

Hsu, Carolyn. 2006. "Cadres, Getihu, and Good Businesspeople: Making Sense of Entrepreneurs in Early Post-Socialist China." *Urban Anthropology and Studies of Cultural Systems and World Economic Development* 35 (1): 1–38.

Hsu, Carolyn L. 2007. *Creating Market Socialism: How Ordinary People Are Shaping Class and Status in China*. Durham, NC: Duke University Press.

Huang, Yasheng. 2003. *Selling China: Foreign Direct Investment during the Reform Era*. New York: Cambridge University Press.

Huang, Yasheng. 2008. *Capitalism with Chinese Characteristics: Entrepreneurship and the State*. Vol. 1. Cambridge: Cambridge University Press.

Hung, Ho-fung. 2013. "Labor Politics under Three Stages of Chinese Capitalism." *South Atlantic Quarterly* 112 (1): 203–12.

Kuriyan, Renee, and Isha Ray. 2009. "Outsourcing the State? Public-Private Partnerships and Information Technologies in India." *World Development* 37 (10): 1663–73.

Italian Trade Commission. 2008. "Let Yourself Be Charmed by an Italian." PR *Newswire*, January 17.

Jacka, Tamara. 2005. *Rural Women in Urban China: Gender, Migration, and Social Change*. Armonk: M.E. Sharpe.

Ji, Zhaojin. 2003. *A History of Modern Shanghai Banking: The Rise and Decline of China's Finance Capitalism*. Armonk: M.E. Sharpe.

Kalb, Don. 2009. "Conversations with a Polish Populist: Tracing Hidden Histories of Globalization, Class, and Dispossession in Postsocialism (and Beyond)." *American Ethnologist* 36 (2): 207–23.

Kamat, Sangeeta. 2004. "The Privatization of Public Interest: Theorizing NGO Discourse in a Neoliberal Era." *Review of International Political Economy* 11 (1): 155–76.

Kao, Caroline. 2014. "New Capitalist Work Ethics and the Spirit of Socialist Utopianism in Silicon Valley." Presentation, Society for Cultural Anthropology Conference, Detroit, May 9.

Kao, Caroline. 2016. "My Boss, My Soulmate: Affective Economies in a San Francisco Startup." Presentation, American Anthropological Association Annual Meeting, Minneapolis, November 19.

Keliher, Macabe, and Hsinchao Wu. 2016. "Corruption, Anticorruption, and the Transformation of Political Culture in Contemporary China." *Journal of Asian Studies* 75 (1): 5–18.

Kelliher, Daniel. 1992. *Peasant Power in China: The Era of Rural Reform, 1979–1987*. New Haven, CT: Yale University Press.

Kerber, Linda K. 1988. "Separate Spheres, Female Worlds, Woman's Place: The Rhetoric of Women's History." *Journal of American History* 75 (1): 9–39.

Kerber, Linda K., Nancy F. Cott, Robert Gross, Lynn Hunt, Carroll Smith-Rosenberg, and Christine M. Stansell. 1989. "Beyond Roles, Beyond Spheres: Thinking about Gender in the Early Republic." *William and Mary Quarterly* 46 (3): 565–85.

Khurana, Rakesh. 2007. *From Higher Aims to Hired Hands: The Social Transformation of American Business Schools and the Unfulfilled Promise of Management as a Profession.* Princeton, NJ: Princeton University Press.

Kipnis, Andrew B. 1997. *Producing Guanxi: Sentiment, Self, and Subculture in a North China Village.* Durham, NC: Duke University Press.

Koga, Yukiko. 2016. *Inheritance of Loss: China, Japan, and the Political Economy of Redemption after Empire.* Chicago: University of Chicago Press.

Kraus, Willy. 1991. *Private Business in China: Revival between Ideology and Pragmatism.* Honolulu: University of Hawai'i Press.

Krug, Barbara. 2004. *China's Rational Entrepreneurs: The Development of the New Private Sector.* New York: Routledge.

Kunz, Grace I., and Myrna B. Garner. 2007. *Going Global: The Textile and Apparel Industry.* New York: Fairchild.

Kuruvilla, Sarosh, Ching Kwan Lee, and Mary E. Gallagher, eds. 2011. *From Iron Rice Bowl to Informalization: Markets, Workers, and the State in a Changing China.* Ithaca: Cornell University Press.

Lardy, Nicholas R. 2002. *Integrating China into the Global Economy.* Washington, DC: Brookings Institution Press.

Lardy, Nicholas R. 2012. "Financial Repression in China." Policy Brief, PB08-8. Washington, DC.

Layton, Christoper. 1972. "State Entrepreneurship in a Market Environment." In *The State as Entrepreneur: New Dimensions for Public Enterprise,* edited by Stuart Holland, 45–55. London: Weidenfeld and Nicholson.

Layton, Christopher, Michael Whitehead, and Y. S. Hu. 1972. "Industry and Europe." *International Executive* 14 (2): 5–6.

Lee, Ching Kwan. 1998. *Gender and the South China Miracle: Two Worlds of Factory Women.* Berkeley: University of California Press.

Lee, Ching Kwan. 2005. *Livelihood Struggles and Market Reform: (Un)making Chinese Labour after State Socialism.* Geneva: United Nations Research Institute for Social Development.

Lee, Ching Kwan. 2007. *Against the Law: Labor Protests in China's Rustbelt and Sunbelt.* Berkeley: University of California Press.

Lin, Chun. 2006. *The Transformation of Chinese Socialism.* Durham, NC: Duke University Press.

Lin, Chun. 2013. *China and Global Capitalism: Reflections on Marxism, History, and Contemporary Politics.* New York: Palgrave MacMillan.

Linder, Stephen. 1999. "Coming to Terms with the Public-Private Partnership: A Grammar of Multiple Meanings." *American Behavioral Scientist* 43 (1): 35–51.

Litzinger, Ralph. 2013a. "Labor in China: A New Politics of Struggle." *South Atlantic Quarterly* 112 (1): 172–212.

Litzinger, Ralph. 2013b. "The Labor Question in China: Apple and Beyond." *South Atlantic Quarterly* 112 (1): 172–78.

Locke, Richard M. 1995. *Remaking the Italian Economy*. Ithaca, NY: Cornell University Press.

Logan, John R., ed. 2008. *Urban China in Transition*. Oxford: Blackwell.

Lu, Hanchao. 1999. *Beyond the Neon Lights: Everyday Shanghai in the Early Twentieth Century*. Berkeley: University of California Press.

Luraschi, A. 2010. "L'evoluzione recente del distretto serico comasco: Una reinterpretazione, 2010/12." http://eco.uninsubria.it/dipeco/quaderni/files/QF2010_12.pdf.

Mah, Feng-hwa. 1971. *Foreign Trade of Mainland China*. New York: Aldine Atherton.

Manning, Paul. 2010. "The Semiotics of Brand." *Annual Review of Anthropology* 39: 33–49.

Mansfield, Becky. 2009. *Privatization: Property and the Remaking of Nature-Society Relations*. Oxford: Blackwell.

Martinelli, Alberto, and Antonio Chiesi. 1989. "Italy." In *The Capitalist Class: An International Study*, edited by Thomas Burton Bottomore and Robert J. Brym, 140–76. New York: Harvester Wheatsheaf Brighton.

"Material Fitness: How Europe's Leading Home for Makers of Clothing and Shoes Is Adapting to Low-Cost Competition from China." 2006. *The Economist*, February 23.

Maynard, Margaret. 2004. *Dress and Globalisation*. Manchester: Manchester University Press.

Mazzaoui, Maureen Fennell. 1981. *The Italian Cotton Industry in the Later Middle Ages, 1100–1600*. Cambridge: Cambridge University Press.

Mazzarella, William. 2003. *Shoveling Smoke: Advertising and Globalization in Contemporary India*. Durham, NC: Duke University Press.

McCarthy, James. 2004. "Privatizing Conditions of Production: Trade Agreements as Neoliberal Environmental Governance." *Geoforum* 35 (3): 327–41.

McKinnon, Susan. 1991. *From a Shattered Sun: Hierarchy, Gender, and Alliance in the Tanimbar Islands*. Madison: University of Wisconsin Press.

McKinnon, Susan. 2013. "Kinship within and beyond the "Movement of Progressive Societies." In *Vital Relations: Modernity and the Persistence of Kinship*, edited by Susan McKinnon and Fenella Cannell, 39–62. Santa Fe, NM: SAR Press.

McLafferty, Sara. 1998. "The Geographical Restructuring of Urban Hospitals: Spatial Dimensions of Corporate Strategy." *Social Science and Medicine* 23 (10): 1079–86.

Medearis, John. 2013. *Joseph A. Schumpeter*. Major Conservative and Libertarian Thinkers Series, Volume 4. New York: Bloomsbury.

Meisner, Maurice. 1999. *Mao's China and After: A History of the People's Republic*. New York: Simon and Schuster.

Menkes, Suzy. 2011. "The Overcoat as Object of Design." *International Herald Tribune*, October 24.

Moore, Jason. 2015. *Capitalism in the Web of Life: Ecology and the Accumulation of Capital*. New York: Verso.

Mora, Emanuela. 2009. *Fare moda: Esperienze di produzione e consumo*. Milan: Bruno Mondadori.

Moreton, Bethany. 2009. *To Serve God and Wal-Mart: The Making of Christian Free Enterprise*. Cambridge, MA: Harvard University Press.

Munn, Nancy. 1976. *The Fame of Gawa: A Symbolic Study of Value Transformation in a Massim Society (Papua New Guinea)*. Durham, NC: Duke University Press.

Munro, John H. 2012. "The Rise, Expansion, and Decline of the Italian Wool-Based Cloth Industries, 1100–1730: A Study in International Competition, Transaction Costs, and Comparative Advantage." *Studies in Medieval and Renaissance History* 9: 45–207.

National Bureau of Statistics of China. 2014. "China Statistical Yearbook 2014." Beijing. http://www.stats.gov.cn/tjsj/ndsj/2014/indexeh.htm.

National Bureau of Statistics of China. 2015. "China Statistical Yearbook 2015." Beijing. http://www.stats.gov.cn/tjsj/ndsj/2015/indexeh.htm.

Naughton, Barry. 1995. "China's Macroeconomy in Transition." *China Quarterly* 144: 1083–104.

Naughton, Barry. 2007. *The Chinese Economy: Transitions and Growth*. Cambridge, MA: MIT Press.

Naughton, Barry. 2008. "A Political Economy of China's Economic Transition." In *China's Great Economic Transformation*, edited by Loren Brandt and Thomas G. Rawski, 91–135. New York: Cambridge University Press.

Naughton, Barry. 2015. "The Transformation of the State Sector: SASAC, the Market Economy, and the New National Champions." In *State Capitalism, Institutional Adaptation, and the Chinese Miracle*, edited by Barry Naughton and Kellee S. Tsai, 46–72. New York: Cambridge University Press.

Naughton, Barry, and Kellee S. Tsai, eds. 2015. *State Capitalism, Institutional Adaptation, and the Chinese Miracle*. New York: Cambridge University Press.

Nee, Victor, and Sonja Opper. 2012. *Capitalism from Below: Markets and Institutional Change in China*. Cambridge, MA: Harvard University Press.

Neubauer, Fred, and Alden G Lank. 1998. *The Family Business: Its Governance for Sustainability*. London: Palgrave Macmillan.

Niessen, Sandra. 2010. "Interpreting 'Civilization' through Dress." *Encyclopedia of World Dress and Fashion* 8: 39–43.

Oakes, Tim. 2000. "China's Provincial Identities: Reviving Regionalism and Reinventing 'Chineseness.'" *Journal of Asian Studies* 59 (3): 667–92.

Oi, Jean Chun, and Andrew George Walder. 1999. *Property Rights and Economic Reform in China*. Stanford: Stanford University Press.

Ong, Aihwa. 2006. *Neoliberalism as Exception: Mutations in Citizenship and Sovereignty*. Durham, NC: Duke University Press.

Osburg, John. 2013. *Anxious Wealth: Money and Morality among China's New Rich*. Stanford: Stanford University Press.

Pargendler, Mariana. 2012. "State Ownership and Corporate Governance." *Fordham Law Review* 80 (6): 2917–72.

Parris, Kristen. 1993. "Local Initiative and National Reform: The Wenzhou Model of Development." *China Quarterly* 134: 242–63.

Peet, Richard. 2003. *Unholy Trinity: The IMF, World Bank and WTO.* New York: Zed Books.

Perry, Elizabeth J. 1993. *Shanghai on Strike: The Politics of Chinese Labor.* Stanford: Stanford University Press.

Perry, Elizabeth J. 2008. "Chinese Conceptions of 'Rights': From Mencius to Mao— and Now." *Perspectives on Politics* 6 (1): 37–50.

Piore, Michael J., and Charles F. Sabel. 1984. *The Second Industrial Divide: Possibilities for Prosperity.* New York: Basic Books.

Pírez, Pedro. 2002. "Buenos Aires: Fragmentation and Privatization of the Metropolitan City." *Environment and Urbanization* 14 (1): 145–58.

Pistrui, David, Wilfred Huang, Dolun Oksoy, Zhao Jing, and Harold Welsch. 2001. "Entrepreneurship in China: Characteristics, Attributes, and Family Forces Shaping the Emerging Private Sector." *Family Business Review* 14 (2): 141–52.

Polanyi, Karl. 2001 (1944). *The Great Transformation: The Political and Economic Origins of Our Time.* Boston: Beacon.

Postone, Moishe. 1993. *Time, Labor, and Social Domination: A Reinterpretation of Marx's Critical Theory.* Cambridge: Cambridge University Press.

Poutziouris, Panikkos, Yong Wang, and Sally Chan. 2002. "Chinese Entrepreneurship: The Development of Small Family Firms in China." *Journal of Small Business and Enterprise Development* 9 (4): 383–99.

Pozniak, Kinga. 2013 "Reinventing a Model Socialist Steel Town in the Neoliberal Economy: The Case of Nowa Huta, Poland." *City and Society* 25 (1): 113–34.

Pringle, Tim. 2013. "Reflections on Labor in China: From a Moment to a Movement." *South Atlantic Quarterly* 112 (1): 191–202.

Pun, Ngai. 2003. "Subsumption or Consumption? The Phantom of Consumer Revolution in 'Globalizing' China." *Cultural Anthropology* 18 (4): 469–92.

Pun, Ngai. 2005. *Made in China: Women Factory Workers in a Global Workplace.* Durham, NC: Duke University Press.

Pun, Ngai. 2016. *Migrant Labor in China: Post-socialist Transformations.* Malden, MA: Polity Press.

Pun, Ngai, and Jenny Chan. 2013. "The Spatial Politics of Labor in China: Life, Labor, and a New Generation of Migrant Workers." *South Atlantic Quarterly* 112 (1): 179–90.

Pun, Ngai, and Huilin Lu. 2010. "Unfinished Proletarianization: Self, Anger, and Class Action among the Second Generation of Peasant-Workers in Present-Day China." *Modern China* 36 (5): 493–519.

Rapp, Rayna. 1978. "Family and Class in Contemporary America: Notes toward an Understanding of Ideology." *Science and Society* 42:278–300.

Rapp, Rayna. 1979. "Anthropology." *Signs: Journal of Women in Culture and Society* 4 (3): 497–513.

Reiter, Rayna R. 1975. "Men and Women in the South of France: Public and Private Domains." In *Toward an Anthropology of Women*, edited by Rayna R. Reiter, 52–82. New York: Monthly Review Press.

Ren, Xuefei. 2013. *Urban China*. Cambridge: Polity Press.

Riello, Giorgio. 2012. *La moda: Una storia dal Medioevo a oggi*. Rome: Gius. Laterza and Figli.

Riello, Giorgio, and Peter McNeil, eds. 2010. *The Fashion History Reader*. London: Routledge.

Riskin, Carl. 1987. *China's Political Economy: The Quest for Development since 1949*. Oxford: Oxford University Press.

Rofel, Lisa. 1999. *Other Modernities: Gendered Yearnings in China after Socialism*. Berkeley: University of California Press.

Rofel, Lisa. 2007. *Desiring China: Experiments in Neoliberalism, Sexuality, and Public Culture*. Durham, NC: Duke University Press.

Rofel, Lisa. 2012. "Between Tianxia and Postsocialism: Contemporary Chinese Cosmopolitanism." In *Routledge Handbook of Cosmopolitan Studies*, edited by Gerard Delanty, 443–51. Oxon: Routledge.

Rosaldo, Michelle Zimbalist. 1974. "Woman, Culture, and Society: A Theoretical Overview." In *Woman, Culture, and Society*, edited by Michelle Zimbalist Rosaldo and Louise Lamphere, 17–42. Stanford: Stanford University Press.

Rosaldo, Michelle Zimbalist. 1980. "The Use and Abuse of Anthropology: Reflections on Feminism and Cross-Cultural Understanding." *Signs* 5 (3): 389–417.

Rose, Nikolas. 1999. *Governing the Soul: The Shaping of the Private Self*. London: Free Association Books.

Ross, Andrew. 2004. "Made in Italy: The Trouble with Craft Capitalism." *Antipode* 36 (2): 209–16.

Rubin, Gayle S. 1993. "Thinking Sex: Notes for a Radical Theory of the Politics of Sexuality." In *The Lesbian and Gay Studies Reader*, edited by Henry Abelove, Michele Aina Barale, and David M. Halperin, 3–44. New York: Routledge.

Rutherford, Danilyn. 2003. *Raiding the Land of the Foreigners*. Princeton: Princeton University Press.

Sanchez, Andrew. 2012. "Deadwood and Paternalism: Rationalizing Casual Labour in an Indian Company Town." *Journal of the Royal Anthropological Institute* 18 (4): 808–27.

Schneider, David M. 1964. "The Nature of Kinship." *Man* 64: 180–81.

Schneider, David M. 1984. *A Critique of the Study of Kinship*. Ann Arbor: University of Michigan Press.

Schneider, Jane, and Peter T. Schneider. 2003. *Reversible Destiny: Mafia, Antimafia, and the Struggle for Palermo*. Berkeley: University of California Press, 2003.

Schumpeter, Joseph Alois. [1911] 1934. *The Economics of Recovery Program*. New York: McGraw Hill.

Segre Reinach, Simona. 2005. "China and Italy: Fast Fashion versus *Prêt à Porter*. Towards a New Culture of Fashion." *Fashion Theory* 9 (1): 43–56.

Segre Reinach, Simona. 2010. "If You Speak Fashion You Speak Italian: Notes on Present Day Italian Fashion Identity." *Critical Studies in Fashion and Beauty* 1 (2): 203–15.

Shatkin, Gavin. 2008. "The City and the Bottom Line: Urban Megaprojects and the Privatization of Planning in Southeast Asia." *Environment and Planning A* 40 (2): 383–401.

Siemiaticki, Matti. 2015. "Public-Private Partnership Networks: Exploring Business-Government Relationships in United Kingdom Transportation Projects." *Economic Geography* 87 (3): 309–34.

Sklair, Leslie. 2001. *The Transnational Capitalist Class*. Oxford: Blackwell.

Skov, Lise. 2011. "Dreams of Small Nations in a Polycentric Fashion World." *Fashion Theory* 15 (2): 137–56.

Smith, Adam. 1998 [1776]. *An Inquiry into the Nature and Causes of the Wealth of Nations*. New York: Oxford University Press.

Smith, Graeme. 2013. "Law of the Land or Land Law? Notions of Inequality and Inequity in Rural Anhui." In *Unequal China: The Political Economy and Cultural Politics of Inequality*, edited by Wanning Sun and Yingjie Guo, 184–99. London: Routledge.

Smith-Nonini, Sandy. 1998. "Health 'Anti-Reform' in El Salvador: Community Health NGOs and the State in the Neoliberal Era." *PoLAR* 21 (1): 99–113.

Solinger, Dorothy J. 1999. *Contesting Citizenship in Urban China: Peasant Migrants, the State, and the Logic of the Market*. Berkeley: University of California Press.

Solinger, Dorothy J. 2013. "Temporality as Trope in Delineating Inequality: Progress for the Prosperous, Time Warp for the Poor." In *Unequal China: The Political Economy and Cultural Politics of Inequality*, edited by Wanning Sun and Yingjie Guo, 59–76. London: Routledge.

Song, Jesook. 2009. *South Koreans in the Debt Crisis: The Creation of a Neoliberal Welfare Society*. Durham, NC: Duke University Press.

Song, Ligand. 2015. "State and Non-State Enterprises in China's Economic Transition." In *Routledge Handbook of the Chinese Economy*, edited by Gregory C. Chow and Dwight H. Perkins, 182–207. New York: Routledge.

Stack, Carol B. 1974. *All Our Kin: Strategies for Survival in a Black Community*. New York: Basic Books.

Stanfill, Sonnet. 2014. "Introduction." In *The Glamour of Italian Fashion since 1945*, edited by Sonnet Stanfill, 8–31. London: V and A Publishing.

Staples, David. 2007. "Women's Work and the Ambivalent Gift of Entropy." In *The Affective Turn: Theorizing the Social*, edited by Patricia Ticineto Clough and Jean Halley, 119–50. Durham, NC: Duke University Press.

Star, Susan Leigh, and James R. Griesemer. 1989. "Institutional Ecology, 'Translations' and Boundary Objects: Amateurs and Professionals in Berkeley's Museum of Vertebrate Zoology, 1907–39." *Social Studies of Science* 19 (3): 387–420.

Stark, David. 2009. *The Sense of Dissonance: Accounts of Worth in Economic Life*. Princeton, NJ: Princeton University Press.

Steele, Valerie. 2003. *Fashion, Italian Style.* New Haven, CT: Yale University Press.

Stenning, Alison. 2000. "Placing (Post-)Socialism: The Making and Remaking of Nowa Huta, Poland." *European Urban and Regional Studies* 7 (2): 99–118.

Strathern, Marilyn. 1988. *The Gender of the Gift: Problems with Women and Problems with Society in Melanesia.* Berkeley: University of California Press.

Sun, Wanning. 2014. *Subaltern China: Rural Migrants, Media, and Cultural Practices.* Lanham, MD: Rowman and Littlefield.

Sun, Wanning, and Yingjie Guo, eds. 2013. *Unequal China: The Political Economy and Cultural Politics of Inequality.* London: Routledge.

Tadiar, Neferti X. M. 2009. *Things Fall Away: Philippine Historical Experience and the Makings of Globalization.* Durham, NC: Duke University Press.

Tang, Beibei, and Luigi Tomba. 2013. "The Great Divide: Institutionalized Inequality in Market Socialism." In *Unequal China: The Political Economy and Cultural Politics of Inequality,* edited by Wanning Sun and Yingjie Guo, 91–110. London: Routledge.

Tang, Yingkai, Shuanghong Ye, and Jing Zhou. 2013. "Political Connections, Legal Environment, and Corporate Valuation in Chinese Public Family Firms." *Chinese Economy* 46 (6): 32–49.

Thompson, Edward P. 1974. "Patrician Society, Plebeian Culture." *Journal of Social History* 7 (4): 382–405.

Todorova, Maria, and Zsuzsa Gille, eds. 2010. *Post-Communist Nostalgia.* New York: Berghahn Books.

Tsai, Kellee S. 2004. *Back-Alley Banking: Private Entrepreneurs in China.* Ithaca, NY: Cornell University Press.

Tsai, Kellee S. 2007. *Capitalism without Democracy: The Private Sector in Contemporary China.* Ithaca, NY: Cornell University Press.

Tsang, Eric W. K. 1996. "In Search of Legitimacy: The Private Entrepreneur in China." *Entrepreneurship: Theory and Practice* 21 (1): 21–31.

Tu, Thuy Linh Nguyen. 2010. *The Beautiful Generation: Asian Americans and the Cultural Economy of Fashion.* Durham, NC: Duke University Press.

"Tutto in Famiglia: Italian Luxury Goods." 2007. *The Economist,* April 12. http://www .economist.com/node/9005244.

Van Eekelen, Bregje. 2010. "The Social Life of Ideas: Economies of Knowledge." PhD diss., University of California, Santa Cruz.

Walder, Andrew G. 1986. *Communist Neo-Traditionalism: Work and Authority in Chinese Industry.* Berkeley: University of California Press.

Wallerstein, Immanuel. 1974. *The Modern World-System I: Capitalist Agriculture and the Origins of the European World-Economy in the Sixteenth Century.* New York: Academic Press.

Wallerstein, Immanuel. 1980. *The Modern World-System II: Mercantilism and the Consolidation of the European World-Economy, 1600–1750.* New York: Academic Press.

Wallerstein, Immanuel. 1989. *The Modern World-System III: The Second Era of Great Expansion of the Capitalist World-Economy, 1730–1840s*. New York: Academic Press.

Wang Hui. 2003. "The Historical Conditions of the 1989 Social Movement and the Antihistorical Explanation of 'Neoliberalism.'" Translated by Theodore Huters. In *China's New Order: Society, Politics, and Economy in Transition*, edited by Theodore Huters, 46–77. Cambridge, MA: Harvard University Press.

Wang Hui. 2009. "'Politique de dépolitisation' et 'caractère public' des médias de masse." Translated by Guillaume Dutournier. *Extrême-Orient Extrême-Occident*, no. 31: 155–77.

Wang Shaoguang and Angang Hu. 1999. *The Political Economy of Uneven Development: The Case of China*. Armonk: M. E. Sharpe.

Wang, Yingyao. 2015. "The Rise of the 'Shareholding State.'" *Socioeconomic Review* 13 (3): 603–25.

Wang, Zheng. 2005. "'State Feminism?' Gender and Socialist State Formation in Maoist China." *Feminist Studies* 31 (3): 519–51.

Wank, David L. 1998. "Political Sociology and Contemporary China: State-Society Images in American China Studies." *Journal of Contemporary China* 7 (18): 205–27.

Wasserstrom, Jeffrey N. 2008. *Global Shanghai, 1850–2010: A History in Fragments*. New York: Routledge.

Wedeman, Andrew Hall. 2005. "Anticorruption Campaigns and the Intensification of Corruption in China. *Journal of Contemporary China* 14 (42): 93–116.

Wedeman, Andrew Hall. 2012. *Double Paradox: Rapid Growth and Rising Corruption in China*. Ithaca: Cornell University Press.

Weeks, Kathi. 2011. *The Problem with Work: Feminism, Marxism, Antiwork Politics and Postwork Imaginaries*. Durham, NC: Duke University Press.

Weller, Sally. 2007. "Fashion as Viscous Knowledge: Fashion's Role in Shaping Trans-National Garment Production." *Journal of Economic Geography* 7 (1): 39–66.

Welters, Linda, and Arthur C. Mead. 2012. "The Future of Chinese Fashion." *Fashion Practice* 4 (1): 13–40.

White, Nicola. 2000. *Reconstructing Italian Fashion: America and the Development of the Italian Fashion Industry*. Oxford: Berghahn Books.

Wiesner-Hanks, Merry. 2014. *Christianity and Sexuality in the Early Modern World: Regulating Desire, Reforming Practice*. 2nd ed. New York: Routledge.

Williams, Patricia. 1991. *The Alchemy of Race and Rights*. Cambridge, MA: Harvard University Press.

Wissenger, Elizabeth. 2007. "Always on Display: Affective Production in the Modeling Industry." In *The Affective Turn: Theorizing the Social*, edited by Patricia Ticineto Clough and Jean Halley, 231–60. Durham, NC: Duke University Press.

Wolf, Margery. 1972. *Women and the Family in Rural Taiwan*. Stanford: Stanford University Press.

Wong, Kwan-Yiu, and David Chu. 1985. *Modernization in China: The Case of the Shenzhen Special Economic Zone*. Hong Kong: Oxford University Press.

World Bank. n.d.a. "China." Accessed May 12, 2017. http://data.worldbank.org
/country/china?view=chart.

World Bank. n.d.b. "GDP Growth (Annual %)." Accessed May 12, 2017. https://data
.worldbank.org/indicator/NY.GDP.MKTP.KD.ZG?locations=CN.

World Bank. n.d.c. "GINI index (World Bank Estimate)." Accessed May 12, 2017.
https://data.worldbank.org/indicator/SI.POV.GINI?locations=CN&view=map.

World Wealth and Income Database. n.d. "China, 1978–2015." Accessed May 12, 2017.
http://wid.world/country/china.

Wu, Juanjuan. 2009. *Chinese Fashion: From Mao to Now.* New York: Berg.

Wu, Weiping. 1999. *Pioneering Economic Reforms in China's Special Economic Zones:
The Promotion of Foreign Investment and Technology Transfer in Shenzhen.*
Farnham: Ashgate.

Xiao Lu, Pierre. 2008. *Elite China: Luxury Consumer Behavior in China.* Singapore:
John Wiley and Sons.

Yan Hairong. 2008. *New Masters, New Servants: Migration, Development, and Women
Workers in China.* Durham, NC: Duke University Press.

Yanagisako, Sylvia Junko. 1977. "Women-Centered Kin Networks in Urban Bilateral
Kinship." *American Ethnologist* 4: 207–26.

Yanagisako, Sylvia Junko. 1979. "Family and Household: The Analysis of Domestic
Groups." *Annual Review of Anthropology* 8: 161–205.

Yanagisako, Sylvia Junko. 1987. "Mixed Metaphors: Native and Anthropological
Models of Gender and Kinship." In *Gender and Kinship: Essays toward a Unified
Analysis,* edited by Jane Fishburne Collier and Sylvia Junko Yanagisako, 86–118.
Stanford, CA: Stanford University Press.

Yanagisako, Sylvia Junko. 2002. *Producing Culture and Capital: Family Firms in Italy.*
Princeton, NJ: Princeton University Press.

Yanagisako, Sylvia. 2012. "Immaterial and Industrial Labor: On False Binaries in
Hardt and Negri's Trilogy." *Focaal,* no. 64: 16–23.

Yang, Hongjian [杨宏建]. 2007. 温州人想的和你不一 温州人为什么会成为富人
*[Wenzhou People Think Differently Than You: How Wenzhou People Become
Rich].* Beijing: 时事出版社.

Yang, Mayfair Mei-hui. 1994. *Gifts, Favors, and Banquets: The Art of Social Relationships in China.* Ithaca, NY: Cornell University Press.

Ye, Min. 2010. "Foreign Direct Investment: Diaspora Networks and Economic
Reform." In *China Today, China Tomorrow: Domestic Politics, Economy, and Society,* edited by Joseph Fewsmith, 129–48. Lanham, MD: Rowman and Littlefield.

Yurchak, Alexei. 2006. *Everything Was Forever, until It Was No More: The Last Soviet
Generation.* Princeton, NJ: Princeton University Press.

Zhan, Mei. 2009. *Other-Worldly: Making Chinese Medicine through Transnational
Frames.* Durham, NC: Duke University Press.

Zhang, Li. 2001. *Strangers in the City: Reconfigurations of Space, Power, and Social
Networks within China's Floating Population.* Stanford: Stanford University
Press.

Zhang, Li. 2010. "Marginalization of Rural Migrants in China's Transitional Cities." In *Asian Cities, Migrant Labor and Contested Spaces*, edited by Tai-Chee Wong and Jonathan Rigg, 246–64. New York: Routledge.

Zhang, Li. 2012. *In Search of Paradise: Middle-Class Living in a Chinese Metropolis.* Ithaca, NY: Cornell University Press.

Zhang, Zhen. 2000. "Mediating Time: The 'Rice Bowl of Youth' in Fin de Siècle Urban China." *Public Culture* 12 (1): 93–113.

Index

branding (continued)

166, 191, 199, 202, 289–90; names used in, 30, 98, 164, 170, 174–75, 184, 251, 262, 277; national identity and, 2, 32, 93, 97–100, 174, 193–94, 199, 312, 342n3; provincial family origins and, 93, 215–16, 227–28, 240; subcontracting and, 245, 286–87

Bretton Woods agreement, 110

BRICS, 311

bureaucracy: difficulty of navigating, 88, 103, 212, 234; import-export corporations and, 117–18, 125, 291, 305, 331n13; Mao's efforts to break, 342n6; ownership and, 326n12; privatization and, 11, 24, 115, 138–39, 321n16, 333n26

business schools, 3, 53, 59, 268; English taught in, 80, 267; management models taught in, 94, 224, 228, 239

Cai brothers, 44, 172–73, 176, 207–8, 210, 238, 300, 314; diverge from Wenzhou model, 276–80

Camera di Commercio, 242–43

Camisca Tessitura Serica, 255–56

capitalism: affective attachment to, 124, 127; in China, 11–12, 16–17, 24–25, 52, 60–61, 121, 138, 146, 321n22; collaborative ethnography and, 3–5, 45, 303–5; corruption and, 271, 331n10; culturally and historically situated, 6–7, 10, 15–16, 36, 66–67, 111–12, 263, 306, 308, 319n6, 321n19; inequality and, 83, 145, 158, 265–66; kinship and, 17–19, 94, 218–19, 224, 228–32, 265, 304, 338–39n11; labor and, 37–38, 163, 169–70, 179–81, 225, 263; neoliberal, 8–9, 115–17, 308–9, 321n16, 329n2, 333n26; periodization of, 110–11, 114–15, 168, 184–85, 304, 307; as process, 159–60, 263, 312, 324n2; revisionist history and, 120–22; states and, 12–13, 19–20, 115–16, 133–34, 138–39,

144, 309, 321n16, 327n26; transnational, 319n3; universality attributed to, 41, 66, 99

Casati, 243, 251, 263

Chandler, Alfred D., 219–20, 234, 238–39, 251

Chen Rongfen/Nicole, 69, 85

China: as competitor to the West, 3, 23, 26–27, 83, 311; disidentification with, 64–65, 70, 88, 104; global fashion and, 193, 210, 215–16, 305–6; growth of domestic consumption in, 53–54, 56–57, 83, 135, 163, 165, 171, 173, 191, 280, 311, 326n16; history of entrepreneurs in, 130; inequality in, 119, 311, 326n14; international criticism of labor conditions in, 343n19; Italian perceptions of, 48–50, 62–65, 76–83, 91, 167, 181, 196–98, 202–3, 208, 223, 261, 307; "opening" of, 21–22, 102–3, 330n4; "rise" of, 25, 29–30, 33, 311, 323–24n36; silk industry in, 135–36; state involvement in economy of, 11–12, 19–20, 24, 39–40, 53, 88, 115–16, 124–25, 132–46, 212, 265, 272, 288, 298, 309; tourists from, 83, 173, 312; transition to capitalism in, 16–17, 24, 52, 60–61, 120–23, 138–39, 150, 221–22, 326n18, 333–34n28; WTO admits, 17, 20, 25, 136–37, 203, 316, 334–35n36

Chinese Communist Party (CCP), 75, 118; anti-corruption campaign within, 173, 312, 337–38n3, 342n4; Confucianism promoted by, 331n15; consumerism promoted by, 16–17, 311; criticism of, 17, 79–80, 228, 332–33n25; entrepreneurs admitted to, 154, 326n11; entrepreneurs suppressed by, 128, 130, 274, 332n23; foreign direct investment promoted by, 322–23n29; historical narratives of, 121, 129, 156; inequality and, 60–61; kinship attacked by, 342n5; officials and cadres of, 51–54,

cultural capital, 15, 39, 53, 217; brands
and, 93, 207–8, 211–12; Chinese-
Italian competition over, 202–3, 307;
of elite fashion dynasties, 240; reconversion strategies of, 252–54, 263, 308
cultural mediation. *See* mediation:
cultural
Cultural Revolution, the, 52, 128, 332n23;
Chinese inflexibility attributed to, 79;
corruption attributed to, 123, 267–68,
342n5

Dai Jianyuan, 292–94
danwei (work unit), 52, 281, 342–43n9
decentralization: in Chinese economy,
24, 88, 135, 141; in Italian industry, 23,
59, 111, 168–70, 179, 241, 304, 309
delocalizzazione. See outsourcing
Deng Xiaoping, 24
department stores, 48, 72, 118, 128, 175,
199; location important in, 63, 162,
210–12
design: celebration of, 29, 39–40;
Chinese-Italian relations and, 190–91,
307; vs. copying, 62, 82, 202–4,
212–13, 283, 289, 338n2; Italian claims
of supremacy in, 202; vs. production,
82–83, 204–8, 257, 323–24n36
developers, 210–12
development: Chinese state and, 11, 22,
122, 281, 311, 321n17, 337n55; entrepreneurship and, 196–98, 325n7; family
firms and, 214, 342n2; international
trade and, 23–24, 311, 333n26; Italian
industrial, 12, 111, 115, 167–69, 216; as
justification for inequality, 134, 144,
329n1; rural/urban divide and, 20,
27, 145, 150–51, 157, 337n55; Wenzhou
model of, 223, 272, 275–76
diversification strategies, 167, 173–77,
179, 183, 195, 248, 255
division of labor: between Chinese and
Italians, 41–42, 44–45, 77–78, 81–82,

104, 166, 172, 176, 196, 307, 314–17;
gendered, 99–100, 151, 176, 236–38,
295–97, 310, 324n2, 328n36, 336n46;
between mental and manual labor,
323–24n36
divorce, 118, 252, 258, 261–62
domestic sphere: dynamism of,
339–40n4; feminist critique of, 9–10,
308, 320nn10–14
domestic workers, 48–49, 57, 93, 287,
324n1, 337n51
Donghua University, 3, 51, 53, 67, 204,
228, 268, 272, 286, 293
dormitory labor regime, 336n48
downsizing, 156, 184, 221, 259, 261,
289–90, 335n42

Eastern Europe: outsourcing to, 164;
postsocialism in, 121–22, 322n27
"eating bitterness" (*chiku*), 156, 274
economic vs. noneconomic, 6, 17–19,
21, 101, 229–32, 306
economic reform, 24–26, 59–61, 131, 134,
170, 286–87; entrepreneurship and,
54, 196, 223–24, 274–75; family firms
and, 264, 281, 290; global fashion and,
193; migrant workers and, 148; silk
industry and, 135
economic sociology, 167, 229–32
education: of Chinese designers, 82;
Communist, 79–80; as cultural capital, 49, 53, 57, 251, 254, 341n12; *guanxi*
and, 268–69, 292, 302; vs. innate
competency, 64, 329n38; of managers
and entrepreneurs, 42, 46, 51, 53, 56,
59, 71, 79, 187, 257, 277, 283, 287–88,
293, 295, 298, 325n3, 335n44, 340n5;
nationalism and, 40; of workers,
270, 336n47. *See also* business
schools
efficiency: Chinese work culture and,
80; kinship as impediment to, 94,
219, 224, 229–30, 267, 271, 284; as

fashion (continued)
193–94, 213–16; produced for export vs. Chinese domestic market, 151, 155–56, 207, 286–87, 310; shows, 1–3, 205; studies, 31
Fashion Power, 267
feminism: and labor power, 324n2; and public/private distinction, 9–10, 116–17, 133, 138, 320nn10–14
Ferragamo, Salvatore, 98–99, 191, 210, 216
Ferrari, Luciano, 47, 56, 118, 180–84, 195, 197–200, 260–62
FGS, 43–44, 57, 72, 82, 117, 197, 207, 235, 314; as a family firm, 237–40, 262, 308; historical evolution of, 170–76, 278–80; statements from CEO of, 199, 215
Fieramosca, Eduardo, 228, 316
finance: in Chinese history, 130, 323n31; fashion industry and, 32, 185, 214; kinship and, 13, 239–40, 248–51, 277, 291, 293–94, 296, 299, 302, 340n9, 342n2; privatization and, 124–25, 138–41, 334–35n36; in silk market, 187–88; states and, 8, 13, 115–16, 309, 320n9, 327n26, 334n33, 342n4; Wall Street, 329n38. See also banks; foreign investment
financial crisis: of 2008, 12, 54, 164, 173, 334n32; Asian, 323n31; and collapse of Bretton Woods, 110–11
five-anti campaign, 332n23
Float, 117, 136, 315
Florence, 98, 186, 193, 215–16
Fordism, 168–69
foreign investment: Chinese dependence on, 323n30; the Chinese state and, 20, 23–26, 30, 33, 40, 53–54, 134, 306, 311, 314, 322–23n29; privatization and, 11, 116–17, 136–37; resistance to, 146, 166; in special economic zones, 333–34n28

Foucault, Michel, 102, 129
French luxury conglomerates, 98, 196–97, 211, 214–15, 328n33
friendship stores, 200
FuHua Co. Ltd. (Grand China), 69, 316

Galbiati, 252–55, 263, 308, 341n18
gender: capital and, 18, 253; education and, 254; entrepreneurship and, 257, 260–62, 274, 331n12; among expat managers, 48–49; fashion sense unaffected by, 64; labor and, 10, 99–100, 151, 176, 181, 183–84, 236–38, 290, 295–97, 310, 320–21n15, 324n2, 328n36, 336n46; public/private distinction and, 9–10, 116–17, 133, 320nn10–14
generation: brand authenticity and, 227, 240; in definition of family firm, 339n2; outsourcing and manufacturing decline impact, 220–21, 234–35, 238–57, 262–63, 308–9; succession between, 18, 94, 222, 228, 235–38, 246–49, 251, 256, 341n14; two processes of, 33, 220, 232–33; younger vs. older, 52–53, 61–62, 72, 158, 237, 250, 279, 285, 292, 296–97, 302, 336n47
gentrification, 86–87, 335n37
globalization, 21, 49, 83, 110–11, 114–15, 307, 323n31, 333n26; celebration of the local and, 92–93, 215–16; in fashion, 192–93, 200, 210, 214–16, 235, 240, 306; immaterial labor and, 101–2; inequality attributed to, 145; kinship and, 218; "rise of China" and, 311; in Shanghai, 95; in textile industry, 146–47, 184–85, 189, 241–42
Great Leap Forward, 332n23
guahu (hang-on household), 275
guanxi (connections), 3, 17, 67–68, 125, 127–28, 264–71, 286, 291, 295, 312, 342n7; classmate vs. kinship, 292–94, 297, 302

Hangzhou, 26, 50, 96, 134, 157, 287, 298, 336n46
Hardt, Michael, 100–101, 330n7
history: as branding, 93, 342n3; capitalism and, 6, 110–11, 118, 304–5; category of labor and, 37–38; inequality and, 20, 119, 145; migrant workers' perception of, 147, 149–50, 154; rejection of socialist, 16, 24, 54, 102–3, 127, 149, 333n27; revisionist, 32, 113–14, 116, 120–23, 127, 129–32, 134, 144, 158–60, 264, 304, 329–30n2, 330n4, 330n7; of Shanghai, 95, 122, 128–32
holding companies, 13, 137, 140, 225, 248
Hong Kong: as conduit of trade with the West, 23, 26, 135, 196; distributors from, 63, 171, 210; English names used in, 321n21; property rights protected in, 188
household industry, 23, 99–100, 148, 168, 275, 281, 288, 336n46
Huang Huaming, 88–89, 109–10, 112, 161–62, 165–67, 201–2, 204–6, 222, 280–82, 304, 309
Hui Hua Yi/Silk Nouvelle, 51, 54, 117, 134, 136–38, 140–42, 269, 305
Hu Jihong, 3, 203–4, 272, 288–90
hukou system, 149–50, 337n55

identity: brand, 191, 204, 210; entrepreneurs' sense of, 166, 181; of family firms, 217–18, 237; national, 31–32, 65, 93, 97–100, 145, 174, 193–94, 199, 213–16, 312, 342n3; Shanghai, 42, 94–97, 114, 116, 122, 130, 132, 330n4; translation and, 73; transnational construction of, 4–5, 14–15, 35–36, 208, 304, 307–8; workers' sense of, 20, 335n43
imitation, 62, 82, 202–4, 212–13, 289, 338n2

immateriality: of fashion, 163, 199, 206–8; labor and, 101, 104, 163, 323–24n36, 328n36
impannatore. See converter firms
import-export companies, 69, 289–90; ambiguous status of, 11; *cohong* merchants and, 332n20; pyramid schemes, 222, 291–93, 308, 310, 331n11; state-owned, 27, 51, 53–55, 59, 67, 73, 84, 88, 96, 117–18, 123–27, 134, 140, 148, 159, 286–87, 305, 313–15, 323n29, 327n26, 331n14
industrial districts, 167–70; class mobility in, 112, 163, 177, 221, 256; diversification strategies and, 175–76, 179, 183; kinship and social networks in, 58–59, 111, 178, 220, 234–35, 259, 262–3, 304; transnational expansion and, 172, 185, 228, 234, 241, 245, 308–9, 315
industrialization. *See* development
inequality: capitalism and, 6–7, 16, 60–61, 158; in China, 311, 326n14; contested meaning of, 119, 121; corruption and, 224, 266, 269, 271; development and growth used to justify, 134, 144–45; in global fashion industry, 29–31, 310; kinship and, 17–18; rural/urban, 20, 24, 150–51, 157–58, 267–68, 305, 337nn54–55; socialism blamed for, 19, 113, 127, 132; in Wenzhou, 276. *See also* asymmetry between Italians and Chinese
inheritance, 127, 236–37, 239–40, 249, 252, 254–55
innovation: entrepreneurial, 54, 223; in fashion, 29, 169, 213
inside vs. outside siblings, 252–54
Institute for Foreign Commerce, 197–98
International Monetary Fund (IMF), 12, 117, 121, 146, 311, 329n1
iron rice bowl, 272–73

Istituto per la Ricostruzione Industriale (IRI), 12–13, 115

Italianità (Italianness), 41, 61–70, 78, 97–102, 106, 165, 227, 307, 312, 328n37

Italy: Chinese perceptions of, 67–68, 83–91, 208, 215–16; Chinese residing in, 68, 298–301, 328n35; fashion of, 21–22, 29, 97–100, 174, 190–94, 209, 305–6; food from, 50, 91, 259; industry and manufacturing in, 22–23, 111, 167–78, 184–86, 215; provincialism of, 91–94; state involvement in economy of, 12–13, 39, 115–16, 225, 304, 309

Jiang Li/Nico, 44, 69, 73–75, 85–86, 105, 276–80, 300–301, 305, 311

Jiaxing Style Silk Company, 148, 186–89, 258, 306, 313–14

job security: elimination of, 61; entrepreneurs' lack of, 272, 325n9; in government and state enterprises, 60–61, 124, 268, 273, 298; workers' lack of, 147, 152

joint ventures: advantages and drawbacks of, 89, 171, 201–2, 205; Chinese partners' autonomy in, 104–5; with Chinese state entities, 25–27, 53, 136; cultural mediators in, 52, 70–72; dissatisfaction with, 316; division of labor in, 81–82, 166, 172, 176, 207; replace comprador system, 332n21; tensions within, 74–75, 90, 109–10, 112, 161–62, 177–78, 238, 278–79, 304, 306; types of, 117–18, 313–15

karaoke, 71

Kering, 214–15

kinship: biological vs. cultural models of, 320n11, 339n3; capitalist modernity and, 18–19, 94, 218–19, 224, 228–29, 232, 304, 338–39n1, 308; in China vs. Italy, 32–33, 166–67, 217–18, 221;

definition of, 231; family law and, 236, 252; generation and, 220, 232–34, 243, 248; glass ceiling created by, 41, 57–58, 83, 256; as index of corruption, 222–25, 266–71, 342n5; metaphors employed in business, 136, 176, 287, 292; and the "noneconomic," 6, 17–19, 21, 230, 306; productive force of, 58–59, 111–12, 163, 169, 178–79, 234–35, 257, 262–63; vs. school connections, 292, 297, 302. *See also* family firms; marriage

kinship enterprises, 18, 220, 230–35, 246–47, 263, 308; vs. family firm as a legal entity, 243

knowledge economy, 25, 30, 36, 40, 101, 330n7

labor: abstract, 15, 37–38, 42, 45, 99–100, 106–7, 324n2; affective and immaterial, 101, 104, 122, 323–24n36, 328n36, 330n7; capital and, 111–12, 163, 169–70, 179–81, 225, 263; entrepreneurial orientation toward, 147–48, 156, 310; estrangement or alienation of, 38, 106–7; of family members, 58–59, 112, 163, 169, 178, 234–35, 257, 263, 309; protests in China, 322–23n29, 336n48; reproductive vs. productive, 10, 306, 324n2; in the textile industry, 143, 146–48, 151–54, 170, 283–84, 287, 289, 293, 305, 326–27n20; unions, 21, 23, 77, 93, 113, 169–70, 180–81, 309. *See also* workers

labor power: abstraction of, 99–100; cosmopolitanism and, 42, 103–4, 307; managerial and entrepreneurial, 36–38, 41, 55, 59, 84, 100–102, 105–7, 163, 307; as product of negotiation in transnational encounters, 14–16, 31–32, 35, 45, 75–76, 306; reproduction of, 324n2, 336n49

laoban (boss), 325n8

layoffs, 156, 184, 221, 259, 261, 289–90, 335n42

Li Linfeng, 51–52, 60–61, 134–42, 144–46, 269–70, 292

literature (field of study), 56, 64, 71, 325n3, 335n44

Liu Shufeng, 285–88, 291–93

Li Yue, 68–69, 105, 298–300, 305, 311

Lou Huayan, 140–41, 213

Louis Vuitton, 196, 199, 210–11, 214, 328n33

Lou Jingxiao/Maggi, 50–53, 69, 72–73, 87, 105, 118, 124–29, 228, 291, 305, 311, 331n15

Luo Ming, 155

luxury: brand image and, 74, 328n33; Chinese consumption of, 56–57, 83, 135, 170–71, 173, 191–92, 199–200, 210, 216, 312, 326n16; corruption and, 337–38n3; in Europe and U.S. markets, 57; finance and, 214–15; malls, 211; subcontracted manufacturing of, 299, 327n22

"Made in China," 47, 174, 207–8; as undesirable for Chinese consumers, 171, 173, 279–80

"Made in Italy," 31–32, 191; Chinese domestic market and, 40–41, 165, 171, 173–74, 191, 207, 279–80, 312; Chinese-Italian inequality and, 202–3, 208; fabric, 340n11; false labeling as, 93; history of, 97–100, 193–94, 199; myth vs. reality of, 98, 100–102, 211, 216, 327n22, 338n3; outsourced production of, 116, 163, 209, 213–15, 337n2

malls. See shopping malls

managerial capitalism, 220–21, 229, 234

managers: become owners, 143, 270; Chinese, 51–53, 59–61, 72–74, 83–84, 86–88, 284–87; Chinese-Italian relations and, 41–42, 52, 61–70, 74–76, 77–83, 89–91, 100, 109–10, 117, 166,

172, 176, 201–2, 222, 244, 258–59, 278–79, 295–96, 303–4, 307–8, 310, 313–17; defined historically, 36–37; family vs. professional, 94, 178, 219, 229–31, 238–39, 245–46, 299–300, 340n5; firms opened by, 58–59, 179, 221, 225, 234, 256–57, 263, 305; government, 120, 314, 326n12; Italian, 47–50, 55–59, 70–72, 105–7, 163, 212; Italianità and, 100–102; owners criticized by, 91–94; workers in the eyes of, 151, 259

Maoism: Chinese lack of creativity attributed to, 79–80; entrepreneurship discourse and, 127, 274, 325n10; poverty under, 329n1; repudiation of, 16, 24, 54, 102–3, 333n27; temporality of, 159; valorized workers, 153; workers' attitudes toward, 149

Marini, Luciano, 148, 186–89, 197, 306, 313–14

marriage: business partnerships and, 47, 59, 109, 118, 166, 176, 180, 182–84, 257, 259–63, 296–300; cosmopolitanism and, 68, 74; cultural capital and, 252–54; among expats in Shanghai, 48–49; globalization and, 218–19; inheritance and, 236–37, 240, 252; workers' imagined futures affected by, 154–55

Marx, Karl, 14–16, 37–38, 99–100, 103, 105, 320–21n15, 324n2; replaced by Western economics, 228

Max Mara, 191, 204, 216, 289

May Fourth Movement, 342n5

MB, 174–75

McKinnon, Susan, 218

Meda, 180, 182, 194, 213

mediation: cultural, 44, 70–76, 84–85, 300, 307; entrepreneurship and, 50–52, 67, 105, 311; firms specializing in, 69, 105, 118, 309, 315–16; between foreigners and Chinese state, 88

merchants, 127, 130, 168, 186–87, 321n19, 332n20, 333–34n25

mergers, 125, 243, 246–47

methodology, 3–8, 35, 45, 303–4, 324–25n2; of data collection on family firms, 242–43; of encounter, 330n5; supply chains and, 324n1. *See also* collaborative ethnography

migrant workers. *See* workers: migrant

Milan, 93–94, 98, 183–84, 193, 213, 215

Ming'er Dress Company Ltd., 203–4, 207, 288–90, 316

modernity: China seen as lacking, 50, 62–63, 181, 196; consumption as signifier of, 157; kinship and, 18–19, 94, 218–19, 224, 228–32, 237, 239, 304, 338–39n1

Mollona, Franco, 212

Molteni, 67, 195, 244–49, 263, 308, 315–16, 341n18

Molto Bene Ltd., 68, 299, 316

monopoly, 24, 132–33, 140, 327n26

Motte, Alfred, 249

Multi-Fiber Agreement (MFA), 25, 323n32

Mussolini, Benito, 97

Naldi, Gianfranco, 46, 50, 64, 71, 81, 171, 201–3, 211

names: as brands, 30, 98, 164, 170, 174–75, 184, 240, 251, 262, 277; Chinese vs. Western, 72–73, 290; firms changing, 135–36, 243; pseudonyms, 319n1

nationalism: branding and, 2, 93, 97, 193, 199, 342n3; CCP encourages, 16, 20, 40; against colonialism and international capital, 20, 40, 130; cosmopolitan, 17, 131–32; of government officials, 113, 120, 145–46; Italian, 280; labor power constituted through, 99–102, 306

Negri, Antonio, 100–101, 330n7

neoliberalism, 7–9, 12, 36, 110–11, 115–17, 121, 160, 218, 308–9, 321n16, 329n2; corruption discourse and, 123, 330n9

networking. *See guanxi* (connections)

New Democracy, 332n23

Nike, 344n20

nostalgia: for preindustrial Italy, 216; for prerevolutionary China, 95, 114, 122, 128–32, 145, 159, 266, 332–33n25; for socialist past, 121, 331n16

One Belt, One Road, 311, 333n26

orientalism, 62–65, 77–83, 85, 190–91, 196, 200–203, 330n9, 341n1; "opening" of China and, 102–3

originary accumulation, 139–40, 143–44

outsourcing, 22–24, 27, 116, 164–65, 184–85, 304; classmate *guanxi* and, 293–94; class mobility of managers affected by, 58–59, 221, 225, 234, 305; improvements in Chinese production and, 76–77, 181, 197, 201–2; of inequality, 19–21, 309–10; Italian industrial districts impacted by, 58–59, 187, 196, 221, 241–42, 244–45, 255, 257, 263, 308–9; knowledge economy and, 101; labor blamed for, 21, 77, 113, 180–82

owners: absentee, 86–87, 91; become professionals, 254, 341n17; of factories, 30, 67–68, 83–84, 153, 156, 183, 187–88, 249–50, 279, 283, 293, 299–300, 310, 335n44, 336n48; labor and, 77, 82, 153, 180–84, 261; managers' relation to, 10–11, 41, 44, 50, 55–59, 91–94, 101, 239, 256; vs. manufacturers, 24; mediators' relation to, 71–72; relation between Italian and Chinese, 74, 87, 88–91, 260–62; responsible for employees' welfare, 143–44, 183–84, 287, 293, 310

Panerati, Alessandro, 1, 3

patriarchy, 180, 236–38, 249, 253, 260–62, 274

reproduction: of capitalism, 6, 219; family firms and, 116, 179, 232–33, 236, 242, 308; vs. production, 10, 306, 324n2; of social class, 217, 254, 336n49; of subcontracting firms, 256. *See also* generation

retail: branding and, 63–64, 81, 210; Chinese tourism and, 173, 312; FGS's success in, 170–71; Rinaudo's success in, 164–65; store placement and, 88, 162, 211–12

revisionist histories. *See* history: revisionist

Rinaldi, Paolo, 43–44, 46, 70–71, 78–79, 278, 328n37

Rinaudo, 89–90, 109–10, 112, 117, 161–62, 201–2, 204–8, 282, 308; Elisabetta, 201, 208, 212, 236, 241, 281, 304, 314; as a family firm, 235–40, 262, 294–95; FGS compared to, 170, 174, 176, 237–38; production and distribution chain of, 164–67, 194–95

Rossellini, Isabella, 98

rural/urban divide, 20, 24, 27, 60, 145, 150–51, 157–58, 267–68, 284, 305, 310, 328n31, 336nn49–50, 337nn54–55; vs. Shanghai/non-Shanghai divide, 96

Salvianti, Sylvia, 47–48, 78, 211–12

Schumpeter, Joseph Alois, 54

securitization, 139, 334–35n36

Segalini, Vittorio, 118, 174–75, 209, 305, 316

sent-down youth, 128, 155, 267

Seripro, 174–75

Shanghai: expatriates in, 48–50, 59, 73, 86, 93; gentrification of, 86–87, 332n24; *guanxi* in, 268–69; as identity, 42, 91, 94–97, 116, 122, 132; Italians' need for Chinese guidance in, 87–88; model of development, 223; nostalgia for presocialist, 114, 116, 128–32

Shanghai Sun Garments Co. Ltd., 292–94, 316

Shenzhen, 26, 298, 333–34n28

shifu (master craftsperson), 149, 151, 277

Shi Qian, 288–90

Shoar, Antoinette, 230–31

shopping malls, 48, 130, 199, 296; bureaucracy in, 88; store placement important in, 63, 162, 210–11

Shu Hailun/Antonio, 75, 282, 294–97

silk: branding, 204, 289–90; consumption of, 27; industry privatization, 134–46; international sourcing of, 186–87, 195–96; prestige of working in, 285–86; production of, 22–23, 26–27, 181–82, 188, 288–89, 336n36; road, 21–22, 289, 333n26

socialism: vs. capitalism, 16–17, 24, 51–52, 60, 113, 124–25, 160, 274; Chinese lack of creativity attributed to, 79–80; corruption and inequality attributed to, 19, 113, 127, 132–33, 265–66, 271; developmentalism and, 22–23, 134, 145–46, 337n55; entrepreneurs suppressed under, 128–30, 332n23; gendered division of labor under, 336n46; illegal economy under, 274–76; intergenerational relations and, 292; local collective enterprises and, 275, 281–82, 344n21; nostalgia for, 121, 331n16; public/private distinction and, 221–22; repudiation of, 54, 102–3, 116–17, 120, 123, 126–28, 305, 333n27; workers' attitudes toward, 147, 149–50, 305; workers valorized under, 153, 325n10

Soci, Massimo, 49, 71, 75, 166, 294–95

sourcing, 69, 186–87, 194–200, 244–45. *See also* outsourcing

Soviet Union, 21–22, 121, 322n24, 330n3

special economic zone (SEZ), 333–34n28

tourism, 83, 173, 298, 312, 327n23

trade agreements, 311, 333n26

translation: as cultural mediation, 44, 70–76, 103–4, 307; difficulties presented by, 79–80, 244; entrepreneurship and, 55, 105, 182, 222, 260; during participant observation, 28–29; as women's work, 294–95

transnational industrial drag, 100, 310

United States: China compared to, 25, 127, 326n19, 343n10; family firms in, 224, 239, 339n2, 339n4; fashion consumption in, 41, 56–57, 98, 173, 185, 337n2; in fashion supply chains, 118, 182, 244–45, 279, 315–16; intellectual labor and, 323–24n36; international policies of, 135, 185, 291, 329n1; perspectives on China, 12, 23–24, 79

urban/rural divide. *See* rural/urban divide

value: as culturally and historically mediated, 6, 35–36, 66–67, 183–84, 321n20, 324n2; as immaterial, 163, 199, 206–8; negotiated in transnational encounters, 14–16, 31, 45, 61–62, 75–76, 103, 303–4, 306–7; transnational inequalities and, 19, 83–84, 102, 104

vertical integration, 23, 58, 111–12, 117–18, 167–68, 174–75, 179, 183, 250

Vinimoon, 43, 46, 56–57, 85, 117, 171–76, 201–2, 223, 238, 300–301, 314, 338n4; cultural mediation in, 44, 73–75; division of labor in, 44–45, 78, 81–82, 172; Pure Elegance compared to, 205, 207, 304; as a Wenzhou firm, 276–80

Wallerstein, Immanuel, 4–5, 114–15

Wang Shiyao/George, 67, 73, 96, 105, 124–28, 140–41, 292, 305, 331n15, 334n34

welfare: devolution of responsibility for, 60, 139, 142–44, 310, 337n1; as rationale for capitalist development, 134, 144–45; rural/urban inequalities in accessing, 150, 337n55

Wen Jiabao, 267

Wenzhou: as model of entrepreneurial development, 223, 272–76, 297, 343n14; as a "third level" city, 50; and Vinimoon, 276–79

workers: become shareholders, 139–40, 143; Chinese vs. Italian, 21, 76–77, 181–82, 259; college graduates becoming, 269; effacement of, 101, 104, 130–31, 310; firms opened by, 177–78, 225, 276–77, 281, 283, 289–90; inequality and, 114, 144–45, 308–10; in Italian artisan firms, 337n1; Marxist theory and, 37–38, 99–101; migrant, 2–3, 20, 26, 40, 60, 96, 113–14, 139, 146–50, 152–4, 157–60, 305, 310, 321n22, 325n9; in post-Mao China, 153, 325n10; prestige hierarchy among, 285–86; in state-run work units, 52, 342–43n9; temporality and, 120, 122, 147, 149–56, 305; transnational encounters with, 157, 197–98; turnover of, 284, 287, 293; vs. "Wenzhou people," 272. *See also* labor

work ethic, 77, 113, 181–82, 199, 228, 259, 270

work units (*danwei*) 52, 281, 342–43n9

World Bank, 12, 117, 121, 146, 311

worlding projects, 87, 102, 159, 330n4

world systems theory, 4–5, 114–15

World Trade Organization (wto), 17, 20, 39–40, 136–37, 316, 323nn31–32, 333n26, 334n36; import/export quotas and, 25, 51, 59, 125, 203

Xiao He, 150–53, 156

Xiao Hu, 284

Xiao Lan, 148–50, 153

Xiaoyu Ltd., 50, 124, 291, 305, 309, 316
Xiao Zhan, 155–56
Xi Jinping, 342n4

Yufei, 89, 165–67, 281–82, 295–96

Zegna, Ermenegildo, 98, 199, 211, 227
Zhang Hualing, 224, 266, 280, 283–85, 309
Zhao Houming, 288–90

Zhejiang New Dawn Group Ltd., 148, 224, 266, 280, 283–84, 309, 315
Zhejiang provincial silk bureau/ Zhejiang FuHua Silk corporation, 51–52, 117, 134–46, 148, 315, 335n39
Zhejiang Yafeng Fashion Co. Ltd., 285–88, 290–91, 316
Zhenfu silk factory, 96, 142–43, 152, 222, 270–71, 316, 335n37, 337n51, 342–43n9